MW00964038

NO FLOWERS
on the DESERT

NO FLOWERS
on the DESERT

Lawrence Wiener

Power Publishing

Toronto, Canada

Canadian Cataloguing in Publication Data

Wiener, Lawrence, 1937-
  No flowers on the desert

Includes bibliographical references.
ISBN 0-968-31130-X

1. Wiener, Lawrence, 1937-   - Childhood and youth. 2. Kibbutzim.
3. Young volunteers in Kibbutzim – Biography. I. Title.

HX742.2.A3W5 1998   307.77'6'092   C98-931804-4

Cover Photography © Roda / First Light

For information:

Power Publishing
7 Vanhorn Court
Thornhill, Ontario
L3T 5P9

Printed in Canada

This book is dedicated to
Samuel Wiener, Rose Wiener,
David Wiener and Auntie Rose Wiener

PART ONE

Toronto

The year was 1957 and...
once upon a time there was Rock 'n Roll

In the beginning... rock... and Martha

It was 1957 - every last Monday of the month was the Rock 'n Roll review at Maple Leaf Gardens. Buddy Holly, Paul Anka, The Platters, The Rondelles - every month there was a different guest star. People like Little Richard, Chuck Berry, Jerry Lee Lewis, and Richie Valens, were just a few of the big names who would appear at the Garden.

I always had front row seats for the show. The ticket cost five dollars. My mother would give me three dollars and I made up the other two from working at my part-time job at Goldblatt's Drugstore at St. Clair (near Atlas - if you know the City of Toronto). I delivered prescriptions after school from Monday through Friday night and occasionally on Saturdays.

I was so wrapped up in the 1950s, it was like I was mummified. I felt as if I was living on the *really* raw edge of the beast - the beast being, of course, Rock 'n Roll. I felt it in every inch of my body and soul (I used to have one, once). I wore Buddy Holly glasses, a James Dean jacket, pink shirts like Elvis Presley, and big, yellow cufflinks like Jerry Lee Lewis. My shirt collar was perpetually turned up. I was like some crazy walking time capsule of the era.

The first time I heard Bill Haley and the Comets play 'Rock around the Clock', I was gone, man - like Elvis used to say, real, real GONE! I went on a dancing frenzy that eventually landed me on the Buffalo bandstand television show for almost seven weeks straight. I would go on to knock Louis the Frenchman and Dapper Dan clean off the dance floor. Right after I heard Elvis Presley's recording of 'Heartbreak Hotel', I went out and bought my first ever record album for the unheard-of-price of $2.98.

It was a good thing, for me anyway, that Rock 'n Roll came along when it did. I mean that. Really. Because up until then my life had been, like they say, in a little bit of a rut. Monday to Friday, I went to high school and when school let out, in the evenings, I worked at the drugstore. Remember that tall, skinny kid always stepping out of your way at Goldblatt's? That was me.

On Sunday, I would go to the Bloor and Spadina branch of the Young Men's Hebrew Association, where I'd lift weights in the afternoons, and maybe have a swim. Sounds like a pretty idyllic life, doesn't it? The only relief I got from this routine, though, was the Sunday night dance that was held in the main hall of the 'Y'.

It was at one of these Sunday night dances that I met a girl named Martha. Now I know you don't want to hear about all of this preamble. I can hear you, already, in the background, saying, "C'mon, Larry! Get to the point, okay?" Okay, I'm doing my best. But all of this preamble is for a reason, believe me. Like they say today, trust me, and have a bit of faith.

Martha. She wasn't exactly what I might have called a knock-out, but I thought she was cute, and I regarded myself as something of a wallflower. I liked to dance, but maybe I was a bit shy, afraid of being turned down, you know - that sort of thing. Almost everyone back then had some sort of problem when it came to things like this. Well, those of us who did, thought so anyway.

Martha didn't turn me down, though. She seemed happy to let me dance with her and so, right in the middle of our first dance, I got the crazies and started to cut loose on the dance floor. Whenever anyone did that, and it didn't seem to matter at times how good they really were - when a couple got the crazies and started dancing in almost any way that was different (and faster) than anyone else - a crowd inevitably gathered around them.

I remember vaguely wondering if maybe this wouldn't make Martha embarrassed and make her hate me for it afterward, but no - instead, her feet kept the beat, her body shook in time, and before we knew it she had a great big smile on her face like you'd have thought nobody had ever noticed her before. Oh, yeah. She loved it.

Even though she was only sixteen years old, she seemed very well built to me. In the little poodle dress her mother had made her, and with her pony tail, white sneakers and matching socks, she was a very nice little package all around. Of course, I was only sixteen years old myself, so I can say things like that.

Anyway, we spent the rest of that night dancing and I walked her home afterwards. She seemed to like me. Once there, she invited me inside where I met her mother and she seemed to like me too. We made arrangements for me to pick her up on the following Sunday. Suddenly life didn't seem to be as dull as it was only a few hours earlier.

I was afraid of making the wrong move and blowing the relationship (kids were a little less forward then than they are today, that's for sure!) but that next Sunday I finally worked up enough nerve to kiss her during a slow dance song. So, while the disk jockey played the song, 'I'm Just A Lonely Boy', by Paul Anka, I made my move. From then on, whenever we were apart, Martha was about all I was capable of thinking of.

She was just perfect for me, too. She wasn't after my mother's money or eager to hang around with the Forest Hill crowd... not that the boys in the Forest Hill crowd would have anything to do with her - their parents wouldn't be overly pleased with them if they started bringing home girls from Kensington Avenue.

Yes, she seemed just right and under my tutelage I made sure Martha became a full-fledged Rock 'n Roller. She slowly began to come out of her shell, like a turtle sniffing salt air for the first time. She had her own inner fantasies about romance, too, mostly culled from popular ballads played on the radio. Was there ever such a time as the 'fifties?

Riding around town in my Chevy, Martha thought it was a romantic song come to life, with its purple sex lights that came on whenever the headlights were shut off, the imitation pine Christmas tree deodorant hanging beside a short raccoon tail, the plush-looking but obviously fake fur car seats, and matching steering wheel cover - not to mention a big pair of dice bouncing off the rearview mirror every time the car hit a bump in the road. Paradise by the dashboard light? You bet.

I took Martha to delis such as Switzer's or Shopsy's and there we would dine on hot dogs and in true 'fifties style drink a couple of cherry cokes through red and white striped plastic straws.

Every once in a while, too, as a special treat, I would take her to The Sign of the Steer. This was a restaurant owned by a man considered by many to be the "Steak King of Canada" - my own Uncle Hans. His establishment was regarded as a pricey enclave of the rich and hungry. Show business celebrities and so-called captains of industry from all over the country would dine there on a regular basis. After all, The Sign of the Steer had won the Canadian Restaurant Association Award for four years running.

The place was no dive, and Martha was thrilled to death to eat there with me. She loved the ambience, loved the soft lighting, loved the steaks served on huge wooden platters, not to mention the liquor served rather surreptitiously on account of there being no actual liquor license.

And, of course, she loved the little black boy who brought bread and butter and later the dinner bills to the patrons. The part I loved more than all of this, though, was the bill the boy brought to my table. It always read "No Charge". The staff liked our visits, and especially liked Martha. They treated her like a homecoming queen, even presenting her with a rose when we were leaving. Yes, those were the days, all right.

Aside from Martha, though, Rock 'n Roll was about the only thing I really enjoyed during those high school years. Everything else was all right, I suppose, but it all seemed to be just on the surface. Nothing could get under my skin the way the music of the times did. I wasn't academically oriented like my brother David, so it was decided I would attend a vocational school instead of shooting for the stars.

I'd been enrolled in Warren Park, a school in the Humber District, where it was expected that I would learn a trade that wasn't available in a regular school. That was all well and good, I decided, but my impressions of the school on a scale of one to ten wouldn't even have hit the five mark and so I played hooky every chance I could.

I didn't think the teachers really cared much about me or any of the other kids in the class. I sat at the back, generally overlooked, feeling at times like I was invisible. Of course, I didn't help make things any better by refusing to go on school field trips, unless they were to Niagara Falls, or some other destination I considered at the time to be of importance.

Instead, I'd go on my own field trips. They were unauthorized, but more fun. I'd take in the latest movies or go to places like the Rio or the Biltmore where I could see two or three recent films for only half a dollar. Hey, even then I knew the value of a buck.

The Death of A Friend

The only friend I had at Warren Park was a guy called David Fisher. He lived only three blocks from the school on Oakwood Avenue, and was - if you can picture it - the classic, I mean like *perfect* 1950s nerd type. He took sardine sandwiches to school, greased his hair back with great messy lumps of Vaseline, and chomped on the backs of his fingers when he was angry.

David had a pronounced limp, due to a bout with polio when he was in his early years. This limp earned him the nickname "Hop along Cassidy" from his fellow classmates - kind jerks that they were. I stood up for him once when he was being teased by three boys from a more senior class than ours. Just because they were in a higher grade, I told them, it didn't give them the right to look down on other people. They just looked at me, scowling, until I went on to add that what they were doing only proved, in fact, they had minds that were on a much lower level than ours, and no doubt had only gotten into a higher class because it would mean they'd soon be pushed out of school altogether and the place could go back to enjoying its previous good reputation. Maybe I didn't say it exactly that way, but the intent was there, and soon we were in a scuffle - until one of the teachers came out and stopped it before any serious damage was done.

After that incident, David and I became even better friends - some kind of bond of trust had been established, I guess. We took arts and crafts together, and made little figures out of plaster of

Paris - I would cast the moulds while David put the finishing touch on the painting. David shared my interest in the movies. We'd go off together to the pictures every week, taking turns paying the admission prices at The Grand on Oakwood Avenue.

One Monday night, David and I went to the Oakwood Theatre to see a double bill of *Excuse My Dust* , starring Red Skelton, and *Travelling Saleswoman* also with Red Skelton and co-starring Lucille Ball. After the shows were over, and we were coming out of the theatre to make our way back home, David turned to Larry and asked me, "Hey, Larry, would you buy me some rope?"

I smiled and said, "Well, sure. What do you want it for - to hang yourself with?" Both of us laughed at the little joke, but sure enough, the next day, on the way to school, I went into the Oakwood Hardware Store and paid two dollars for a one and a half inch thick piece of marine rope. The joke wasn't over yet, I thought.

Meeting up with David in the schoolyard, I handed it to him. "Here's your rope," I said. "Have fun." David asked me what it had cost and I told him and said not to worry about it, he could pay me back the next Monday - our usual night for going to the movies. He agreed that would be the best thing, and stuffed the rope up under his jacket. I had no idea what he really wanted it for, and didn't ask. Maybe he was building something special. Maybe he was going to string up some of those stupid little plaster figurines we made at school and drop them from the trees on the heads of the three bullies we'd managed to embarrass.

After school that evening, I went home and David said he was going to Keelesdale Park to watch a football game - something I wasn't overly keen on. I had music, remember? At about ten o'clock that night, the telephone rang. There was a police officer on the other end, telling me that he was very sorry to have to be the one to convey the sad news, but my friend David had hanged himself in the park after the football game.

Just before midnight, a uniformed cop and a detective in a cheap grey suit and porkpie hat came to see me at the house. The detective did all of the talking. He wanted to know how long I had known David. I told him we had been friends for about three years, ever since I began going to Warren Park School.

"Well, being such good friends and all," the detective said, "you fellas sure had a strange sense of humour."

I asked him what he meant by that, a strange feeling of fear and anxiety suddenly coming over me, starting to tie a knot in my stomach.

"David left this for you," the detective said, pulling something out of his pocket. He fumbled with it for a few seconds, opening it up. It was a piece of paper.

"Has your name on it, son. Name, telephone number and address. Want to hear what it has to say?"

Somehow, I gulped out a positive response.

"It reads, 'Larry, you're a good friend. Thanks for the rope.' "

I laughed nervously. "It was just a joke," I said. "He asked me yesterday if I'd buy him some rope. I didn't think he'd do something like *that* with it."

The cops, however, didn't seem to think it was very funny, the detective telling me I could be charged as an accessory to suicide. About the time I began to shake in earnest, he said they had decided there was really no point in taking the matter any further.

I was "all shook up" about David's death, though anyone knowing me at the time might never have thought so. In the fifties, we were being trained to keep things to ourselves, to live on the surface, so to speak. But what the hell David had gone and done a dumb thing like that for, I couldn't figure out, and as there was nothing anyone could do about it now, anyway, I didn't think about it much. Hey - it was the fifties. A guy had to keep his cool, right?

David's hanging was the most exciting event of the year, but no one talked about it much. What was there to say, except to wonder who might be next?

"Jewboy !!!"

Warren Park was an all boy vocational school for slow learners, and like any school it had its bullies. In my class there was a boy named Doug who liked to pick on anyone smaller than or different from himself. Because I was Jewish, he particularly disliked me, and took great delight in giving me a hard time whenever he saw me.

I wasn't afraid of him, but he had a brother named Bob, three years older and larger than he was, who picked him up from school every day. This allowed Doug to say whatever he liked to me, and he certainly took advantage of the opportunity, calling me "little Jewboy" and other, worse names.

Bob, for the most part, ignored the situation. Whether or not he was aware that his younger brother was using his presence as a deterrent to open warfare between us, I never knew. I vividly remember, though, Doug's yappy little mouth letting loose with a steady stream of ragging and cursing, and always ending up with, "You can't touch me. My big brother will knock your lights out, you dirty little Hebe!"

One day, in woodworking class, Doug's bad nature got the better of him and he pushed me into a spinning plate I'd been making for my mother on a wood lathe. It ripped my sweater, the shirt beneath it, and cut into my side. I was rushed to Humber Memorial Hospital, where they bandaged me up and gave me a tetanus shot. The doctor there told me if I hadn't been wearing such heavy clothing, I might easily have been killed. "Yes, Lawrence," he said, "killed. Like dead."

I didn't think too much of that idea and thought to myself that this time Doug had gone too far and I was going to put a stop to it once and for all, even if it meant fighting his older brother Bob at the same time. I'd get them both if I had to, somehow.

I stewed over it for a couple of days, keeping to myself. At home, I couldn't even listen to the radio without hearing Doug's needling, vicious little voice superimposed above the announcer's. "Jewboy, Jewboy, Jewboy! Na-na-na-naah-na!"

"Fuck this shit," I thought, "I can't even think!" And began planning my revenge. I confronted Doug in the schoolyard.

"I'm going to get you and your brother, too, if I have to. I'm not afraid of you. You're just a yellow-bellied little coward, hiding behind your brother, but you haven't heard the last from me."

Doug looked a little stunned. I'd never spoken up much for myself before, but there's only so much anyone can take. Doug pretty well left me alone for a while after that, until almost the end of the school year, when he started up with the name-calling again. He'd lean out of a window and call, "Wienie, Wienie the Jewboy!" and then, he'd try and spit at me from above. He never got me, but I got the general idea. We probably wouldn't see each other over the summer holidays and he wanted to have the last word.

Okay, I said to myself, the next time I see you... bang!

It didn't happen that way, though. The next time I saw him, we got into a pushing match and were stopped by the school principal who'd seen us from his office window and had come outside to see what the trouble was.

He knew there was bad blood between us - the whole school knew. There could never be any mistaking Dougie's little rat-voice when he started in calling me names, and the principal, as it turned out, had heard it once too often.

"Boys," he said, "you're going to get this over with. I'll not have this nonsense going on in my school any more. You're going to fight it out after school and I am going to be the referee."

He arranged for us to meet behind the school after class, at 3:15. There were to be no holds barred, and winner take all, though why he said that I don't know. There was nothing for either to "take", except maybe to be able to walk away afterwards with some semblance of what they call pride. The one thing the principal would not allow was for us to take it out of the schoolyard. Perhaps he had seen how vicious Doug really was, and how he at times threw rocks at kids from other schools.

A crowd gathered, and of course big brother Bob was standing at the inner edge of it, waiting, I imagined, to kill me if I so much as laid a finger on his precious little Dougie. I also imagined the crowd was there to finally see the end of the little blond Jewboy - namely me. Yes, I had blond hair, and this fact didn't sit well with others. A Jew shouldn't look like that, I was repeatedly told, along with the statement or question, "We know you're a Hebe, but what else are you?" Not to mention a few other slanderous remarks about my mother. Oh, they knew how to make me boil, all right.

Ringed in at the rear of the schoolyard by every kid, as it seemed, that I ever knew, all waiting for me to be slowly and painfully slaughtered, I wanted to suddenly run. Just run, get out of there - to hell with all of them, I thought. But it was too late for that. Not that I was so frightened, really. I just wasn't prepared to be the centre of attention in a spectacle like this.

The principal's voice brought me back to the reality of the situation, as he addressed the whole crowd. "All right, boys, this is it. There's just one more rule - no one can step in. If the fight has to be stopped, I'll stop it."

As I looked around the crowd, trying to keep my eyes away from Doug, who was taunting me with words again, I was surprised to see his brother Bob staring at me, a crazy, lopsided grin on his face.

"It's okay, kid. Go get him. If you beat him, if my brother loses, you know what? I'm going to laugh. This is a fair fight, what's your name - Larry? He's all yours."

To this day, I don't know why he said that, but he did, and it changed everything. There would be no running, not for this Jewboy, not that day!

Standing there waiting seemed like forever, but finally the principal searched us for weapons, stood back and said, "Okay, boys. Go to it."

Doug rushed me before the words were out of the principal's mouth, and gave me a punch in the eye. It started to swell up before the fight was over, which only took about two minutes. This was my chance. I knew there'd never be another.

Doug took another swing, screaming something about how my father must have been a Nazi - "Little blond Jewboy... " and that was as far as he got. If Doug had spent more energy on actually fighting me instead of screaming his filthy insults, he might even have beaten me. As it was, I grabbed him by the throat and threw him to the ground, put my knees on his chest and pummelled him, just pummelled him, bang-bang, one-two-three! "You bastard!" Someone told me later, that's what I yelled back. "You bastard, you're the fuckin' Nazi around here! I'll show you Jewboy right up your ass, you dried up little prune!"

Somehow, maybe as we crashed to the ground, my nose was bloodied, but I had him cold. My knees were on his chest and I moved them out onto his arms, pinning them down. And smashed him, hard, again and again in the face. He couldn't defend himself, couldn't keep my punches from hitting him.

The principal had to pull me off, and when I stood up, the whole schoolyard was cheering. I hadn't, apparently, been the only one who was sick and tired of Doug's bullying. Well, you get what you deserve. Looking at his little brother's bloody face, Bob didn't laugh as he said he would. He just sort of grimaced, and helped him to his feet and led him home without a word. No one had ever seen Doug so quiet before. Quiet, because he was struggling against the tears that had formed in his eyes, all the fight gone out of him now.

The principal declared me the winner, fair and square. Later, though, Doug (or his parents) called the police and they came around to visit me, but wrote the episode off as simply "just another teenage fight, no reason to do anything about it."

I saw Bob a few days later, and told him thanks for not interfering. He shook my hand and said, "I don't know nothin' about you, kid, but I know my brother. I'd say he had it coming to him."

I never again heard the word "Jewboy" at school, not even in a whisper. The victory brought me a new respect from everyone. Even the principal seemed to be more of a real person than before, when he'd merely seemed like some kind of figurehead to watch out for if you messed up in class.

And what of Doug, you ask? How did he react when he came back to classes? Well, he got himself expelled from school soon after the fight - for what, we never knew. Then, one night he made the mistake of stealing a car from Hutton Plumbing (at Rogers and Weston Road). He was drinking at the time and at 4:00 a.m. the next morning decided to try to outrun a train at a crossing. He almost made it but didn't.

The train sideswiped the car but good, killing him. And that was the end of Doug.

Young Love

The next thing that happened to me in those early, wildly exciting but depressing days - was Marlene B. She lived over on St. John's Road near the Islington bus terminal, and she told me she liked my blond hair, and gave me her address and phone number without blinking - or thinking!

Marlene was a year or so older than I was, and we met at the Beaver Theatre, where I was working at the time as an usher. Maybe she thought I was older because I had a part- time job. I don't remember her asking and if she did I might have agreed with her.

We spent a lot of time together, skipping classes and meeting here and there, though mostly we went to her house when her parents weren't home. We'd go to her room - this incredible room filled with teddy bears, like they were breeding or something! - and squirrel away the daytime hours together, listening to music, talking and... whatever else you can imagine a couple of hot-blooded, oppositely-sexed teenagers doing when there's no one else around to tell them not to...

No one, that is, until four months of this had gone by, and her father came home unexpectedly one afternoon and caught us, more or less, with our pants down! I heard him coming in the back door and tried to make it out through the front but alas and alack, didn't quite succeed. I got out through the front door, all right, but because I was still trying to get my pants done up properly, I wasn't moving as fast as he was, and he caught up with me on the front porch, and there, no questions asked, we fought it out plain and simple, just like in the movies.

Marlene and I used to talk about getting caught and she told me, "You know, if my dad ever catches you around me, you're a dead Jew." Her father, apparently, had a strong dislike of the Jewish race. I'll never tell who won that fight we had, way back when, but until his dying day, I'll bet Marlene's father had an even stronger dislike of the Jewish race - especially if they happened to be blond!

None of us ever saw each other after that, though, so when a friend informed me, a few months' later, that Marlene was pregnant, I of course had to disclaim any and all knowledge about how something like that might have come about. It was just one of those things that happened to teenagers in those days - there was never any intention of having it last. Neither of us pretended it was a romance. - it was just a couple of kids doing their thing.

When my mother wanted me, she knew enough to call Marlene's house and she'd always say, "Whatever it is you're doing, it's your affair. Just don't bring it home with you!" I never did. And anyway, if she was pregnant from me, I never found out. I wouldn't have cared, anyway. Should I have?

Whatever your reply to that, Marlene sure was good in bed. Even today, when I see more than ten teddy bears all together in one place, I start to get a bit sentimental and wonder what ever happened to my misspent youth, where did it go so fast, and all that jazz. But, that's life. It happens to us all.

A luscious, zuftig solid lover, my Marlene, a kosher dinner with milk on the top and meat on the bottom. Having sex with her was something else. She was very rare for her time, not afraid of her body - or of mine. (She should see it now, I think to myself - she'd say she never knew me!)

Marlene was the fuel for my fire. She made my sex drive come alive. We'd go on all day sometimes, from 9:30 in the morning till 4:30 in the afternoon, no holds barred. When things got too exhausting, we'd take a break, have something to eat - I'd smuggle food in, so we wouldn't eat from her family fridge. The less questions, the better.

She stuck with me because I wouldn't boast of my conquests. I didn't start rumours about her. Rumours could ruin a girl like her in those days. The littlest hint that a girl was messing around could put everything in jeopardy. Most girls her age, back then, went so far, then drew the line. She pulled me across the line! She taught me the longest word I knew, whispering into my ear that she was a (gasp! my good fortune!) a nymphomaniac.

Remember now, I was only fifteen and a half at the time, listening to Rock 'n Roll, daring to take the leap, take the chance to be the animal I'd always knew I could be, after being such a goody-goody little virgin Jewish boy. I was up to no good, doing no good, and being no good - and I knew it. Knew it? I relished it, revelled in it, loved it!

Love ya, Marlene, whoever you are now... remember Larry?...

Dancin' My Life Away

Bill Haley and the Comets, The Platters, Paul Anka... the music... how I loved it

On the way to my first concert, I was in such a rush, I lost a gold ring, going up an escalator. I didn't care - it didn't matter. To me, Rock 'n Roll was everything. Well, next to girls, everything. Certainly, it was ahead of gold rings!

I sat out my first dances at the 'Y', turned off by the mush and the hush and the wishy-washy early fifties pop music that was everywhere to be heard on the eve of the Rock 'n Roll era. I'd just sit there and waited, not even knowing what I was waiting for.

Then there was "Frenchman". He was the guy who always wore the flashiest clothes, had the neatest hair, the spit-polished shoes, the smoothest moves, got away with calling all the girls "sweetheart", and - made me hold his glass while he danced.

I couldn't grasp, for the life of me, what Frenchman was doing out there on the dance floor, waltzing with all the nicest looking girls, but then, I didn't much like the Frenchman anyway. I didn't even like the 'Y'.

Maybe I hated Frenchman. Certainly I was extremely jealous of him. I got to dance, when I did, with only the uglier girls, the wallflowers (like myself?), the ones who reminded me of "Foreign Legion rejects"... I wonder where we got those crazy expressions?

I just wasn't in the groove, I guess, but I *was* there to meet a nice girl, wasn't I? However, if Frenchman was like Little Lord Fauntleroy, I was kind of like the Mud Lark, stuck in my own whirlpool of chaos.

On the good side, though, Frenchman was my buddy. It's just that everything I did around him was wrong and everything he did was right. People would stick to him like flypaper, and avoid me - like flypaper. It was hard to figure. He was hip right down to his socks. I always wore the other kind.

He danced with all the prima donnas, the art exhibits who, if they'd smiled and meant it, would've cracked into a billion bits… meanwhile poor little Larry only wanted someone who cared, was maybe a little lonely, who wanted a little action, who could appreciate a good guy when she saw him.

Maybe Martha filled the bill, maybe. The volcano was there, inside - waiting. It just hadn't erupted yet… That's how I look back on it all now. It's the only way it makes any sense!

Anyway, Frenchman - he married Sheila, met her at the 'Y' - where else? (Much later on, she was murdered.)

I was going regularly to the 'Y' for eight or ten weeks before the bomb dropped and landed smack right on top of my cute little Jewish stupid blond head - but I'm getting to that part, don't worry!

Where was I? Oh yeah. At the 'Y'. (You can Rock it, you can Roll it, at the Hop. Bop. Bop.) So. There we were, the Frenchman and I, him whipping out a fresh five dollar bill (which was actually worth something back then), and sticking it under my nose. "Betcha this five bucks against five of yours you won't go out there and start tearing off your clothes like Johnny Ray does!"

Johnny Ray. He'd been on the *Ed Sullivan Show*. He sang, and he tore at his clothes. What could I say? Was I some idiot who would never take up a bet - or a dare? Whoever the girl was that Frenchman was trying to impress that memorable evening, she was more than willing - almost eager - to hold onto two five dollar bills until it could be proven one way or the other what I, really, was all about.

Ah, what things would we not do for youth, when we ourselves are young, and full of truth?

What a joke. I waited for a while - for some reason, they always played slower dance numbers first - then casually walked over to the jukebox and dropped a coin into the slot. Plink. Pushed the right buttons for Johnny Ray's song 'Cry'. Whirr.

I'd chosen a fifteen year old girl to join in the number, first warning that she "might be a little embarrassed" at what I was about to do.

Except for the girl with him, l'il ole Larry was totally alone on that dance floor. The bet had been made in the same way Frenchman did everything - flashily, just loud enough so everyone could "accidentally" hear what was going on.

I began to pull at my shirt, but only succeeded in getting its tail out of my pants. Grabbing both ends of my collar, I ripped it down the middle, losing all the buttons. Pop. Pop. Pop. The crowd loved it. I was the centre of attention for once, and I liked the idea. If Frenchman had thought I'd have gone out there and actually done it, I doubt if he'd have made the bet. Like I said, he always seemed to do the right thing.

Not this time. This time, I did the right thing. I'd broken through, somehow, and came away five dollars richer, too.

Even my young dancing partner didn't mind. After all, people were looking at her, too - and she was with me, the DANCIN' fool!

I practised in front of a mirror all the next week to blow Frenchman clean off the dance floor but still I needed my weekly fix of film. Down the road, at Lowes Theatre, a movie was playing starring Sidney Poitier, called *The Blackboard Jungle*. It seemed imperative that I see it, at least once.

During the opening, it was stated that the movie was restricted due to the amount of violence in it, *and* a new song called 'Rock around the Clock', by Bill Haley and The Comets.

Well, I didn't know what to make of that. The film was banned in many places because in it a teacher gets knifed and the America of the time was very fearful of the dawn of Rock 'n Roll, which, of course, was marked by the Bill Haley tune. The time also spawned the dawn of something even creepier, I thought - those awful teen films Hollywood made, where every boy has a smooth look, a fast car, a slow girl and a mediocre monster chasing him... none of which was very true to life - except the part about the monster.

Thanks to that theatre warning about 'Rock around the Clock', I of course rushed out first thing early next morning and bought the record. Yes, a convert was born! And I played it and played it and practised dancing some more. No way Frenchman was gonna out-step *moi*!

So the bran'new Larry, the hep-cat, goes on down to the 'Y' dance feeling like a new person altogether, like I'm really with it, ya know?

Oh yeah! I'd bought a whole new outfit, to prove it, too - hey, a charcoal suit, pink shirt with starched collar, black and pink striped tie, big, ugly cufflinks, yellow in colour (read fake gold) and, natch, a pair of ultra cool, new blue-blue-blue suede shoes - don't touch 'em!

I made the grand entrance a bit later than usual (final primping in front of the washroom mirror, Larry?) like I had to just throw myself at the crowd at just the right moment, eh Frenchman, ole buddy? You know how it is, right? With my hair all greased back, stuck together with Brylcreem or Vaseline or Lanolin or Dustbane or whatever it was, you know?

What a smash!

Poor Frenchman didn't know what hit him, but his little protégé Larry was very gallant and polite (for once) about asking a girl to dance. He stuck a hand out in front of her and said, very quietly, "Would you please teach me how to Rock 'n Roll?"

She was much better looking than the one that was with Frenchman who, upon seeing this, didn't know what to do except let his jaw drop a foot or so.

Not missing a lick, I flipped a quarter to someone and said, "'Rock around the Clock', on the jukebox, doc," - and it was, as they say, a done deed before Frenchman's jaw could push itself back into place.

And I - I simply went mad. I went crazy, nuts, flying all over the place, girl in tow, trying to keep up to whatever it was she must've wondered I was doing and from then on at that 'Y' dance, I was known as "rubber legs".

When the song was finished and we were catching our breath, the kids said if I would do it again they would throw money. "Never mind that," I said, "I'll get a girl to pass a hat around!" It was just so crazy, the whole thing, but there I was, doing what I loved, and getting paid for it!

Paid, indeed. The kids dared Frenchman to get out on the floor and do what I'd been doing - and he couldn't! He just couldn't do it. Oh, he tried. But when you normally would twirl the girl, I'd flip her, and just when you got used to that, I'd twirl her - but from behind and through my legs! Not even Frenchman could do something like that.

As I said, though, he did try. He tried to upstage me but the girl he was with was too snooty to get lowdown like she would've had to get and Frenchman, he fell right on his ass for lack of cooperation. We stayed "friends", though, and he asked me a week or so later where did I ever learn to dance "like that"?

"Easy," I told him. "Just… taught myself."

The *Toronto Star* newspaper, by the way, ran a picture of my dancing on the front page, a picture taken outside the downtown City Hall. It was during Dominion Day festivities (do we still have a Dominion Day festivity, anybody know?), and the MC asked if anyone wanted to dance on stage. I jumped at the chance, as nobody else had wanted to try, and there I was - on stage, all alone.

Someone said into the microphone, "Well now, all he needs is a girl to dance with!" - and a lady from the audience came up and joined me. The DJ of the day said, "Your pleasure, sir?" - and I said (you guessed it)'Rock around the Clock!'

My mother owned a cottage at Crystal Beach, and I liked to go there whenever I could. There was a joint called The Swing Inn that had an outside dance floor that filled up on weekends. Its patrons mostly came down from Buffalo. The parking lot would fill up with hot rods and cars with lake pipes running along the sides, dual exhausts, chromed everything. These American kids had a head start on everything, it seemed, and we Canadians did nothing but follow. I think we still do that. Show me an original Canadian thought, and I'll show you an American influence somewhere.

But anyway. One weekend I went up there and after getting settled in our cabin, headed on over to The Swing Inn about 7:30 p.m. or so, just when the dancing got underway. It was an extremely cool place, and I don't mean the temperature. At the time, Sammy Davis Junior was all the rage on the radio. Whatever he was singing wasn't Rock 'n Roll, though, and the Yankee kids weren't having any of it, not on that dance floor.

They only wanted to hear two songs, and you know what one of them was... Bill Haley's 'Rock around the Clock', of course. The other? Elvis Presley's 'Heartbreak Hotel'. Yeah. Now that was music.

I hit the dance floor and it was the beginning of a truly unforgettable summer. I met this very pretty little blonde girl named Diane. She was seventeen years old, she was cute, and she liked my dancing. I've never been known to be shy, so I may as well say that the American kids liked it too.

In those days, there were two beaches - one you paid to get on, the other was free. The former had a curfew, the latter didn't. The first night Diane and I met, after the dance (about eleven o'clock or so), we went down to the free beach or what was locally called "Makeout Heaven". And make- out, we did. Well, you can't just sit there and watch the waves roll in, can you? Not when you're that age! You're experimenting, you've got to check everything out! So anyway. After a very heavy necking session, and full of love and sand, I told her I liked her, walked her home, thanked her for the evening and went back to the cottage to fall asleep dreaming of tomorrow.

Tomorrow came, and Diane and I went swimming at the pay beach. The strap on her bathing suit broke and I remember giving her a safety pin. I always kept one on my own bathing suit, you see, just for emergencies like this. I should have been a boy scout. Always prepared, that was me.

Pet names were a big fad in those days. It seemed everyone had a nickname, and I started calling Diane 'Pixie'. I have no idea why. I used a letter-pressing set, which was another fad, to make her a key chain that read: "I LOVE PIXIE". With a display of love like that, we became quite a hot item around the beach that summer. ("Here come Larry and Pixie! Clear the dance floor! Make way for the lovebirds!")

One night, back in the city, Pixie drank a little too much and her parents threw her out. She showed up at my place on Oakwood Crescent and my Mom gave her a place to sleep. I'm just telling you this part because I wouldn't want anyone to get the impression we spent all our time on beaches, or didn't have anything to do with one another in any other way. Actually we became pretty good friends and went to all sorts of places together.

Once, after returning to Crystal Beach late after a day trip to Buffalo, I drove over to the cottage, half expecting Pixie to be there. The feud with her parents was still on, and she couldn't go home so had gotten into the habit of dropping by unexpectedly - which was fine with me. But this time, no Pixie, which seemed a little strange, knowing how she didn't like to miss a weekend trip under almost any circumstances.

I went down to the beach by myself, and walked along the shore awhile. It was dark and in the distance I could see the light of a fire and headed toward it, figuring maybe there was a party going on that I could invite myself to. As I came nearer the perimeter of light, I could make out figures sitting around the fire, couples mostly, and there was Pixie. Her head was sticking out from beneath the shoulder of a huge football-player type. She was "Oohing" and "Ahhing" and running her fingers through his hair and I was devastated.

I couldn't bear to watch and no longer feeling in a party mood made my way back to the cottage. Life was so cruel. I waited for her until 2 a.m. and when she still hadn't shown up I gathered her belongings together and threw them, one by one, out onto the lawn.

About 2.30 a.m. the side of beef pulled up in a bright yellow convertible and she slipped out of it, after a long and engaging hug session while the car quietly idled. As she let go of the guy and slid out of the door, the fella looked up and seeing someone (me!) standing in the doorway of the cottage, suddenly stepped on the gas and *vroooooooommm!* - got the hell out of there, almost sending Pixie flying.

It was quite the scene that followed, believe me!

"Why are my expletive-deleted clothes out here on the lawn!?"

"Hey! You eat my food, you sleep in our bed, and now you've gone and pissed me off royally. Who do you think you are, anyway? Guess you were hoping I stayed in Buffalo, huh? So, you go off with some effin' quarterback when the cat's away, is that it?"

She started to cry, or at least made like she was crying. "Well, what am I supposed to do? Where'll I go?"

"Do I care? Just get your stuff off our lawn. Go down to the beach and sleep there. Maybe there are members of the team you haven't met yet, who knows? Personally, I don't give a damn what you do. Just don't do it around here, got it? Goodbye!"

I never saw "Pixie" again, but I still have one of her little bell earrings. (I knew you'd be interested!)

The summer kept on moving into what later I would call "the past".

❀❀❀

Back in the city, I had the terrible feeling that my life was becoming much too bland. My schooling certainly was a washout. I had that bored, senseless feeling that creeps into the life of every kid, only in my case I seemed more senselessly bored than most of my peers. Maybe it was because I went through periods of having no girlfriend. Dances were one thing, but they didn't happen every day.

❀

Fate Steps In – At the 'Y'

Sundays were a particularly dull routine for me… I'd go to the 'Y' and work out on the weights, grab a cherry coke and a hot dog in the cafeteria, talk to the guys awhile. Nothing special about that. It was all done in the name of socializing. One thing a teenager can't be and that's a social reject or a hermit. You've got to get out and be a part of the gang.

One Sunday evening, about six, I was in the showers at the 'Y' after a workout, and this guy Irving Rodstein was there.

"So, what are you doing these days?" he asked.

I told him "not much", but at the moment I was getting ready to go to the dance. "Exciting life," I added. "How about yourself?"

"Me? I'm studying Marxism and Leninism. Zionism, too."

"Is that enough?" I asked. "Have you checked out Nazism yet?" I always had to be fast with a good reply. It's one of the things teenagers are good at.

Bernie was there, too, scrubbing his back and listening to us. He joined in the conversation with, "I'm recruiting volunteers who can commit a year to go and live in Israel. Why study Zionism on paper when you can go there and live it firsthand?"

Irving said, "If you mean it, count me in. I'm serious."

Bernie looked at me. "What about you, Larry? Want a free trip to the Promised Land?"

"You're kidding," I replied. Then, "No, you're not. You're serious, aren't you? Well, they wouldn't take someone like me, would they? They want believers. I'm just a schmuck."

I dropped a bar of soap smack on my toe when Bernie said, "Don't worry about it. If you want to go, I can get you in. You want in?"

Well, I wanted a free trip. But what I said was, "Sure. I'll go and fight for Israel." I knew that was what he wanted to hear, but after telling him that, I put the idea out of my head. There was no way I was going to believe him. Who would want to send someone like me anywhere? A kid with nothing on his mind but girls, cars and Rock 'n Roll? A kid whose main ambition was to be Elvis on the dance floor? And that was how I agreed to go, and the three of us shook hands.

As the summer came toward an end, though, it became more and more clear that there was no fooling about this trip. We *were* going to go! I didn't know what to think, but was becoming excited at the prospect. What had started as a joke was soon to come true.

So much for Crystal Beach that year. At home, I went about my business, went to the 'Y', saw Martha, and then called her one evening shortly before we were due to leave for overseas - and said goodbye. She was mad, because she'd somehow gotten it into her head that we were going to be a pair, go steady or something. I hated to disillusion her, but as I tried to explain, "You've gotta do what you've gotta do, and this is what I've gotta do!" Somehow, it didn't wash very well - she figured I had another girl.

I never saw her again, either. It was, looking back on it now, the end of an era. So I called everyone I knew and told them all good-bye. Not really understanding what I might be getting myself into, I simply told them I was going on a holiday. I didn't even mention Israel. I doubt if anyone would have believed me, anyway. If I'd said, "Memphis, Tennessee," well... that would have been more plausible. But, Israel? Forget it.

The countdown was on and a week before our scheduled departure Mom threw a goodbye party for me, inviting Bernie, Irving, Uncle George, Auntie Shirley - a big, family affair.

Uncle George said, "You're not going to last over there. Your type never does." I wasn't sure what he meant by that, or if it was meant to be sarcastic or just a joke. He said it while handing me a one hundred dollar bill, adding, "Don't look at me that way. You're going to need this, you know. You aren't going to last more than a few weeks, that's all. I can see you won't last. You can't do it, kid."

I remember staring at his outstretched hand and wondering, what the hell does he know? What does he know about Larry Wiener that I don't know? I wanted to tell him what I thought he could do with that hundred dollar bill, but I didn't have the nerve. Besides, it was money. Who was I to look a gift horse in the mouth? Today, I might, but then - I was the ultimate rebel, right? I'd make it to Israel, all right, and I'd stay there, too, as long as I had to.

"Listen, Uncle George, I don't really need this," I started to say - but he was insistent and I didn't get any further. Well, what the heck - if he was so eager to give his money away, it was fine by me. Besides, you never knew... maybe somewhere down the line I would need it.

Did I?

I'll never tell.

⊗⊗⊗

The sendoff party was in name only, because no one believed I'd be gone very long. I didn't exactly inspire anyone to have faith in me in those days. After filling ourselves with chicken soup, roast chicken and roast beef, there was a wine toast. "Have a good time, Larry! Don't forget to write!" - and all the rest of it. But, behind all the words and sentiment, beneath it all, was a sense that not one of these people figured I'd be away any longer than a few weeks or at most a month. I didn't know myself, really, what I was getting into.

The next day, I was summoned to appear at the Zionist offices over at Lawrence Avenue and Marley Street, along with everyone else who was going to make this wondrous journey. I knew most of the people, except a man named Saul, who was extremely religious, verging on the fanatical, and a girl by the name of Judy, who hailed from Winnipeg. I wasn't impressed with this crowd, and wondered what their motives for going really were.

For their part, the Zionists started pumping us with information - hype and propaganda - telling us we would be "pioneers" working the earth and building up a country that was only ten years old in the eyes of the rest of the world. They reminded us, of course that, being Jews, we knew it was much, much older than that, and that official recognition only meant the fulfilling of prophecy.

I wondered what they were talking about, but kept my mouth shut, listening to them rave on about how important a work it was we were setting out to do, not to mention how expensive it would be to send us off to the Holy Land - they made sure we heard that part! Most of the people, though, were pretty gung-ho. Filled with Zionist fever, they couldn't wait to set their feet down on that holy ground. "We have to build up the Motherland!" I wasn't buying any of this, but kept my thoughts to myself.

We were told we would have to learn to speak Hebrew and assimilate to the ways of kibbutz life. They didn't tell us which kibbutz we were headed for, but already, we were told, a large group had been sent to religious kibbutzim, people whose hearts were into never having to return to Canada. I thought, well, maybe Canada is better off without them. After all, they would have been, to degrees, fanatical sorts, older kids planning to marry Sabras - and marry the land. Which might come first, I figured, probably didn't matter.

Bernie was a member of a Zionist organization, and I don't know what he thought of me - maybe he believed I'd become a convert - he prayed three times a day and it struck me that he was dedicated not so much to Zionism, but to whatever beliefs his family had instilled in him. However, he'd crossed the line into zealotry, and I could see he was well on the way to becoming one of those sorts who, rather than going to actually work and develop the new state through physical means had more of an idea of praying it all into being.

Personally, I didn't know or care much about what might be ahead for us, and developing the new state was about the furthest thing from my mind. I wondered what kind of music they had over there... did they know about Elvis? Did they have dance halls where you could twirl the night away? *Everyone* wasn't religious, were they?

We were informed that we were to be part of a so-called "splinter group", gathered from across Canada through an ad in the

Jewish News. Of course, they were really looking for mercenaries, whatever that may have meant at the time. Looking around the room at the rest of my fellow travellers, the gathering, and the idea behind it, seemed slightly unreal. Did any of us know what we were doing? Were these people just being used? What was the deal, really? While the others seemed to be going along with whatever was said, Rock 'n Roll had altered my sense of innocence to the point where I was becoming pretty cynical.

Cynicism, though, was what they seemed to be after. The more discontent you were, the better. You'd fit in better, into the plans of the new state, whatever they were. What the Zionists didn't realize was that some people were more cynical than others, and it would only be natural for someone like that (me!) to be cynical about the whole operation. In fact, if they had been able to read my mind, they never would have let me into their office.

I couldn't help wondering if people who already lived in Israel were as religious as these Canadian Zionists, and somehow I didn't think so. I mean, here we were, this little group of would-be pioneers, the girls with their hair cut off, shaidles or kerchiefs wrapped around their heads, most of the guys with full beards and wearing long, black coats, the adopted Hasidic style... standing around chanting their all-day prayers like a bunch of beatniks waiting for the wine bottles to be opened and the crazy poetry to begin. I mean, that's what it appeared to me to be like and, I think, even to some of the Zionists who were sponsoring the trip. They never did advertise for recruits in the *Jewish News* again, not after seeing this sorry-looking crew.

In reality, of course, Israel wanted newcomers, but they were looking for workers, not dreamers, and these kids would be out of place wherever they might turn up. They didn't fit in here, and they certainly wouldn't fit in there. Why did they sign up? Why were they so enthusiastic? For one thing, they couldn't carry on the family businesses here at home, for whatever reasons. Maybe their families realized it, and encouraged them to be a burden to someone else for a change.

There might have been one or two of them who were genuinely wanting to do something, but whatever it might have been, it wasn't to go to work. Israel, to them, wasn't a country or land where actual labour took place; it was a mystical territory where the miraculous happened, and these self-styled utopian missionaries wanted to be in on it, right in the front lines, to make sure they got their share of the spiritual spoils.

I couldn't believe it.

I couldn't believe, either, that I was one of them, but I was.

One More Meeting...

There was one more meeting with the Zionist organization, and then, if all went well, we'd be on our way to the Promised Land. They thought of it in this way too. My mother went with me (I suppose she couldn't believe I was doing this crazy thing, either, and had to see for herself what kind of lunatics would send her little Larry off across the sea to terrorize strangers with his passion for hot dance music). We visited with a Mr. Rosenthal, who represented the Zionists. He told us that what they were doing was "looking for Paradise Lost".

"If they don't come back within a year, we'll have gotten our money's worth," he said. His smile was like a big slice of watermelon. "If they're true to their calling, I know I'll never hear from them again. We all have to do our part in this, Mrs. Wiener, even if your son Lawrence here doesn't see the truth - if his eyes tell him he's seeing something different than what is - you and I will know beyond any doubt that he has seen our Paradise Lost." Mother just stared at him, wondering, I guess, which one of us was crazier. As for me, I couldn't help wondering if he'd see the movie, *Lost Horizon,* too many times.

Rosenthal was a huge man, weighing about three hundred pounds. I mean, he was *large.* He was the glitzy type, with gold rings. One had a flashy diamond in it, the other had his initials sticking out so you had to know who he was, even if you only saw his hand. This man was rich, super rich. You could smell money, if you got too close to him. I liked the idea - even though it was all

B.S. - I knew that from the beginning. Still, all these signs of wealth, even down to the big cigar he smoked, impressed me no end. I wouldn't mind being like that, I thought. Then I took a closer look at him and decided no, I wouldn't want that at all. Just give me the money, honey...

He was very impressive, though - a super hustler, rich and powerful - just like Uncle George. We spent four or five hours there in the Zionist office with Rosenthal, going over everything two, three times - just to make sure everyone knew what was going on. I knew, all right! But I'd learned a long time ago to keep quiet, to listen to the music and, if I liked it - to dance! So, I danced.

I danced to Rosenthal's trying to tell us we were protecting his country. "What you are going to do, my children, is build a *new* country!" We were all his children, it appeared, like he was Abraham. Hell, he was like Chuck Berry. "You are all my children!" I wondered which of us was to be sacrificed first.

I danced, too, when he made it clear we would be well provided for, but would receive no pay. "It isn't a money deal, you understand. You will be acting strictly on a volunteer basis." Yeah, like Isaac on the mountain.

After a long description of what was expected, and describing us as "religious kids setting out on a pilgrimage", he said he wanted to speak privately to "each of my children of Israel", and one-on-one interviews followed.

"What are your motives for going? What do you think of Israel? What's your opinion of people living in a land where there's warfare twenty-four hours a day?" And on and on into the afternoon, he played this music and we all danced to it.

What would we be doing when we got there? Well... Judy, for example, would be doing domestic work or maybe teaching children English. Her mission would be to spread the propaganda, and to find a nice Israeli boy and "multiply the children of Israel", to help set the stage for the development of the new state, the "Promised Land". It left Judy feeling "high", she said, high and important. She bought it all and was going to Israel to conquer whatever and whoever got in her way - a modern Joan of Arc. Each one of us had a separate job to do, but when you broke it down, it all came out as the same nonsense - spread the Zionist message.

So what did Irving think of all this? Irving was one hundred percent a scholar, an avid reader, spoke good Hebrew, knew the geography of the Middle East. He didn't smoke, drink, swear. He wouldn't go out with girls, let alone go to a 'Y' dance. He wanted to go to Israel, marry a proper woman and never come back. He'd read anything he could get his hands on, as long as it had the word "Israel" somewhere in it. A real fanatic, he was Rosenthal's golden boy. The man loved him. How could he help it?

All the B.S., the propaganda - none of it bothered good old Irv. Sold on the whole idea before he ever set foot in the Zionist office, he wallowed in the stuff. He'd do anything he was asked to do. To Rosenthal this was proof they were doing the right thing. Whatever strings were pulled, poor Irv the puppet danced without moving his own feet. He was the epitome of Canadian Jewish Zionist youth, the perfect subject.

He was also a Communist, and had the idea he could go to the Holy Land and conquer the entire country with no more than a glance. And maybe a couple of guns. Like Genghis Khan, was all set to march right in and help take over. Liberate the people! Set them free from tyranny! Colonize the captives! Do whatever it takes, but do it! He was also from a poor family, which helped explain his dream. The strange thing was, he wasn't what you'd call a very religious person. He was simply rebellious. He wanted a revolution, a real one. And Rosenthal, however he might have misinterpreted Irving's longings, loved him for it. Just loved him.

Irv was pure as a mountain stream used to be, a true Zionist, not a fake like the rest of us. Nothing could turn his head from getting the job done, and done well. It didn't matter to him what anyone said about Israel - he knew the truth. His only goal, aside from changing the world, was to kiss the wailing wall.

When Rosenthal asked him, "Well, what do you think about Israel?" Irving's reply brought tears to his eyes: "Listen, if there's blood to be spilled, I want to spill it on the sand!"

Rosenthal told him he was exactly what Israel was looking for... youth with spirit! Oh, man! The propaganda and the blessings fell from Rosenthal's lips that day, all neatly mixed together so you couldn't tell them apart after a while. He was so impressed with Irving's dead-serious belief in Israel and his soldierly oath about spilling blood on the sand. "What a boy! Just what God's looking for!"

❀❀❀

What did Bernie, who had been the recruiter for the group, think of it all? Now that we were all together, and getting set to leave Canada, had he changed his mind at all? Was he even beginning to have doubts, after listening to Irving's outburst of misguided patriotism? Not on your life.

If anything, it reinforced and strengthened whatever convictions he might have thought he'd had. Bernie, you see, was more of a realist than a dreamer. If someone like Irv could say things like that, so could he. Bernie was big and burly, a macho sort of fellow - a fighter, not what you'd call a thinker. Brawn, not brains, was his specialty.

He was the oldest of us all. At twenty-two he'd already decided he wanted to be a war hero. He liked the idea of being known as a big man in a small land - sort of a modern-day David, even if he had too bulky a body to seriously qualify.

Rosenthal, who of course had known him beforehand, thanked him in front of everyone for bringing together such a fine group of candidates. "There's not much to say to you, Bernie. We know each other so well. You're my right hand man."

He asked him a couple of predictable, stale, routine questions to make it look good in front of the rest of us - all things had to be equal, you know, and praised him for doing such a wonderful job for Israel. "Such commitment! You'll make your family proud!" He asked none of the long, probing questions he'd asked the rest of us.

Bernie had gone to the same public school I'd gone to. He also went to the 'Y' on Sundays to work out. Not what you'd call a good example of a social creature, he spent a lot of time to himself, thinking God-only-knows what. Although he was the one who'd asked me in the showers if I wanted to go in the first place, he had some second thoughts about this later. He didn't push it, though, because he was too hungry to please Rosenthal and recruits weren't that easily come by. He did whisper in my ear once, before I met Rosenthal, telling me there was no way I'd pass the test, and that I may as well forget about going anywhere.

My reply was, "Well, to hell with you, Bernie. I've decided I want to go, and that's it. I'm going. I'll pass his test all right. You think I'm stupid? You want to hear some bullshit, you just listen to me. I'll make it sound like I'm Joseph, searching for his coat. Maybe I just want to go to get a free trip, and maybe I don't. How do you know? After six months of listening to you and your crap about building up a new state, I'm already in one. You can't try to get me to back out now. Fuck you."

And that was that, except that Bernie kept asking, "Don't you care about Israel at all?"

I had to look up at him to reply, because he was bigger than me, but I eyeballed him all the same. "Hey, Israel could sink into the desert for all I care, and you with it. But I want to see it first, and I'm going to!"

End of conversation.

❋❋❋

I was the last to be questioned.

Rosenthal lit his cigar, sucked on it, splayed his ringed and sparkling fingers out on the desk in front of me - making sure I knew he was every bit as rich and powerful as anyone could imagine - and asked, "Well, Lawrence, tell me. Why do you in particular want to go to the Holy Land?"

"You see, sir, it will be a great opportunity for me to help our brothers and sisters build up a new and expanding country. I have the thought that I'd like to work the land like a Sabra, what else?"

Bernie, who had been standing off to one side with a little smirk on his face, suddenly changed his expression. his mouth opened so wide at this demonstration of dedication, you could have stuck a donut into it.

"I also would like to turn my life around," I added, "and going to Israel seems to me to be the perfect way to do it."

Rosenthal smiled. "And do you believe in what you're doing, really? What do you think you will be doing for the country?"

"Mr. Rosenthal, sir, I know I can be of value wherever I go, whatever I do. I want to be of service to the people of Israel. It's our heritage and I want to be a credit, not a debit, to the Jewish people."

"And exactly what do you believe you can offer to the people of Israel?"

"Honesty, sir. There can never be enough of it, whoever we may be. I'm a very honest person."

Meanwhile, I'm thinking, "Well, yeah, I can teach 'em how to Rock 'n Roll. If I'm going to have to dance, it'll be to *my* kind of music, not someone else's!" For the past six months, after all, I'd been dreaming about being the first real rocker to hit Israel. I'd show 'em a thing or three, for sure! It's a good thing, isn't it, no one has learned how to read thoughts yet? Well, except maybe Uri Geller, when he isn't busy bending spoons.

I think Rosenthal had a few doubts, though, even if he couldn't read my mind. He always spoke to the others as if it had been written somewhere on their birth certificates that going to Israel was a part of their destiny, like having a bar mitzvah or something. With me, though, it was different. Maybe my blond hair threw him off, maybe I didn't look Jewish enough. Maybe my nose didn't have a big enough crook in it.

He reminded me quite a lot of Uncle George. Instead of looking at you straight, one eye always seemed to want to roam toward the glitter of the rings, or gaze at the cigar, like he wanted your eyes to follow his, so you'd see what he saw - the riches, the power - and not the real person behind it all. Every time he spoke to me, when I answered, he'd look over to Bernie. I had the impression his idea of talking directly to me was about the same as it would have been if he'd been addressing a dead fish or a bank teller. Like, no eye contact whatsoever. I wasn't really there, or he didn't like the idea that I really was...

I was convinced he knew I was a screwup to the operation, but he needed bodies badly.

"But what do you know about Israel today?"

"Not a lot, sir. About as much as I know about China, I suppose. What I've read, that's all. But I believe in our heritage."

"Well, let's see. If they put you out to work in the fields, Lawrence, what would your reaction to that be?"

"I'd work as hard and as long as I had to. I want to be a benefit to Israeli society, sir."

"So you would do whatever you were told?"

"Of course. If they sent me into the desert to plant flowers, I'd do it."

"And you would learn Hebrew? Would you do guard duty, too?"

"I'll do whatever is required of me."

Oh, Rosenthal knew I was lying, all right. But what could he do? I had all the right answers, and it all must've sounded very nice to him - exactly what he wanted to hear. If you tell people what they want to hear often enough, you know, they'll wind up believing you. And it flowed out of me like it flows out of an actor who's perfectly familiar with the lines to his script.

Then, it began to get a little frightening. Rosenthal's mind went fully into the clouds, and out popped the big questions:

"So, Lawrence. Do you go to the Synagogue regularly?"

"Sure I do."

"And did you have a bar mitzvah?"

"Well, not exactly."

"Not exactly?"

"No."

"I see. Are you a religious boy?"

"I don't pretend to be religious, but I am Jewish and I do believe in what I'm doing. Maybe I'll learn some religion when I get there."

I could see Bernie, off to the side. The donut hole had disappeared, and the smirk was back. He figured I was finished. Rosenthal, however, continued with one final question.

"Do you really and truly want to go to Israel, Larry?"

I said I did.

Rosenthal's fingers pulled away from the desk, and he looked around the room. He fixed Bernie with a look that asked, *so, where'd that donut go?* and said, "This is the kind of young man I want in Israel. He will make a *wonderful* convert."

I thought Bernie was going to choke on the crumbs, and I gave him the sweetest little Jewish boy smile I could muster without laughing out loud.

"Well, I think that's all we have to say for today," Rosenthal announced, standing up. "Everyone has been accepted, yes, you too, Larry. You will get your papers in a couple of weeks. The papers will include any directions you'll need, what you'll have to take with you. You'll have to have your passports by then, of course. And - good luck to all of you. I know Israel will be blessed with your presence." This last bit, he said to everyone, individually, calling us all by name and shocking me slightly when it was my turn by adding, "Say hello to your Uncle George for me, Lawrence. I know him. He's a good man. We're both members of Variety Village, and the movie business, too."

And just like that, it was over. Rosenthal said goodbye again to the group as we trooped out of the office. Once we were out of earshot, I sidled up to Bernie and dug him in the ribs with my elbow.

"See, asshole? I told you I'd make it. Well, don't trip over yourself before the boat leaves."

Maybe I shouldn't have said anything, but it was too hard to resist. He glowered at me in return, but said not a word. This marked the beginning of a long rivalry between us.

I wondered, as I went to bed that night, "Are you ready for this?" Whether I meant was Israel ready or was Larry Wiener ready, to this day, I really don't know.

Honest.

Bound for the USA

Finally, after what seemed like ages, a letter came via registered mail from the Zionist organization.

"To L. Wiener," it read. "We have accepted you as a volunteer to spend one year in Israel."

"Hooray for Hollywood!" I said aloud to no one. "Now, I'm going to be on my way. Ready or not, here I come... like it or not!"

The letter further instructed me to ensure I had a passport. Okay, fine - I already had one. They also wanted a couple of character references - one from my rabbi, another from the local police department. The Israeli government wanted to make certain the Canadian contingent didn't include any criminal types. They needed the signatures of no less than three people to this effect. Well, I had no criminal record. I'd never been busted, not even for dropping a candy bar wrapper on the sidewalk or for jaywalking.

So, I went to the central office on old College Street for letters of referral from the police. This had to go through the Royal Canadian Mounted Police. Everyone had to swear to my good standing with the law. Then a Justice of the Peace had to sign it and just like that I officially became a good, solid, upstanding, law-abiding citizen. How many people can say that - and have the letters to prove it?

The whole process only took three days. Times were much simpler then. Can you imagine how long it would take today to get all the paperwork done, and to have the right people sign? It's amazing what the computer age has wrought! Things were much smoother before they came around, believe me.

The rabbi had to confirm that I was indeed a member of his synagogue, was of Jewish origin, and, I guess, that my blond hair wasn't a sign of my being related to Attila the Hun. Everything had to be verified to the nth degree. This was demanded by the Israeli government. They had to make sure everyone coming over was as pure as Abraham.

I had to have three copies of this documentation - one for myself, one for the Zionist organization, and one for the kibbutz I would be going to. At this stage, I didn't know where the latter would be, but I suspected they did. Everything had to remain a big secret until we were officially notified of our ultimate destination.

A second page of the letter told me what I would need to bring with me. It was like a list of things to take to a summer camp, but would have to do me a year.

The list included:

Light, long-and-short sleeved shirts, for night and daytime wear, respectively.

Sweaters for the cool night air.

A couple of zippered jackets.

Long shorts for working. I didn't like the idea, and had never worn a pair in my life, but I went out and bought a few pairs anyway. I didn't want anything to put a snag in the free trip I was going to have.

Suntan lotion and bug repellent. I never understood why we had to lug items like this all the way across the ocean when we could just as easily have gotten them upon arrival, but if this was what was wanted, who was I to argue?

Plenty of socks.

Light-weight shoes, for working in.

Toothpaste. When I asked why we would have to carry enough toothpaste for a year with us, I was told the reason was quite practical - toothpaste in the Middle East had an off-taste to it. (As it turned out, a lot of things had an off-taste, but you'll see what I mean later on.)

Cigarettes. If people smoked, they would have to supply their own. I didn't smoke, but figured it would be prudent to bring along a couple of cartons for resale. Israeli cigarettes, we were told, were not at all like Canadian brands, and probably smokers wouldn't like them very much. Larry the capitalist, that's me!

We were also told to bring a camera and a flashlight.

A note at the bottom of the list said that used clothing would be available to us if we needed anything during our stay.

Another page - the third and final one - included a parting shot of pure, unadulterated hype. It reminded me of a morale booster for a cub or scout pack.

It listed all the rules we would have to comply with, and told us how we would be expected to work six days a week, with Saturdays off. It wasn't as bad as it sounded, really, because this meant work would stop at noon on Friday, and we would also have Sunday morning free. The letter pointed out we would have plenty of chances to go into the city if we wished.

Everything sounded kosher, except for the line that stated because we were pilgrims of a sort, pioneers building the new state, there would not be much pay involved. We were, after all, looked upon as volunteers carving out a bit of history, and as such, should be quite happy to do our bit for the motherland. I wasn't very happy with this, but there was nothing I could do about it, and if I complained or said anything, I thought that my application might be reconsidered. Not everyone was delighted with the fact of my being included.

I was beginning to wonder if I shouldn't chicken out, too. When I pondered my future - an entire year working for almost nothing in a foreign country, even if it was the land of my roots - I began to have second thoughts. However, with the arrival of this final letter from the Zionist organization, I realized I had committed myself to the "cause", and couldn't back out now, even if it was their cash and my ass on the line.

The closest thing I'd ever come before to signing any kind of contract was when I put my Jacob Esau on my driver's license! Now I was signing away a year of my life to a group of idealists I didn't even believe in. By this time, though, almost everyone I knew, including my immediate family, had become involved on one level or another, and I felt I couldn't let them down, as much as I may have wanted out, and at this crucial point, I *did* want out!

I couldn't, however, forsake my - and everyone else's - credibility, and so said nothing about what I privately felt. Looking at a map of the world, one night, it suddenly hit home that this was for real and I wasn't going for a bagel in the sun! Although I said next to nothing about this sudden discovery, my mother must have sensed some of the uneasiness I was feeling, because she pointed out one afternoon, "Listen, Larry. I hope you're not thinking of backing out on this trip of yours, not now. Not after I held a party for you. Remember, if you signed the papers, you can't leave them at the altar!"

When she said this, I told her, yes, I had some misgivings about the whole affair, but knew I'd committed myself and I'd go even if I really didn't want to. I'd been toying with the idea of writing the Zionists a letter of apology or something, saying I'd come down with Arab fever or some other weird, incurable disease. When I mentioned this to Mother, she really hit the ceiling. "No son of mine," she told me (as only a mother can) "is going to do a meshuga (crazy) thing like that. You made your bed and now you'd better lie in it. No letter, Larry. You're going to follow through. You gave your word, and you're going to keep it!"

Much against what I thought was my better judgement, I decided she was right, and started packing.

While I was going through all this inner turmoil, another letter arrived, informing me that I would be leaving in a week, that I would be expected to be at downtown Toronto's Union Station at 6:45 a.m.

During the final week in the city, nothing much happened, except that my adrenaline rose due to my anticipation of spending the next year in Hell. I was really frightened. Here was little Larry headed out into the real world - this was no dance floor. Probably the only thing that stopped my adrenaline from jumping clean off the chart was the satisfaction I had for having been able to con my way into getting a free trip to Israel. Dedicated to the cause, that was me! And, after the blowout with my mother, there wasn't a thing I could do about it. The gates were definitely closed, and there was no way out without losing my self-respect. Oh well, onward and upward! There was no other way of looking at it. I'd made my choice, and I was going to have to stick by it.

Came the fateful day of departure, and I kissed my mother - and my life in Canada - goodbye. Of course, she was crying. "Have fun on the farm," she said. Sure, Ma. "Don't you forget to write me!" I will, Ma. So long.

The train left at 7:30 sharp, with little Larry safely on board, headed across the border into the States. If there was such a thing as "freedom" at that point in my life, it must have begun as I was settling into the seat. I remember thinking, "No more six o'clock dinners, no more Martha, no more..."

But then, my revelry was quietly put to rest by a sudden, jogging memory of a little boy staring out a window and his teacher tugging on his shoulder, saying, "Why are you looking out that window? You think maybe you're going somewhere?" I was the little boy, and reality, it turned out, was the teacher...

So there I was, headed off on a trip halfway around the world on a scammed free ride. I found, not much to my surprise, by the way, my conscience was living in a completely guilt-free environment, proving - to me, at least - it paid to daydream.

The train lurched, knocking my suitcase over onto the floor, and we were on our way, pulling out of the station. Goodbye, Toronto, so long, world-that-I-know! The adventure begins, and there's no way back now!

The train trip took nine to ten hours. I felt quite alone, sitting there watching the fields go by. It was like walking to the gallows, sort of - the shock was beginning to settle in. As the miles faded into the background, I knew beyond any doubt I was in the wrong place. What, really, was I doing there? Why was I on this train? I was destined to be a third wheel for the next year. This feeling of being the outcast, of ostracism, was not imagined. It was real, all right.

There was a lot of difference between the other kids and myself. Maybe, somehow, they knew what I was up to. True believers can ferret out the blasphemers, after all. It doesn't take a lot of figuring, when everyone in a group is all hepped up, and one person moodily stares out a window, saying next to nothing. There was plenty of tension in the air, though everything was left unspoken.

It's amazing, isn't it, what a sideways glance can say? And there were lots of them, all directed my way.

As the train took me further from home, I was starting to hate Bernie with a real passion. All he had to do was say, "Okay, that's it. Larry is out" - and I would have been out. He had a lot of pull with the higher-ups. He could have done it earlier, I thought, but he didn't. Did he suspect — or did he *know* - how much I was hating this? Maybe he was letting me come along in order to extract some kind of revenge. My thoughts were really having a field day, and despite the exhilaration of "freedom at last", I began to sink into a self-dug tomb of depression.

Killing time while the train rumbled and roared its way on toward my new life, I sat there trying to dissect Bernie in my mind. He liked Peggy, the girl from Winnipeg. She was a schoolteacher and I could see she believed in teaching by rote. Every twenty minutes or so, she'd remark in a very Pollyanna manner on how wonderful it was we were all going to the Promised Land to build a new country.

To my way of seeing things, she was quite plain in appearance, and I supposed Bernie thought she was another Lana Turner. She was much too thin for my taste, and at the risk of sounding crude (don't worry, I can be a lot cruder than this!) I'll just say that Bernie must have liked sliced chicken for his sandwiches, while I wanted something with some real meat to it.

Peggy-the-Pollyanna must have known how I felt, and made it very, very obvious how much she held me in disdain - by telling me so! Nice people Israel was getting, I thought, but wondered if her dislike for me was due more to Bernie's influence than to any real thought she herself had given the matter. Well, I didn't like any of them much and had decided to spend as much time away from them as I could.

Rodstein went so far as to ask me how the organization could waste so much time, effort and money in sending a schmuck like me anywhere, especially on such an "important" mission as this. He pointed out that I had never even gone to a Jewish school, and the fact I was unable to speak Hebrew made him address me not as "Larry'" or even "Lawrence" but "you idiot". That's nice, I thought. I don't even rate a name with some of these people.

He went a little too far, though, when he told me everyone figured on my "selling out to the Arabs for money". This petty attempt at painting me a traitor to the righteous cause of the young pioneers did not help put Rodstein in a favourable light, and resulted in my never being able to forget what he'd said.

I told him, as much as he might like to, he wasn't going to be able to make me into a Dreyfus, and that we were going to Israel to do a job. "That includes me," I said, "and if you want to be a friend, it's all right with me. On the other hand, well, if you don't, you know that will be just fine, too. But know this, Rodstein - you're nothing but a dumb rich kid with a fancy education and a yen to have people listen to you. You've got nothing to say, though. The first time they stick a gun in your face, you'll run back to Canada with full pants and even less to say."

He was too little to start a physical fight with, so I let him have it verbally, loud enough so everyone else in the car could hear the discussion. When I'd finished, I rubbed it in by refusing to give him an opportunity to defend himself, and got up from my seat instead and left the car - and clique. I snuck into a first class section a couple of cars away, and sat there awhile staring again out through the window, wondering for the ninety-seventh time what the Hell I had gotten myself into.

A man sitting across the aisle from me asked where I was going. I told him "to Israel, as a volunteer, to help build up the new nation." Then I offered him a peanut butter sandwich, which he accepted, saying that he hadn't had one of those in twenty years.

"Haven't you ever been broke?" I asked.

"What, me? T. W. Andrews? Broke? You must be kidding."

He then began asking questions about Israel and why I was actually going there, what my real reasons were. Not one to betray my own inner questions to a stranger, I gave him the Zionist treatment, making the volunteer-pioneers sound like young Elijahs heading off for Moonbase Two in their first fiery chariot. Andrews ate it up. He was as hungry for zealotry as he was for the peanut butter sandwich.

He asked for my address in Toronto and I gave it to him. He said he would write to my mother and tell her he met a true pioneer on the train, adding he was glad to know I was going off to build the new state, that it made him proud, that he wished he could come with us. I almost asked him if he'd like to trade places...

With that out of his system, T. W. Andrews then settled back in his seat and began to tell me his life story. He had started working during the Second World War, he told me, selling dollar-a-week insurance to Southern blacks. The plan was that for their money, after twenty years, they would receive $1000 back or, in the meantime, a thousand dollars if there was a family death. It sold, he said, like wildfire all over the United States.

I did a quick bit of figuring, and thought, well, unless someone died, you'd come out a loser by a few bucks. I didn't say anything, though, because I really didn't want to hear the spiel that would probably come up. Aside from people hoping some relative or other would die before the twenty years was up, maybe it was a good plan for people who couldn't save money any other way. Anyway, I didn't care. We were just passing time.

Andrews was now, he told me, vice-president of North American Life Insurance. At least someone has come up in the world, I thought, privately wondering how the blacks made out. I didn't think it would be prudent to ask, especially when he was now in the process of inviting me to the dining car to have a good meal, to help me remember, he said, that folks back home were pulling for all the young Jews working for God and country in the land of their forefathers. Or some such gibberish, which I didn't much listen to. I wasn't exactly the most grateful person in the world. Andrews, however, went even further in his praise, offering to take me to dinner.

"You know, Larry, for a kid like you to have the guts to go to Israel and work for a year with such little reward," Andrews said, "at the least you deserve a decent meal. Let's go into the dining car, and you can order anything you like from the menu. I'm paying. You'd better do it," he added, "you never know but it won't be your last good meal for a while." I didn't need a lot of persuading, believe me.

I wasn't complaining, though. Walking with Andrews back to the dining car, which meant going through the young Zionist party while they munched on their wilted lettuce and dried cheese sandwiches, gave me a great deal of pleasure. I smiled all the way through their stares.

Steak! With all the trimmings... who needed to go to Israel? I was already in Paradise! With every bite, I thought of my pitifully patriotic comrades, back in the cheap car, eating their stale bread. It looked good on them, I thought. Of course, I couldn't say any of this to Andrews.

He was busy, anyway, chatting away, telling me more and more of his life, motioning every once in awhile to the steward to "bring more for the kid, more, more. Eat all you want, Larry!" And I did. He asked me where my mates were. Between mouthfuls, I said, "Oh, they're back there, playing poker. Me, I don't like to gamble. I don't even know how to play the game."

"So, how did you get up here to the first class car?"

"I got bored watching them, and decided to take a walk. When I got to the first class section, I sat down. What were they gonna do, throw me off the train you know? It's much nicer back there."

Andrews drew a circle in the gravy with his fork. "Well, young man. You've got balls, haven't you?" Then he ordered wine, and toasted me, my travelling companions, all the youth of Israel wherever they might be in the world, and the success of the pioneering venture.

I had put away two Porterhouse steaks and a couple of pieces of coconut cream pie that day, not to mention several glasses of wine, when Peggy came into the dining car and, noticing me, came by our table. I half-expected her to say something like, "Well, well, here he is, the boy wonder, scrounging a meal from a total stranger..."

She had a little more class than that, though.

"So you've made a friend, Larry," she said.

I introduced them, and when she had gone, thanked Andrews for the meal and the conversation, told him I'd remember him in my prayers, and excused myself from the table, explaining that I had best get back to my friends, who were obviously wondering where I'd gotten to, sending the young lady out as a sort of search party as they must have done. I made it all sound very pretty, and he swallowed it. I said goodbye and headed back to my rightful place, back to the cheap seats with the cheap people.

Rodstein was furious when he saw me. Peggy, of course, had

told him what I'd been up to. I could imagine the conversation, told in flaming words no doubt, words everyone in the car would have listened to.

When I sat down in my seat, Rodstein started in on me. "So," he roared, "Larry's been up to his old tricks, I see. Now he's gone and mooched himself a meal. His friends sit in the cellar, he decides to go first class - at someone else's expense." I realized the reason for his anger was pure jealousy, and I laughed.

"Well, you were the one who said I'm stupid," I told him. "You might have the school smarts, but I've got street smarts - not to mention a full belly. How was your sandwich, by the way? Was it dried out enough for you?"

Bernie naturally had to have his two cents worth. "He'll probably do this all the way through. I'll give the kid this much - he certainly knows how to talk and buy his way in and out of things." I smiled in reply. He wasn't telling me anything I didn't know. It was truer than Bernie knew, too. I had a plan to make money once we got to wherever we were going. I had it all figured out. My Mom was going to send me Maxwell House coffee and cartons of cigarettes that I figured I would be able to turn over at a pretty good profit. I'd heard that in Tel Aviv there was a flourishing black market and I planned to be a part of it.

I had another reason for not replying, except with a smile. I was talked out and tired. With a stomach as full as mine was, all I wanted to do now was sleep. I laid back, stretched my feet out as far as they'd go, closed my eyes, and just like I didn't give a damn, which maybe I didn't, began drifting...

PART TWO

New York

The Hachsharah

When I awoke, slightly groggy from the wine, I asked one of my compatriots where we were, and was told we were almost there - in New York. I could see buildings in the distance and a half hour later the buildings started getting more and more numerous (and much taller!) and we pulled into Grand Central Station. It was about seven thirty in the evening.

A man who was waiting for us there with a stubby little school bus herded us aboard like so many cattle and announced in a rather impersonal way that we should settle back and relax as we had another hour and a half to go before we reached our destination - the "Hachsharah" in New Jersey.

The Hachsharah was a farm that contained one of the largest apple orchards in the United States. When we arrived there we were taken inside the farmhouse, where sandwiches, milk and cookies awaited us - as well as groups of other volunteers from all over North America. While we ate and awaited further instructions, I managed to say hello to some of them, asking where they were from and what they thought about leaving home, but I didn't attempt to make any friends. I was a loner, I knew it, and I liked it that way.

This was a meeting of the clan, where everyone mingled, asked the same questions and got essentially the same answers. It seemed to me to be a rather convoluted bunch, one that lacked any team spirit, but that may have been because no one, really, had much of an idea of what we were in for.

Finally, we were shown to our rooms - a sort of barracks affair, with bunk beds. It made me think of pictures I'd seen once that had been taken inside a county jail. My bunkmates were thrilled at the prospect, however. Somehow, the arrangement made them think, "Well, now we're real farmers for sure," or something. I'd never heard of a farmer who lived in a barracks, but kept my opinion to myself. I'd decided it would be the best policy at least until we got overseas. There might still be a way to bump me from the list and I didn't want to have to return to Toronto with my tail between my legs.

After showing us our digs, they told us to return to the main farmhouse, where duties would be handed out. Rodstein got assigned to the barn, appropriately enough, I thought. Bettle was to become an apple picker. Peggy drew kitchen duty, while I, not really crazy about the thought of picking apples all day, was chosen as an egg grader. (This consisted of choosing the right sized eggs to fit into "Grade A" and "Grade B" cups or cartons. If there were any that were too small for these, guess what we ate for breakfast?)

One fellow, Dave, who was markedly older, was given no duty at all, as he was headed for a religious kibbutz. Instead of working, he was allowed to walk around all day carrying his Bible, praying for the rest of us. He was heavily bearded and looked the part, too, so people basically left him alone with his conception of whatever version of God he felt he might be serving by doing nothing.

There was a bit of a clash between the Canadians and Americans, too. Not much, but noticeable, and our group wound up thinking the latter weren't very friendly - something the Americans, I imagine, thought about us.

Tired as we were from our train and bus rides, no one got a lot of sleep that night. The whispering went on until almost dawn, the air filled with expectation and speculation, even a kind of excitement. The next morning we dragged ourselves out of bed and after breakfast were quickly ushered into the routine of farm life: "early to bed, early to rise, and doing chores will make you wise."

Well, I surmised, we were only going to be there for ten days, so the best thing to do seemed to be to try and make it look as good as possible. I've never believed in promises, and never had much faith in people, especially organizations, when I wasn't an organizational type. Therefore lurking in the back of my mind always was the suspicion that if I didn't act out the part perfectly, before we set sail, it might be that I would never be permitted to set sail, that I'd be hauled into the office and drummed out of the place.

So, I did as I was told. We got up at five o'clock in the morning and then it was off to the henhouse to work from six until lunchtime. Putting eggs onto a conveyor belt and watching them roll along it and drop into appropriately sized cups, to my way of thinking, was the sort of job that could drive a fella crazy after not too long a time. I kept remembering, though, that ten days would go by quickly enough, and tried to make light of the work, asking one of my co-workers where the "D cups" might be... This didn't draw much of a response, though. I'd asked one of the more serious types, who only grunted a reply and kept on rolling the eggs without looking up.

To tell the truth (this book *is* about truth, you know), I kind of liked the job. It was easy enough, and was the sort of work you could do and daydream at the same time - something I did a lot of. I wished the henhouse had a radio or record player so I could listen to drums pounding or guitars strumming madly, with the voice of Jerry Lee Lewis belting out the lyrics for us to liven the place up a bit with, but of course that would never be permitted. Think of all the eggs we'd break! Still, I could play the songs in my head, and that was okay. Like I said, it was only for ten days, it was no big deal.

Most of the time, I worked alone and I liked that. I had it set firmly in my mind that I was *not* a part of what was going on - I was there for the free ride, that was it. Whatever I had to do in the meantime to get there, I'd do, but if it didn't involve being with the others, so much the better. Everyone got the message, too. At least, they got some sort of message - I was the loner of the group, I didn't fit in well, and no one, it seemed, liked me. I didn't have to wonder why. I didn't *want* to be liked.

The eggs had to be graded and off the farm by 8 a.m. They were picked up by a local hotel and that was the last we saw of them. Goodbye, eggs! I thought of fat tourists, enjoying a late breakfast, all because of Larry's newly acquired egg knowledge...

I was told how important my job was - the commodities market couldn't do without egg graders, after all, and the amount of eggs properly graded daily across the U.S. directly affected the stock market. Playing dumb as usual, I joked about wondering how the sale of pork bellies affected the stock market. After the first few days, it began to look like I wasn't going to be sent back, so my jokes got bolder and bolder - or worse and worse, depending on how you look at it. Of course, to Bernie and his buddies, they must have seemed simply staler and staler.

I liked the farm, though. I liked the work. The air was brisk, the mornings were beautiful, with dew on the grass, hay stacked in the fields for the cattle to munch on and, in the background, all around us, there were the apple orchards. The aroma was delicious, the sky was clear, and all of nature seemed to be in harmony. Maybe, I thought, this was the Holy Land. Maybe I didn't have to go any further to find it.

It *was* beautiful. Glorious, even. I'd never spent much time in the country before. It was a city boy's dream - a dream most city boys never have, or if they do, they don't get the opportunity to try it out. I felt lucky. For all my scheming, too, I felt clean. The air made you feel that way, like nothing could go wrong. It was the kind of place where whatever had happened in the past sort of faded away, and questions about the future, too, had a way of disappearing - at least temporarily.

Bernie had a way of making the pastoral life itself disappear. He dropped by the henhouse one morning to comment on the job I'd been given. "The barn's the place, Larry. No sissy work there, like you're doing here. You do fit right in, though. Maybe you were a chicken in a past life."

I kept on working, ignoring him as best I could, but I had to ask, "So Bernie. How could you eat your breakfast this morning, knowing your eggs had to pass through my hands before going down your gullet into your stomach? Did you like them? I set aside a couple of them especially for you. I'll never tell you what grade they were, though. So why don't you go back to your barn and eat some hay or something?"

I didn't want any trouble, but he really knew how to aggravate me. I figured if there was going to be trouble on this trip, there'd be enough to go around once we got to Israel. I began to pray that Bernie would leave me alone, and that I'd be able to shake him and the whole group once we got there. Yes, pray. I know it sounds strange, me not being religious and all, but still, I was brought up with the background, and knew how to do it if I had to. Whether it would help or not was another question. Like I said, I've never had a lot of faith in anything.

The days passed uneventfully after that, so maybe the praying hadn't hurt. The simple rhythm of life on the Hachsharah was enough for me in the beginning, but as time went by I began to become bored, and wanted to get off the farm for a day and see a movie. I was still a film nut and watching the sun set over the apple trees every night wasn't my idea of something to sit and eat popcorn by. There was no way to leave the farm, I knew, so I had to be content with thinking about bits and pieces of flicks I'd already seen. Of course, there was no television set at the farm to watch. We weren't there to enjoy ourselves, were we? We were there to learn how to work.

For some reason, I was becoming increasingly distressed because of the easy okay I'd gotten to go on this trip, after lying through my teeth so glibly. Bernie and a couple of the others, I was sure, knew what I was up to. I wouldn't have been surprised if Rosenthal knew, too. They must have said something to him. But, everything was kosher, signed and sealed. Why did I have this haunting feeling that at the last minute, when the ship came in, I'd fall off the dock and get shipped back to Canada?

No one with any real authority had said a word, and on the farm I was treated the same as everyone else. It didn't make any sense. Maybe it was guilt, I reasoned. It really did bug me, the feeling I had that something wasn't quite right, that there was something right before my eyes and I just couldn't see it. I tried to shrug it off, and the only solution I could see was that I shouldn't pray any more. Maybe I'd tapped into something by praying to be separated from Bernie and his crowd - and, along with an "Okay, Larry" response, some kind of deal had to be made to confirm it? "Okay, Larry, but now you're going to have to live with your conscience!"

Is that the way God works? I don't know. Anyway, it was an

unsettling, upsetting time. Why Rosenthal hadn't grilled me like he'd done to all the others puzzled me. If I was really such a zero nobody as Bernie thought, why the Hell had I been chosen to go with them? I didn't know then what I knew thirty-three years later, when my Mom told me about the thousand dollars Uncle George had paid Rosenthal to get me out of everybody's hair, to get me a life, to... whatever the reason was. It must have been like, "Here's the deposit, but there can't be a return!"... and that's how it was.

That was the reason they didn't kick me out. Uncle George had been very specific, and Rosenthal hadn't minded the "donation" to the cause. I didn't know anything about it then, but the truth was, there was only one way I was going to be returned before the year was up, and that was if the Israeli government bounced me.

So there I was, stuck with this creeping guilty conscience or whatever it was, and it was all Uncle George's fault - and I was blaming it on whatever I'd prayed to! So I had good enough reason to be disturbed - but I didn't know what it was. Getting bounced by the Israeli government and sent back to Canada would have been, to my family, one step below one of those infamous "Chicago rides" people were taken on for not complying with the rules, i.e. when they went wrong - or, for the sake of argument, right.

Everyone waited nervously for the days to go by. Although everyone seemed to like life on the Hachsharah, still, we wanted to get on with the trip. Our luggage had already been sent ahead to the ship we'd been booked passage on - the famous *Queen Mary*. The day before we were scheduled to leave, I noticed an advertisement in the newspaper: the film *Giant*, starring James Dean, Rock Hudson and Elizabeth Taylor, was playing at the Roxy in New York. For me, this was temptation at its worst, so I went into town and saw it - twice. Maybe a fitting end to my stay, maybe not. James Dean was a favourite actor of mine - the rebel. That was me, I thought - Larry the rebellious one.

At 10:30 the next morning, I took a taxi to the docks, after missing the bus all of the other recruits went on. By the time I arrived, everyone else of course had already boarded. If I'd delayed much longer, I would have missed sailing time. As it was, I had to endure a few smart remarks like, "So, Larry - what happened? You have to kiss your chickens goodbye?" and "Well, Wiener, we figured you'd chickened out," and "You figure the *Queen Mary* should wait for you, or what?"

Well, maybe, I told them, I was a little late on purpose, just to destroy their hopes at the last minute by showing up. If this had been the nineties, I would have been more direct and told them, "Get a life," but it was the late fifties, and the art of the insult hadn't been quite perfected yet.

I'd made it on time, and that was the important thing. The others were all so afraid they'd miss something, they did everything by rote. They had to be the perfect little Zionists in all they did. Me, I didn't care less, but I couldn't let it show too much. Not yet, anyway, so I didn't say any more. Besides, my Mom had sent me flowers and my two New York cousins Ronnie and Ellie were waiting on board the boat to see me off.

Cousin Ronnie handed me a fifty dollar bill, plus an envelope from Uncle George - which contained another hundred. There was a note enclosed, reading, "Do yourself a favour, kid. Spend this in the biggest whorehouse in Paris." Ellie smiled and in her innocence, asked, "What's the note say?"

I told her Uncle George wanted me to plant some flowers on the desert for him when I got to Israel. "Sentimental old guy," I said, adding that I didn't know where he got these crazy notions, but I supposed it must be hereditary. Folding the note and putting it in my pocket, I added, "You know, he thinks the nation of Israel is still in the wilderness."

If I'd known then what I know now, I would have known how close to the truth that statement really was.

Cousin Ronnie nodded wisely, indicating knowledge of Uncle George's romantic ways, and said, "I guess something like that was to be expected, but he might have given you a bit of money for yourself, too." I had to think fast, and assure him that Uncle George had been plenty generous before I'd left. I didn't want any weird rumours to start based on what I'd told them the money was for, so I relayed to them in a hushed voice that of course, Uncle George had expressly said he didn't want anyone to know how he felt about the motherland, so naturally, they'd forget I'd ever said anything, that if word ever got back to the family he would be embarrassed beyond tears, et cetera, and that the only reason I was even mentioning it to them was because I knew I could trust them. I didn't - I didn't trust anyone in those days (you could say I was thirty years ahead of my time) - but they never said another word about it or if they did, it never got back to me - which was, I suppose, all I really cared about.

I kissed Ronnie and Ellie goodbye, thanked them for the fifty bucks and we said our goodbyes as the sound system announced that all visitors were to head for the shore and when I got to my room I found another surprise awaiting me - a huge box of chocolates sitting in the middle of the table with a note, "Bon Voyage. Have a sweet trip." It was signed "T. W. Andrews". It was a nice touch, and made me think that any friends I had, I was leaving behind. Andrews wasn't a friend, really, but he'd treated me well. Although he wrote to my mother, I never saw him again.

A horn began blowing somewhere in my immediate vicinity as I stood at the railing and looked, for what might well be my last time, at the city, and I knew this was it. I would be alone for the rest of my journey, no matter how many people I might find myself with. My trip into the unknown had begun.

PART THREE

HMS Queen Mary

On Board *the* Queen Mary

The room was very plain, but not bad by a lot of standards. This was, after all, a very ritzy ship. The only drawback was that it was shared accommodations, and the roommate I drew certainly wouldn't have been my choice. At that stage in my life, though, I don't know who or what sort of person would have been acceptable. I was a loner, and didn't like having my space invaded. That's how I felt about a lot of things, and there wasn't much I could do about it, except maybe conform and be like everyone else - something I flat-out refused to do in any event.

There was no avoiding the others, though. It seemed they were everywhere on the boat, wherever I went. I wanted to explore this most amazing of vessels before it hit an iceberg and went down like the *Titanic* - and before you start thinking, "the kid really did have a negative attitude" - remember whom I was travelling with and our reason for going! It wasn't exactly a paid vacation. I had day-dreams at times about the *Queen Mary* hitting an iceberg, too, complete with visions of eager, young Zionists sinking beneath the icy waves, while I moved peacefully away in a lifeboat. In reality, of course, I'd never wish that sort of thing on anyone, and tried to be as friendly as possible with everybody. Well, sort of...

Just to make conversation, I asked my roommate, whose name was Morton, if he had left a girl back in Canada. He looked at me strangely and shook his head. He'd never had a girl friend. He did-n't have time for such things - he had to study, you know. I figured, by the look of the library he was building around his part of the

69

room, he must have brought books along instead of clothing. I motioned to the now-opened box of chocolates. He shook his head again and chided me for what seemed to him to be my attachment to useless, unnecessary things. "You should be honing up on The Land," he said, "instead of wasting your time talking." I could almost see the capital letters rising from his lips as he spoke the two words.

What the Fuck is wrong with this Morton guy, I wondered. Obviously, somebody's already brainwashed him... done a nice job, too. I stared at him for a moment, thinking of the others. It was like all of them, with the exception of yours truly, had been cranked out like so many nuts and bolts from an assembly line someplace. Well, that's nice, I thought. Pretty dumb, though, to go along with it. Picking up a handful of chocolates, I left Morton to his propaganda and went back out on deck to start my exploration of the ship. I just knew I was going to have a ball.

Like I said, there was no getting away from the others. I'd been only out of my cabin about a minute, when I bumped into Rodstein, who kept telling me, over and over, how much of a hero he thought Bettle was. He just wouldn't let it go, until I told him to change the subject, he was boring the hell out of me.

He had a one track mind, though, and started in on "our future, our wonderful future", by asking me what sort of job I wanted once we got to Israel. I deadpanned him and said that, well, Prime Minister might be okay for a while, and other than that I wasn't much interested. He ploughed on about the importance of our mission, how everyone was depending on us to do the right thing. He wasn't giving up on me, figuring somehow he could stir me into thinking his way. I couldn't be so easily encouraged, and turned the topic to one of my favourites, one I knew was one of his least preferred... to that of girls.

Rodstein knew what I was leaving behind - my claim to being the playboy/dance-hero of the Y. "You've been wasting your time, Larry. Who cares about girls and dancing and music? You've been going nowhere, kid, don't you know that? You think we're travelling across this ocean for the fun of it? On second thoughts, I guess that's what you do think, isn't it? You don't care about the cause one bit, do you, Wiener? You're just an opportunist, but wait 'til we get there - you'll sing a different tune then, when you're out in the fields all day digging up a new life for yourself, one, I might say, you're very badly in need of."

"Don't hand me that jazz," I countered. "'Y' know, Rodstein, it strikes me that you think every goddam Jewish kid on the planet is an Einstein like you. You think a girl's place is in school all week, then staying home on weekends helping their parents prepare for the worst, like they're all going to go bankrupt one day and the glorious state of Israel is gonna save them - but only if they followed directions and didn't go to dances, didn't listen to the real news or listen to good music, didn't do this or that... I know how gung ho you feel about this going to Israel thing, but you're not Moses, you know. You're not leading anyone out of anywhere, and if you think you are, I wouldn't be a bit surprised if it's to a worse place, not a better one. So how about shutting up for a while with all this stupid indoctrination bullshit? Maybe it's all a farce. What do you know? You haven't even seen the place, but anyone would swear you were born there or something. What if it's not what you think, eh? I could be right, you know."

He didn't like that, and let me know what he thought of such treacherous talk. I was turning into a traitor to the cause, he said. I reminded him none of us knew, really, what the "cause" was - and wouldn't, until we'd been there to see for ourselves. He was adamant, though. There was no opening his mind. He kept it under lock and he'd thrown away the key. He was a good teacher, despite his lack of worldly knowledge. He certainly taught me ...

He taught me this... that his version of Zionist was next to Nazism, and that if he'd been born in Germany, he'd have aspired to be an officer in the SS. He was one of those people, I surmised, who, wherever they were, would have been perfect material for whatever the latest in brainwashing techniques were, pertaining to almost anything, as long as he could feel he was born into it. I didn't dare tell him this. To tell someone like that what you really think is maybe to sign your death sentence, to be carried out at a later date, in one form or another.

I did give him a few clues, though.

"I know you don't like me," I said, " and you know I don't like you. But, we're going to be stuck together for awhile, and there's not much either of us can do about it. So. Such is life. But at least, let's keep out of each other's way as much as possible, okay? You know… just so we don't kill each other."

He wasn't listening. "Larry, you know you only got to go on this trip because Rosenthal thought he could make something out of nothing. Rosenthal was wrong, wasn't he? Even your buddy Bernie is sorry he ever mentioned a word about this trip to you at the Y. If he could have prevented you from coming, he would have, believe me. All you are doing is stealing from the Israeli government."

"Like it's never stolen from anyone?" I replied. "But you can ask the Palestinians about that, if they'll talk to you, which they won't." Rodstein's face flushed a little at that, but it only made him angrier. I hoped he wouldn't start a brawl on the deck. I also hoped that, if he did, he'd be the first to hit the water. I didn't care. I'd taken enough of this religio-political nonsense of his, and couldn't help myself. I went on.

"Listen, Rodstein. What you do when you get to your Promised Land is your business. As for me, I don't see the Promise. Maybe I will, but right now, it all looks like mud, and I won't tell you what I think it's mixed with. But, hey, we've got to stick together at least while we're on this boat trip, or one of us is going to be overboard. I'm not threatening you, it's simply a fact. So. Look at me. I don't care what you do, just leave me out of it. What we have to do together, we will, but apart from that …

"You can work the ground, till the soil, dig graves for all I care. You're right about me in a way, too. Now that I've been around you long enough to pick up on a few things, yes, I would sell you out. But I imagine you'll do that yourself somehow. The world doesn't need any more zealots. The world knows this. Your fate is sealed, I suspect, and one day your own zealotry will make you break the seal yourself, and it'll be all over for you."

He tried to stop me, to get his own two shekels in, but I wouldn't let him. I can talk, too, when I want to. I told him as much, and he looked away, but his ears were eating it up. All I was doing was stoking the fires of his zealotry, not that he needed it, but that's what I was doing. Unintentionally, of course. It only occurred to me later, that would be the only effect.

In my mind, I was trying to soft-soap him, by stroking the "working together" aspect of all of this. I figured if I could get that through to him, that we could get along when we had to. As long as he kept his ideology to himself, everything would be fine. I didn't know how to keep my own counsel, though, lighting into him as I was doing. But I wanted to make it clear, and there was no way I was going to let him have the last word. He was determined to become a sort of Israeli kamikaze once he got there and we both knew it, but that was no reason everyone else had to join him. At least, I didn't think so.

"Okay?" I continued, "We're on this trip together, you and me, the whole group of us. We don't know Israel from a map of Central Russia. I don't want to argue all the way across the Atlantic Ocean, all right? Get that in your head, Rodstein. Eat it for breakfast. Remember it in your prayers. I'll level with you, okay? What you want is what you want, so go ahead and be a martyr. Me, I just want to be left alone. I've got my own agenda, my own priorities. I've decided I want to have a good time - is that your business? No, it isn't. Got it? Look, this isn't a jail term, and you've not my keeper. I don't care what your opinions are - just keep them to yourself. I don't want to hear them."

With that, I walked away, off to watch for whales and dolphins, something with more of a playful attitude than Rodstein. I'd wanted to straighten him out, but trying to get something through to him was like waking up with a pillow over your face. He just wasn't listening. Years later, when I heard the expression, "My mind is made up - don't confuse me with the facts", I always thought of him. He was in pretty sad shape, if you get down to it. He had no mind of his own.

Anyway, it didn't work. He followed me up the stairs where I'd gone to another deck. I was staring out to sea, but nothing was out there to be seen except twelve foot waves.

A much larger, unwanted wave that went by the name of Rodstein blew up behind me. The wind that drove it could only be called blustery.

"Jesus Christ, Larry," it said, "when are you going to grow up? Don't you understand what's going on here? You know Israel needs to be rebuilt, don't you, that it'll go under if people like us don't pitch in? What's the matter with you? Why is it you're so self-centred? You're from a good Jewish family, even with your blond hair, which makes you look like a schmuck. But you owe something to Israel. Why can't you act like it? Why can't you understand that?"

I think, for the first time, he was genuinely trying to understand my position. He made the mistake, though, of trying to understand it from *his* position - a way that was bound to fail. You've gotta lift your foot from the first step to get to the next, you know? He wasn't willing to do that, so he wasn't going to get there. He would never understand, but I think he tried that day, I really do. he just couldn't see beyond whatever had been pumped into his head, maybe from the first day he started absorbing knowledge - who knows? I felt sorry for him.

I put my hand on his shoulder, like a buddy. "Listen," I said, "you know what I think? I think it's great that you were chosen to go to Israel. I mean, it's right up your alley. It's opportunity. It's a chance to do something for the things you believe in. The country needs scholars, but they don't need someone like me. I'll do what I have to do, but as for the rest of it - count me out."

I was bound and determined to enjoy myself on this trip, and didn't need some crazed radical fanatic extremist dogging my every step. I wanted to make some sort of compromise, like Bob Dylan later sang about - "You go your way, I'll go mine."

I tried every line I could think of to get rid of Rodstein. He was trying to listen, I think, but his ears were closed - I'm sure you know exactly what I mean. Whoever had helped turn him into whatever he had become had done a pretty good job of it. It was in a way, very sad, like I said.

"So, throw your books down the toilet, Rodstein. You know something? The fish wouldn't even read them. They know better. Learn to live, man. Enjoy it. You'll never have a trip like this again in your lifetime, you know. Think of it that way. You're only here once. You want to see the land of Israel turn into a garden, with every kind of fruit-bearing tree? What's the point? You know, right beneath our feet, there's more food swimming around than Israel will ever need. They've got money, Jews have been known to trade. Why develop a land that's probably going to glow in the dark one day, anyway?

"Besides, I'm sick and tired of you always harping about what a lowdown person I am, how I'm a faithless son about to turn into a desert rat or some such crazy thing. Maybe I will, maybe not. How about getting the subject of Larry out of your brain? You're not going to convert me. I'm a reject. Face it. Face facts. Face life. Look it, and me too, straight in the eye, Rodstein. Let's talk about something serious. Let's talk about... Rock 'n Roll and its effect on whales, dolphins and the American way of life ..."

"I don't like Rock 'n Roll, Larry. You know that."

"No kidding? I had you figured for a real cool cat, an old jiver from way back. You have to prove me wrong, eh? You don't like Bill Haley, you don't like the Comets, you've got no time for 'Rock around the Clock', you don't even like Elvis. Man, where have *you* gone wrong? Don't talk about me, for Chrissakes! You're the one with problems!"

"Only wild animals dance to that type of music, Larry. Wild animals, not human beings. Do you like being identified with the beasts? You probably do."

"Rodstein, I don't think I want to talk to you anymore. I'm going to go and look around. This is a big ship, and not everyone is headed for your Promised Land, you know. I'm going to see if I can't find a girl somewhere. I'm sure she'll be more entertaining than you. So why don't you go and play Jesus and walk on the water for a while? Israel is that way, I think." I pointed out over across the bow of the ship. I wanted out of this conversation, and wished he'd leave me alone.

"Oh, I'm going to Israel, all right, Larry. But not like Jesus did. I'm going to be a Moses and help lead my people."

"Where you gonna lead them? Back into the sea? Moses walked the wrong way, didn't he? He didn't even know where he was taking them."

"What do you mean, he walked the wrong way? What are you talking about, Wiener?"

"If Moses had walked the other way, all of the Jews would be rich. Stinking rich. We'd have the oil, right? So, who has the oil? Tell me about Moses going the right way. It's pretty obvious to me, he went the wrong way altogether. Grind that up and put it in your pipe."

Rodstein said nothing, but I could tell the conversation was getting to him, too. Maybe that's what I had to do, introduce a little blasphemy into his religious belief. Maybe then he'd go away.

"Okay, Rodstein. If you want to think Moses knew what he was doing, it's all right with me. I don't care, anyway. This Zionist thing is all based on superstition and politics. Who's making money out of it, by the way? Not us. Not me. Not you. Rosenthal? He's already rich. Maybe he's not rich enough. Who knows?"

"Don't be absurd. We're all in this - with the exception of one Lawrence Wiener - for the love of our homeland. Money's got nothing to do with it."

"Oh yeah? It seems to me there's something fishy about this whole thing. Like, all these young people being exploited, working for next to nothing, committing themselves for a year to The Cause. And you tell me nobody's going to gain anything out of this?"

"Don't twist my words, Wiener. I didn't say that. I said money's not the reason we're :"

"I cut him off in mid-sentence. "Sure, Rodstein. Okay, have it your way, but do us both a favour, huh? Let's pretend we don't know each other, that we're strangers who met on this tub. We've got two boat trips to go through, you know. We may as well enjoy it. If we're going to be at each other's throats the whole time, it's hardly worth it, is it? Neither of us is going to agree with the other. If we pretended we were strangers who just met, maybe we could work out some kind of compromise to leave the sore points alone. What do you say? I'm trying to be friendly with you, Rodstein, but you're not cooperating."

"God forbid," was his only comment.

I left him standing there gazing out to sea. Whatever it was he was seeing, I figured it had to be quite different from what I saw. Maybe he detected a golden glow in the distance, but all I noticed was fog. I spent the rest of the afternoon and evening cruising the ship, looking for some kind of action - or at least something or someone who wouldn't leave a sour taste in my mouth. My search that day turned out to be in vain, but I got a good sense of what was happening from deck to deck, and where the likeliest places were to maybe look in the future.

Like everyone else, I probably should have been tired, but the dreamlike quality of the first night on board such a huge ocean-going vessel as the *Queen Mary* kept me awake, and it was just as well. About two o'clock in the morning, there was a knock on my cabin room. It was Bernie, "just checking", he said, to see if everyone was all right, if things were in order, and so on. He was very excited, and wanted to spread his enthusiasm.

He knew that Rodstein and I didn't get along, and was probably just sticking his nose in to see if I'd elaborate on the rivalry. Maybe he thought it was a soap opera. He was also a bit green looking, and had already been sea-sick three hours into the trip. Still, he had his duties to perform, and nothing was going to stop him from taking inventory of his subjects. I remember thinking, "Such responsibility - he should have joined the Post Office." I also wondered what he would be like if, for some reason, he ever came under fire in the military sense. He'd probably close his eyes and wait for orders.

He seemed to be happy enough, despite being under the weather. His recruiting job was over and done with, and he slid back into just being another one of the bunch of lunatics making the crazy pilgrimage to whatever awaited us. He had his eyes on Peggy, too, all the way, and made it obvious to everyone that he wanted to spend some time with her in the sack while he had the chance. None of us knew what would happen once we docked on the other side, and this seemed as good an opportunity as any. Besides, the chance might not come again.

Making his rounds, he had a word for everyone, even Rodstein. It was funny, because what he had to tell him, was the same as I'd been saying all along…"Relax, Rodstein, enjoy yourself, have a bit of fun. Find a good girl. Nobody's going to look in the window, you know. Get your rocks off, who cares? You'll be sorry later if you don't."

Bernie gave a really solid speech about having sex while on the boat - well, to the guys, at any rate. There was nothing wrong with it, he told us. It reminded me of a locker-room type pep talk by a football coach ...

"Your mother gave it to you to use, not abuse," he'd tell us. He had all kinds of sayings, some kind of cute, others downright dirty. He wouldn't let up on the subject. Really, I think it was because he had some inner guilt association over his desire to sleep with Peggy, and figured if he could convince everyone else having sex while bound for Never Never Land was okay, he could justify his own advances.

The group went for it, too. They were young and a boat trip somehow equated in their minds with a sex festival. Well, I thought, at least in some ways, they're still "normal", whatever I thought that meant. And so, the girls, who had all come from good, decent backgrounds and who would never perhaps have dreamed of being lusted after - not on a trip like this! - suddenly became a group of unattached, sex-starved women, all searching desperately for nothing more than a good time... in the minds of the young men, that is.

When some of them were approached by these passionate young lions of Judah, though, godliness and duty was forgotten for the time being. Who could blame them for that? It was a natural setting for sex, with the rise and the swell of the waves, the open sky above, and of course, no chaperon. There's something to be said for having sex on board a boat, too - you don't have to push too hard.

Bernie's arrival that first night - or morning - was in a way a welcome break for Rodstein. Probably, having someone besides me tell him to relax was just what he needed. That way, he could pretend I hadn't said a word. When Bernie finally said goodnight, about 3 a.m. he pointed a finger at Rodstein and pronounced: "Okay, that's it. You're on your own now, you're free."

I passed the chocolates around and was somewhat surprised when Rodstein took a couple. Maybe he didn't hate me as much as he made out. Then again, maybe he accepted them just so I'd have all the less for myself. That last bit's really not fair, though - he knew I wasn't the type to care about things like that. If I had something, everyone was welcome to share it. Some of the others had been given last minute gifts, and had stashed the goodies away, but not me. I wanted everyone to know I wasn't as bad as they'd painted me.

We talked for a few more minutes, and after Bernie's preaching, the conversation turned onto a lighter note. What were we going to do, now that we were on board? There were so many ways to pass the time - shuffleboard, swimming pools, movies, plenty of drinking spots. The drinks on board were all tax-free, as were the tobacco products. I liked the idea. "See," I said to Rodstein, "sometimes it pays not to be too patriotic!" Whether this was too subtle a joke for him or not, I had no idea. If not, he didn't reveal any secrets about what he might have thought of it. I babbled on about how much I liked the Tom Collins and the Singapore Slings, all those "sissy" drinks. I didn't like the hard stuff, I said, because I didn't like getting smashed out of my gourd. It was too hard to get laid when you were smashed, I told Rodstein, who for some reason was peacefully listening to all of this.

There were dances every night, too, and I said we'd have to check them out. Maybe we'd meet some new chicks. Rodstein nodded, yawning, and said he had to go to sleep. I kept talking for a minute. Besides the many activities, there were tons of free food, all you could possibly eat. Rodstein yawned again, this time louder. The thought struck me that he was relenting a bit, trying to be civil at last and that was good. I said goodnight to him, too, and he left the cabin. I thought as I finally drifted off to sleep, yes, I was definitely going to make a point of enjoying the trip.

Day One on board the *Queen Mary* saw me getting up about 6 a.m., before any of the others. I was dressed and out on the bow before breakfast, eager to gaze out over the ocean - it was so peaceful, with a beauty all its own, and I began to see why people ran away to become sailors.

I could barely believe I was actually there. My luck had been pretty good, after all - one slightly ostracized phony among the dedicated believers. I knew I wasn't fooling anyone. It didn't matter, though. I was beginning to fall in love with the boat, the largest ocean liner in the world. Standing on the bow, I could catch the spray flying up as we plowed through the deep, and with every crashing wave I felt a thousand feet closer to my destination.

Really, I thought, if we could just keep sailing...if we were to go in circles forever, it would be fine by me. The *Queen Mary* could do that to you, and with every surge I loved it more - I was tingling with the sense of freedom. No Uncle George ordering me about, no mother demanding I do this or that, no six o'clock dinner. I was entering virgin territory, and didn't mind it a bit.

I caught my first sight of porpoises leaping along beside us, and wondered why I'd never thought of going to sea before. They were so graceful, as if they hadn't a care in the world. I realized that what I'd been taught in school about them was true - they travelled together in schools. There were seven or eight of them travelling alongside us, curious, maybe - sightseers come to find out what this huge, strange thing with smoke coming out of its top was...

Ten minutes later, I saw my first whale. The books had been right about them, too. It was enormous, splashing up out of the sea like some crazy Biblical monster, spouting, blowing water high into the air. I wondered, if I fell overboard, would it come and swallow me up and deposit me, like poor Jonah, on some foreign shore with a new way of looking at life?

From where I was standing, the whale's big, black head looked to be about the size of a '56 Buick. It was harmless looking, though, and I got the impression it, too, was curious and had come up simply to see what the big shadow going along the surface might be. Satisfied, perhaps, that we weren't the grandmother of all the whales that had ever lived, it began to frolic, diving and then emerging again, its immense tail bobbing and seeming to wave to us. The porpoises got into the act, too, following the whale. It really was quite a show they put on! I was amazed, thinking they must be doing this deliberately.

I don't know why, but I felt a certain affinity with that whale. He was a loner, like me, and though he had the porpoises to play with, still he was no porpoise, and somewhere there were boats out on the ocean searching for him, their captains and crews wishing nothing more than to have him in their sights so they could slaughter and put an end to him. I felt sorry for him, and angry that people would want to kill him. It wasn't fair.

I was thinking this as the whale was under the water, and I

wondered where he'd surface. It was like a game, and one of the stewards told me later that often passengers would make bets on which side of the boat one of these behemoths would come up on. "Yes, sir, I've seen thousands of dollars change hands over the years, all depending of where a whale broke water."

Seeing the whale and porpoises had a dreamlike quality to it, and I wondered for a moment if they could read my thoughts. It seemed so. When I started thinking about the wholesale killing of these beautiful monsters of the deep, the whale came closer to the ship, the porpoises trailing after him, leaping and cavorting in his wake, like a bunch of schoolchildren at recess.

I got the distinct impression the whale knew what I was thinking, and somehow knew he had made a friend. Just as I was about to leave to go and have some breakfast, he came up right alongside the part of the bow where I was standing looking down. He leaped once, and disappeared into the blue, flicking his tail as if saying goodbye.

There were three dining rooms on board the *Queen Mary*, and I was lucky to find the largest one on the middle deck in time for breakfast. Then my luck changed. Bettle, Rodstein, Peggy and the rest of the group were there ahead of me to snap me out of my oceanic daydream, and I felt out of place as usual. I decided to say "Good morning" and nothing more, if possible. Just seeing them took away from the trance I'd been in.

I tried to forget they were there, and concentrated on the dining room itself, looking around to see what sort of a place I'd landed in. There were huge crystal chandeliers hanging from a high ceiling, and the tables were made out of mahogany. Talk about luxury! All of the plates had been especially made for the boat, and had Queen Mary's picture on them. The silver was real.

The waiters wore formal clothing, complete with full jackets and bow-ties. The table settings were complemented with the whitest linen I'd ever seen, anywhere, and a giant portrait of Queen Elizabeth graced one wall, looking down on us, as if expecting to be prayed to.

In the "Israeli section", there were about ninety of us, whisperingly referred to by the other passengers as "adventurers and heroes". There were a few snide remarks, but mostly we seemed to be the object of quite a lot of admiration. We were young, we were headed into the unknown, and we were full of faith and belief in what was right.

We were full of it, all right. We also didn't have a clue about what we were getting ourselves into.

The Captain made his grand entrance, all dressed in white with gold braid and stars on his cap. He was maybe thirty years old - an age that, to me at the time, seemed almost ancient. He had a neatly trimmed British-style beard and a warm smile, inspiring great amounts of respect from all quarters, a sort of grandfather figure. His stature, decked out as he was with all the trimmings, and in the beautifully luxurious setting, made you forget his age. It was easy to believe he'd been Captain of this proud ship for, well, at least twenty-five years, a descendant, probably, of Captain Nemo himself...

"Good morning, ladies and gentlemen. My name is Captain So-and-so, and I'd like to welcome you aboard the *Queen Mary...*" He went on, informing us of all the things that were available to us on the ship.

"Along with having a social convenor, who will be pleased to have his staff assist you in any way possible, and lo, and behold, we also have an operating room with six nurses, four doctors, two of whom are qualified surgeons. We have an infirmary for people who become seasick. More people have been sick over the side of this ship, by the way, than died in the war. We have seasickness pills available from the dispensary, but people seem to put off taking them until they are just a little bit too late to help.

"Also, we have a theatre on board if you'd like to watch a film. Showtime is two p.m. and seven or eight o'clock at night. We have shuffleboard, too. You can run around the decks as much as you like to kill some time, as the journey may become monotonous to some. At 8:30 p.m. we hold a nightly dance which lasts until 11:30.

"Now, for the happy part - as far as cigarettes and liquor are concerned, no taxes are applicable on the high seas, so you may purchase these items to your heart's content and have a good time. There are a few rules that we do observe, however. Every morning before breakfast, we say a prayer and give a blessing to the vessel, which will carry us safely to our destination. In honour of the ship, too, we play 'God Save The Queen' daily. If you wish to avoid this, you can try sleeping in - but you'll also miss breakfast. In fact, if you do this, it may help with seasickness. As the old sea salts say, nothing down - nothing up.

"Before we begin our breakfast on this glorious morning, there's one last thing I would like to say to you... if any of you, as passengers, ever finds a need for any of us, the crew - from the Captain to the shoeshine boy, please don't hesitate to let us know. We are here to serve you in the best manner possible, as if, in fact, you were already in England. While you are on board this vessel, you may consider yourself a part of the British fleet.

"The rules are every bit as British here as they would be if you were out walking the - at times - foggy, foggy streets of England herself. And, yes, if any of you may have wondered - we do have a brig. This vessel operates on an honour system, and we neither condone nor tolerate thievery, which is considered to be the among the worst violations that can occur on the boat. Of course, this looks to me like a very honest group, and I am sure no more along these lines will be needed to be said during our voyage.

"I would like now to thank you all for being here with us on this transatlantic crossing. Everything on the boat is of course open, so I ask that you enjoy yourselves as much as you can, and have a fine breakfast. I hope you will find it cooked to your satisfaction."

And with that, he bowed slightly, and went to his table. To follow up, the grand formal order carried on. The breakfast bell rang and the waiters marched in single file, as if they were indeed in the Navy, breaking rank to serve differently numbered sections.

Our physical place in the general scheme of things was called Blue Section 21, and there was an Israeli flag hanging over it and a sign with the words "Reserved for Israeli Tourists".

Moved by the spirit of brotherhood, I wanted to break the ice we seemed to be forever stuck in, so decided to make the attempt to talk to everyone. I started with Peggy - who looked exceptionally good that morning. Her hair was freshly done up and she'd plied her face with makeup and lipstick. Not to mention the tight-fitting pair of jeans she was wearing...

"Hi, Peggy. Beautiful day to start off on a voyage, isn't it?"

"Good morning, Larry."

"Well, what do you think, Peggy? Isn't it great, us being on a marvellous boat like this, being waited on all the time, being served like some kind of royalty? How do you like it?"

"It *is* the *Queen Mary*, isn't it? So what did you expect from a queen?"

"Nothing," I told her. "Nothing but the best service in the world, and that's exactly what we're going to get. Hey, you can be sure that once we get to Israel, we're not going to get service like this there. We'll be treated differently then, so - when the going is good, you may a well accept it, all right?"

"What are you ordering for breakfast, Larry?"

I was somewhat amazed she'd even bother talking to me. Like all the others, I assumed she'd been warned off me by the Prophet, Rodstein.

"I've got a few minutes yet to decide before the waiter comes around," I told her. "Let me see what they have." I picked up the menu.

The menu was beneath the plate, sitting on a bright white linen tablecloth. It was printed on a sort of parchment stock with a layer of onion-skin paper in between each of its three sections - Breakfast, Lunch and Dinner. On the inside of the back cover was a listing of available desserts. The entire presentation, I thought, was done on a level of elegance and class I figured we would never see again, if we lived to be ten thousand years old. It really was something - a final glimpse of yesterday, like finding yourself in the middle of an Edwardian time capsule.

But, uh, oh, look who's coming.

Enter the Prophet - making for the end of my conversation with Peggy.

Of course, it was only natural for Rodstein to begin the day by rejecting outright the pomp and polish of the *Queen Mary*, but to do it in such an outlandish, self-righteous way as he was wont to do made his exhibition seem even more ridiculous. Couldn't this guy enjoy *anything* ? I wondered.

When the waiter arrived at our tables, Rodstein took it upon himself to stand up and speak for all of us. He wanted - he *demanded* - that everything be served kosher. Privately, I thought that wasn't what he wanted at all. Kosher meant nothing to him in the long run. What he was after, I reasoned, to myself, was recognition for his communistic-style "virtue", mindlessly naive as it most certainly was.

He became very loud as he made his demand known, so that everyone in the room, of course, had to listen to him. He revelled in the attention. None of the rest of us would have dreamed of asking for special treatment.

The waiter looked slightly baffled, the other passengers looked away, smiling if not a little shocked, and my old pal Bettle did the honours, turning to Rodstein and saying, "Why do you always have to be such an ornery cuss? We're all very satisfied with what's being offered, you know. Everybody pisses downstream, and you've gotta piss upstream!"

The heads of the other passengers turned back to face us at this loud outburst.

Peggy said to Bettle, "Well, you know, he's got a point there. It says right here on the menu: *If you would like kosher, please state.* You're the one, Bettle, who's pissing up the stream. He can eat whatever he wants. You're not paying for his trip."

And that seemed to be the end of that stupid little conversation.

Saul was sitting a little away from us with a bunch of genuinely religious Hasidics who davened or prayed at each meal. They were wearing religious shawls, yarmulkas, had bowls of water at the table with slices of lemon with which to wash their hands. Lemon was seen as a symbol from God that meant no matter what anyone might think, in reality, the world is not all made of sweetness.

The group swallowed Saul up. He was in his element, all right, but other than that, he had no connection with them - all he knew was that he was going to a religious kibbutz. They were neither for nor against him, but they certainly weren't compatible with his higher ideals. He was older than they were, and viewed them as mere children who had plenty to learn before they would ever be in as good a standing with the Almighty as he obviously was.

I was interrupted from this train of thought by the waiter, who was quietly trying to make Rodstein understand that if he wanted kosher, he'd have to order from a "special" kosher waiter. This meant, he said, waiting a few minutes. I could see he was anxious to get away from this lunatic. Besides, he tried to explain, he had other tables to serve, and people were beginning to get impatient. (If he had been allowed to say what he really thought, he'd probably have told Rodstein to go out on deck and throw himself into the great wet. I know I would have.)

"Well, why don't you put my order in first?" Rodstein boomed. "That way, by the time the others are ready, mine will be, too."

The waiter was very polite, given the circumstances. "Yes, sir. And what would you like to order?"

"Let's see. How about some orange juice, a bagel with cream cheese, some lox and tea with lemon."

At this point, I think the waiter had begun to read my mind. He was ever so cordial as he spoke.

"Very well, sir. And will that be it? Are you certain there's nothing else? Some olives, perhaps?"

"That sounds interesting. What colour do you have?"

"Well, sir, we have green and we have black."

"I'll take the green. And, ah, some of the black, too."

The waiter, absolutely stoney-faced and as pleasant as all get-out, asked, "And would you like an olive branch, too, sir?"

I'm not sure Rodstein even caught the sarcasm, or if he did, knew the reason for it.

"Just bring me my breakfast," he said, "Jesus, I'm starved!"

Peggy ordered the standard fare - cornflakes, toast, juice, coffee. Bettle wanted grapefruit, grapenut flakes, milk, toast and jam. I asked for a blonde on rye.

The waiter smiled. I think he was glad to know at least one of us had a sense of humour. "Don't you think it's a little early for that, sir? You *can* get that particular dish from room service, you know, later on in the day. But, I don't have much time for kidding. What would you like for breakfast?" I told him orange juice, cornflakes, scrambled eggs and toast.

"How many eggs, sir?"

"Three, sir, would be plenty."

"Will there be anything else?"

"I'll have some coffee and if you have any tea biscuits, that would be nice… on my first order, anyway."

So, now that you know what we all were eating (why I mentioned that, I don't know - just to give an idea, I suppose, of the sort of food to expect on the *Queen Mary* in case the reader ever gets caught in a Twilight Zone episode and wakes up hungry)…

The food wasn't long in arriving, and everyone was too hungry for talk. It's amazing what the sea air can do for you - if you don't succumb to the waves. Of course, Rodstein had to try to have the last say as the waiter laid the food out on the table. "See, I told you. I can get anything I want here."

Peggy surprised everyone, even the waiter, who I'm sure had seen and heard a lot of strange things on these Atlantic crossings.

"Christ, Rodstein - what do you have to be such a prick for? You, the big preacher of diehard Zionism. All you are is a pile of bullshit."

"Oh, leave him alone," interjected Bettle, "We're going to be on this tub for a while, so let's try to live in peace. I don't want to have to start yelling MAN OVERBOARD! just yet!"

I'm just sitting there wondering how I might be able to fix him without even saying anything. I have a desire to see how mad he can really get. I'm such a nice guy, I know, but this dope is really asking for it. As I gaze at the relatively blank faces around me, I strike upon a way.

I get Rodstein to go and ask Saul for a cigarette, knowing he doesn't smoke. As he did as requested, I told the rest of the group what I thought we should do, and the blank faces were lit up momentarily with smiles, as one by one, they agreed my plan seemed like not a bad idea, after all.

Everyone dumped their remaining bacon on top of Rodstein's kosher plate, and made a fake trip to the washroom, like a boy scout troop on an outing. We stayed away for five minutes or so, giggling and guessing at his reaction. Then, we went out to see for ourselves what all the hollering was about, for by that time he had returned to his place and we could hear him in the distance, ranting and raving.

"Who did this!? Who put this goddam bacon here on my plate!? I want to know who it was!" Blah blah blah.

Trailing back into the room in single file, we pretended to look surprised, and said, almost in one voice, "I don't know. I wasn't here."

That really set him off. He looked at us in pure disgust and began calling for the waiter, as if it had somehow been *his* fault. "I want another breakfast! On the double, too!"

The waiter, who had seen the whole thing, tried to suppress a smile as he calmly regarded his wrist-watch and said, "I'm sorry, sir, but breakfast time is over now. The kitchen closes at ten a.m."

Rodstein turned to me, in a rage. "It was you, wasn't it, Larry? I *know* it was you! Well, I'll get you back for this." He was beginning to splutter, and really looked foolish, even to the few admirers he had. Everyone was laughing. It had worked. His self-righteousness had been defeated, soundly.

And so with that accomplished, we all went our separate ways to see what else might be done on this, our first day at sea.

As I left the breakfast table for the main deck, I stopped a deck hand and asked where the writing room could be found. I'd decided to send a few postcards.

"Just follow the signs on the doors, sir, and when you get to the smoking room or the games room, go in. You'll find a little room off to one side, behind them. The postcards, by the way, are free."

I did as he told me, and followed the signs, which led me to the exact spot I was looking for (today, you usually get sent in some weird kind of circle and wind up back where you started - or just plain lost). The room was small, but large enough for five or six desks, complete with typewriters and pens for those who preferred writing in longhand. The stationery - letter paper and envelopes - had the ship's logo on it, a great advertising device - free publicity for the cruise line and a bit of ego boost for the passengers. (Look, Ma, here I am on board the best of the best!)

I wrote out a card to Mom, saying basically the above and adding that I wasn't seasick (yet), and was eating everything available. I told her I wasn't getting along with the people in the group very well but was enjoying the trip anyway. Knowing me, she'd understand. I *did* have opinions of my own, and she was quite aware of it.

On the way in, I passed a small store carrying various tourist goodies. They had cards there, but they weren't much good for writing on. Basically, they were more free advertising for the ship - just a picture of it on the open waters, and not a lot of space on the back. I used the free cards, which were much better, and wrote out a few more to friends back in Canada I thought might get a kick out of receiving something with such an exotic postmark.

When I was finished, I went out into the First Class Smoking Room. First Class, yeah. I loved it. None of the merry little group of pilgrims would expect to find me in here, so I plunked myself down in a comfortable looking armchair. Looking around the room, I noticed how some of the other passengers were sending the porter for cigars. When he'd brought theirs, I waited a few minutes, and motioned to him to come over. It took him about three seconds.

"Would you care for a cigar, sir?"

I asked him what brand they were. I'm not particularly partial to cigars, but a really good cigar is something else.

"They're 'Punch Lily', sir."

Only the best for this boy. A decent first-class cigar in a first-class smoking lounge, you know, was one thing I thought I could indulge in. Having gotten deathly sick one time after smoking a junky, cheap cigar taught me a bit of a lesson. The higher the price, the better the quality. Besides, I wanted to be served and waited upon. Maybe, I thought, it would help me to meet some of the elite.

"The cigars are seventy-five cents apiece, sir. A lovely smoke, they tell me."

I bought six dollars worth. It would be worth it, my reasoning told me, to make a bit of an investment. This way, I had a sure excuse for disappearing when I liked and also get to spend some time with first class company instead of the rat's nest of zealots I was supposed to be a part of. I didn't want to hear any more third-class talk! Besides, I'd get to embellish the facts a bit about the heroism involved in going on the volunteer Israeli adventure. Maybe I could find a friend...

The cigars were the ticket, all right. This was definitely the way to go. Maybe I could cadge a few drinks out of someone, terrible person that I was. Maybe I could get to meet another good listener like Andrews, and show him off to the zealots. I really did need some new company, and at the same time, I wanted it to be known Larry Wiener wasn't just some fly-by-nighter who got lucky once in a while - he was the real thing, a *pro* con.

So, there I was, sitting in one of the best seats in one of the best rooms, on board one of the best high class vessels in the entire world - sitting there with a stupid cigar in my stupid mouth just like one of the best characters, I thought, from one of the best movies I'd ever seen, having a nice, restful drink. Just relaxing, you know, with the best of them, trying to look like I actually fit in. I was hoping, too, for some nice, white-haired gentleman of stature and status and all the rest of the things bankers and con men like to see in their victims come along and say, "Good day to you, son. Who might you be, and do you mind if I sit in for awhile? You look like you have a story to tell," - or whatever he might want to say while I smiled back from my throne of luxury and relaxation, urging him on...

Mr. Johnson

I must've been doing something right, because it wasn't long before the gears began to move. Looking around, I saw an old gentleman, sleeping his passage away. To his immediate right, a couple of others were reading. Nothing too promising in that corner.

But, wait! There, on the other side of the room, sitting alone, an interesting looking man with a great mop of white hair, pretending not to notice me - but you can't con a con. He was sizing me up, all right, so I thought it might be best to give him the benefit of the doubt by moving my head nonchalantly and then letting my gaze-across-the-room stop when it caught his eye, as it had no trouble at all doing.

"Ahem," he said, when my gaze wouldn't go away. It made him uncomfortable, and he got up and walked toward me. "I say, I haven't seen you in here before. My name is Johnson. What is yours, sir?" What a wonderful accent, I thought. Thoroughly British, this one.

"You may call me Mister Lawrence," I told him, thinking, what the Hell, why tell him the complete truth?

"A very outstanding British name," he said, gripping my hand and shaking it vigorously.

"Actually, my Mother gave me the name," I replied, deciding he might somehow find out my real name, after all. The *Queen Mary* was big, but she wasn't *that* big! I didn't want to wind up on the Captain's hit list or in his little black book because of a little white lie. I remembered what he'd said about the ship having a working brig, and there was no way I wanted to get labelled as a thief - which I wasn't, of course - but I figured the Captain might think that if someone lied about as simple a thing as a name, he'd be a likely candidate, too, if anything went missing.

"Yes," I continued, "My Mother gave me the name Lawrence, but it took me fifteen years to learn how to spell it, because everyone else just called me Larry."

There was a silence for a moment or so after this exchange, and I wondered if I'd said something just a bit too juvenile for a young man so far from home with such a huge cigar sticking out of his mouth. I tried another tack.

"Well, Mr. Johnson-from-England," I said, "you had some very famous Lawrences in your country."

"To which Lawrence are you referring?" he asked politely.

"Why, to Sir Lawrence Olivier," I told him. "Only the greatest movie star in the world! Who else?" I could see he liked this, so I added, "Oh yes, and you also had the famous adventurer Lawrence."

"The adventurer...?"

"Lawrence of Arabia, of course." Seeing he hadn't been expecting this, I threw in what little else I knew by telling him I had read "the famous book he wrote, *The Seven Pillars of Wisdom*...."

"Brilliant man, that," I added.

He stared at me incredulously, as if he had never dreamed anyone as young as I must have appeared to be to him could have such knowledge about the Lawrences of England. That's what I thought, anyway, until he cleared his throat.

"We of English extract are not that big, you know, on Lawrence of Arabia. It is the rest of the world who consider him a kind of hero. To the British, he was merely one of a long string of glory-seekers. One hell of a showman, I'll grant you that. But you are correct in assuming his greatness, albeit in another area indeed. He did prove himself, you see, by writing one hell of a book, didn't he? Yes, brilliant fellow, but a bit of a charlatan at that."

Johnson then asked if it would be all right with me if he joined me for a while. I nodded, and he pulled the next chair over a little closer to mine, and proceeded to enlighten me, giving me the best description I was ever to hear of Lawrence of Arabia.

"He was, you see, the English Custer - one hundred percent qualified showman. But, like all great heroes, he had to fall. Napoleon fell at Waterloo, Custer fell at the Little Big Horn...

"Lawrence believed, as I understand it, that he was a godsend, but we had plenty of other generals equal to the task he laid out for himself. Oh, indeed. There was the fellow who went to Khartoum - General Gordon, who was known as 'Pasha', which meant *King* ..."

I'd really picked a live one this time. I liked him, though. History wasn't my strong suit, but what he had to say was interesting, and I liked the way he said it. He went on to speak about many people - some from direct experience, and I believed him - why not? Just because I told the odd lie, didn't mean everyone did.

He talked of many who, through war or prayer (Ghandi, for example), had made a name for themselves. It's funny how conversations get started, but my dumb remark about my name rang all the right bells, and the old fellow was off like the turtle in the proverbial race. Old Aesop didn't mention it, but the more Mr. Johnson droned on, the more sure I was that the original turtle had won his race by putting the hare out of the running by talking him to sleep!

I didn't mind, though - I wasn't falling asleep. I was busy stirring and nursing a drink, and watching, out of the corner of my eye, the pretty young things coming and going, passing by outside the door. And, sure enough, when a porter came by to ask if our drinks were all right, Johnson ordered another, and there! - I'd scored my first free drink!

Johnson reminded me of Uncle George and his knack for storytelling. There was just enough bragging in it to make you wonder if any of it was true or not, but just enough truth instilled, too, to cause you to realize it wasn't bragging you were hearing, but just the story of someone who was probably on the fringes, of someone who knew what he was talking about and who exaggerated his own importance or role in the story. It was harmless enough, and vaguely interesting. Besides, I knew if I listened to much more of it, I'd be having a First Class lunch!

According to Johnson, General Allenby, who had fought for the real Lawrence of Arabia, was by far much more revered. In comparison, he said, Lawrence was nothing but a clown. A good showman, maybe, but still a clown. Johnson had fought with Allenby and Lawrence of Arabia when he was a nineteen year old soldier. He told me that Allenby had died on Ali Mountar, the mountain at the east end of the Gaza Strip.

He'd read in the papers of the bombings of Nachal Oz, he said, but wasn't much impressed by it. "Fear tactics," he said, "that's all it is." He presented a good case to me, and if he wasn't impressed by the way people did things, I was beginning to be impressed by him. He had plenty of knowledge about Lawrence of Arabia, anyway.

As a young soldier, I imagined he would have looked the part, and pictured him in my mind with a handlebar moustache, his head held high and with a stiff upper lip and all that. He remembered Lawrence of Arabia as a white-robed rebel who would go out of his way just to thwart British protocol as much as he possibly could.

Was it true, I asked, that Lawrence had walked across the Sinai alone as a young boy?

"Oh yes," Johnson replied, sniffing. "He did that to raise money for his forces' ammunition and of course to further his lifelong profession as a glory hound. He was quite a small chap, though, and as everyone knows, drove a motorcycle. It was all for show, I fear. He was nothing more than a warmonger, always trying to overstep his power. He was, remember, only a Colonel.

"In a way, I can see why he felt as he did. The British army was the same, I suppose as all other armies - if you won a battle, you did it for England. If you lost, they denied they ever sent you."

The conversation began to branch off into other areas then, the comment maybe causing him to decide he'd let his private feelings show a little too much to someone he really didn't know. He changed the subject, asking about me. "And now, my boy, tell me a bit about yourself. Where are you going?"

"I'm off to Israel, as a volunteer…"

"Ah yes, I might have suspected. My kind of fellow, an adventurer." I could see he liked the idea. It was time to push on, though, and I said so long for now, and we agreed to meet again, later on. It was getting close to lunchtime, and so we went our separate ways.

Back out on the main deck, I noticed the social agenda posted on a wall. Some movie that didn't interest me was playing that afternoon, but my eyes lit up at the announcement at the bottom of the sheet:

"STARTING TOMORROW, FOR TWO DAYS - 'GIANT', STARRING JAMES DEAN." I knew where I could be found the next two afternoons!

Pleased at the thought, I walked along and across the deck to the Dining Room and met the gang at the table. They were already reading through the menu. I was late, having been daydreaming about deserts, soldiers and Hollywood. Someone asked me where I'd been all morning. I told them.

"I was in the Kosher Room, of course! Where else? Down in the First Class section, in the smoking chambers, talking to an old English gentleman." I laughed, adding, "So where did you think I'd be - hanging around with you guys? Hey, this is Larry..."

Maybe I shouldn't have put it quite that way, but I wanted to remind them I didn't fit in. Bettle was the first to wax indignant.

"Yeah, right. So what's the matter, Larry? Isn't our company good enough for you? Are we too poor, maybe?"

"Naw, not too poor - just too boring. Look, lets get something straight while we're at the table here. I'm not under your thumb. It's my trip as well as yours. You didn't pay for it, and as for your company, if I didn't have to have something to do with you, I wouldn't have anything to do with you. Am I being clear enough about this? I mean, y'know?

"So, we eat at the same table, because that's where we've been assigned. See the sign? Welcome, our Jewish friends! That's you, that's me. but, you're not my keeper. I mean, if I wanted someone to watch over me, Bettle, I could've stayed in Toronto and gone to the Don Gaol for a while, eh?"

Rodstein couldn't resist that one.

"That's pretty big talk, Larry, coming from a little man like you. Without Bernie, you know, you probably would be in the Don Gaol by now."

"Listen," I said, " if I end up in the Don, I'll send you a postcard. This trip is for a year, and either we're going to have to have some kind of pact to get along, or you're on your own. When you wind up in shit, don't look for me to back you, 'cause I won't be around. I'll be busy, minding my own business. Got that?"

"Well, Larry, that just isn't true," said Bettle, banging his finger into his chest. "I'm responsible for everyone on this trip, and that includes you. You're on this expedition, and it's not a holiday. It's my business to see you get there safely, and arrive back home in the same condition. Much," he added with a phony sigh, "as I care. But that's my duty.

"And that goes for you, too, Rodstein. You two guys are nothing but screwups - anybody can see that. You with your almighty Communist talk and Zionist bullshit. Yeah, the last of the holy warriors, that's what you are, Rodstein. Or what you think you are, anyway! And Larry - get that stupid grin off your puss. What are you? Just a Rock 'n Roll kid, a young punk who has about as much right to be going to Israel as A-for-Asshole Hitler, I don't care what his mother thought.

"Probably, you know, none of you will ever amount to much of anything over there, well, except maybe Saul. So what am I doing, bringing nothing but a bunch of misfits with me? I feel sorry already for the locals."

There was silence for a few seconds, but I was never one to let that get the better of me. "So what ever gave you that idea - me, a misfit? I'm a nice guy, so how can you think something like that? Hey, I went the same way you did - I went to the farm, I did my job, I worked hard, I looked after all those eggs, you know. At least, I did some real work for a change. Don't forget, though - the work we did there earned money for that farm. It wasn't all for us. I didn't suckhole for the easy jobs like some people did. You think looking after eggs is easy - try the smell!

"So what did you do, Bettle? You picked a few apples while your pal Rodstein shovelled manure. He's been doing it all his life, that's easy for him! And you probably ate most of the apples. Don't think I don't know what you're all about. You guys wouldn't take five o'clock in the morning jobs, oh no. Heaven forbid you ever should do anything like that! And don't forget, either - every egg you ate, even the tainted ones, I handled! Okay, so there were no tainted ones - I'm just having a bit of fun, can't you see that? Anyway, while you guys were busy sleeping, I was out there working. Not too many people would eat what you were shovelling, Rodstein."

Finally, Bettle had had enough. "Stop this craziness," he said, "here comes the waiter."

Peggy, whose eyes had been bugging out while I was telling them what I thought, agreed. "Yes, let's order before you three get into a fight."

I wasn't very hungry, and ordered a couple of egg sandwiches, soda pop and a dessert I liked - coconut cream pie. Wherever they'd gotten the chefs, they sure knew how to cook. Peggy turned the conversation into some light banter about the other wonders of the ship, helping calm us down. We avoided looking at one another, ate, then went our own ways.

I thought about what there was to do with the long afternoon and the coming night. I wanted to do something very different, something I'd never done before, so I went to the darts room. Daring, wasn't I? But, I'd never played darts before, so I tried it, gave up after an hour or so and stood there for a moment in the empty room, considering.

As I was lost in thought (or was I just lost?), a young man came into the dart room, said "Hello". He sounded like he was from New York, with one of those thick accents, Brooklyn maybe, or the Bronx, you know, down by the "wah-tta". He asked if I liked to play darts. I told him I didn't much care for it at all.

"So how about if we go and shoot a little pool? You game for that?"

It wasn't hard to tell this guy knew what he was up to, and was trying to hustle a quick buck. There was a pool table on the other side of the room, and I nodded toward it. "Rack 'em up," I said.

He was a pretty good shot, too. As we played, we talked a bit, and I realized he, too, was Jewish.

"So, you going to Israel?" I asked. He told me he was, but not as a volunteer. He was going to work for a company there.

"Why would someone work for free?" he asked. He had me

there. He also won the first game, played just for the fun of it. I knew what was coming, though.

"You wanna play for a little action?"

"Well, how much?" I asked.

"Say, two dollars a game?"

I agreed, and quickly lost ten dollars. This guy was a real shark. I asked him if he played cards, thinking I'd be able to win my money back some other way, maybe a way where he couldn't (or wouldn't) have more than a half a chance. I was pretty good at cards - poker was my game. He agreed - what did he have to lose? I won my ten bucks back plus forty more. The kid didn't like that.

It was getting late in the afternoon, and I thanked him and got up to leave. He was a little upset that I didn't want to continue playing.

"Look," I said, "it's after three p.m., and all you're doing is losing your dough. You beat me in pool, I beat you in poker. You should be glad, you've learned something, too - you can't hustle a hustler. There's always someone just as good, maybe better."

He didn't pursue it. I left and went up on the deck to watch the ocean roll on its way, carrying us to France. So what did I really leave behind, except my family? What were the good times? Martha? It was all over with her. If I'd stayed, maybe we'd have married. Not that it was such a terrible thought, but inwardly, all the same, I shuddered. Marry, and lose my freedom? I wasn't sure at all that I liked the idea.

I missed Mother, though, and my little brother. Okay, I missed Martha, too. I also missed my times at the Y, and the music and dancing, and driving around in my car; but this trip was something new and different - it might turn into a real adventure, or at least I hoped it would. I don't know what kind of adventure a person could have, running around with a pack of crazy Zionists, but here I was, and I was going to make the best of it, whatever happened.

For all of those people and things, sure, I missed them, because there could be no replacement - still, life was to be lived, wasn't it? I'd be gone a year, a long time. Staring out to sea, thinking these thoughts, was no good. It was just making me depressed, so I tried to cheer myself up. Forget the lunatic Zionists. I'd just won a bunch of money, and the day was still young. I wondered if they played Rock 'n Roll music at the boat dances...

I couldn't believe it, but I was actually getting bored - and on the first day! Instead of going full-tilt, exploring the ship's resources, there I was, staring morosely out to sea, half homesick already. A year I'd be gone? For the first time, I wondered if I'd make it. All I could see ahead of me was water. Something was missing, but what?

Suddenly, I knew. I needed to find someone - someone with maybe a ponytail, wearing bobbysocks and a poodle skirt... I figured this would be hard to find on a boat that seemed to be filled with British snobs and Jewish crazies, but then again, if I looked hard enough, I just might get lucky. Yes, that was it! Check out the ship's resources!

I ambled away, feeling cocky and self-assured, cruising the Third Class section, knowing that a lot of the people in that area were refugees who'd been turned down in their attempt to get into the United States. Israel was the only country that would take them, but just because it was in need of the labour. Oh, they'd work for the privilege, all right! Knowing that I probably wouldn't, I felt even better, and went off, this time on a quest.

The difference between the First and Third Class was almost shocking. Being in Third Class meant living at the bottom of the boat, in cramped quarters, and eating whatever the First and Second Class had left over. It was almost like being in jail, and had none of the beauty and amenities of the rest of the liner. The only relief, really, was that you could walk the decks freely.

Third Class, too, was filled with girls, men, babies - some of the adults going to prison kibbutzim to do manual labour, the price they would have to pay for getting away from whatever background they had come out of. Whatever hell their homeland had been, I wondered if it would be much better. This policy was nothing more than a thinly disguised form of slavery. Their passports were stamped, "ISRAEL - NO RETURN."

There were other not-so-classy rules, too. You couldn't take your food back to steerage, for example, unless you paid off the deck hands. I took some down anyway, figuring this would help break the ice with everyone. I swept all the leftover rolls into a bag, and took the jars of jam, jelly and peanut butter from the tables.

The people I jokingly called "peasants" were more than thrilled to get the food - what a godsend this fellow Larry could be! Most of the old men were Rebbitzins (True Russian Orthodox Jews), dressed all in black, with side curls. Israel was the perfect place for them - the "Promised Land" for sure, all prophecies fulfilled!

One of the old women asked, "vilsdu a maidel?" which means, "Do you want a girl?" Well, what could I say? Of course I did! I played it cool, though, hoping I didn't let it show. All I had to lose was whatever dignity I thought I might have had, which in retrospect, really didn't amount to a hill of beans, all things considered at the time.

So I was introduced to this cutie with beautiful, dreamy eyes and curly black hair. The old woman told me her name was Raizel (Rose) and said to treat her gently - she was a little bit seasick already. The family was of Russian-Jewish extraction, and I spoke just enough Yiddish to be understood - the last thing in the world I wanted, as far as Raizel was concerned, would have been to be misunderstood - as to my intentions!

I invited her to the next night's dance, and she accepted. As I looked her over, I thought my chances of making it with her were about 60/40 to my advantage. I didn't know any Russian, so figured that if I tried, and said something wrong, there was no way she could feel insulted. I could claim, even with my elementary knowledge of Yiddish, that I'd simply gotten my words mixed up. Ignorance, you know, can be of some benefit in the pursuit of bliss - in certain situations.

The old woman's motivation for matchmaking (Shadchin) us was to keep the supply of extra food coming down to the lower levels, I was pretty sure of that. Her eyes began to gleam and her nose twitched every time I appeared with a bag under my jacket. She was a nice lady, an old- school-type peasant who wore a long, black dress and had her hair done up in a bun. She reminded me of an oyster or clam, but she'd open up if something free was coming her way.

I decided I wanted this little Russian girl. If we hit it off, she'd provide me with a new story to tell - and more! I also knew - as did she, I hoped - we would never see each other again. Raizel didn't seem to take much notice of any of the men in the Third Class section. She, too, liked the idea of getting some free food, and, for a time, a little better living. She also liked being invited to attend a dance in the First Class section.

The next day, when I went down below, Raizel seemed friendlier than she'd been the day before. I wondered at this at first, then realized it must have been the old lady's influence. (Get closer to him, dear. Play up to him. Think of all the extra food he'll bring us, extra food for everyone!) Sure, I was taking advantage of the situation, but they were taking advantage of me, too. I didn't feel guilty. I don't think they did!

Later that evening, I went down to their quarters to pick Raizel up and take her to the dance. She was wearing a long peasant dress fit for a Russian wake. I was embarrassed to take her into the First Class section, knowing everyone's eyes would be on us, but what could I do? Besides, my nefarious motives definitely outweighed any social embarrassment either of us might suffer. Scratch up another blunder to wayward youth, but what the hell? I knew, underneath that ugly gown, earthly delights might await me, if I played my hand right (pun definitely intended).

At the dance, Bettle, Peggy and Rodstein quickly spotted us.

"Larry! Who's this? Where'd you find her? Are you crazy, or what?"

Rodstein, realizing she was of Russian extraction, got the hots for her right away. It was quite funny, watching him, knowing that here it was, the moment of truth - his café communism suddenly confronted with the real thing, and all he could think of to do was try to figure out a way to get her away from my corrupting influence - so that *he* could corrupt her instead!

He started in on her right off, speaking in broken English, sign language and a bit of Yiddish. Raizel seemed totally indifferent to his advances, wondering, probably, what lifeboat he'd crawled out of. In her simplistic way of viewing life, she equated people with what they'd done to be helpful to her and her people. Rodstein, of course, had done nothing at all.

He didn't like being brushed off so quickly, so, pretending

aloofness, he turned his back on us and walked away, as cool as a wind from Hell.

Then Bettle started in on her, talking in very fluent Yiddish: "du bist a shayna maidel" (You are a pretty girl); "Fun vanen shtamsdu?" (Where are you from?). She startled him a little by replying, just as fluently: "ich shtam fun Moskva". This wasn't some dumb farm girl. She had class, but was unfortunate enough to be poor as well.

Bettle, smiling his best, asked, "vilsdu tansn?"

She shook her head, "Nayn. Ich bin mitn 'Blondie'." (I'm with the blond.)

Bettle stared at me, dying of envy. This young, beautiful Russian girl who was obviously meant for him - what was she doing with a tramp like me? What could I possibly have done to deserve being with her? He shook his head sadly, and, like Rodstein, walked away from us. Peggy, who had said nothing all through this, followed him.

At about seven forty-five, the band came on stage. Raizel's face broke out into a smile as big as you'd ever want, as if she'd never seen anything like it before, and maybe she hadn't. I half expected her to exclaim, "Wow! This is really living!" but she kept her thoughts private. It was easy to see, though, she'd never, in her life, been to such a fancy affair.

Glancing over at Rodstein and Bettle, I smiled, too. Then, taking Raizel by the hand, said, "kum, lomir tansn. Velche tans vilsdu-fox trot, tango, waltz...?"

I was almost floored by Raizel's answer.

"Ich vil tansn 'Rock 'n Roll'!"

On our way out into the middle of the dance floor, we passed by the front of the stage. I asked the bandleader if they knew any Rock, told him the reason - I had, here with me, right by my side, the most amazing phenomenon, a young Russian girl who wanted to dance to some good old American Rock 'n Roll. The bandleader was just as astounded as I was, and nodded his head, "Yes, of course!"

This was my chance to show off, not only to her, but to everyone, to the whole boatload - I'd be hailed as a king, or dismissed as a fool. I'd taken the chance before. It was only a matter of being crazy now or looking stupid later. I was betting though, if I won, if everything went off okay, it would be from the dance floor to the bedroom! It was something I didn't mind gambling on. So, if she wanted Rock 'n Roll, I'd give it to her, all right.

I asked the band to play 'Rock around the Clock' and slipped a five dollar bill into the leader's hand. On our way back into the centre of the floor, I asked her if she was sure "Rock 'n Roll, *real* Rock 'n Roll" was what she wanted. It was as if a light had turned on somewhere, and it beamed out from her shining face: "Ya, ya ya!"

The bandleader adjusted the microphone stand to get everyone's attention, then announced... "I have been requested by a young Canadian volunteer to Israel to play something for his Russian sweetheart. He would like to start tonight's dance off with a Rock 'n Roll song. So, for all of the young at heart aboard the *Queen Mary* tonight, we'll begin with the number one worldwide hit song, Bill Haley's 'Rock around the Clock'."

Raizel was so happy! She jumped up and down, clapping her hands together, as if beating off flies. (I imagined my friends the flies in the background, Bettle and Rodstein, watching and grinding their teeth in disbelief.) Raizel was cool about it, though. She wasn't intimidated by this new element - it was exactly what she wanted. And so, the dance got underway...

The lights went down, the mirrored ball started turning, twirling around and around, sending silvery squares of light everywhere. It was magical. Gentle washes of blue, red and yellow cast over the crowd, lit them up, then went their way. Faces were there, then gone, lost in the mesmerization of the moment.

A roll of drums started it, then, "One o'clock, two o'clock, three o'clock, rock!" - and with this opening line from the tune, everything broke loose. most of the people on board were young enough to appreciate the song and the dance floor began to fill up. I had to prove my stuff, and it was now or never.

We already had the crowd's attention, but I wanted everyone's eyes aimed in our direction. What is it they say today? The best thing about being a paranoid schizophrenic is, you're always the centre of attention... It was a schizophrenic atmosphere, all right...

and I wanted people to notice us - me! I loved it, every minute of it! The women swirling around to the beat, their skirts flying up… the men bent low and gyrating, imitating every move the Canadian Kid was making.

Well, I felt that way, anyway. You know what it's like when you're young and you can do something well. You're hot, you know it, and you want everyone else to know it. Your ego won't get fried, it's okay to let people flatter and tell you how good you are, you eat it up!

The band did a great rendition, and our dancing came off perfectly. The second tune the band did was 'My Prayer' - a slow one, but very popular. Raizel fell into my arms, or I fell into hers - we fell together, as if we'd been with each other always. At first contact, how could I resist? She was as solid as she looked, despite the loony dress she was wearing. He body, I mean - was definitely for real. I was in love at the first touch of her breasts, pointed and pushing into my chest. I thought I'd faint on the spot.

She really was one beauty of a diamond in the rough, like some unadorned Sophia Loren, the Queen of the Ball, Queen of the *Queen* - I must have been reading too many newspapers or something, and began to imagine her as a kind of sex bomb grenade - pull the lever and she'd start exploding, which was fine with me, as long as I got to be the one to pull it …

The more the band played that song, the more 'My Prayer' began to come true. Her body pushed into mine - the word "suggestively" didn't fit, it was much more than that! The very heat of her was like a furnace. She was burning up, and so was I. The closer she got, the more she pushed, the firmer she felt, rubbing against me… the firmer everything felt! I didn't want to break away from her. Maybe I *would* be embarrassed, after all!

She began nibbling at my ear, whispering: "You like my body?" I lowered my hands, sliding them around onto her tush, pushing her even closer, stroking her. She was hungry for affection, this one. It wasn't difficult to figure out what was on her mind - the same thing that was on mine. I was in big trouble now, and would have to stick close to her, not wanting anyone - except her, naturally! - to notice the nature of the "trouble".

The next dance was slow, too, and I began to ease my hands up her sides, slowly working my thumbs around to her front. She had such a luscious-looking chest area. How black bread and borscht could have created something so divine, I didn't know... My thumbs brushed her breasts, pushing against them. Every time they sank in, she gave a little sigh, and pushed back, digging them in ever further. I thought I'd explode right there.

I'd turned into a grenade, too... but what could we do? This wasn't the back seat of a Chevy, or a field somewhere. I had to get her out of there, away from the dance floor, out onto the deck, take her under a lifeboat, anything. Maybe the dark, empty games room. I started thinking of playing darts and shooting pool, cigars, anything to get my body back to a more normal stature. There was no way I could walk out of there in the condition I was in. Down, boy, down! Quick, think about whales or something!

It worked, enough that I wouldn't look too stupid, anyway. I'd had to back away from Raizel for a couple of moments, my eyes probably glassy and staring into space. She was puzzled at first, as I took her by the hand and dragged her off the dance floor, out the door, and down along the deck.

"Where are we going?" she asked. "What is wrong?"

"Yeah," I told her, "something is wrong. Me, I'm in big trouble. You don't know what it is? I think you do. How long do you think we can keep it up, dancing out there, going crazy, with everyone watching? I think you're in big trouble, too, aren't you, Raizel? You're Russian, and you're rushin' and we'd best get gone outta there for a while, what do you think?"

"You want me to help, I know. I know boys - and I understand what is wrong with you. I noticed at the dance, too. I have read *Peyton Place*, you see."

"Hey, look. You know what you do to me. You know that I like you. I think you're beautiful, Raizel. But, nature plays funny tricks. I didn't expect this to happen. I'm a boy, yeah, and you're a girl - a very pretty girl, at that. Too pretty! And I think - I hope -I know what your next line will be. You want to make love with me, don't you?"

She turned her head to one side, like a bird, and smiled. Her eyes, though, were just as glazed-looking as mine must have been,

I could see that. "Well, I have nothing to lose, what about you? We're good friends, on a voyage together. And, making love - isn't that what they say boat cruises are for?"

I held her close then, and kissed her. A vision of Mother flashed through my mind. What would she say if she could see me now? Her little Lawrence, bound for the Promised Land, not even halfway there and already being seduced - and he loved it!

Holding Raizel as tightly as possible, I managed to move my hands up inside the top of her dress and lay her head back on the couch. It was a teenage dream come true, and the only thing missing was an on-site camera so I could play the action back to Rodstein and company later on.

I unbuttoned the top of her dress and slid its shoulder straps down over her pretty little shoulders. She didn't try to stop me. She was enjoying this as much as I was, and wiggled a bit when one of the straps refused to move for an instant. Raizel wasn't about to display any of the phoney North American girl resistance every teenage boy had seen too much of. She wasn't going to play any games, not at this point. She wanted to have sex. She liked it, and wasn't afraid to let me know.

Once we'd gotten the top of the dress down, I discovered this luscious little Russian hadn't bothered to wear a brassiere, and I got to thinking she'd known all along what the result of our going dancing would be. As I stared down in the semi-darkness at the sight of her well-formed, beautifully peaked breasts, I almost began to drool. Larry the lascivious, that was me all the way! I lowered my head, kissing her on the mouth and neck, working my way toward her chest.

Raizel was a boxer's dream, and I soon had a real "bust in the mouth". I was right in my guess that her bosom was soft. Funny how something so soft can cause something else to become so hard, isn't it? She was "Ohhing" and "Ahhing", too, grabbing at my body, loving every minute of it. Although in one way, I wasn't in any kind of a hurry, in another I couldn't wait to get to the main course. Lapping at her nipples like a babe in arms, I wondered why I had ever been hesitant about ever leaving home...

She was experienced, I knew that now. I'd always wondered

what it would be like, going down on a girl from another country, especially one who was completely unlike a North American. Well, I decided, I was about to find out. My hands were already all over her thighs, and her hands were encouraging their movement, pushing them along, here, there and everywhere.

In the back of my mind, I kept hoping no one would come in! I figured no one would, as they were all at the dance, but you never knew about the crew, who might turn up on their appointed rounds just when you didn't want them. But I didn't think we'd be disturbed.

We managed to squirm and wriggle around on the couch enough so that by now the upper part of her dress was down and the lower part was up, all gathered together at her midsection, and I, of course, was in Heaven, kissing and licking her thighs, slowly arriving at my target. I gave her a complete tongue bath, one I knew no Russian boy had ever given her, and by the way she began to thrust her pelvic area around, it was being appreciated! Hey, this, to her, was America - sex and Rock 'n Roll!

As I came nearer and nearer to the object of my affections, she began to spread her legs apart, pulsating and throbbing, pushing herself up, as if to say, "Well, here it is! Almost in your face!" It was an open invitation, one I wasn't going to turn down. I took both of my hands, and, putting one on each of her legs, nudged them together, and hooked my thumb into the top of her panties. She got the idea, and lifted her butt, just long enough for me to pull them down over her knees and then off completely.

Then, I stroked the place where her long, exquisite legs met, and as I did that, they spread apart like the Welland Canal, and as I lowered my face and touched my lips to her magic button, she began to flow like a fountain, like Niagara Falls... and quickly, expertly, her hands went for my zipper. She knew what she was after, all right.

Having found it, she pushed my pants down, peeling me like a banana, and rushed to meet it. I took her head in my hands, rustling her hair, and kissed her once, long and gently. She broke free in a frenzy, twisting her body around, and took a six-second, loving look at the now rock-hard, elongated "banana" in her hand. She squeezed it once and looked up at me. Her lips were half-opened, her eyes filled with desire. If there had been a question in them, the answer was silently supplied as the banana answered her hand with a kind of squeeze of its own. Then, she lowered her head, and slowly took it in between her lips, running her tongue along its top.

I couldn't take it. This girl was everything I'd ever dreamed of. I had to pull her away - slowly, mind you - but firmly. I wanted more, and so did she. Her eagerness, though, surprised me, and I had to count to ten twice while pulling her away - she didn't want to let it go, and kept trying to pull herself back to it. Playfully, maybe, but like I said, she knew what she wanted! She wanted it so badly, though, I wasn't sure I could give it to her without having that banana burst before its time.

"Raizel," I whispered, "wait!" She finally let me pull her away. My fingers were busy, running up and along the insides of her legs, touching and probing at the top, moving in and out... talk about being on fire! Then, we were lengthwise on the couch, our feet sticking crazily over the edge, and I was sucking on her tits again while she was guiding the banana, like a missile, into its lovely destination. I knew I had to let her have her way, that if I'd had mine instead, there would have been almost no lovemaking or foreplay at all, that I would have shot like a bull in a cattle barn after a long, cold winter.

It was amazing no one heard us. While we pleased each other, pumping up and down like a couple of wild animals, I began to grunt in earnest, and Raizel, God bless her, started letting out high-pitched, long shrieks each time I plunged inside her - when I withdrew, all the way a couple of times, just to tease her - she'd cry out, "Laarry, Laarry, mooore, please, Laarry!!"

Then, all of a sudden, it was over. We had both come at the same time, just like the sex manuals said you were supposed to. I was surprised later to learn that the boat hadn't lurched at that instant! We settled into a warm, huggy embrace after that, and slowly got dressed again.

Raizel would have liked, I think, to go at it again, but the banana was bent and tired, its owner in a state of bliss already. In any event, we wouldn't have had time anyway. Raizel said she had to get back to the Third Class section, and we straightened ourselves up. She left the room alone, not wanting anyone to provide an opportunity for anyone to guess where she might have been or what she'd been up to.

I stayed where I was, in a kind of dream state. I stretched my legs out until I heard the joints crack pleasantly, laid my head back on a cushion, thinking, "Wow. What a night this has been!" - and promptly fell asleep. I'd be Raizel's dancing Russian bear anytime.

Just Like James Dean...

Early the next morning, about 7:30, I woke to the sun blazing down on me through the porthole. I stretched, yawned and decided it would be a good day to take a stroll on the deck before breakfast. On deck, I checked out the news of the day - the "Daily Bulletin Boar", to see what had been planned for our social agenda. I noticed the movie *Giant*, with James Dean was listed. I'd seen the movie twice, four days before, at the Roxy in New York.

The listing of the film brought on a strange feeling to me, a sense of loss somehow. James Dean, the alienated, the teenager's teenager. the lost young man, the misunderstood. Just like Elvis, in a way. But Elvis was still alive, and would be for many more years. Dean had been dead for, what, two years already? I thought about the time I'd met him ...

It was in 1954, and I'd been in New York at the time, at Romeo's Spaghetti House on Broadway. It was no big deal - I'd just gone in to get something to eat, when lo and behold, as I was looking around the room, and not really seeing anyone recognizable, my gaze came to rest at the table right next to me, and who should be sitting there, trying not to be recognized by anyone, but Dean, as hungry, probably, as I was.

I saw him later that evening, too, in the Village at the Ports of Call, which was a jazz club with a sawdust covered floor, like you might expect to see at a barn dance. Dean was a real vilder man - a wild one. Even after his death, the image he portrayed in his three films embodied the nightmare of every Jewish parent. I loved him for it, really admired what he'd done. I saw him as the original rebel, the one guy who could say "screw you" to everyone, and get away with it.

James Dean was definitely my hero in those days, and the role model he showed me - and so many others - set the pattern for the Larry of years to come. What can you say about his life that hasn't been said already? He lived fast, and died young. He had it all in the palm of his hand and let it all go. He left the memory of his magic for us to relate to, and I think kids still do, even now. I don't know why they wouldn't.

There was an innocence and a sort of timelessness about him, and when you're young, you see one of his films, and something clicks inside. When I heard about his death, as tragic as it was, I didn't know whether to cry or laugh. I knew right away he'd left a fantastic legacy. As I looked away from the bulletin board and out to sea, I fancied I saw him, larger than life, like on a huge screen that had suddenly appeared on the horizon, and he was floating out over the waves, just kind of drifting... but enough of this brooding, I thought. The guy's dead, and I'm alive. I'm also hungry, and it must be time for breakfast...

Afterwards, I decided to go to the Smoking Room again, and see if I couldn't find my English buddy Mr.. Johnson. He wasn't there, but in his regular chair sat a lady, in her sixties, puffing away on a long, glamorous looking cocktail cigarette. She had a couple of American bills on the coffee table next to her, her change from whatever little vice she'd been indulging in before I showed up.

She had style, and was very well dressed, with a chinchilla stole wrapped around her neck, its poor, dead, little head's mouth opened as if ready to attack her, not that I could blame it. But that's what they wore in those days, teeth, eyes, nose and all.

She couldn't contain her curiosity when she saw me come in, but asked what I was doing, where I was going, all the usual boat questions. The con guy in me rose to the occasion. Sure, I'd play her game. Why not? Maybe I could avenge the chinchilla. So, after giving her the customary speech about being a volunteer Canadian headed for Israel to help save the country or put it together or whatever it was we were supposed to be doing, I thought maybe it was a good time and place to put my "poor kid" act on for her (and my) benefit. I could see she was the motherly type ...

When I told her I was from Toronto, she responded by saying she had friends in Forest Hill, but of course, she was from "New Yawk". She was also Jewish, so I figured she'd play right into my hands if everything went right. She and her husband had a shmata (clothing) business, she told me. I asked why she was in the Smoking Room - which was still a bastion for men, and she replied she was travelling with non-smokers, and thought she might slip into the room for a few minutes, to get away from the others, maybe have a nice chat with someone different for a change. Her answer reminded me of my own predicament. I was doing, more or less, the same thing, though it wouldn't have bothered me to light up in front of my group, that was for sure!

I didn't tell her any of that, though, but I was thinking it. She interrupted my thoughts, and asked, just like any Jewish mother would, "Why did you leave home? Israel is not exactly going to be a loaf of bread, you know that?"

"Well," I said, trying to be nonchalant about it, "Israel will be the best education in the world for me. A year in Israel will be a fabulous experience. I can't think of a better place to go." I really believed it, too.

"I wanted my son to go to medical school in Haifa, but he refused to go there. I'm very proud of him, though. He went on to become a doctor and married a nice girl, and I've been left all alone in the world." She was actually being quite funny, waving her hands around and rolling her eyes, and for a moment I wondered which of us was doing the acting.

"Yes, my son's a wonderful doctor, but he left me, and I have a daughter, but she's out in California, and my husband's in Parklawn. My kids are just "chalishkes" (stuffed cabbages) - they wouldn't carry on the family business my poor husband Sam worked so hard for and left them. Oh, no, not them! It was only worth forty million dollars, but that wasn't good enough. Oy vay! Such a bunch!

"So, what do I do? I had to sell it to my brother Benny, who worked for us for thirty years. He was the plant foreman. Thirty years! And now his sons are running it, and I get one million dollar annually, every year until I die, heaven forbid!"

She was happy, telling me this. Sometimes it's easier to talk to strangers - they don't have to listen. I wondered why, though, she was spilling all of this onto me. She wanted one of her children to listen, not me. I could be her friend for a little while, but that wouldn't do it. Thinking it best to get her mind going in another direction, I asked why she was going to Europe.

"It's time for a cruise," she said. "I brought my maid along with me. It'll do her good." She laughed, and continued. "You know what I have? I have what every boy your age longs for. A twenty-five year old French maid to take care of all my needs."

This, too, sounded strange, coming from such a stately-looking lady. Again, I tried to change the subject.

"I've been to New York," I told her. "I know a little bit about it. Where do you live?"

"Well, dear boy! Park Avenue, where else?"

"Do you live at The Plaza?"

"Well, that's a pretty good guess, but no, I don't live at The Plaza. I have a nice place on Park Avenue." I realized she didn't want me to know exactly where. She was just being cautious. I couldn't blame her for that. She was a bit exasperating, though, and I admit I did want to ask, "Well, then, can you tell me where that animal draped around your neck used to live?" But, I didn't.

To my surprise, she said that this was her first real travelling. Before now, she'd only been to Miami a few times, and once to Hollywood. She didn't consider, she said, anywhere you could get to in a day "real travelling". I agreed with her. So, she was doing some "real travelling" on her doctor's advice - and went into a little pantomime, waving her arms around in front of me. "It'll be good for your nerves, my dear. The ocean air, you know, there's nothing like it, anywhere. And as for your heart, well! You know how frantic the city can be. Take my advice and get away from this for a while. Yes, yes, a trip across the Atlantic would be just the thing, just what the doctor ordered, ha ha ha... Well, you see, I suppose he was hoping I'd never come back! But, I am getting on a bit in years, and I want to show my maid I'm not as much of a nudnik (a bore) as she thinks, by taking her to France to visit her parents. A nice surprise for her, don't you think?"

She really was pretty funny, when she went into one of her routines. Her dead husband Sam, she said, had been a true New Yorker - and had never travelled at all. He'd started in the garment industry as a dress designer in one of the places that had burned in the great "Triangle Fire".

He was a union man, one hundred percent concerned with safety conditions for his workers. He'd even paid the rent on a doctor's office, she told me, so his employees could get free treatment when they needed it, if they stuck a needle up their rear end. (Don't ask me how or why, but that's what she said!)

Sam had built his business on loyalty, and everyone was valued equally - from the coffee boy to the auditor. When Sam died, he left her, among other little items, a 1937 Rolls Salon with a bar and a sterling silver steering wheel. It was, she said, "his prize possession - his own wife should be so important!"

She went on."Sam had bought it (the car, not me - me, he rented!) in 1951 for a mere $85,000. He hired a chauffeur to drive him everywhere, as he'd never learned to drive. He sent the chauffeur to Rolls Royce school in England for six months to learn how to maintain the vehicle, and upon that newly-educated chauffeur's return, why, Sam Swartzman was the envy of everyone on Eighth Avenue, as he rolled by, huddled in the back seat, smiling at the devil..."

She told me more and more as the morning passed.

Her husband Sam had instilled working values in their children, God bless him. He'd give them five dollars apiece to sweep the floors every Sunday morning.

"My Sam wasn't what they call dirt-rich, though - he was sweat-rich, and there's a world of difference!" I could well imagine, I told her, that indeed there was.

"He was a Polish Jew, you see, an immigrant who'd never gone to school. Well, who could blame him? And look at the result! A beautiful wife, his own factory, loving children... and he believed in the fundamentals of his religion, too. I'll never forget him saying, 'Early to bed, early to rise, and you'll make a good investment ...'

"He wouldn't take the time off work to go anywhere. Not to Europe, not to Connecticut, not even to New Jersey - though, God forbid, I don't blame him for that! But now that he's gone, I'm going to go *for* him. He would have enjoyed the *Queen Mary*, I think."

I said to her, rather affectionately (and I wasn't acting), "Well, don't worry, Mrs. Swartzman, your husband Sam's going right along with you. Think of it that way, and enjoy it. You know what you should do? Well, if I were you, what I'd do - take one of those flowers they bring you and throw it out onto the ocean. For Sam. Throw it to him. He's here, you know. You think he won't get it? He will."

This surprised her, and she gave me a funny look, with her eyebrows knotted, like she was puzzled. As for me, I realized we'd been (that is, she'd been) talking... for at least a couple of hours. I excused myself, as it was getting on time for lunch. She smiled sweetly as I left the room. I couldn't help thinking about that line, "you can't con a con". I wasn't sure, but she'd sure stolen some time from me, and hadn't even bought me a drink as I sat there listening, listening, listening. I wondered who was fooling who. This one was light years ahead of me - I could learn from her!

I joined the gang for lunch and we got into our usual little scraps, everyone very concerned about where I'd been and who I'd been with and why. They all seemed quite well informed about my little fling with Raizel - or thought they were, anyway. Well, let them think whatever they want, I decided, it was me having the fun, not them.

Bernie of course had to stick his big nose into business that wasn't his by ordering me to stay away from Third Class. That drew a laugh out of me. He was worried about my bringing food down there, he said, but I knew his real worry was that if I was "caught", he and the others might somehow be implicated. They wouldn't want to be known as people who had any compassion, after all!

"I said you'd get in trouble, Wiener, and you will. Mark my words."

"Yeah? Well, so what?" I replied. "So what are you gonna do, send me home? I'll catch the first shark back. You know, you can say what you like on this trip, but with me it won't wash. It doesn't mean anything to me, you and your righteousness - which is all self-oriented anyway. I'll tell you, though, and you should mind your own beeswax. If you take it too far, one day I'll get even with you. So just leave me alone, and I'll leave you alone. Stop trying to interfere in my life."

That shut them up, and I was able to eat the rest of my lunch in peace, without anyone saying another word. When I was finished I got up and said, "So long, see ya later, guys and gals. I gotta go jump off the ship now, just to make Rodstein's day."

I headed off to the film room - and talk about a plush place! It seated at least one hundred people, and it was packed. I found a seat right up front, two rows away from the screen, and buried my face in the film.

You already know that James Dean was my hero. In *Giant,* a story about the founding of Texas, he played the part of young Jedd Rink, a guy who stumbled across oil on a piece of land in that state. On the anniversary of his striking the oil, he passes out in a cake after a fight with Rock Hudson while 'The Eyes of Texas are upon You' played in the background.

I was there, right in the film, standing on Texas soil, feeling the oil gush up between my toes. I could really project myself into it, totally. When Dean mumbled (he always mumbled, it seemed), "I'm rich, I'm Texas oil rich!", I was right there with him. The film was three and a half hours long, and when it was over, I came out singing about Texas' eyes watching, watching, watching everyone...

High on the story and my hero's part in it, I hummed that tune the rest of the day. It was the first film that really put across a depiction of the mean and ugly core of power, and how ill-fitting wealth can sit on youth - actually, the story presented an eerie parallel to Dean's real life and death.

The only other movie that had the same sort of impact on me was, though you may not believe it, *Gone with the Wind.* Maybe I just liked long films. On my way out of the theatre, I noticed an advertisement for the next day's showing of Marilyn Monroe in *Gentlemen Prefer Blondes.* I wanted to see that, too. Marilyn Monroe was - well, Marilyn Monroe - and I was a hot-blooded, can't miss that type of guy.

Walking out on the deck, I thought maybe I'd play some shuffleboard awhile, but realized it was almost five o'clock and nearly time for supper. As I turned to go back, a voice called out from one of the deck chairs.

"Hello, son."

It was old Mr. Johnson. I said hi, and asked him how he was getting along now that we were far out to sea. Had he seen any whales?

"I'm doing just fine, my boy. The ocean is quiet today, nothing rising at all. I guess you saw your boy Dean today, did you?"

"Oh yes. I'd seen the movie before, but it's a good one."

"I watched it, too. You wouldn't think it, perhaps, but I'm a fan of young Dean, too. It's a shame he didn't live long enough to become an adventurer. Like Lawrence, I believe his calling was to live fast and die hard. A real man of his time - America's first young hero."

I wasn't going to argue with that.

"By the way, son, would you like to drop into the Smoking Lounge after you've had your dinner? I have a treat for you tonight - something I think you might enjoy."

I said, sure, I'd meet him there. I liked the place, and felt I belonged there, no matter what Rodstein might say about my mixing company.

I said goodbye to Johnson, telling him I'd meet him later, and went off to dinner, wondering what the "treat" might be. I wasn't asking for favours, but wouldn't turn one down if it was to my advantage, nice guy (or is that opportunistic youth?) that I was. Anyway, I knew that the conversation would be interesting, and I might learn from him. Johnson had been where I was heading and I wanted to know what Israel had been like as Palestine in 1914 when he'd been there. Talking with Johnson was like listening to my old Romanian grandfather - here was a walking, talking history book.

I thought, too, that by hearing Johnson out, I'd get at the truth of someone's experience in the Middle East, rather than the self-serving propaganda I'd been getting fed by Bettle and our holy sponsors.

Group Dynamics

At dinner, Peggy and Bettle were babbling away about what they planned to do in Israel. She wanted to work with the Sabras' children. Being a school-marm type, she seemed best suited for that, she said. Bettle was very moved by her sense of purpose. Her mindset was appropriate, and it was good to see someone, he said, glancing in my direction, with serious plans and a decent work attitude.

Peggy's hope was to take care of the children in the daytime and early evenings - and also to teach English to the Sabra, and maybe make herself a little extra cash. Her native Winnipeg had a large Jewish community, she said. Her parents were Reform Jews who always observed the Sabbath, and went to synagogue regularly. Her reasons for going to Israel were varied, but her main interest seemed to be in looking at the trip as a great adventure, the opportunity of a lifetime to do something worthwhile.

She'd always wanted to go to Israel, she said, and was so happy about being included. Maybe she'd even settle down and stay there forever. "Anything would be better than the blasting winds of Portage and Main!"

She then asked Bettle what his dreams were. Well, he wanted to work in the electronics field when he arrived. I don't know if he had his papers, but he claimed to be an electrician, and seemed to know plenty about it.

"I might join up with the army," he said. I could just picture him in uniform. He'd be right in his element! "Ever since I was ten years old, I felt I wanted to grow up with Israel," he claimed. What he really meant was he wanted to become a macho type figure, some kind of a "leader of men", a legend - the guy who leaves home a nobody and later takes on the role of a returning hero.

Peggy wasn't going to let Rodstein get away, either, and directed the same question to him.

"Well, Peggy," he answered, slowly, as if she should know already, like it was super obvious or something. "I want to work the land, get down and get my hands dirty, do things for Israel! I'm an idealist, you know, and I'd make a good leader, wouldn't I?"

A leader? Maybe a leader in the B.S. field. I knew what he was, and what he wanted. He saw Israel like someone sees a mirage in the desert. It was a mystical place, not a real place at all. He always had a book with him, either in his hand or in a pocket. He'd believe everything he read in the book, but he'd trip over the real item. He'd never done anything much in his life before now, but saw himself as a trailblazer, a Moses, an Isaac. He told us he was going to change his name to make himself a real Kosher Sabra. He'd call himself "Israel Rodstein". Talk about imagination! Really inspired, he thought.

At about this point, the dessert arrived, and I started in on it. The waiter had asked me if everything was all right, and I missed a part of the conversation, picking it up again as Bettle was asked what he thought of the part I'd missed. I guessed they were talking about the idea of the trip itself.

"Well, it's close to Irving," he said, "so I guess it's all right."

"I think it's a little bit too nationalistic," Peggy remarked. "But, I suppose that's what is wanted..."

I'd noticed Peggy glancing at me when I was talking to the waiter, figuring I hadn't been listening, I guess, so now she turned to me. It wasn't the usual course of events, someone from the group wanting my opinion on something.

"Well, Larry? What do you think we've been talking about?"

"You really want to know? I've been listening. Are you sure you want to know what I think?"

Bettle spoke up. "Yeah, Larry. I want to know, because I'm the one who got suckered into bringing you along with us."

"All right, I'll tell you. I'll tell you exactly. Personally, I think you're all a bunch of overly idealistic schmucks. The country - Israel - is like, ever heard that old joke about the hereafter. Ever heard that one?"

Of course, nobody had, so I made them listen, glad to let them know old Larry had a sense of humour.

"It's a pick-up line I often use. You walk into a bar, see a pretty girl, and go over to her and ask, Do you believe in the hereafter?

"Usually, she'll ask what you mean, and even if she doesn't, you can change the wording around a little, and still get your point across.

"You tell her - If she's not here after what I'm here after, she'll be here after I'm gone.

"It's the same with Israel. It's already there, and it's gonna be there after we're gone, won't it? We're not pioneers, no matter what we've been told. The only reason you're taking this trip, though you won't like my saying so, is that you didn't want to work back where you came from - you're too damned lazy. You think this going to Israel thing is going to be a big piece of cake, that you'll be worshipped and paraded around like heroes.

"I don't think so. Don't stop me, Bettle - you asked me what I thought, and I'm telling you! Look, here's this free trip, so you can get out. A nice chance to pile up Brownie points, while you're at it. You, for instance, Bettle, wouldn't be going anywhere if your daddy had bought you an electrical store. You'd be back home splicing wires together.

"And you, Rodstein - why, if anyone had given you a soapbox and you could preach your Communism or Judaism or whatever it's supposed to be, you never would have left. Trouble is, in North America, nobody's listening to that crap. It's all old hat to them, but you think it's something new. The smartest one of the group is Saul, and he left. At least he knew where he belonged, didn't he?"

When I'd finished, Bettle started in on me first.

"So, you just ripped us off for the ride. A free trip. eh Larry?"

"Is that what you want to believe? Well, no, Bernie, I didn't rip anyone for a free trip. You invited me, remember? Remember that day in the shower? *You* wanted *me*, right? So don't blame me for taking you up on it, which is all I've done. You know, I'm going to have to do the same work as you, on a kibbutz. If you don't do your share, you're the one that's gonna stand out. The slaves never get noticed. Anyway, we've got a year to be together in Israel, Bernie. So, we either start off on a new foot, else you're gonna need me one day, and I won't be there for you. It's as simple as that, isn't it? Take me as I am or not, but you can't leave me behind."

Peggy spoke up in my defence, sort of. "He's right, Bernie. You don't have to like him, but you are going to have to live with him, so you should settle things now. Israel doesn't want us to bring problems there, it's got enough of its own to deal with. Then, when the year is over, you can come back home and never have to see him again. But while we're there, we're going to have to at least try to be compatible with each other."

Peggy, the peacemaker. But I couldn't let it go at that.

"And who knows," I added, "maybe one of us won't come home at all. Maybe you, Rodstein, will leave your blood on the sands like the martyr you think you'd like to be."

Bettle belched and threw in his two shekels worth: "Smart talk from a mooch. Suckered himself into a free trip and now he's preaching like a friend of the Almighty."

"No, Bettle, you've got it all backwards. *You're* the Almighty in this outfit. You're the one who dragged us all along with you. Me, I just piggy-backed a ride. I'm the hitchhiker in the crowd, the loner, the outsider. Am I getting too heavy for you to carry? Think about it, buddy - twelve months, fifty-two weeks, three hundred and sixty-five days, how many hours? - and you're lucky, Bettle, it's not a leap year. It'll go by quickly enough, and all be over and done with.

"If you don't like me, then stay out of my way. Once we're in the Promised Land, you'll have no responsibility for me whatsoever. Your part will have been done. I'll be the kibbutz' problem then. And as for you, Mr. Rodstein - Mr. Israel - if you want to talk to me, speak English, please. If you feel the same way Bettle does, well, do the same thing. Stay out of my way. I'm not going to be your mental punching bag. I might punch back. I might turn you over to the Arabs. It'd all probably be for the best, too - maybe where you belong."

Peggy looked up and asked, "And so. What do you think of me, Larry? What am I to you? How do I fit in?"

Getting up from the table, I told her, "Well, I've said enough already, more than I wanted to. I gotta go to the can. I gotta leave a leak. Don't worry - I'll see you all later."

Secretly, I was gloating as I left. I usually had somewhere to go, even if it was only to the can. They just sat around and mooned over Israel and what a wonderful thing they were doing. Hell, they were getting the trip of a lifetime and weren't even enjoying it. What a sad, pathetic bunch. If that was what religion and politics did to you, I wanted no part in any of it.

So, I went to the washroom, did my business there and went out onto the deck, and ran directly into Saul, good old Saul. He actually seemed glad to see me.

"Hi, Larry. How are things going?'

"The usual," I told him. "We just had another argument in the dining room. Irving, Bernie and Peggy versus the teenage virus here."

Saul smiled. "I'll bet you won the argument."

"I don't know if there can be a winner, Saul, but I sure as shootin' got to speak my piece."

Saul didn't like Bernie very much, and asked how I'd handled him. Maybe he had plans of his own?

"That was easy," I ventured, but couldn't explain further. How do you explain something you don't have to think about? To me, Bernie's brain was on fire and all I was doing was tossing some water on it to cool him off a bit. Saul chuckled at this weak reply. I asked him about himself. How was he doing? Was he, unlike the others, enjoying the trip?

"Love it, Larry! I've always wanted to learn our religion from the bottom up, and these people I'm with are teaching it to me that way."

"Gee, I'm real happy to hear that, Saul." I knew he wouldn't catch the sarcasm in my voice, but thought instead I meant every word. "Maybe you'll be the only one of the entire group to actually get something out of this mishmash of a trip."

"You know, Larry, I've always liked you for what you are. You've got guts, you know, more guts than they have. I knew you'd find a way to get to Bettle and Rodstein."

"The Master of Israel, you mean."

"Yes, and by the way, I heard about what happened the other night at the dance. That's not bad, you're the talk of the ship. You're ruffling their feathers but good, I like that. It's time someone did. Well, I've got to go now, and do my prayers. Goodbye."

And just like that, he was gone back into the woodwork.

Lawrence... of Canada

I headed off for the smoking lounge, remembering what Johnson had said, and wondering what his surprise was. Sure enough, when I got there, he was sunk back in his favourite studded-leather wingchair, waiting for my arrival.

"Hey, good evening, Mr. Johnson. So, how are you? Have a nice dinner?"

"Very pleasant, thank you. And how was yours? Satisfactory, I hope?"

"Well, ah - it could have been better. I got into a little argument with the guys I'm travelling with. You know, all they've been doing the whole time I've been with them, is pick on me."

"Picking on you? Why is that, Larry? You're all going to the same place, for the same reasons, aren't you? You'll be working together for the same organization, won't you?"

"Yes, but they think I'm too young, you see. They say I'm not dedicated enough to the cause, and that I'll just be a burden to their great expedition."

"Well, son, my advice is to hear them out. Listen to what they have to say to you, and if it makes sense, do something about it one way or the other. But if you don't believe they're making sense, maybe they aren't. Everyone is entitled to be themselves, and you have to be yourself, too. What's the worst that can happen? If you really can't fit in, or don't want to, don't feel you have to. I'll tell you what - if that turns out to be the case, then to hell with them, that's

124

the only way to think. There's trouble in the Middle East, too - big trouble. There always has been and perhaps there always will be.

"Also, if you do what everyone tells you, you might be shipped home in a box - you never can tell. Go ahead, Larry, and live up to your namesake, Lawrence of Arabia! England wrote the book, and he ripped it up and threw it back in England's face. However much some may not like him for what he did, at least the man stood up for his own convictions. I hope you'll do the same."

The old man's countenance almost began to glow as he began to recount the methods of heroism of a man he'd personally known, who was now legend. He launched on into an account of the famous guns of Accaba, and the blowing up of Turkish trains, a story about a British photographer being captured.

"Take no prisoners, Larry, leave not a living soul!" Johnson suddenly shouted, bolting upright in his chair, making me jump slightly. I hadn't really been listening - my mind had been drifting back to thoughts of Raizel. And then he was going on excitedly about some massacre or other, the telling of which I took no interest in at all, though I wouldn't have let him know that. I'm sure I had a very studious expression on my face, young disciple of history I was pretending to him to be.

Then he was back to Lawrence of Arabia again. "It's too bad, son, that he died on his motorcycle, but I suppose it was a fitting way to go. Heroes never like to die in bed, I suppose. But, he'd written his book. *The Seven Pillars of Wisdom,* and the world won't forget him, will it? No, it won't. Never!"

He relaxed his grip on the arm of the chair and took a deep breath. "No one, Larry, becomes famous for being a follower."

I liked old Mister Johnson. He made me feel comfortable and accepted for who I was. Besides, we had a kind of kinship - one of rebellion, but that was all right. Here was someone who sided with my way of thinking. It reinforced my previous beliefs about the individual. In some ways, Johnson and I fed off each other. I'm sure that if he had broached some of these topics with anyone else on board, he would have been pretty quickly dismissed as a passenger to get away from as quickly as possible. But as I said, I liked him, and he liked me. In Johnson I had a secret mentor the others didn't know about. I had an escape.

Johnson reached into his jacket pocket, and said, "Well, son, I told you I had something for you, a surprise. I think you'll like it."

His hand came back out, with a package of Winston Churchill cigars in it - at that time worth about five dollars each. There was no way I would ever have bought them for myself, and I thanked him profusely, shaking his hand, pumping it hard, as if by doing so I could make more things appear from his jacket pockets.

"I'll tell you, Mr. Johnson," I said, "if I never, in all my remaining days and nights, smoke a fine cigar again - I will *always* - and I mean always - remember when I smoked a pack of Winston Churchills. Thanks a lot, sir. I certainly appreciate it."

If you'd been there watching, you'd have been able to smell the honey dripping from my words. He was just trying to be nice, and although it's true, I would have probably accepted anything he offered, I did enjoy his company and I did, in my own way, appreciate what he was really doing - extending his friendship. to me. So, in a feeble attempt at being thoughtful toward him in return, I asked about his past, what line of work he'd been in before he retired.

He regarded me attentively before replying. "Well, sir, I was a Judge at the Central Criminal Court in London for quite some while, among other things."

"And if you don't mind my asking, what were you doing in America?"

"Visiting. I have friends there, and I've always wanted to see that part of the world."

I wasn't listening again, and hoped my face didn't show it. My mind had gotten a bit stuck, when he'd told me he'd been a Justice. "So, Mr. Johnson, you've been at the head of the court in London. I've always wondered what it would feel like to sentence a person to death."

The old man leaned forward in his chair, raised his eyebrows and fixed me with a cool stare. "Well, sir, I will tell you what it is like. Indeed. The first time you do such a thing is very difficult, of course. But as you must realize, 'cold-blooded murder' is just that - cold-blooded murder. And, according to the law, that means you must mete out the full punishment, which is cold-blooded death.

And the conscience rests easy, at that. It was not I who imposed death on the guilty party, but the law, and the law is the public's will, is it not? I merely carried out that will. Everything is dictated by law, Larry. Otherwise, there can be no justice. So my part was acting in accordance with what the law dictated."

Johnson was about five feet, ten inches tall, had a medium build, and was trim enough for someone his age. Wealthy and slightly eccentric (was that why I liked him?), he had thick, white hair - a bit longish for the time - with lamb-chop sideburns. This, combined with a pair of black horn-rimmed glasses, was enough to give anyone pause to wonder who he might be. The long, probably lightly waxed moustache gave him the appearance of a human mountain goat, and I liked that - most people usually all looked same to me, dressed in the same clothes from the same shops, and wearing their hair all styled with Brylcreem, all brushed in the same direction.

Johnson's apparel was as distinctive as the rest of him - grey flannel pants, a blue wool jacket, dark tie complete with a diamond stickpin, the end of which had been turned into some sort of symbol I couldn't quite make out, but figured was possibly a family insignia, as he always seemed to have it on. I wondered if he slept with it.

The reason I'm mentioning his appearance is to give you more of a sense of the sort of person one was likely to run across on a vessel like the *Queen Mary*. And remember, this all happened in 1957. Times are very different now. You're not likely to run into someone like Johnson today, unless you venture into the Twilight Zone; and even if you do, I think his conversation will be a little less open. He might not say much to you at all. Of course, that's just my opinion. I wouldn't blame him, either. Today, the world is filled with con artists, much more uncaring and even vicious than I'd ever been. I wasn't out to hurt anyone, but only wanted to have a good time.

"You know, Larry, I believe you are going to like Palestine - Israel today. Where I once rode a camel, there are quite possibly towns now, and cities. But all of the ancient sites are there, basically unchanged by time. Jerusalem never changes, only the people do that. I will probably never set eyes on it again, but you will - and it's a lovely place.

"I remember walking through the streets of Bethlehem, searching for the birthplace of Christ, and how the only thing I found was a sign saying that here I was, this was it. But there was nothing there to be seen, only the sign itself. And I remember, in Jerusalem, walking along the famous Wailing Wall, watching the old men in their orthodox robes, crying and stuffing its cracks with prayers and requests they had written, as if the wall was God's mailbox. Yes, and King Solomon's Temple of the Golden Dawn - amazing, simply amazing.

"I hope you know that Jerusalem, today, is split in half - like East and West Berlin. There is an arch in the centre of the city, near the Wailing Wall, called The Mandelbaum Gate. It divides the city of Jerusalem, sundering it from the Arab Nation. Those people who live around it, however, are neither Arab nor Israeli. It is a strange thing, but they are known as Yemenites. They live in mud huts and have little or no means of income at all, so they send their children out to steal, though it may be that some of them, fearful of being caught, borrow or beg instead. They are fearful not simply of being caught and held guilty of thievery, but of never returning to their homes again.

"The shopkeepers, you see, are quite free to do as they wish with these little child-thieves - and very often they kill them. You will recognize them when you see them in the streets, sitting and playing the balalaika, hoping the tourists will toss them a little change. The parents of these street children, some of them, once were famous as jewellers, who would bribe their way in and out of Israel in order to purchase silver and other valuable metals and stones. At times, they would leave their children behind as collateral. It was, and still is, quite a difficult - and terrible - way of life, as I'm certain you will agree. In the daytime, they would sell their wares to tourists who had come to see the Wailing Wall, not the local facts of life. And these self-motivated street merchants, if I may call them that, would have to get out of the city before nightfall, before the changing of the guard, who could mean real trouble for them if they hadn't previously been paid off. Sometimes I wonder why Lawrence of Arabia didn't run them all off - Yemenites, guards, tourists and all!"

This wasn't my notion of Israel at all, and while I found it fascinating, I wanted to change the subject back to something I knew more about. Lighting up one of the big Winston Churchill cigars,

I puffed and puffed on it, blowing smoke in every direction, letting (I figured) Mr. Johnson know how much I appreciated his buying them for me (and secretly hoping he'd go a step further, and maybe buy me something else).

Just to make sure he knew, I told him how much I enjoyed "a good smoke like this" - even if my face probably was turning a bit green around the edges!

"So, Mr. Johnson," I asked, music-crazed North American teenager that I must have appeared to him to be, "Mr. Johnson, have you ever heard any Rock 'n Roll?"

"Of course I have, son, of course. We all hear it, you know. Can't help but hear it. You're talking about this fellow Bill Holly with his 'Rock Around the Clock tonight', who is 'number one in England' with his swivelling hips and rotating pelvis and his 'Heartbreak Hotel' song... Well, Larry, as I see it, I suppose it has to be considered 'music', although to me, you realize, it is only noise. I suppose, too, with the way the world has been going lately, it will last, too. But let the young have it, I say. They will soon enough be old."

He smiled at my obvious surprise at his knowledge of Rock 'n Roll, even if he hadn't gotten things quite in the right order.

"Well," he said, "what were you thinking? That England was swallowed up by the ice age? We have radios, you know, and television sets. The island isn't *that* isolated. Of course, we have Rock 'n Roll. Before sailing to America, I had to purchase my grandchild a recording by some fellow called, I believe, Little Richard. The recording, as I recall, had a very strange title - something along the lines of 'Beee-dop-bee-dula-bee', I think. Am I close?"

When Johnson laughed, it was more like a chortle, as if he knew something you didn't. While he was being as pleasant as he could be, there was something underneath his tone that told me he really didn't think much of either the title, the singer's name, the idea of having to buy a child a Rock 'n Roll record - and the whole idea of the music itself. Maybe the something was scorn, I thought.

He told me his favourite American bandleader was Glenn Miller. He also liked Johnny Ray, the deaf singer.

❁

Stormy Seas

As he said this, a glass that had been sitting on top of a small coffee table suddenly slid a length of about two feet before it hit the little raised gutter that ran around the edges. Something out there wasn't right. If I'd ever told myself the idea of travelling across an ocean was nothing, that there was no reason to have any fear whatsoever on a liner this huge - well, now was the time I started to contradict myself.

"Uh, Mr. Johnson," I blurted, "I - I hope we're not going to sink or something! But, something's wrong, I can feel it. The room is moving. Look at that chandelier, it's swaying! This definitely feels funny, doesn't it? I mean, we weren't moving like this three hours ago. It must be very choppy out there."

Johnson looked up at the chandelier, cocked his head and stared at the floor a moment, trying to feel how the boat was, through his feet, like some crazy doctor. "Yes, you're right," he said after his diagnosis. "Let's get ourselves a drink before we go down."

"Wow, this is just great," I announced, feeling my fear subside a little at the thought of having a free drink. "If we sink, we'll be shark bait, won't we, and all those beautiful meals we've eaten on this ship will be sitting in some satisfied shark's belly."

"A cheery thought," said Johnson. "You have an odd sense of humour, Larry, but I must admit I don't mind it one bit."

We never did order the drinks, though. The sound of the waves was coming to us much more clearly now, as they crashed across the deck, and I knew things were getting - probably already were - fairly serious. This was no little twenty minute fall of rain. Johnson had been consulting with his shoes again, and now, startled by hearing the crashes, he lifted his head and looked me straight in the eye, like a man who has just discovered a terrible secret.

"It's going on ten o'clock, Larry, and we've been the only ones here all evening. This is going to be a big one." By the look on his face, he was definitely worried.

"What do you mean," I asked, "by a big one? A big one what?"

"Why, this is no piss into the wind, son. This is a big blow!"

"I want to go up and watch this," I told him.

"That's not such a bad idea, Larry. You go and do that. Get the feel of being a real sailor. I'm going to my cabin. I'll see you tomorrow, hopefully."

"It'll be all right, Mr.. Johnson. This is a big ship."

"So was the *Titanic*," he said. He smiled at me in a gloomy kind of fashion, and slowly left the room, hanging onto the railings.

I left the room, too. It was very hard to walk, and I could feel my supper sloshing around inside, slowly, from one side to the other... I couldn't believe this - the power of the storm was immense! If you didn't hold onto the rails... tightly - you weren't going to get where you wanted to go, that was one thing for sure! The ship was bouncing and lunging like a huge roller-coaster, pounding ahead into the wind and waves.

So there I was, inching my way along, trying to keep my supper safely where it was supposed to be, wanting to get to my room to grab a coat so I wouldn't be drowned by the splash-offs. We were stuck, it seemed, right in the heart of the storm and. queasy as I was, I wanted desperately to see what was going on. I *had* to get into the middle of it if I could, don't ask why - there's no reasonable, sane answer to a thing like that. It was just that I knew I'd never have the chance to see, to be a part of, such a drama again, that was all. This wasn't watching *Mutiny on the Bounty* - this was the real thing.

I made it to my room by having to literally crawl along the sides of the wall, hand over hand, knee over knee, but I got there. I pushed the door to our quarters open and saw the gang, sitting there, holding on for dear life. As I stood up, trying to get my balance again, I asked, "Hey, who wants to join me for a walk out on the deck?"

Rodstein was already turning a murky greenish- yellow colour, and was in the process of vomiting all over the place as I spoke. Bettle, excited by the sheer force of the storm, said he'd liked to come but was afraid. "But, you, Larry, you're crazy, your going out there proves all of my theories about you, you're a bona fide nutcase if I ever saw one, and no, Larry - nobody wants to join your madness, so go ahead and take the dive! Have a nice swim, looney-toons!"

"Oh, come on!" I yelled back. "Come on up and get the feel of the storm. There's nothing wrong with it - this is the best part of the trip! We're not gonna be life-raftin' it, you know. We aren't lifer Navy boys, this is your once-in-a-lifetime chance to see something like this. It's great!"

"You really *are* meshuga, aren't you?" Bettle cried. "One of those waves will wash us… it'll wipe us clean off this tugboat. This is only the beginning, Larry. There's worse to come, I can feel it. We're not back home on Sunnyside Beach, you know. No, we're out here… and this is the fucking centre of the fucking Atlantic fucking Ocean! And you want to find God or something, right in the middle of everything. Well, good luck, I say! But don't expect me to go with you!"

"All right, fuck it. I'll go by myself."

I got my jacket from a hook on the wall, put it on and started back out the doorway.

"Well," Bettle yelled over the roar of the wind, "if you're not back in an hour, we won't have to go looking for you."

"Goodbye …"

I took the stairs.

I hoisted myself up, clinging onto the railing. Up - and down! Each time the ship rose out of the water, I'd have to hang on with all my might, and then, when it was going down again, hold on even tighter so I wouldn't be smashed into the floor. As I was pulling myself along this way, I heard, over the constant crash and smash of the water, someone yelling at me,"Hey, you! Get back down there! You'll get yourself killed!"

I ignored the voice and went on, picking my way as best I could out onto the deck. Finally, after what seemed a short eternity, I got to where I'd wanted to be.

I was completely alone, the night surrounding me, black as midnight ink. It made me think of being in the bottom of a mine, one with no lights. Above me, the sky had gone crazy. I could see nothing but what looked like swirling soot, the air dark and menacingly wild. I felt like I was inside a giant eggbeater. The sky was lacerated by huge forks of lightning, of a kind I'd never seen on land, bright enough out on the open ocean to light up an entire city. It was simply amazing, and I loved it.

Still, it wasn't enough. I wanted more - to get myself right into the heart of it. I pulled and dragged myself all the way along the side of the ship to the front edge of the bow. Holding on to the railing for dear life, up there at the nose of the *Queen Mary*, it was like riding a roller-coaster, only forty or fifty feet higher in the air. The boat was lunging ahead, up and down like a harpooned whale. Then, it surged straight up like a javelin, taking about ten seconds for the front half of the boat to get held up in mid-air.

A ghostly pause then ensued, lasting about thirty seconds (or so it seemed), holding it motionless before gravity kicked in and we started the long, gut-wrenching trip down again. During those thirty seconds we were poised in this treacherous hold where the sheer weight of the near-submerged stern could have sucked the vessel under in much less than half the time it took the *Titanic* to sink... at least, that was the thought rolling around in my head as I waited.

Then, suddenly, the bow would dive down again, crashing like a huge iron pan into the water, throwing sixty to eighty foot waves back that covered the entirety of the ship. I shuddered as we began the descent, wondering each time if we'd ever come up again. The first bang of the waves hitting the deck washed all around me, drenching me, sucking at me. I imagined the waves themselves were giant stretched-out hands, their fingers searching for victims, grabbing at me, wanting to carry me down into the watery depths.

Being this close to winding up as shark bait, I snapped out of my childlike bravado, as I began to realize how serious the situation actually was. Taking one last look at the maelstrom, I decided I'd had enough. Any longer and the sea and the storm would have mesmerized me, and maybe one of those wave-fingers would snatch me overboard and goodbye, Larry. I began to grope my way back, knowing that if I didn't get out of there, it would mean the end of me. The storm was getting worse.

I made it to the Smoking Lounge, too seasick to get back downstairs to my cabin. I was startled at the sight of old man Johnson sitting there with a big smile on his face, as if he'd been waiting for me.

"How are you, old boy? You're looking a little wet. Have you had your jollies?"

"Well, aside from whatever's rolling around in my stomach, it was great out there. I loved it. Never seen anything so wild, so pure. The power of nature, can't beat it, Mr. Johnson."

"There's nothing like it, is there?" he replied, looking me up and down. "But, my word, Larry - you're soaked. You'd better take off your jacket and shirt. Here, put my jacket on so you don't catch your death of pneumonia!" He removed his jacket and handed it to me as I began peeling my wet clothing off.

"You certainly had your fun out there, didn't you, son? that's what adventure is all about - doing the unusual. Doing what other people regret they've never done, people who just don't have what it takes. So many people are primed for a lifetime built around when to eat, when to sleep and when to work. Adventure, I believe, is the essence of human life, but not many people actually live it, do they? Perhaps I should call you 'Lawrence of Canada' from now on."

I chuckled a bit at that. "Yes, I know what you mean. Just look at me - I'm drenched to the gills and nearly fell to the sharks - but, I've got something to tell to my grandchildren, if I ever have them. I'll tell them I had an experience that those chickenshits I'm travelling with will never have!"

Mr. Johnson grinned and got up and made his way over to the bar, making us each a Tom Collins, doing, I might add, a fine job for someone who surely had never tended bar. It was now past midnight and the storm seemed to be getting worse. The floor of the

Smoking Lounge was getting wet with the wash-over of the pounding waves that pummelled everything. The walls were creaking and the ship was beginning to take some pretty hard sideways leans. In the distance, mixed in with the noise of the wind and waves, I could hear a metallic-sounding crashing at intermittent intervals.

"Do you know what kind of cargo we have below decks, on the bottom of the ship?" Johnson asked.

"Not really," I replied. "Aside from luggage, I didn't know the *Queen Mary* took anything but passengers."

"Well, we do. Automobiles, Larry. Bentleys and Rolls Royces, going back to England for specialized repairs. By the time they get there, I'm afraid there might not be much left of them. A bunch of elegant looking junk, maybe. I've been to sea before, and have been in a number of storms. One like this might only hit the Atlantic once every fifty or one hundred years. In the thirty-odd passages I've taken in the last forty years, I have never seen anything quite like this."

We chatted on, drinking Tom Collins' until, about 12:30 a.m. Peggy appeared in the doorway. I was surprised to see her. She must have fought her way up the stairs like I had. I asked her what she thought she was doing, wandering around in the storm. Didn't she realize how dangerous it was?

She was bored, she said, and sick, too.

"I just thought I'd come up here. I've never been here before, you know. It's nearly the end of the trip - I hope! - and I thought I should at least see the Smoking Lounge. Besides, getting away from downstairs might do me some good. Everyone's sick down there, sicker than I am."

"So what's with Bettle and Rodstein? You're always with them. Where are they? Why come and talk to me? You never do that."

"For starters, they're both as sick as dogs. I knew you went out on deck, and thought, well, you can't be as seasick as they are. All they do is vomit and groan. I had to get away."

"Peggy, this is Mister Johnson, a friend of mine from England."

Johnson took her hand and smiled. "You must be one of the group Larry's travelling to Israel with. He's mentioned the name Peggy. He speaks very highly of you.

"The other two that you say are 'as sick as dogs', I take it they don't like Larry very much. They run him down, he says, and since he can't be bothered with that sort of treatment, he comes up here to hide. They're a bit older than Larry, aren't they? They don't seem to know a great deal about life, it would seem to me. They don't know what tomorrow is going to bring their way any more than Larry does.

"They pick away at Larry, from what I can understand, like birds on a loaf of bread, but one day he will turn on them when they need him. They'll be in a bit of a sling then. You know, Peggy, you're all going to a strange land, to a country where petty squabbling is not tolerated - it's too dangerous. There are no allowances for age, either, you see. A twelve year old might shoot you, a ten year old might stick you with a knife - just because of a wrong word, or a misinterpreted action.

"You're going there, in a sense, as revolutionaries, but do you really know what revolution is all about? The country of Israel is in a state of revolution all of the time. Since its inception, it has been. Any personal differences you may have within your group will matter to no one once you get there.

"Your friends are picking on someone who is in the same shoes they're in. As I take it, all of you were asked to go to Israel, and you all accepted in the same spirit. Larry here, being the youngest, is taking the greatest risk of all. The rest of you are at an age when you should be thinking of getting married and working, settling down. You had all better face the truth, my girl - you are running away from home, in a sense, as discontented misfits.

"Now, what do you expect to get out of this trip, Peggy? Tell me honestly."

I hadn't expected Johnson to start in on this, but was glad he did. Maybe Peggy would convey some of what he'd said back to the others, and they'd have a bit more respect for me. Fat chance, the pessimistic side of me said, but maybe ...

"Well, I... I think you're right, really. I'm looking for the elusive dream."

"Yes," said Johnson, "but you must have a goal, mustn't you? You didn't come along just because someone offered you a job.

There are plenty of those back home. And, a girl like you - I can see you have high ideals, Peggy - you wouldn't have come just because you were offered a free trip. So, why?"

"I thought it over when I was asked in Winnipeg, and I couldn't see a better arrangement. Going to Israel is better than standing at the corner of Portage and Main in January, waiting for a bus in the wind and cold. I couldn't think of a better way out. I'm Jewish and from a religious family, for whatever that means. Besides, how often in a lifetime do you get a chance to go somewhere like Israel?"

"Or a free trip?" queried Johnson.

"How do you know so much about this?" Peggy asked. "Larry must have told you quite a lot."

"It's my business, young lady, to know things. In knowing people, one comes to know many things. I haven't spent my seventy-odd years beneath a rock, you know."

Peggy smiled with the pureness of her youth, and decided to play along.

"So, what did you do for a living, Mr.. Johnson? Did you hold down some high-falutin job in a London bank, maybe?"

The old gentleman smiled right back. "If it would really interest you to know what I did for a living... a part of my living was made by playing a major role in the ending of other people's lives."

Peggy gave a start a second or so before the boat lurched into the next wave. Thunder crashed and lightning struck at the same time. Mr. Johnson's smile continued throughout. The little girl was puzzled. She didn't know everything, after all...

"I'm not sure I understand," she said. "Do you mean you were - er, in the army or something?"

"My dear lady, I was a Judge at the London Criminal Courts and a large part of the duties I performed during those years had to do with hanging people who had been tried and found guilty of crimes punishable by death. I have seen many, many people hang - that is to say I have *sentenced* them to hang by the neck until dead. Now, would you say that I might know people, and how they think and what they are capable of?"

He let the question hang, too, for a moment, letting the idea sink in, and then continued, "I have been to Israel, as you may have guessed, and I daresay I am not speaking out of turn when I say that you indeed have much to learn, young lady, about this life. Perhaps your journey to Israel and your stay there will help ease you out of the cocoon you seem to have got yourself wrapped up in.

"You people, you see, are all so worried about Larry here. Don't make that mistake. He isn't worrying about any of you. He's going because he wants to go. He's looking forward to having a good time, if I judge him rightly. Isn't that true, Larry?"

He didn't give me a chance to reply, though I found myself nodding my head "yes" anyway. He could be very persuasive, this Mr. Johnson, judge and executioner.

"Now, Peggy," he went on, "you see, if you look at it in that light, which is the only true light, why then - there's no earthly reason to be angry with him, is there? He's following his star, and doing what he wants. He's not pretentious about it, and doesn't espouse high ideals he doesn't have. He's a realist, you see. And anyone venturing to the land of Israel today had better be a realist, or be ready to be made into one."

He sighed, and gave her the opportunity to say something back to him, maybe offer some sort of defence. She had none to offer, though.

"Well," he said, "as we used to say in the dangling business, the hanging's the easy part. It's the bringing them back that's difficult. So, you remember what I'm telling you, and perhaps one day when Larry here has decided he's had enough of being kicked around, you or one of your group will find themselves alone and in need of help - and it may be that Larry, because of who and what he is, would have been the only one to provide the sort of help needed. But he won't be there. He'll have vamoosed, as the Americans say, into the wide blue yonder. And there will be no help. You will have already chased the help away.

"The only person you have to worry about is yourself, you see. The people there won't bother to protect you. Why should they care about a group of young, naive westerners? Over there, it's a rugged existence, and every man for himself when the shooting starts. It won't be like being in one of your Hollywood films. Instead, you'll get to see firsthand who comes home and who doesn't. Or who does, but in a box, or confined to a wheelchair or worse for their remaining days.

"Now, my dear, I've probably said enough, having nearly bored you to tears. But, you are polite to an overly talkative old man who needs his sleep and can't get it for the pounding and smashing of the waters upon the hull of this ship we're aboard - so I will say only one more thing to you before 'Good night'. WAR is the dirtiest three letter word known to mankind, and there are no heroes."

With that, Mr.. Johnson quickly polished off the last of his Tom Collins, bid us good evening, and cautiously edged his way out of the room. We said goodnight to him as he left, Peggy's voice quiet and subdued, mine as loudly proud to know him as ever. When he was gone, I couldn't help getting a dig in.

"Nice guy, eh Peggy?"

She wasn't biting, and when she didn't, I realized that what the old man had said to her made sense.

"Smart man. Maybe I shouldn't have said what I did to him. He is right, I guess. Maybe we're all pulling our strings too hard. Maybe Bettle and Rodstein don't have a clue what they're talking about, but just think they do.

"When I think about it, I have to say, I really don't know what Bettle's ideas are, but I think he's a sort of war-monger. He likes to provoke people and get them to fight, and he likes to fight. Maybe, for him, it's got nothing to do with Israel at all. I don't know. And Rodstein, he's just a paper Communist. If it ever came down to it, he'd probably babble like a newborn baby, and a pacifier or placebo would shut him up, and he'd think he'd won everybody over. Vain glory, I guess you call it.

"You're probably right about him, Larry. He'll end up, as you like to say, with full pants and empty arms, whatever that means - and don't bother telling me, I don't want to know. But nothing will come of him. He'll rant and he'll rave and it'll be a wasted trip. He'll be able to tell his children he went to Israel, but he'll have to make up the stories. Besides, who wants to fight a war? That's not why we're going, it isn't why *I'm* going!"

I didn't get the impression that Peggy was softening - she'd been soft from the beginning. It was just the way she was, but the old man had made her think. It's hard to ignore a man like that when it's almost one o'clock in the morning and the seas are so high you're ready to place bets on what time the ship starts breaking up.

"Well, look at it this way, Peggy. Me, I've got nothing against you. I like you. You've done me no harm, and I don't think you would. I just don't want any problems with any of the group. If I want to go to Israel for my own reasons, what's wrong with that? I could pretend otherwise, but would it help matters? Then I'd be a liar as well as a deserter of the cause. Except, I'm not a deserter because I don't have a cause. A rebel without a cause, that's me - just like James Dean. So, I go for my reasons, you for yours, them for theirs. Everybody's on their own, that's all that really counts.

"I'm not out to steal anybody's thunder. I got thunder enough of my own, it follows me around. If Bettle wants to think he's a hero, so what? Let him. There are lots of heroes buried on Boot Hill and plenty of other places, Israel included, so who cares? If he wants to push his weight around, that's all right - I don't have to listen. He didn't pay for this trip. If I went and got myself shot, believe me, he wouldn't so much as bat an eye...

"He wouldn't even blink - too busy studying himself in the mirror, that guy. You see what I mean? You see what Mr. Johnson meant? That's how it is. I don't have to answer to anybody except myself. I came on my own and I'm staying on my own, that's it. I feel the same about Rodstein, too, only worse. I'll get even with him, don't worry.

"So, Peggy. Your trip to Israel belongs to you and you alone. I've got nothing against someone like you, and what you do, it's your own beeswax. Me, I've got nothing to do or say about it. But I'd rely on flypaper before Bettle or Rodstein. When it comes down to the crunch, those guys will be there for no one but Bettle and Rodstein. You can kiss them goodbye if the bullets ever fly. They won't hang around, looking after you or anyone. That much I know, so don't ever put yourself in a position where you have to depend on either of them. And together, they're worse. If you leave them as your last exit, you'll find they've locked the door. So, anyway, Peggy... whatcha gonna do with your time, once we get to Europe? Just to change the subject...?"

"The idea is to have a good time, Larry - same as you!"
That was nice to hear. Finally, a bit of truth.

The storm began to abate around 2:30 in the morning, and the Captain made an announcement saying that we'd passed through the worst of it and that everything would be fine by morning. The only damage, apparently, was to some of the cargo. No one was to worry about anything and passengers should, if they were able, go to sleep, presumably to dream about peaceful waters.

He said he was sorry to have had to wake those who had already been asleep, but felt it was his duty as Captain of the vessel to keep passengers informed, especially when the news was good. Then he thanked us for our cooperation, and said goodnight.

I doubted if the announcement had actually woken anyone. Anyone who could have slept through all the banging and crashing would have slept through the announcement, too. I decided I'd had my share of the storm, and went off to try to sleep. We were still rolling with the waves, but I managed to get a few hours, falling asleep to pleasant thoughts of not winding up as shark food after all. The next day would be our last on board the *Queen Mary*, and I didn't want to miss anything.

Saying Goodbye

Somehow, I got up early enough to see the sun rise. The sea was calm and you never would have guessed there'd ever been more than a whisper on the waters. The storm, however, had held us up some twenty hours, giving us an extra day on the ocean. Everyone I met seemed very happy to be alive that morning, and I had the feeling that many a Bible had been opened during the night, and many a prayer read. Some people told me there were points in the storm when they thought the ship would surely tip over in the high gales.

The porpoises were running alongside the ship, the sun was coming up, the air was warm and refreshing and I was feeling kind of glad to be alive myself, when I turned my head and had the spell broken by Bernie, who had somehow managed to make it through to morning.

"Good morning, Bernie. I see you're still with us."

"No thanks to you, Wiener."

It was such a nice way to start the day.

"So, Bernie, I hear you had some bad luck last night."

"What do you mean? Everyone was sick, not just me."

"No, I mean real bad luck."

"What was that?"

"You didn't get swept overboard like I'd hoped you would."

"That's your bad luck, chump, not mine. I guess we're stuck with each other for the year, in that case."

"Rodstein's still with us, too, I guess," I said, pointing out to sea.

"I'd sooner be stuck with those porpoises than with you guys, but they're smart - they're sticking with the tides."

Bernie sniffed, and changed the subject, trying to get some sort of upper hand on me.

"Hey, Larry, tell me something. Are you still messing around down in the lower parts of the ship? You still gettin' laid for a lousy piece of bread?"

"I dunno," I told him, "if it's any of your business. But how about you? Are you still messing around with the teacher? Is she any good in the sack, or would you even know?"

"Never mind that, Larry. Are you still sucking up to the old man in the Smoking Lounge? What's he give you - free cigars, free food, a couple of drinks? You're a real cooz 'n booze boy, aren't you? Sucking up to a poor little refugee girl in steerage and a lonely old man in First Class. You're a first class ass, you are, Wiener. What a joke!"

"Well, Bernie, maybe you're right. I may be a first class ass, whatever that is, but you're a bigger one. And you're not first class, you're at the bottom of the ladder. You're a sucker, pal. You're the one who set me up for this trip, and now you've gotta live with it - and me. I may have talked my way on, but you talked my way in. So if you can't live with it, you've only got yourself to blame."

"For once it seems you may be right, Larry. I never should have done it."

"But, you did, and now you'll have to suffer the consequences. All I was doing, Bernie, was having a shower at the Y, don't ever forget that. You approached me, I didn't go to you. Maybe you liked the way I looked or something - what do I know? You asked me if I was interested in a free trip, you didn't ask if I was a religious zealot... remember?

"I heard you out and agreed to go, that's all. Now, you wish you hadn't asked. But it's too late, and anyway - there's no reason why we can't get along, now that we're on our way. All I want from you is an even break. Do you remember, at the Jewish Agency in New Jersey, when you were my boss? I picked the apples and potatoes and shovelled the shit that you wouldn't touch with a fifty-foot pole. Remember, Bernie? Well, you're not my boss any more, and when we get to Israel, believe me, I'm going to do exactly what I want... just as *I* please, not as *you* please. Got it? In Europe, too, I'm going my own way, and you can't stop me.

"And when we arrive in Israel... you won't be my boss there, either. If you make any mistakes about that, I'll be the first one to jump down your throat. So, we'd better make peace now, don't you think? Or do you think? Y'know, Bernie - over there, we'll only have ourselves to rely on. We don't even speak the language, and the people there aren't going to give a sweet damn about us. We'll be strangers in a strange land. So, let's shake hands for once and get it over with. Live and let live is my philosophy. How about you?"

He stared at me for a moment, not expecting such a speech so early in the day - but I could see it made sense to him. He offered his hand, and I shook it.

"Let's go for breakfast," he said.

"Okay," I replied, "good. We'll keep the peace. It's the best way."

So, waving goodbye to the porpoises, we went down the stairway to the dining room, buddy-buddy.

After breakfast, I was asked to join the group in a game of shuffleboard and then some swimming. I turned it down, saying that I had something to do. I thought I should go down and talk to Raizel, realizing we would probably never see each other again. I can be a sentimental schmuck at times.

Down below, I bumped into an old man, a typical bearded Jew, and asked him, "Vu iz di shayna maidel?" (Where's the pretty girl?)

He stared into the air a second as if getting directions from above, shrugged and pointed to over his shoulder. "Dortn." (Over there)

I walked through steerage feeling like I was entering a Nazi prison camp. It was dark as a dungeon, and the men and women were decked out in their best plain black peasant garb, reminding me of crows. They had no money, no food to speak of, and were mostly Russian, Polish and Hungarian peasants, as religious as all get-out. I could hear their mumbled prayers as I passed them, and the atmosphere had an eerie feeling to it, as if we were on board a train headed for Dachau...

The difference was that the war was over and these people were going to a "homeland" they'd never seen, where some would end up farming or return to the crafts and trades they'd known before the war. At least they were getting a new start in life, and having their dreams fulfilled, not to mention the prophecy they'd lived by - the promise of a new land. There were about two hundred of them in all.

I knew I'd never feel such an atmosphere again, and somehow, I began to understand some of the anguish and pain that must have attended the war camps... as I walked along, I couldn't help but think of the groups of herded strangers going off to their deaths and worse in Dachau, Auschwitz and Buchenwald. These people had been a part of it, I could see the numbers tattooed on their arms. The ghosts of the death camps, people who had survived, but only barely - here they were, the gloomy aura surrounding them wherever they went... making me shudder as I passed through.

It struck me, suddenly, how different life in the west was. Here they were, "going home" to a land they'd never seen - coming from places they never wanted to see again, but would never be able to forget. And here I was, a young kid riding on the coat-tails of a rich organization, as Bernie would say, "out for a free ride", knowing next to nothing, really, about things that went on in the rest of the world.

Well, I was learning.

I went around a bend in a hallway, and there was Raizel, dressed in black like the rest of them. It was hard to imagine her hopping around on the dance floor the way she had. There was no way to be alone down there, as people were coming and going, back and forth along the passageway. I asked her if she'd come up on deck with me for a while. "I want to say goodbye to you," I told her. She said, "Only for a few minutes. I can't stay away long. We are getting ourselves ready for the leaving of the ship."

We left the dark, melancholic air behind us and went out onto a stairway leading up out of steerage. She smiled at me, and began talking about the storm and how she thought they were going to wind up at the bottom of the ocean. I smiled back, and she went on, bringing herself around in her own way to the point she wanted to make...

"Larry, I want to say thank you for what you've done for us. It may seem small, even nothing to you, but we had nothing and you brought us down some food to eat. It meant a great deal, what you've done. You helped turn what was very difficult for my people, into something more enjoyable. It wasn't only the food, but also the company. No one else on board this ship came down here to talk with us. Only you.

"When we stop and get off this boat, I know that what you said was true - we will never see each other again. But, the time we did have together will be a memory for a lifetime. I will never forget you. I only wish I could have done more for you than - well, go to your dance."

"Raizel, just knowing you was more than enough to teach me what hardship is all about. I know if I was half the man I'm supposed to be, I would cry because I know that if you were in my country, Canada, I would never let you go. But listen - whenever you think of me, think of the tough times and the good times as well - remember that some Canadian boy thought of you as the great person you really are. Remember what we did together, if only for a little while. It was good, wasn't it?"

In the distance, I could hear the old man telling someone where we were, and then another voice calling Raizel.

"I have to go," she said, lowering her eyes, not wanting to look at me. I put my finger to her chin and lifted it. There were little tears forming in the corners of her eyes.

"I want to kiss you goodbye," I said.

And I did.

I saw in her face at least a little glow of the joy she would (hopefully) feel when she finally reached her "homeland". And so, we kissed and parted, and that was it. I turned and walked away, never to see her again.

I went back upstairs to see if I could find old Mr. Johnson. I wanted to say goodbye to him, too. He'd been very nice to me, and had treated me as an equal.

He was sitting in his favourite armchair, relaxing with an unlit cigar in his mouth.

"Hello, Mr. Johnson. How are you today? Quite the night, wasn't it?"

"Good morning, Larry. Did you get some sleep?"

"A bit," I said. "Well, Sir, I guess this is our last day on board the ship. The trip is coming to an end and you'll be going your way, I'll be going mine. We had some good times, though, didn't we?"

"That we did, Larry. Remember me in the days ahead, and I'll remember that I met a young man who turned out to be a pretty good bloke."

"What's that? What's a bloke, Mr.. Johnson?"

He took his big Winston Churchill cigar out of his mouth, looked at it for a moment, took another one from his vest pocket, handed it to me and said, "Sit down, Larry, and I'll tell you what a good bloke is."

He lit the cigars with a solid gold Dunhill lighter, the appearance of which infected me with the desire from that day on to have one of my own. I sat down, puffed on the cigar, waiting for what he'd say next, although I certainly wasn't prepared for what was about to happen.

Mr. Johnson signalled to the waiter, and told him, "Two glasses of champagne, please - one for my buddy and one for me." The drinks arrived, and then he turned to me.

"I just want to tell you, Larry - *buddy* - that it has been great fun meeting you. You provided me with some very good company, and an old man like me needs that once in a while. A *bloke* is simply a nice fellow, someone like yourself, or as they say in your country, a buddy.

"I suppose, Larry, we will never meet again. But, I will always remember my trip to New York and this boat trip. You will probably meet a nice young Israeli girl once you get to your destination. Unless I miss my guess, I imagine you will become a Lawrence of Arabia, in your own way. Maybe you'll become the Lawrence of Israel."

I was a little bit stunned, not having realized Johnson thought so much of me.

"Well, I could never be a Lawrence of Arabia. I don't even know what I'll be doing once I get there. The people I'm with say I'll be working on a farm, which I know I'll hate. I mean, I don't want to be a farmer."

"Yes, but Larry - farming is right at the heart of any country. In Israel, there's the farmer, and there's the soldier. Unless you plan on becoming a gentleman prophet, well... look at it this way: as a farmer, you'll be building a new state, being a pioneer. If you became a soldier, you'd forever be at odds with your own position - would you be a builder or a destroyer? It's better to be someone who toils at the soil, providing a necessary good, than to be a man with a gun and provide a necessary evil, isn't it?

"And anyway, tomorrow you'll be able to look back. You may not see what you have done. Nobody will know your name after you're gone. No one will care whether you've been there or not. Maybe, too, you won't last out the year. It is entirely possible you might be killed there, even in the first week or month. It is a killing ground, you know. However, Larry... win or lose, you will have done your part. A flower or vegetable may grow somewhere on that desert, and it will have been a seed you yourself planted. It's a bit like Flanders Fields. Who knows who is buried there? But the dead ones, they know they did their part. And you will, too. Of course, I trust you won't be dead.

"I'm saying this to you as a friend, you see. You're going to a country that was built out of a dream, but built out of sand nonetheless. It's a place where, I believe, you being the type of fellow you are, you'll survive. You won't have to steal or lie, and wouldn't if you had to - I don't believe you're the type. Remember, I'm a good judge of people, so when I say this, I mean it. Don't mistake my meaning, then, when I say that I can see that you will have to do a bit of conniving to survive.

"If there's any way to make life easier for yourself, you'll find that way, and make use of it. You'll do whatever you have to do to attain that easier life. You're a believer in the *ask and ye shall receive* syndrome, and that's all right. If I may be a bit more blunt than usual, I'll tell you something else≥you're a typical bullshit slinger. You came, you saw, you talked. You talked an old man out of a cigar, you drank his liquor, and you gave me good entertainment in exchange. Not a bad trade, and I may be the luckier of the two. You were well worth the little you received from me. Who else would have taken the time to talk with an old fellow like myself?

"I don't walk around with a sign on my forehead saying, *Judge Johnson. Please speak to me.* You came and talked to me, anyway, and whatever you thought you were after doesn't matter. It's immaterial, you see. And so, I liked you. It's as simple as that, Larry. To say it like an American, I thought you were a swell guy. Or, to put it in terms better to my liking, you've been a good bloke. Now, what do you have to say to that?"

I was a bit flabbergasted at his honesty, and the correct way he'd judged me. I didn't mind, though. Sometimes, it's good to see yourself through someone else's eyes - especially when they're right.

"I realize that what you just said about me probably sums up my whole life - ninety percent bullshit, ten percent heart. I think, though, that's what makes me a survivor. I'll say one thing for sure - I would never want to stand in front of your bench! You'd have me hanged before I knew what to do. But forget that. You know, I did really enjoy your company and will think of you wherever I go or whatever I'll be doing in the future. I will always remember the man who'd known Lawrence of Arabia and General Allenby."

"When we get across to Europe, Larry, remember that your Mother's not there. Have a good time. You have everything in your favour, son - youth, time and enough money to get by on. That's all anyone needs, but not everyone has. You may think you don't have much, but you'll have enough to have yourself a good time. I think you'll do that, won't you?"

I told him I sure was going to try.

"Yes, Larry, you will. As for me, I am not at all sure if I'll live long enough to ever return to America. I am over seventy years old now, and my time is running out. But I understand what you are going through. Age understands youth, believe it or not. I've been there. Now, you told me you were the youngest in your group. That must mean you're about twenty years old?"

"Nineteen."

"Well then, would you be embarrassed if I wanted to give you a little gift in honour of our friendship?"

"I don't need a gift from you to prove our friendship. It was fun just being with you on this trip. You're a very interesting man."

"Well, thank you, Larry. I suppose, then, I will have to force this upon you by using my power as a judge of the court. And as you have pointed out, I am a hanging judge."

He smiled, stubbed his cigar into the ashtray and got up and went over to the bar. I watched him, thinking he was getting more champagne, although that didn't make sense as the waiter was standing not far away from us. As I was wondering why the bartender wasn't turning around to get the bottle, I realized they were exchanging more than words. Johnson seemed to be handing the bartender something… a tip, I suppose - and the bartender was handing something - a small package - to Johnson. They spoke for a moment or two, then Johnson returned to his chair. As he sat down, he extended his hand, indicating that I put my hand out, too. I did so.

"Now, Larry, I don't want any sentimentality about it. This is strictly a man-to-man gift. If you would like to open it, all well and good. If not, that's fine, too. Just put it into your pocket, and open it up later."

"No," I said. "I'll open it now. Who knows if we'll see each other again?"

Johnson beamed when I said that, and I set to the business of opening the little package. It turned out to be a box of twenty-five Winston Churchill cigars with a fifty pound bank note tucked neatly around it. In those days, fifty pounds would have been worth about one hundred and fifty dollars.

There was also a note:

"To a simple friend from a simple judge. Have a good time. You have only one life to live. Live it to the fullest. Sincerely yours, Judge Johnson."

I rose and shook his hand, thanking him warmly for the gift. I felt bad that I hadn't gotten anything for him. He seemed very fragile and lonely at that moment, but he spoke first.

"I know you have to go back to your group now and pack your things. So, let's finish off our drink and maybe someday, you'll think back on this trip and remember the best and the worst of it."

"You've been the best," I said. "You and the storm, no matter how bad it was. I don't care about the worst."

We shook hands again and I left the room. I didn't know what else to say. Sentimentality, I think, would have insulted a fine man like Judge Johnson.

When I got back to our room, Bernie and Rodstein were already packed and ready to leave the ship come morning. I knew they resented my spending time with the old man, so I thought I'd dig it in a bit.

"Hey, guys, look at the nice gift I got."

"Big deal," rumbled Bernie. "So the old guy gave you a box of cigars, did he? He wouldn't give you any cash? That's what you were after, wasn't it?"

"Wrong again, Bernie. How does a fifty pound note sound to you?"

"Yah, sure, Wiener. He gave you fifty pounds like God gave the desert to the Arabs."

I showed him the crisp note, and smirked. "Who said God didn't give it to the Arabs, Bern? *They* say He did. So, as Roosevelt would say, happy times are here again. It's gonna be a lot of fun in Europe."

"Yeah, I guess you're right. The way you wangle people, Larry, you'll have yourself a real ball there."

Rodstein couldn't help sticking his nose in, too.

"So you did it again, eh Wiener? Bullshitted your way into a fifty pound note and a box of nice cigars. You think you're such a smart-ass, don't you? First, you mess around with the girl down in steerage, then you fool around with a millionaire. Well, buddy, we'll get even with you, don't worry."

"You couldn't get even with me if you had a six foot ruler, Rodstein. What do you have to get even with, anyway? What I do is my business, not yours. I'm just telling you how it is. Every turn you take, I'll be there, but I won't be doing what you'll be doing. We can have it out later, if that's what you want. Right now, I just want to have a good time when we dock in Europe. I'm going to have it, too, despite you, despite everything about you. We'll be there tomorrow, you know. Just watch me."

Bernie spoke up, whether in my defence or not, I wasn't sure, given the way he phrased his words.

"Don't mess with him, Rodstein. The guy's like a cobra. He'll strike when you're not looking if it takes him six months to get to you. And he'll get to you, never fear. I didn't know he was going to turn out to be such a little bastard when I asked him along on this trip, but I know it now, and it's too late. Just let him be, and he'll let you be. Let him have his good time - it's no skin off your ass.

"Y'see, there's something real fishy about Larry here. He didn't have to go through the grilling we did to get on this trip, did he? I've been thinking about that. It's almost like someone paved the way for him first. Probably, to get him out of their way, I'd say. He's not exactly the world's most lovable guy, is he? If that's the case, Rodstein, if that's the way it is with him - then, he's dangerous, don't you see?

"So the best place to be is as far away as possible from him. Let him go his way if he wants. He'll be doing us all a favour. Even when he's around, you don't have to sleep with him, do you? You just have to put up with him. So don't feel too bad, Rodstein. None of us likes him."

Bernie my big buddy unknowingly was maybe solving our problem for us. I didn't know whether to start clapping at his little speech or get angry with him for saying there was something fishy about my getting on board so easily. I'd thought I'd smelled a rat, too, earlier - but there wasn't any proof, so what was there to say about it? Anyway, I was saved from maybe putting my foot in my mouth, by the opening of the cabin door.

It was Saul.

"Hey, hi fellas. Have you packed your things? All ready for Europe?"

I decided to be nasty.

"So, Saul. What are you gonna do - hunt down the nearest syn-agogue and pray for our friend Rodstein here? But I guess you'd better pray for all of us - long prayers, too, heartfelt ones - even if we are all headed for Hell."

Saul's ears, like those of most overtly religious people, made no sense out of my words, and so he couldn't respond to them. Instead, he started rambling on about how wonderful it would be once we got to Israel, to the Promised Land.

"It'll be fantastic! Just think - we'll be in the country of our forefathers! Aren't you excited?"

"Who the fuck do you think *you* are - Abraham Lincoln, or just Abraham?"

"Israel," said Rodstein. "Well, we'll be there in another week or so, won't we? We'll see what it's like then."

"Israel," I said. "You guys are impossible. I'm going to pack. For good or bad, for better or worse, we're all going to the same place in the end."

Bernie was hungry, and his stomach was growling, making him speak up about lunchtime. It was time to go, he told us. "Our last lunch on board the Big Boat. I thought for sure we'd be at the bottom of the ocean by now, after that storm."

"Last lunch for this bunch," I rhymed back at him. "At least we're still a step ahead of the last supper." (I was quite the little wise guy in those days, and probably had no idea why I said that. Sometimes, if you came up with a quick enough reply, it didn't really matter whether or not it made much sense.)

Saul heard it, though, and he piped up sombrely "Don't forget, we'll be walking those same steps soon enough. We'll be treading on Holy Ground. You'll feel it tremble beneath your feet."

I didn't know what he meant by that any more than the others knew what I had meant by my remark. Maybe Saul was secretly confused. Maybe he was secretly a Christian, or a Moslem. Maybe he just liked the idea of being religious.

Peggy showed up at lunch and suggested we work out a system of meeting each night in the hotel once we'd landed in Europe to make sure everyone was all accounted for and all right. She said we should all meet at three p.m. in the Smoking Lounge on the second deck, so we'd be together leaving the boat, and everyone agreed to the plan.

I killed some time after lunch by playing darts. I had a Tom Collins and after an hour or so got bored and went to the Writing Room to write my Mother. I wanted to tell her about Raizel, the storm, and still being on speaking terms with the rest of the group. I knew she'd be surprised, and happy. I sent along a postcard of the *Queen Mary*, and a note about the story I'd read on the front page of that morning's London *Times* (they'd been dropped on the boat): "*Queen Mary* - Largest Ship in the World, Tips in Storm Overnight."

By the time I finished my writing, I'd whiled away enough time - it was 3 p.m. by my watch and time to meet in the second deck Smoking Lounge.

Once everyone was present and accounted for, Peggy took over with: "I've brought you together here to talk about how we should have a daily system once we land in Europe. It's a big place, you know, and we all have to be kept track of."

Rodstein didn't like that idea, apparently, his rough voice asking "what for?" Bernie, however, was in a more mellow mood.

"Let her speak, for Christ's sake. We've travelled three thousand miles and we haven't heard much from her so far. Maybe she has an idea we should hear."

I joined in, too. "That's right," I said, "it's okay when you want to have your say. You do your best to get everyone to listen, so let's hear from someone else for a change. Go ahead, Peggy, tell us what you want to say."

Her voice ranged high and low, dripping with motherly concern."Well, as near as I can figure out, we will need to meet at least twice a day to make certain no one is sick or has been injured or has disappeared. I know that very soon we'll be in Paris, and we don't really know what to expect. None of us has ever been there before. None of us has been anywhere much. We'll have a tour guide for some of the time, you know that. But, because we'll be on our own most of the time, we'll have to find a way to stay in contact with each other."

"So what happens if we can't meet, and say, can't get to a telephone or for some reason just plain can't get in touch?" (This was from Bernie).

Peggy let out a long, disparaging sigh and I got the feeling that if she'd smoked, she would have blown it in his face. He wasn't trying to be helpful - just annoying. He only wanted to hear his own voice.

"You can always find a telephone," she said. "If you're so preoccupied, break your concentration for a minute and call in. I've heard the phones in France all work. Just get off the girl, Bernie, and tell her you'll be right back. But no kidding, people, I mean this. We have to let each other know what's going on."

"Another thing we have to do," I said, "is get Rodstein laid."

Peggy shook her head. "I don't care what any of you do, really. After spending so much time here with you all, I think I might just go out and find myself a nice French boy."

Saul broke in, taking a moment out from his constant praying, with: "The way you fellows are talking, all you need is a bottle of booze and the back seat of a Chevy. Doesn't anyone realize or care about the importance of our journey?"

Bernie said he did. "You know, Saul, I've read that there are a lot of beautiful synagogues in Paris, and there's a great Jewish district, too. And fantastic champagne. All I know is I'm going to have a good time there, because once I get to Israel, I'll be staying for good."

Peggy broke in again, and explained a bit more of her plan, which really didn't amount to much. It would, however, keep everyone from straying too far off the beaten path. I wondered why she cared, and guessed she wouldn't want to be a part of an arriving group of imports who'd lost some of their members along the way.

"Well, guys," she said, "I guess that's it. I've said everything I wanted to say, and I just hope we can stick to it, because it's important. So let's keep our deal straight. Go and have your good times, but remember we're a team. Just telephone in and let the others know you're alive, that's all. There's a dance tonight, by the way. Can I assume I'll see everyone there?"

There were a few grunts and mumbles and then we began to drift off to our quarters to get dressed for the last dinner on board the *Queen Mary*. When Peggy got back to her cabin, the steward knocked. He had a note for her, an invitation from the Captain for her, requesting the presence of our entire group to sit with him at his table that night for dinner. At the end of the note were the words "*Carte Blanche* - order what you will, it's on the house."

Peggy was overwhelmed by this. She ran from cabin to cabin, yelling that everyone had to wear their very finest. This was a real honour, she said, and we couldn't blow it. She went off to find Saul, to tell him that he would have to join us, and couldn't sit by himself as usual at his religious table, snubbing the invitation. Besides, she told him, he would be able to order anything he wanted, as kosher as he liked.

He agreed, she told us, saying that he figured he owed at least this much to the group. It all hinged on the promise of being allowed to eat kosher, he said, and wanted to know if he could wear his yarmulka and shawl. Peggy told him he could do as he wished, as long as he didn't expect everyone else to act likewise. She told him he could daven over the bread and wine if he liked, that it would act as a mitzvah for the Captain because, after all, he'd brought us safely through the storm.

Peggy said she went on to remind Saul that he wouldn't be alone, that the ship's rabbi and priest would be joining us, too. "You won't feel so much like a duck in a chicken coop, Saul." That girl really had a way with words, especially when dealing with a difficult person like him.

On her way back from making sure we'd be graced by Saul's presence, she hurtled into our room to make sure we'd gotten the message right. She really was like a mother, making the rounds to ensure all her children knew how to dress themselves. "This is it, boys, is everyone ready? Larry, your tie's crooked. Rodstein, tie up your shoe! Bernie, Jesus Bernie! I hope you plan to run a comb through that mop of yours?"

"Yes, ma'am, Sergeant Major, ma'am!"

"We'll be there, don't worry!"

"With bells on!"

"And yarmulkas!"

"Well, maybe Saul …"

"This isn't funny," she reminded us. "This is an *occasion*."

"Okay, okay. We'll be there at eighteen hundred hours, we'll be on the spot, right on the dot!"

She looked us over, seemed hesitant to leave us on our own. "Well, all right. I'd better leave you to finish dressing. And boys - remember your manners, please!"

There was a collective sigh of relief as she closed the door behind her, the first thing, I think, we'd ever done in unison besides argue. I mentioned the fact, adding "maybe it's a good sign." But I didn't believe it.

"Well," Bernie said to no one in particular, "this should be a fantastic supper. It'll be the last time the group will be together as the original party that started out. So let's try to forget our differences just this once. We don't want to look stupid, or embarrass anyone this evening of evenings. Let's talk, dance, drink and celebrate the ending of our trip across this fine and majestic ocean."

"Fine and majestic ocean?" I repeated. "You just finish reading an advertisement for it or something? You're right, though. We should try to keep clear heads. Let patience prevail among us, amen."

Saul let himself into the room just then, looking as orthodox and out of place as his clothing and attitude would permit. "Not bad, Larry, yesterday Toronto, tomorrow Paris," he said, "God is with us on this trip." This remark made me wonder about that - not where God had been, but where Saul had been. I told him maybe we should be more concerned about today than yesterday or tomorrow, and that kept him quiet for a while. If he's still alive, in fact, it wouldn't surprise me if he's still pondering that one.

I decided I'd had enough of this serious stuff, and asked Bernie if he'd do me a favour.

"Yeah? What's that?"

"Well, big guy, you can start with shining my shoes."

"Get lost, you idiot."

"I'm only joking, you know. Ease up a little. The party's about to begin, so get in the right frame of mind."

And then we were ready. I was wearing my 1957 rocker's best: blue suede shoes, a charcoal suit, pink shirt, pink tie and large, ugly yellow, "let's pretend they're gold" cufflinks. Of course, this get-up was because I planned on being a star on the dance floor again...

We made it to the table without mishap. We had five seats, directly opposite the Captain, who sat alongside the rabbi, the priest, the purser and the ship's doctor. The Captain started off the conversation.

"Good evening. I'm pleased that everyone was able to accept my invitation. The steward will be around shortly to take your order. You may order whatever you wish, you know. If we have it, it is yours. Now, which of you is the - er - religious fellow I've heard so much about?"

I wondered what he'd heard - that Saul spent all his time praying for the rest of us... or what?

"You would be meaning me, I think," said Saul.

"Well," the Captain said, "then I'm very pleased to meet you, and I'd like to introduce you to Rabbi Shwartzman here, and this is Father James."

They all nodded to one another across the table, and the Captain continued his sales pitch, concentrating on Saul. (No doubt he'd heard of some of the scenes we'd had with each other, and wanted us to at least be unified in any memories of the ship we later had. He didn't have to worry, though. We all loved the voyage, except for the stormy part.)

"Now, you can order kosher, Saul. I believe I've seen you at the kosher table more than once. If you would like to say prayers, you might like to say them with the good Rabbi."

The steward interrupted the flow of religious niceties, and took the Captain's order, then turned to our side of the table. I order the teenager's feast... a Porterhouse steak, French fries, Coke and ice cream.

Saul, with a silly smile on his face, gave the blessing over the bread and Father James quietly said grace over the wine. The Captain was very genial, and seemed genuinely interested in our little sojourn. He wanted to know who the youngest of our group was. Peggy answered, pointing in my direction.

"Larry, the blonde one."

The Captain smiled at me and said, "Well, Larry, you will have the honour of lighting the first set of candles."

I lit the eight Hebrew candles (the menorah) while Saul mumbled a prayer, then the Captain spoke up again.

"Peggy can light the other candles, as she is the only lady among us."

Father James prayed over the second set of candles as Peggy did her solemn best to accommodate the Captain's wishes.

Dinner was served, and it was fabulous. I sat there, stuffed like a Christmas turkey, hoping the feeling would subside by the time the dance started... at eight o'clock. I couldn't wait to show off my dance floor hi-jinks. I had plenty of stunts lined up for everyone to see.

Because it was the final night of the voyage, the dance was to be open to all passengers - even those down in steerage could come up and join in the free buffet and drinks. There was about an hour's break after dinner, and I decided I could pass some of the time away by sitting and looking important, so I excused myself and went off to the First Class Smoker's Lounge, where I slowly and nonchalantly pulled out one of the Winston Churchill cigars and lit up. I thought maybe there'd be time for a final chat with old Mr, Johnson, but he wasn't anywhere in sight.

Instead, I did as I'd planned - I just sat and puffed, relaxing, letting my gorgeous dinner settle into my gut, hoping someone would notice me and wonder who the significant-looking young man in the armchair was...

Eight o'clock came, and after almost falling asleep from the weight of all that good food, I got up and made my way to the main ballroom. It was fully decorated, with streamers and balloons hanging everywhere you looked.

With high crystal chandeliers overhanging everything, and the gleaming freshly polished brass railings, the old solid oak panelling and newly buffed mahogany tables and gleaming floor - who could ask for a lovelier setting? It had a dreamlike quality to it, like something from another century, a grand ballroom from another age. But, there it was and there I was, in the middle of it. Talk about a life of luxury!

I was feeling a little luxurious myself, so I went over and had my first drink (of many to follow). It was, of course, champagne - Dom Perignon, which flowed like water throughout the rest of the evening. There was a separate pub section set up, which had a large selection of British and European ales. There were even a few American brands available, which seemed somehow out of place. With all this class, I figured, who would have thought of America? But, someone had, probably to appease some of the passengers.

The band was already on the stage, tuning up their instruments and getting set to play, and I went over and started to speak to the bandleader, who remembered me.

"Let me guess," he said. "You'd like us to play 'Rock around the Clock'."

"You've got it," I answered. Sensing they were going to jump right into it, I glanced hastily around, looking for something in a dress. It didn't take me long to spot one that looked available, so I went over and asked if she happened to like Rock 'n Roll. She replied that she did.

"Well, then, you're going to get some," I said, and took her arm as the lights went down.

The Captain came onto the stage and spoke into the microphone, saying, "I've done this, I suppose, a thousand times, you know - and here we are again. This is your final night on board the *Queen Mary*, and I want everyone to have a good time. We will start off with 'God save the Queen' and I would like everyone to stand. Thank you - and please enjoy yourselves to the fullest."

He left the stage, everyone got to their feet and the band began to play the anthem. When it was finished, the band leader took the microphone and said, "We're going to have a good time tonight, aren't we? And to start it off, to get us all in the right mood, what could be better than a little of that new phenomena sweeping the world, Rock 'n Roll? Somebody asked me for a small favour, and here it is - 'Rock around the Clock!' "

I grabbed the girl and we tore up the floor. We spent the entire evening together, dancing and having a great time. I didn't even know her name and I knew I'd never see her again, but it didn't matter. The evening was magical, and I felt as if it had been made especially for me. My wild dancing seemed to shock Rodstein and Bernie. Even Peggy, who was usually more open minded than the rest of them, came across as being disturbed by my crazy antics.

I was everything a religious Jew hated. I was a good (or bad?) example of the worldly enemy. I could see them muttering to one another and shaking their heads as I spun by. They seemed to think my dancing was a sign of some kind, an omen of wilder things to come. I didn't care. To Hell with 'em. If they didn't want to have fun, well... they'd be planting potatoes or yarmulkas or whatever it was they'd be planting once they got to Israel, that was my thought, and who cared? Let them suffer!

The dance wound up about midnight. I thanked the girl, wishing I could sweep her up in my arms and carry her off to a bed of flowers somewhere - but that was impossible. She was with her parents, and they, too, had been watching me very warily. I went to my cabin alone, but happy nonetheless, thinking, "This has been a trip to remember, and tomorrow - Europe!"

I awoke to a sunny morning with the ship already docked at Cherbourg. I turned to Rodstein and grinned cryptically.

"Well, this is the beginning, and I hope we all have a good time while we're here. Parlez-vous Francais and Mercy Buttercups if you don't, eh, Rodstein? We should be off this tub in about an hour or so. You made any plans for yourself once you get to Gay Paree? Gonna hang yourself in the Louvre, or somethin'? Me, I'm getting pretty excited. Jesus, I'm not even hungry. Man, what a trip this is!"

"What's that? You? The great Larry? The dancer from Hades? He's going to pass up a free meal? I don't believe it! Anyway, yeah, I had a good trip, I guess. There was plenty of time to read on board. But, really, it was just a boat trip. Nothing special. So, what's exciting about three thousand miles of nothing but water? Sea sickness?"

"Christ. You know, Rodstein, someone should make one fact clear to you. If you had fallen off the deck in the storm and gotten washed away, I wouldn't even have yelled 'Man Overboard!' You're such a jerk at times. You would have been shark bait, with my blessings. I would not have cared. I just want you to know that."

"So listen, Larry, I don't like you either. You're just a little chiseller, a leech. You talked your way onto this boat by lying the whole time. Just because you've got a rich Mother, you get away with whatever you like. But you can't do that with me."

"Hey! Keep my Mother out of this, idiot! One day, don't worry, we're gonna have it out, just you and me. Anyway, you're just jealous. I know that you and Bettle don't like me, but I don't care. It doesn't bother me. It's good - and I'm glad you don't like me. Because if you liked me, that'd mean there really is something wrong with me, because that's what attracts you. Things that aren't right. You should listen to yourselves sometime...

"But, listen. Never mind what's eating away at you - we're going to enjoy ourselves here, right? We can settle our differences some other time, and we will! Until then, though - remember my motto? Live and let live! Learn from it, okay?"

Saul, who always seemed to arrive at just the right time, knocked at that moment on the door. "Can I come in? Are you guys ready to go? Everyone is leaving the boat."

"Yeah, we're ready. Are the others ready?"

"Yes, they are. We're all out on deck, waiting for you two to come up so we can leave. Like the book says, Europe today, the world tomorrow."

I wanted to ask, "What book is that, Saul? *Mad Magazine?*" - but really, I liked Saul. His naiveté had an endearing effect on all of us. If he was as full of baloney as the others, at least it was a private baloney and he didn't go out of his way to make others share the sandwich.

And so, without any further ado, we picked up our luggage and went up onto the deck to join the others, Saul mumbling silent prayers behind us, covering our past sins for us, or whatever it was he thought he was doing.

The five of us were together again, waiting for the purser to come and give our valuables back… the important things were the passports stamped NEW YORK - CHERBOURG. Without them, we might wind up as galley slaves, working our way back home. Finally, the purser arrived, all smiles, handing back our things - and goodbye, *Queen Mary*! We walked down the gangplank onto French soil. I looked back more than once at that glorious vessel, completely satisfied with her. Then I turned to the business at hand and wondered what we were in store for.

Well, I thought as I looked around, the sun is shining and the price is right…

PART FOUR

Europe

Paris

Cherbourg, as it turned out, was sort of a lull. Of course, we didn't get to see anything at all... We were dead tired from all that bouncing and the sleep we hadn't been getting. We were only there for an hour or so before the train was to leave for Paris.

The train pulled out at four p.m. It was only about a three hour trip to the so-called "City of Light", and I watched the rolling countryside pass by through the window. I started to think about Martha, for some unknown reason. I was, as they say, stung by regret at the way I'd cold-shafted her. I hadn't even said "Goodbye, so long, it's been good to know you." I'd had a great time with her... sitting on the old chesterfield on Borden Street, watching television and necking and listening to Elvis records. Her favourite song had been "I Was The One".

I was the one, all right. I should have my face slapped for the way I'd treated her, really. Not nice, not nice at all. Was I actually feeling guilty, though? What I really regretted was the fact she wasn't here with me now. When I closed my eyes, I could see her as plain as day... wearing her little poodle-skirt, bobby socks and flowered tennis shoes. She would be off to the 'Y' on Sunday, and loverboy Larry would be nowhere in sight. "Wiener? Oh, he went to Israel to work on a kibbutz. Maybe he got religion." I could hear the remarks, I could see the smirks on their faces...

Martha's Dad had a red '57 Chevy that I absolutely coveted. I would borrow it just to drive around in and show Martha off, as if it was mine, and as if she was a movie goddess I'd picked up because I wanted people to think I deserved it. I liked to show off a little (as I'm sure you've figured out by now).

I liked to pretend I was another James Dean, a cigarette hanging out of my mouth, and we made good use out of the back seat of the car, too. I realized, though, I'd done a pretty rotten thing, just dumping her like that. She deserved much better treatment. Really, she was very special, and would have been the one I probably would've wound up marrying. I was terrified of settling down, though. The malady of the age was upon me like a fever... I needed my freedom, and knew that marriage, for me, would only be the first step toward divorce.

Her parents expected a wedding after a year or so of dating. It was the way things were done in those days. But, Bettle's offer was my out... who was I to turn down an offer to help my mother country? More B.S., I told myself, but there was nothing to be done about it now. I'd chickened out of a good thing, and that was it. Martha was a sweet girl, and I still wanted her, but the bridge had been burned...

I thought to myself that I'd done a really lousy thing, letting her down that way. I'd slept with her Sunday night, and on Monday morning left without warning, bound for, of all places, the Land of Our Forefathers... treating a year-long love affair like a one night stand. I'd kept my plans to go to Israel from her for six long months.

Her father called my Mother a week or so after I'd left, to find out if what Martha had heard through the grapevine about me was true. He'd liked me up to that point, I think, but when he heard I really had left, he blew his stack, told Mother off in no uncertain terms that his daughter had been badly hurt, that this was no way for a young man to act, that I was shameless and who knows what else? Mother said: "I'm sorry, but there's nothing to be done about it. My son felt he had to go to Israel, and so he went."

I'd sold out, that's what I'd done, sold out completely. Staring out through the window, watching the French countryside go by, I knew I'd never get Martha back. I was a traitor. I also knew I would regret it later in life, and it turned out to be true. I still regret losing her, but it was my own damn fault, wasn't it? She was someone I was never able to replace. She had everything I'd ever wanted... she was cute... pretty, but no Hollywood starlet (who wanted a false beauty that faded?); she was a good rock n' roller who loved to dance up a storm; she was fun, sweet, lusty... ah Martha, where have you gone?

The conductor came down the aisle, shouting, "Paris, next stop!" - and I snapped out of my melancholy. It was about seven p.m., and I could see the lights of Paris coming up fast. My stay in Europe wouldn't last long, and I planned to make the best of it. As the train shunted to a stop, we pulled our luggage down from the racks and headed out into the growing darkness. So long, Martha! Goodbye, whatever guilt I'd been feeling!

So there we were, off the train and standing on the platform, wondering what to do next. Rodstein mumbled something about having to hang around waiting for a woman who was supposed to be picking us up. Peggy said she hoped whoever it was would be bringing the letters for us that would let us get settled into the hotel without any problems. She was worrying about there being some kind of a mix-up, and us being left out in the cold.

"Naw," Bernie said, "everything will be all right. They wouldn't send us this far just to let us down. The girl is from the Jewish agency, and she knows were new to the country, tourists, Y'know? They're not going to let us sleep in the streets. Well, maybe Larry... anyway, don't worry about it. Everything has been well taken care of, I'm sure." He just had to get a little dig in, didn't he? I let it pass.

"Well, this agency woman," said Peggy, "will hopefully have money for us, too." She could be a real worry-wart at times. "I hope she has the hotel rooms ready for us, so there won't be any trouble. We'll be here about a week, so I guess she knows that. Maybe there's no reason to worry, but where is she? Shouldn't she be here already? You'd think she'd be waiting for us. We're supposed to have free tours, and get to see the city, aren't we? I wonder if we'll have any time to ourselves? And where *is* that woman, anyway?!"

Just as she said that, we heard a female voice rising over the noise of the hissing steam released from the resting train. "Israeli group from Canada, Israeli group travelling from Canada?"

"Hey, that's us!" Bettle yelled, calling her over. "Hey, Peggy, see? We won't be lost after all. Here she is!"

The woman introduced herself to us as Suzanne, from the Jewish Agency of Paris. After welcoming us to her country, she told us she would be our guide for the next week, but first wanted to get us settled into our hotel. After that, she said she would come by in the morning to pick us up and would give us each an envelope.

I could see Bernie was eyeing her pert little figure, so of course he had to let her know who he thought was in charge. His arm went into the air with a sweeping motion to include us all, and he said, "I'm Bernie. I'm the leader of this group. Let me introduce you to the kids..." Of course, I was last on his list.

Suzanne picked up on his overwhelming persona right away, and I could see she disapproved of pompous people. She looked away from him and winked in my direction, saying, "Hi, Blondie."

I smiled back and told her I was glad to meet her, and that since it was my first trip to Paris, I looked forward to seeing it with her. Peggy spoke up, too, telling Suzanne I was the youngest member of the group... her way of saying, "leave him alone!" Of course, I was thinking maybe I didn't want to be left alone...

"He's cute," Suzanne told Peggy. "I'll make a man out of him by teaching him what Paris is all about. You know, we call it the City of Love."

Rodstein was looking a little frustrated with the lack of attention he was getting. He cleared his throat noisily and stated, like a soldier giving his rank and serial number, "I also hope to have a good time in this city." This was supposed to convey something like, "don't forget about the rest of us", and came out very awkwardly. Inwardly, I smiled. I hoped he'd stumble over every word that came out of his mouth.

"Well," said Suzanne, "Paris is a big city, and I'm certain everyone will have a good time, Mr. Rodstein."

Then she turned to Peggy. "And, young lady..."

"My name is Miriam,' Peggy said.

"... what did you do, before deciding to come here? What brings you on this journey?" This was girl-to-girl stuff. Maybe Suzanne was wondering why a young woman in the '50s wasn't at home getting married or having babies. Instead, here she was, the only female on a male team headed for the land of truce and turmoil. Peggy told her what was what in a nice enough way, but you could feel the friction in the air between the two.

"Before deciding to come here, I was a schoolteacher. When I heard about this opportunity through my synagogue, I applied to go. I've always wanted to see Israel. I was taking a year's sabbatical anyway, and saw this as an adventure, and wanted to go if they would take me, and here I am."

"Yes, here you are," Suzanne said, smiling at her. "And I will see that your adventure continues."

She turned then to the bearded one among us, and looked down at her list. She'd spoken to everyone else already. "You must be Saul?"

It wasn't hard to see, he was the religious part of the group. He was wearing his yarmulka and his prayer belt.

"I will show you some of the main synagogues of Paris," Suzanne told him. "You'll see the Yeshiva (religious Hebrew schools). I'll show you where the Nazis marched and the Monmartre ghetto for Jews during the German occupation."

She turned then to the rest of us. "Now I will take you to the Réveille, your hotel off the Rue de la Grande Armée. Come with me, please."

She hailed a cab, which was an oddly slanted Citroen, the first of its kind I'd ever seen. It was too small for all of us to get into, so we had to use two of them.

Paris was exactly as described, when lit up at night... beautiful. I thought it must truly live up to its reputation as a lover's paradise. As we drove along the streets, Suzanne pointed out a few of the sights... Notre Dame de Paris, the Pont Neuf, the Hotel de Ville

We arrived at the hotel about 8:30 p.m. and let Suzanne do all the talking at the desk. We were given three room keys. Suzanne said goodnight to us and said she would see us at eleven o'clock next morning, and we'd begin our tour of the city. We took our luggage aboard an ancient-looking cast-iron elevator that had to be stick-operated. Peggy got off on the third floor, where she had a room to herself. The rest of us were booked on the fourth floor.

I was to share number 411 with Rodstein (I would've preferred

Saul, but had no say in the matter, as it had all been arranged beforehand). Bernie and Saul were in number 416, right across the hall. On opening the door to our room, I was surprised to see how quaint it was. it reminded me of my Grandma Altman's house, and had an 1800s sort of feel to it.

There was a high porcelain bowl in one corner of the room, half full of water, with a chain hanging from the wall behind it. While Rodstein was unpacking his gear, I went over to take a leak, thinking it must be a French toilet. Midstream, Rodstein yelled at me, "Hey, Larry! Stupid, it's not a toilet bowl, you know!"

I told him I didn't know what he was talking about... of course it was, and finished the business I had set about on.

"Jesus, Larry! Don't try to flush it! Don't pull that chain!"

I pulled the chain.

The water in the centre of the bowl flushed away and then water began squirting up from the rim, all over the wall, the floor and carpet. For some dumb reason, I figured this was a combination toilet and hand basin, and put my hands into the upblast of liquid.

"Don't stick your hands in that!" Rodstein bellowed.

"Too late to stop now," I told him. "What the Hell is this thing, anyway? You can't pee in it, you can't wash in it. So what's it here for, to clean the walls? I don't get it.'

"You don't get anything, do you, Wiener? It's called a *bidet*, stupid. Women use it... they clean themselves after going to the can. Christ!"

"Yeah? So where do we guys go, out the window? I mean, if I can't go here, there's nothing else around."

"Try looking down the hall, Larry. I can see you've got a lot to learn about Europe." He said it in his smartass way, as if he'd lived there for years. Well, one of these days, he'd get his.

So I went down the hall, and checked it out. The washroom was small, and had only a sink and a toilet in it.

Coming back into the room, I said, "Well, you were right for once. Hey, don't you think we should go out and get something to eat before we go to sleep? We haven't eaten for hours, and we didn't have much on the train. There should be a restaurant around this joint someplace."

"You mean a café, Larry, a café. A restaurant here is a very expensive place to go to. Okay, then, let's do it. We'll find a little place for a bite or two before turning in."

We put our jackets on and headed out, taking the rickety old elevator downstairs to where the desk clerk sat, reading a newspaper. We asked him where we could find a small place to get something to eat, and he sent us around the corner to a small café.

It was a cosy enough place, reminding me of a little neighbourhood bar. Rodstein said he knew enough French to keep us from getting overcharged, adding that he could also understand the menu, which might as well have been written in hieroglyphics as far as I was concerned.

The waiter came over and asked us something *en françcais*. Getting no response from me, and a quizzical look from Rodstein, he tried again, this time in broken English, "May I 'elp you?"

Rodstein stuck two fingers in the guy's face and said, in an overly loud voice, "Deux cafés." Somehow, he managed to order a couple of pieces of cake for us as well.

"If I had Saul here," he said, "he'd study this menu like reading the Torah. It would take him forty minutes to order a cup of coffee, and he would part painfully with every franc." At that time, it took four hundred and fifty French francs to make up one American dollar.

"I don't think Saul will survive long on the kibbutz," I said. "He all but snubbed us on the way across, on the boat. He didn't work with us, either, on the farm back in New Jersey. He's like a fifth wheel, isn't he?"

"Jesus, Larry, I think you've finally got something right. I have to agree with you this time. That Saul, he'll screw us up good, all the way down the line. The four of us will want to go out and have some fun, to play around a bit. We'll play and he'll pray. Somehow, it won't work out, will it? He's like a square peg trying to fit into a round hole, and it's just not going to be that easy."

The waiter brought us our coffee and cake, and I tried out my only French on him: "Mercy Bourcoop." It got a slight smile out of the waiter, and a hearty laugh out of Rodstein.

"You really are dumb, aren't you? But, tell me... what do you think of Peggy? Really?" I wondered what he was getting at.

"Well," I said, trying to give my best James Dean drawl, "I suppose she's okay. She ain't no Martha, but she's all right. She'll work out, she'll do her bit, she's part of the gang. You think she'll buck the system? I don't. She wants to meet some Sabra and have Israeli babies so she can write home to her Mom and tell her she's doing just fine, 'xactly as planned, the way it's supposed to be. I don't think she really liked it in Winnipeg, like she thinks life there is for the birds or prairie dogs. She'll stick out the year, all right. What do you think?"

"I think you're probably right again, Larry. That's twice in one night. It almost makes up for your pissing in the bidet. But, Peggy… she's a schoolteacher, she thrives on discipline. She'll make out okay."

"How about Bettle?" I asked. "What do you think he'll be like?"

"Oh, Bernie will try to push his weight around. He'll play Gestapo, you know? He thinks because he's the one who got us all here, he has some kind of hold over us, and he'll use it anytime he thinks he has an opening. The key to him is… don't let him have an opening. But he'll try to work our asses to the ground, believe it. That is, if we give him the chance."

"I'll make sure he doesn't get it," I said. "I may seem stupid to you, but there's one thing about me that neither you nor Bettle know about. I have no fear. He won't be able to scare me into doing anything I don't want to do. He'll find that out soon enough."

"You realize that he'll be made leader over us, once we get where we're going. You know that, don't you?"

"I know, but so what? A leader is only as good as those who follow him. If Hitler hadn't had followers, he'd still be painting houses, the little wart. So, Rodstein. Now that we've talked about everyone else, what do you think of me? We've passed over four thousand miles of ocean together. Know me any better?"

He was quiet for a moment, sipping on his coffee, which looked remarkably like mud. He was studying me, wanting to get his words right.

"Well," he said, without looking up, "I really don't know what to say. I know I don't much like you, that there's something about you that burns my ass, and I know that we'll have to settle our differences someday, one way or another. There will, I think, come a time for it.

"But you'll try and get the softest job you can find, once we get to Israel. Your Mother will send you presents… gifts, and you'll sell them on the black market in Tel Aviv. On top of that, your Uncle will send you money."

"So, what's wrong with that?" I countered. "So I've got the guts and the wherewithal to do it, and you don't. What's the big deal about that? What are you going to be working at… cleaning latrines? Just to avoid hard labour? Or would you sooner be sent to a Russian labour camp? Maybe that's more your style. Look at those books you're always reading… Stalin, Lenin, Marx, Trotsky… Communism is your religion.

"You think you're gonna be able to move from where you're sent, you're gonna start up your own party, or what? Maybe you're on the wrong trip… you should be going to Russia. The Sabras aren't stupid. They'll figure you out. They want to build a country, not a communist state, eh. You're being sent there to work for them… not to change the country, you know."

Rodstein studied his coffee again. "You're trying to be smart, Larry, but it's not going to work. You didn't even know what a bidet was, but you sure know how to talk world politics, like a pro, don't you?" It was obvious to me he didn't have a reply, that I had struck on the truth of the matter.

"Hey, I'm only trying to tell you, Rodstein, that it's a lot easier to go along with the system than it is trying to change it. That's all. It's just my humble opinion."

He sighed, and pushed the coffee away, looked up at me. "You may be right again, Larry. After all, we'll only be guests in someone else's country. They'll be able to toss us out anytime they like, I imagine. That is, if we don't conform to the way things are done. I hate to say it, but you may just be right about that."

"Let's get out of here," I said. "Let's go and have a good time. We should enjoy Paris. Our year doesn't begin until we actually get there, right? So let's make the most of the time we have before it starts."

We left the café and walked the short distance back to the hotel. When we got there, instead of going to bed, we decided to make a surprise visit, and knocked on Bernie's door.

"So where were you guys? I was looking for you earlier."

"We just went around the corner, you know, for a coffee. The man downstairs told us where there was a café. It was a nice little neighbourhood place."

Even after the pleasantness we'd shared over our coffee, Rodstein couldn't keep my stupidity to himself, and started laughing. "So, Bernie, guess what happened to Larry here? He didn't know what a bidet was, and now we have a thoroughly soaked floor."

Bernie rolled his eyes up and grinned. "Yeah, well… what did you expect from a dumb Toronto kid who's never seen anything of the rest of the world? He probably thinks everything works the way it does back on Spadina Avenue. But, he'll learn, don't worry."

"Maybe," said Rodstein. "Hey, have you seen Peggy tonight?"

"No, not a sign of her anywhere."

"Well, I guess we'll just say goodnight and turn in. We'd better get some rest for tomorrow. So, goodnight Bernie. See you in the morning. I hope we can stand to spend the night together. I hope this guy," sticking out a thumb in my direction, "doesn't flood the whole building or something."

❀❀❀

The night passed uneventfully, though, except for a dream I had about dolphins. We were all up at nine o'clock and met downstairs for breakfast. Bernie went over to the desk to ask for a local restaurant. As it turned out, there was no dining room in the hotel itself. As we considered this, I realized how shabby and rundown the place really was, and that our sponsors hadn't gone out of their way to make us feel ultra-comfortable.

The morning man directed us to a local cafeteria down the street and halfway around the block. It wasn't anything like what we might have expected. Seating 1000 people, it reminded me of one of those huge New York cafeterias where you never knew who was going to turn up. We thought it wasn't a bad idea, sending us there, and that the man at the desk must have realized we weren't rich tourists… the cafeteria wasn't expensive, and we didn't have to speak French to be served. All we had to do was point at what we wanted.

The place was packed, filled with locals, and certainly didn't look like any tourist trap I'd ever seen. It sort of had the atmosphere of a 42nd Street diner, brightly lit up… a working man's type of place. I noticed that a lot of the regulars, after eating, didn't pay but simply signed their tabs.

The servings were generous, too, with piles of scrambled eggs, pancakes, bacon and toast, topped off with a huge glass of orange juice. Halfway through eating, Bernie grunted at one of the staff and made a shovelling motion with his hand, asking for more. He got it. Breakfast was the specialty here, served from 6 - 11 a.m., and they wanted to please their customers.

We ate very well, and at a bargain… 600 francs (about $1.50 our money for a hefty breakfast at a clean, cheerful place). It was a very good deal, we thought. You could have as many extra coffees as you liked, too… *gratis*, as they say.

Saul, of course, had to play the odd man out, sulking over his toast and coffee, complaining loudly that the place wasn't kosher, offended by the smell of bacon… even if the only aroma anyone else noticed was that of the delicious coffee. Well, he'd just have to grin and bear it… we weren't going to stick up for his crazy notions… should all the world be kosher, he'd still find something to complain about.

But that was Saul for you, and there was nothing anyone could do about it. The problem was his. I told Peggy in a quiet voice that he probably secretly loved the smell, and was simply jealous because we were enjoying ourselves and he couldn't blow his cover. "Seems to me, some of these sacrifices were more inconvenient than religious," I added.

When we returned to the hotel at a quarter to eleven or so, Suzanne was waiting for us in the lobby.

"I hear you went to *La France* for breakfast. They serve big meals there, don't they? It's a good thing they do, because you'll be needing your strength," she said. "We're going to be doing a lot of walking today, down the Champs-Elysées. We can take a break at the top of the Eiffel Tower... they serve coffee there, and you can look out over the city. It'll be something to tell your children about.

"And, oh... I have to give you your envelopes..."

We were each handed an envelope containing $25 US worth of francs. This was to keep us in meal money a week. We thanked her and left the hotel together, headed out for our first day of Paris... a clear, beautifully sunny day, too. The only thing obscuring it was Saul's carefully set, constant frown.

"Be very careful," Suzanne told us, only half-jokingly, "when crossing the streets here. Drivers get five points if they hit a tourist... ten if they kill one. You'll see some very odd-looking automobiles here, too, so keep an eye out."

We did, too. Many were three-wheelers that had a sort of comic effect as they puttered past... like some hybrid, a cross between a car and a motorcycle, one step above the latter and a step below the former.

Walking up the Champs-Elysées, we saw a lot of street vendors selling freshly roasted chestnuts, ice cream, soda pop and so forth, all from four-wheeled sidewalk carts... some bigger than the three-wheeled crossovers running along the roadways. Suzanne bought everyone an ice cream from one of the vendors. It was incredibly delicious, very rich with heavy cream. Even Saul couldn't say anything about it, though he ate it in silence without as much as a smile. He really could be a sour one when he got his hackles up.

Then Suzanne asked if we wanted to do any "tourist shopping"... if anyone wanted to get anything to send back home while we had the chance. If so, she'd show us where to get the best deals. Bernie, Rodstein and Peggy said they only wanted to get some postcards... Bernie wanted the nudie ones you had to buy on the sidewalks from the street kids. It was perfectly innocent, he said, adding he only wanted to send a few back home to his friends and father, just to show them what "the real Paris" was all about.

Sure.

Suzanne was remarkably game, saying if that was the case, she would get them for him. "If they hear your accent," she told him, "you'll get taken, and wind up with a brown paper bag filled with the kind of postcards you can get anywhere. These kids are swift, too, and you'd never catch them. They know every alleyway in the city, and can be dangerous to try to follow them.

"I know what you want. You want to be able to show off to the folks back home and send some postcards of tushie and pussy, don't you? Let me get them for you, then. It'll cost you a little more, but you'll wind up with what you want."

I spoke up, adding that what he really wanted was to let the kids back home know how demented he really was, so the dirtier the postcards, the better. This set Peggy off.

"Do you think Suzanne and I want to hear this garbage? If you're going to talk like this, do it in your rooms where there aren't any ladies present. I'm sure Saul doesn't want to hear it, either! Do you, Saul?"

Saul's head was in the air, though, his brain millions of miles away, floating with Elijah on a cloud. Peggy's outburst didn't impress any of us, Suzanne included. After all, she was the one who pointed out the specifics of Bernie's quest for the perfect pictures.

"Leave them alone," she said. "They're young, they're in Paris, in the City of Love, and back home they were probably leashed to their mother's apron strings like nice little boys. They'll get over it."

"Well," sputtered Peggy, "how would it be if we talked that way? What if we went looking for pictures of nude men?"

"What do we need them for? If you haven't seen a nude man by now, dear, I'll make certain that you have the opportunity. Besides, they're just trying to show each other how macho they are. They're just guys having some fun."

Peggy gave in at this point, deciding to agree. It was obvious to all of us, Suzanne had been around the block a few times, and wasn't going to put up with any prudishness. I loved her for it, and started having daydreams of climbing into the sack with her. I was sure she would be able to teach me a few things, and I'd be a most willing student, too! It was at this point in my imagining that she turned to me and asked, "And what would you like, Larry? What do you want?"

It took a few seconds to remember what we'd been talking about.

"Well, I think I'd like to get a big bottle of perfume for my mother. There's nothing better she likes."

The others were slightly shocked. None of them had that kind of money.

"Well, how much can you spend on it?" Suzanne wanted to know. I shrugged. "More than anyone else, I guess."

"So there goes Larry, showing off again," Rodstein said. "What did I tell you, Bernie? Watch that kid... he'll try to drive us all nuts."

Suzanne liked my idea of wanting to get something for my mother while the others only seemed to want to look at dirty postcards. "I'll take you somewhere," she said, "where you can get something for your mother that she will never forget. When would you like to go?"

"Now. Today, before I spend my money foolishly. If I get something and send it off today, it won't matter what I do with my money later on, or if I blow it or not. The good deed will have been done already."

"Well," Suzanne said, "only a few blocks from here is the finest place in the entire world to purchase perfume... Coco Chanel's. We'll go over there now, before we go on to the Eiffel Tower."

And off we went, in search of the right smell. As we walked along, I was the object of a barrage of nice comments:

"Larry has a rich Uncle who gave him money before we even left... he has tons of money with him."

"Remember that old man on the boat? I'll bet he's still wondering what made him give Larry anything more than the time of day. He chiselled his way across the ocean, remember?"

"Yeah, and that girl from below decks, the one he ran off with at the dance. Maybe she gave him her life's savings!"

"He chiselled his way into the trip, to begin with."

That was it. I'd had enough.

"Listen, Rodstein... and the rest of you, too! While you're puzzling over my good luck, with your hands in your empty pockets, my hands are on my money. I didn't spend it on booze on the boat, that's for sure. How come you don't have so much, eh? Tell me that, wise guys. What makes you so broke?"

Suzanne put a stop to our bickering with a look and a few simple words: "So, he has more money than you do. You're not jealous, are you?"

After walking a few blocks in relative silence, we reached Coco Chanel's and went inside. There were brass trimmings everywhere, it seemed, and sparkling, glittering countertops. The sales girls were absolutely beautiful... Chanel models. I realized I didn't look the part of their ordinary clientele (if any of their clientele were "ordinary"). I wasn't a well-off Parisian man buying perfume for my mistress, but I approached one of the sales girls, anyway, an overly-attractive painted-up blonde with a bust that would fit into anyone's imagination and all I could do was mumble out a few clumsy words, wishing everyone would disappear so that I could have her for breakfast.

I asked if she spoke English.

"Oui, m'sieur. How can I help you?"

"Well," I said slowly, unable to tear my eyes away from her bosom, and not knowing whether I wanted it to be obvious or not, "I... I'm looking for a gift for my mother... ma mére, you know?"

She looked surprised at this, and smiled sweetly.

"And what sort of perfume does your mother like to wear?"

How the hell did I know? Something fashionable, I guessed, and said as much. "Show me something you would like. I know this much... she doesn't care for either Chanel or Lanvin."

"I know just the thing for your mother," she said. "It is a very fine perfume, with a subtle fragrance. It is on sale at the moment, too, because it is new and we are promoting it. It is called Arpège."

"How much is it?" I asked. This woman could have sold me bottled turpentine, and I wouldn't have known the difference... everything about her spoke of pure sex.

"Would you like one ounce or five ounces?"

"Give me the five ounces."

"Certainly, sir. That will be seventy-five dollars." She seemed to know I'd have American money. Maybe she could smell it.

I took my little bankroll out of my pocket and coolly peeled off a fifty, two tens and a five. Bernie and Rodstein just stared at the money as it changed hands. Peggy wanted to smell the flower water or whatever this stuff was. She seemed to approve of it, telling me she had a small bottle of it herself, but could never afford a whole five ounces.

"Well," I said to the gaping mouths and wide-open eyes around me, "you only have one mother, you know. Price doesn't bother me when it's something for her."

I asked the salesgirl if she could gift-wrap it and have it sent to Canada. She batted her eyelashes and smiled some more, asking me for the address.

"It will be another five dollars," she said, "for the mailing cost. But, please," she added, "forget that amount. I will mail it with no charge. After all, it is for your mother." She winked at me, and bounced away, her breasts jiggling so I thought I'd faint.

"Thank you," I managed to whisper.

We left the shop, me walking out half backwards, trying to get a final glimpse of her, knowing I'd never see her again... and headed off to the Eiffel Tower.

I was glad I'd bought the perfume and sent it to Mother. She deserved something special from her wandering son. I'd sent her Barton's chocolates, too, from New York. I hoped she'd be pleased.

Suzanne seemed very impressed that I, youngest of the group, would do something so thoughtful and generous. She found it heartwarming, she told me. It wasn't something every tourist bothered to do. Usually, they thought only of themselves. Like, for instance, Saul. "First, we go into a worldly shop, and now we're going to a modern idolatrous shrine in a decadent city. When will I get to see my synagogues?"

"Saul," said Suzanne, "if you really feel so strongly about it, and don't want to follow our agenda, well... you don't have to. You can go off on your own if you like. The agency has planned a group tour of the city, but if it really goes against your grain and you're going to be unhappy being with us, I can't force you to stay. However, you'll have to sign a release form stating that the agency is not responsible for you while you're in Paris. Wherever you go, and whatever happens... you'll be on your own, Saul. Do you want to do that? You can if you wish.

"But the rules change in that case. The agency will not give you any more money... or protection. All you will have is the room, since it's already been paid for. No matter what happens to you... healthwise, action-wise or whatever, we will not be able to help you. The form is a release for us... it releases us of our duties toward you, and if something happens we can't be held at fault by the Canadian Jewish Agency. Do you understand this? Does everyone understand?

"If, let's say, you wind up dead, killed on the streets by a car, or... suicide (Suzanne thought Saul had tendencies in this area)... our only responsibility will be to send you home in a pine box. I don't like to use such strong language, but I have to protect the agency, and I want to make certain everyone realizes the repercussions of signing a waiver. You are, in effect, waiving your rights as far as we're concerned. Now, do you want to do this? I can bring the paper tomorrow, if you wish. Is it really what you want, Saul? I can't stop you, but I want to try to discourage you. It isn't a good idea."

"I would like to go on my own," Saul muttered, his head down. It was obvious to us all he wasn't a bit happy with the way things were going, and I started to wonder myself if he wasn't maybe a bit suicidal by nature. He was a loner, that's for sure.

Bernie couldn't let this go by without commenting.

"Saul, what are you trying to do? You don't like us, is that it? You're a schmuck, a real schmuck! You're going to ruin the whole trip for everyone. We could all get sent back to Toronto by the end of the week because of this. If you keep making waves, we'll never even see the Mediterranean!

"You're just lucky... we're all just lucky Suzanne is the way she is... she isn't blaming us for your actions... yet, that is! But if you sign that paper, it's your death certificate, not ours. Remember that next time you say your prayers, okay?"

Suzanne, overhearing this (no one could ignore Bernie's big mouth), spoke up: "Well, I'm certainly not blaming anyone for anything. Saul can do as he pleases... tomorrow. For today, though, the tour goes on as scheduled. We'll begin with the Eiffel Tower."

We weren't far from it, and within ten minutes we found ourselves standing by its base.

I said to Suzanne, "It's true, isn't it? Paris really is beautiful.

Now I know why it's called the City of Lovers. And I still find it hard to believe… a guy like me is walking these streets."

"Look at it as a lucky break, Larry. Me, I've never been to Canada, and I'd like to see it one day. It must be beautiful there, too."

"It's nothing like this," I told her. "Where I come from, it's known as Hogtown… Toronto the Good, not Toronto the Great. There's nothing special about it. The city is divided into camps, just like any other large city in North America… between the rich and the poor, the haves and the have-nots. The rich have their own area and they couldn't care less about the poor.

"The working man takes home his weekly wage, looks after his kids, and drinks his beer. God forbid that he could afford Canadian Club whiskey! In wealthy gentile society, you know, there are clubs where no Jew can belong… or are allowed to go to, even if they wanted. Down along the waterfront, there are clubs where no Jew can join. They might as well have billboards dotting the landscape, with the words in huge letters: SORRY, NO JEWS.

"Like, the Yacht Club… the main WASP club of the city… you won't find any Jews in that joint. Canada, you see, is not the liberated New World country you may think it is. I know Canadians are big over here, after the Second World War, but let me tell you the way it really is… Canada likes to liberate other countries, but won't liberate its own people.

"There are lots of companies that won't hire Jews, and on Sundays, the Jews who know the Jewish merchants on Spadina Avenue… the clothing dealers and the furriers… they go down there and make deals when the places are closed to the public. They bring their kids down to suit them up for school. I know, my mother took me there. All these Sunday sales were illegal, under the table, tax free for the merchants, good bargains for the customers. But the major department stores, they wouldn't hire Jews and they lost a lot of money doing that, because it forced our people to boycott them, so to speak, and go down to Spadina and do business with ourselves…"

I was really on a roll, but some of this stuff had been buried in the back of my mind for a long time. What a strange place to be talking about it, though… in the shadow of the famous Eiffel

Tower! A couple of tourists with their cameras clicking away nearby stopped and stared at me, and I went on, as much for their benefit as anyone else's.

"The Goyim have a lot of beautiful words for us, don't they? 'Kikes', and 'Sheeny-men'. You hear that word 'kike' throughout your whole school life. 'You stupid little Jewboy ratface kike,' they say. The Jew in Canada, you know, is seen as being rich... and he's hated for it. The Goyim don't hesitate to call a Jewish doctor, lawyer, auditor, accountant or professor when they need one... but their kids better not try to marry one!

"The really well-off Jew has to live in a place called Forest Hill because no matter how much money he was worth, he couldn't buy into Rosedale, the bastion of the wealthy WASPs. The Jewish backlash to this was a sort of underground railroad of property-buying that took place in kosher restaurants, synagogues and Jewish golf courses. The biggest dealings, they did at home, when no-one was looking. Through this system, properties that the Jews couldn't normally get near, not openly, anyway, were bought up under names like 'Smith' or 'Jones' or 'MacDonald'...

"The most important thing expected from Jewish kids by their parents is absolute success in school. You have to get a good education, you have to be smarter than the gentiles. This was always the first and last word, and it still is and probably always will be. As long as the kids do well in school, they'll get anything they want. The ones that don't, they get shipped off to Uncle Harry's tie factory to be made gofers, or manual labourers... a family embarrassment, of course, but they're well looked after.

"I'm very lucky to be here, Suzanne. It's because I'm one of those family embarrassments. I never went very far in school, and what did I do before I came here? I worked for my uncle. I was a delivery boy."

"Well, I think you're very lucky, Larry," Suzanne put in. I guess she could see I was starting to run out of steam. "But it's hard to believe you're not smart. If you talked your way into coming here, as they tell me you did, you can't be stupid. You're here, aren't you? Now, why is it I have the feeling that others in the group aren't quite satisfied with you?"

"You're right on that account," I told her. "But because Saul presents a larger problem, he takes the heat off me. What these people say doesn't bother me anyway. To them, I'm just stringing along. It's like them having to take their little sister with them on a date or something. If they can't take me seriously, why shouldn't I return the favour to them? Payment in like coin, I always say."

"You're all right, Larry. Don't worry about them, you're doing fine on your own. But I'm here to show you Paris, and I intend to show you the *real* Paris! Then, maybe if I ever have the opportunity to visit Canada, you'll show it to me."

I nodded that I surely would.

We were still standing at the foot of the Eiffel Tower, the tourists had left, shaking their heads (maybe they were from Canada, I thought, and was glad to have verbally exploded the way I'd done). The group, however, was getting restless. Saul was staring at the skies, waiting for a word from Elijah or whoever, and Rodstein was glad to finally change the subject. His unusual silence during my little tirade made me think he privately agreed with me. But, he wasn't going to let it show.

"That's such a beautiful piece of architecture," he said, a little too loud. "With all of the books I've read about it, the pictures I've seen... I never dreamed I'd be actually here, looking up at it. What I'm wondering, though, is why is it here? What was the reason for building it, or was there one? What does it mean?"

Saul snapped out his revelry long enough to mumble a reply. "God let them build it, like the Tower of Babel, as a sign to the rest of the world. It's a symbol of decadence, that's what it is. It's the only thing it could be."

Suzanne smiled and thanked him for his observation, then turned to Rodstein.

"The tower was built as a celebration. It's an iron structural colossus, built by one of the greatest architects of the time. He intended it to be his showpiece, to mark his own excellence, but also to be the showpiece of Paris, so tall that every traveller would see it from every furthest part and corner of the city.

"It was meant to be a legacy, and it has become that. but Eiffel really didn't expect it would be called 'one of the seven wonders of the world' in his own lifetime. Did you know that Thomas Alva Edison was the man who originally lit it?"

I had something to tell them, too.

"In 1900, my grandfather and grandmother came to Paris from Romania, heading for the United States. This is a true story, by the way, and I can prove it if you don't think so. Anyway, they were headed for the States, but never got there because they took a liking to Canada and stayed there instead.

"When they were in Paris, Grandma and Grandpa Altman thought they would take a short vacation. Really, it was a honeymoon as they'd just been married. They took a hotel in Monmartre district... the Jewish area. Grandpa didn't need a job at the time, because he had some money and Grandma had her dowry. One afternoon, Grandpa went downtown to shop. He was going to pick up a few gifts for his new wife, and so he did. His business finished, he boarded a tram for the ride back to where they were staying. In those days, the trams were pulled along tracks by twelve horses, and the one he got on was very crowded.

"When he got back to Grandma and Monmartre, she asked him for some grocery money and when he reached for his wallet, it was gone. The only thing he could think was that he had been pickpocketed on the crowded tram. All they had was their week's paid rent. He knew he'd have to find some kind of work right away, the next day if possible, but he couldn't speak French. Work, however, meant food and rent money, so he had to do something, whether he knew the language or not.

"The next morning he set out to look for a job. He didn't know anyone... not a single soul... and couldn't speak the language. As he was walking along, wondering what to do, he saw a group of men lifting iron bars. He went over and asked for 'the big man' or boss. Luckily, one of the men seemed to understand him and went and got the man in charge of the work. He spoke a little English, and Grandpa told him, 'I need job'.

"The man asked what he was able to do, and Grandpa Altman made paint brush gestures up and down. Without batting an eye, the foreman or boss or whoever he was nodded and asked him when he could start. He was told, "tomorrow", and Grandpa's new boss asked him to come in at 8:00 a.m. And that's how my grandfather got to work on the Eiffel Tower. His job was to help paint it.

"He worked at it for two and a half years. They put four coats of battleship grey paint on it to keep it from rusting and falling apart. My Uncle George and my Auntie Marie were both born in Paris. Uncle George was born in a horsedrawn cab when they were on their way to hear Enrico Caruso at the Paris Opera. Grandpa was paid well for painting the Eiffel Tower, better than the other workers who did the heavy lifting."

Suzanne laughed when I was finished with telling the tale.

"You must have your grandfather's gift for blarney, Larry... he talked his way into a good job, and you talked your way here."

Bernie simply snorted, and said it was difficult for him to believe that I actually had some kind of connection to the Eiffel Tower. I told him he would be welcome to ask my mother when we returned to Canada. After all, it was her father I had been talking about.

Peggy changed the subject. "Well, Suzanne, you're right. Paris is *the* city, isn't it? I think that if I found a good Jewish man here, I would never leave."

"A good Jewish man?" I asked, frowning. "You mean, such a thing exists?" This brought a couple of interesting glares from my compatriots. "I'm only joking," I said."Don't you guys have any sense of humour at all?"

"I think it's time to go and get our tickets," Suzanne noted. "I'll be right back."

She went to the ticket window and came back and handed out our passes. We lined up by an elevator so old it would only take six people at a time. *Wonderful*, I thought. I was terrified of heights, and as we started going up, began to feel a little queasy, but didn't say anything, knowing the others would probably start to make fun of the fact. It was beautiful, though, rising up out of the heart of Paris in the afternoon sunshine.

The elevator stopped about halfway up and we got off at a platform where they served tea and coffee. The waiters were very polite, knowing they relied on tourists like us for their tips. We had coffee and a sweet. Suzanne made a point of going over to the floor model pay-for-view binoculars and got us all to look through them, showing us the best places to look, to get a really thorough, overall view of Paris.

We each took a turn at the binoculars and were amazed at the sights below where 20,000,000 tourists a year come (and we were a part of it!). I think each of us felt a bit let down when our francs finally ran out and the binoculars went blank. Then it was time to begin the long climb up the stairs to the top. I suddenly developed a bad case of vertigo, and found I couldn't face climbing higher in the open air. Suzanne took immediate note of my plight and grasped my hand.

"Don't worry, Larry. Hold my hand and we'll go up together. I've done it a thousand times. Then, if you're going to fall, you'll have to take me with you. You wouldn't want that, would you?"

I squinted my eyes a bit so I wouldn't have to see below us, and said okay. Suzanne pried me above the platform, and up we went, step by terrible step over the old iron stairs, into the wind. I wasn't feeling good at all, even with Suzanne holding me. Some of the people were leaning over the girders like they were no higher than a backyard fence and I kept thinking, "any minute now, we'll all go tumbling down"... but the sound and feeling of the rushing of the wind through the tower, and the sight of beautiful Paris below us was something else!

"Do you feel better, Larry?"

"Holding your hand, yes. I still don't like the heights, but being with you certainly helps."

"Well, you know what I told you. I said I'd show you Paris. There'll be a lot of free time this week, and I'm going to show you Paris the way it's supposed to be seen... the real Paris."

"Uh, Suzanne?"

"Yes?"

"I really don't feel very good. I'm starting to feel sick. I don't like heights at all, and I can't go any further. Can we go back down to the platform and wait for the others there?"

"Of course, Larry," she said, and squeezed my hand.

She told the others to take their time and that we would meet them down on the platform when they had finished their tour of the top. Inadvertently, I realized I'd set up a chance for us to be alone... just Suzanne and I, while the others were above, tickling the feet of the angels. We climbed back down to the coffee shop where a waiter brought us to a table.

"Do you feel a bit better now?" Suzanne asked.

"I feel a lot better. Thanks for coming back with me. I'm sorry you couldn't go all the way up."

"Don't think about it. I've been, a hundred times."

She called for some coffee and when I tried to pay for it, she wouldn't let me.

"This is my treat, Larry. You know, I like you, so let me pay."

"So, why do you like me?" I asked, genuinely curious.

"Well, you're fun to be with, for one thing. You're not as serious-minded as some of the others."

I jumped right to what seemed to me to be the point of our being along together: "Don't you have a boyfriend, Suzanne? A pretty woman like you? There are enough eligible Frenchmen here, aren't there?"

Suzanne smiled. "A little change never hurt, and you're sort of cute. There's something different about you... you're happy-go-lucky. The others take this as their mission, while you..."

"Look, Suzanne, let's get all the cards out on the table. You just want to put another notch in your gunbelt... a Canadian. Right?" I grinned at my own boldness, figuring that in Paris, why should it matter what you said? This was the City of Lovers.

"What do you mean... another notch in my gunbelt?"

"Well, I mean you want to take a Canadian to bed, you know, for another page in your diary or something maybe... to tell your friends. Am I right? If that's what you want, well, I'm here in Paris to have a good time, not to gaze at synagogues. So, it's up to you. Whatever you want, I'm game."

"I'll bet you are," Suzanne said, in a voice low enough to almost have been meant for her own ears only. "I'll tell you what, in that case, Larry. Tomorrow is a free day for your group, and that includes myself. I'm free, too. How about if I meet you at your hotel at, say, one p.m.?"

Before I could answer, I heard scraping noises from above, and looked up. It was Bernie coming down the stairway.

"Here come the others," I said.

"Don't forget our date, Larry," Suzanne said. Then she announced, when everyone had gotten off the stairs and onto the platform, "We'll be going down now."

I leaned toward her and whispered into her ear, "Already? I thought that event was going to happen tomorrow!"

Her face had turned a little red as she got up from the table to tell everyone about the next day.

"Tomorrow," she said, avoiding looking at me, "should be a good day for you. You'll have it to yourselves, a free day. At six o'clock, we'll meet and go from the hotel to the Place Pigalle and the Moulin Rouge. Just for you, Bernie... we'll take a little tour of the red light district. Is that okay with everyone?"

"Well, what do you think I am," Bernie asked, "a deviant, a pervert, some kind of sex maniac?"

"You've expressed yourself perfectly, Bernie." This came from Saul.

I had to add to that. "You probably never ate pussy in your life, Bernie. Tell the truth, now."

Suzanne's eyes flashed at me in a smiling way, then she turned to Bernie. "Well, you know, that is what a red light district is for..."

"Yeah," I said, you have a bit of money, you spend it. If you want a girl in Paris, I'll help you find one. I'll take you to the right place, then we'll come back and get you when you're done. This may be the City of Lovers, but Parisians are very practical people, too. Not everyone is an artist, or I should say, not all artists play with paints. If you want a girl, Bernie, you can have one, and you'll find it won't kill you. If it does, we can have you shipped back a hero... 'Missing in Action on the Place Pigalle!' It'd look good on you, Bernie, it would!"

"It would look very good, carved on his tombstone," said Saul. The guy was definitely developing a sense of humour, sardonic though it was.

Rodstein, who had been off to one side, lapping up every word, spoke up."So, how do you go about it? Just go up and knock on a door, or what? I'm just curious."

"Well, yes," said Suzanne, with a knowing smile. "You simply knock on the door. The Madame will let you in, if you look like you have the means to pay for the service. She'll ask you what you want, like a waitress at a good restaurant. In fact, the business end of it is very similar to going to a restaurant. She'll present you with a card... like a menu... and the card will explain what services are available, and which girl to ask you. This 'menu' will have everything on it, and some things you may not have heard of. You'll be able to order anything your heart desires."

"I don't see how you can talk like this," Peggy groaned. "It's a filthy practice, the whole thing. And you, Suzanne, especially! How do you come to know so much about it, anyway? I thought you were a tour guide?"

"I am exactly that. I am also a born Parisian, and we are raised not to be shocked or embarrassed about these things, which are a fact of Paris life. A boy is a boy, after all, and a girl is a girl. I'm sorry if these things bother you, but I'm only telling the men how it is. You don't want them to go off to the wrong areas and get into trouble, do you? If this is what they want, I can at least show them to a place that's honest, where they won't be robbed of their every franc, and maybe beaten, too, if they should try to resist."

"Well, what does it cost, at these, er, places?" Rodstein wanted to know.

"It depends on where you go and who you deal with."

"You sound like a Chicago mobster," Bernie put in.

"Have you ever been to Chicago?" Suzanne asked. "Or do you just go to movies? Do you mean when you say, like a Chicago mobster, someone like the infamous Al Capone?"

"Canada," I said, remembering Capone's reply about booze-running, "I don't even know what street it's on."

"But enough of this," Suzanne said, shaking her pretty head. "Today, we have one more place to visit, and it's beginning to get late. We'll take a taxicab to the Arc de Triomphe on the Etoile."

The preceding conversation took place on the elevator ride down, and my stomach was glad when we landed at the base of the tower without incident. Suzanne hailed a cab and we piled into it. "Monsieur," she said to the driver, "Arc de Triomphe, s'il vous plaît!"

"Oui, madame," he replied, and we were off, tearing through the streets of Paris.

"I am sure you've all heard of the Arc de Triomphe?" Suzanne queried. "It contains the tomb of the unknown soldier. The government keeps an eternal flame burning there, and the families of soldiers who died in the world wars come and lay flowers there. They come every day, and there's a donation box, too, for the upkeep of the Arc. Maybe you would like to put something into it, out of respect for the dead. It's up to you, though. You don't have to, but most tourists do."

The cab pulled up at the Arc, and we got out and played tourist for a while. We were there for about a half an hour, and did all of the expected things... signed the guest book, gave a small donation and asked questions of the two guards who were there. They told us of some of the famous people who had been there before us. Some had been infamous, too.

Among the latter, Hitler had deliberately marched his troops through it during the occupation of France. Among the former, Churchill and De Gaulle had walked among the crowds after the liberation at the end of World War II. I tried to picture them being there at the same time, and couldn't. To me, the Arc was a historical remnant of another age, and that was all. It meant nothing to any of us, really, but we listened to the stories about it, and what it meant to the French. You could see the guards were very proud of it, and proud of their heritage.

It made me think about back home in Canada, where about all we had to be proud of were hockey stars and maybe Hank Snow, the "singing ranger"... for the young, anyway. Most Canadian kids worshipped anything American, and not much "made in Canada". It made me think about how young a country we really were, and either how little history we had or how little I knew about it.

At about five o'clock, Suzanne asked if we'd seen enough. We told her we had, and she said, in that case, it was time we were getting back.

"You're not far from the hotel. I'll give you directions... you'll only have to walk a few blocks. I have to leave you, and check in at the Agency. Tonight, you're free to do anything you like, but don't get lost. Paris is a big city, and none of you knows the way around. The cab drivers are friendly, though... as long as you tip them, and they'll help you navigate in case you do want to go somewhere off the beaten track. Remember, too, that tomorrow is your free day, until I meet with you at the hotel at six o'clock, that is. Goodbye for now."

She winked at me as she left, and that got me to dreaming about what might happen with her later on.

On the way back to the hotel, I spotted a little bake shop and went in to purchase a bread stick, some cheese, butter and bottled water... we'd been warned to stay clear of the local tap water. The bread smelled delicious and was hot out of the oven. I had something good to munch on later, so I wouldn't feel like I was starving at night, in case no one wanted to go out and grab a bite or two. Always looking ahead, that was me.

Back at the hotel, I asked the desk clerk if I might be able to borrow a radio. I was dying for some good old Rock 'n Roll, and hadn't heard anything at all since we got off the ship. I needed something to while away the evening, and since there was no television in the hotel room, and the only other thing to listen to would be Rodstein quoting from Trotsky or someone, it seemed like the best idea. I was lucky, too. Yes, the desk clerk had a radio, and said he wouldn't mind loaning it to me.

Rodstein ran it upstairs, along with my food stash, while I talked a bit longer with the desk clerk. When he came back down, we decided to go out for something to eat, and found a nice little restaurant a couple of blocks away. It wasn't touristy or too imposing for the likes of us, and we ordered some pretty satisfying roast chicken, french fries, green peas and coffee. The price wasn't bad, and only cost us about three Canadian dollars.

After eating, we walked around the neighbourhood for a while, seeing what there was to see. We noticed there were more than a few Jewish pawnshops, with Hebrew writing on the windows. This was interesting, and we spent an hour or so peering inside. The shops looked exactly as they did back in North America. I guess a Jewish pawnshop is a Jewish pawnshop, wherever it may be... and a good bet is they're probably everywhere they're allowed.

Rodstein seemed to be fitting into Paris quite well, and said he had read a lot about it beforehand, and had liked what he'd read.

We walked on, checking out the other shops, and generally exploring the neighbourhood. It was a welcome change from our constant arguing, and it was good to know we actually could set aside our differences for a while.

After a lot of back and forth banter about life in Paris, he asked, "So, Larry, what do you think of this Suzanne? Is she something, or what?"

"Yeah," I said, "I like her. She's our tour guide, though, so what chance do any of us have to get near her, aside from being her charges? She's got her job to do... and it's to look after us." I knew what was on his mind. It was on mine, too.

"But, if you think you can get anywhere with her, you may as well try. Who am I to stop you? I'll give you this... she *is* very pretty. She seems pretty easy to get along with, too. So, why don't you talk to her tomorrow?"

"Naw, I don't think I will," Rodstein answered. "I won't have the time for that. I plan to try to get as much out of our free day as possible. I'm going to spend a lot of it at the Bibliothèque Nationale - that's the Library."

"Well, if you want some real French culture, I know how you can get it."

"How's that?"

"Eat some French toast."

"Screw you and your stupid jokes, Wiener. You and Bettle can have the French toast... you'll probably go to a Paris whorehouse tomorrow."

"Hey, now you *are* talking 'French culture'! We'll take you along, too, Rodstein. We'd love to see you get fixed up."

"Only animals get fixed up, Larry."

"So? Don't worry, buddy. We wouldn't let anyone cut 'em off. But, seriously... why don't you come with us tomorrow night, to the Pigalle? You've got a few dollars, don't be afraid to spend it. How many times are you going to be in Paris, the famous City of Love, anyway? So, go all the way, schmuck. You'll be able to write home and tell your mother how Paris made a man out of her little baby boy.

"Come with us, and have yourself a good time. If you're short of money, we can help you out."

Rodstein decided he'd come with us, but wanted to know if the girls were "safe".

"Sure, they're safe. Safest country in the world when it comes to sex. Paris *is* the City of Sex… they don't call it that for nothing, you know. Safe City, pal, this is Safe City!" I was laughing at my own joke, and finally Rodstein got it, and grinned.

"French safes," he said. "Yeah, I see what you mean."

"But, the girls have to have yellow cards, see? That way, you know they really *are* safe. You ask for the card, and make sure it's been stamped. That means the girls have been checked by a doctor every month and they're clean. The card will say so. There's nothing to worry about. This is a civilized country. It's not like back home, where you have to get it in an alleyway behind the local bar, and you don't know what you're getting. This is different. North Americans can learn a lot from the French."

"Yeah, yeah. Okay, it's on. I'll come with you tomorrow night."

"Good," I said, wondering what craziness I'd gotten us into now. "Let's get back to the hotel. I want to hear some decent music before I go to sleep. I wonder if they play Rock 'n Roll over here? You can read your book. I know there's *gotta* be a Rock 'n Roll station somewhere in this town!"

When we got back, I tried the radio, and sure enough, there was an English station playing Rock on the short wave length, probably coming from across the English Channel. So, I was happy for the rest of the evening, and Rodstein, ignoring the music, read himself to sleep. It had been a tiring day.

The next morning, I arose at seven a.m. and went out to see if I could find the bake shop again. I'd eaten all of my bread and cheese, and wanted more. I needed a coffee, too. The place hadn't been far away, and after I got my bearings, I found it and sat down on a park bench and had "breakfast" with the pigeons. There seemed to be pigeons everywhere you turned in this city.

After eating, I decided to take a little walk along the River Seine. I had no idea where it was, though, but figured it must be somewhere near where we were. I walked a couple of blocks and found a traffic cop, and asked for directions. He pointed out the way. I had been right… it wasn't far.

The morning was beautiful... warm, but not yet hot, slightly misty. I was glad to be off on my own... who needed the extra baggage? Let the others go their own way today, while I went mine. That was how I felt, too... the day was mine, mine alone. I could walk as long and as far as I wanted without getting lost... you could see the skyline of the city from almost any vantage point... and I wanted to soak in the feeling of actually being there in Paris, of being a part of it as opposed to being towed around by Suzanne with the others, as mere tourists.

I liked the idea of being alone, being able to think for myself without anyone answering back or telling me what to see or do next. I wanted to find the real Paris, not some imagery inspired by movies, or some American perception or other that wasn't true to begin with. Hollywood has a way of painting everything in colours that are anything but true, just for the sake of selling a ticket. I wanted none of that, and wanted to see the Parisians as they really were.

The city mesmerized me. If the Jewish Agency had suddenly decided to cancel my trip to Israel, I would have been quite content to remain exactly where I was. I loved the place, liked winding my way through the back streets and then up the Champs-Elysées.

It was a fantastic feeling, being on my own this way. The city breathed new life into theßß individual, and you noticed everything, even the singing of the birds. What I mean is, back home, the birds sing, but nobody listens. Here, in Paris, somehow you just can't help hearing them. It's just something about the city itself. It makes you want to hear, taste and see everything. From that one walk that morning, I learned why so many artists want to go there to study, and to paint. I was no artist, but I'm certain I felt exactly the same way. Fabulous, and absolutely alive.

I worked my way home, not even having seen the Seine, not having had to. My walk was so invigorating, I'd forgotten all about it! Back at the hotel, I met up with Rodstein.

"Say, where are you going today? I've just come in from a walk. The city is alive today, it's great out there! So, are you going to see the town today with Bernie and the others, or what? It's a free day, right? You can do what you like. Gonna go have yourself some fun?"

"Yes, and Saul can go and visit his beloved synagogues. If he doesn't come with us, we don't care. He doesn't want to be around us anyway, and he's no fun to be around, either. his mind is always in the clouds. So, the further from us, the better, maybe. If he doesn't get lost. Or if Elijah doesn't come and take him away. He'd feel better if that happened, I'm sure he would. I dunno. But, never mind him... what are your plans for the day, Larry?"

"I'm not sure. A little screwing around here and there, you know... I'll find something to do."

"So how are you going to screw around, as you say? You don't know anyone here."

"Well, what I want to do... you don't need to be tour-guided for." I thought that by saying this, Rodstein would take the hint and realize I wanted to be by myself. It went past him like a three o'clock train.

"Maybe we should go do some sightseeing on our own, is that what you want?" he asked.

"Don't worry about it, Rodstein. I'll be able to find something to do." *Hopefully, without you*, I added beneath my breath. "But, what are your plans? What are you guys gonna do today? You still going to the library?"

He shrugged. "When Bernie knock on the door, we'll head out. You can stay, if that's what you want, but... what do you think?... some beautiful girl's gonna bust in here while we're gone, and ask you to go to bed with her? You can do what you want, though, if Paris is too big for you."

"Don't get smart with me, Rodstein. Look at it this way: when opportunity knocks, I'll open the door, all right. And, you never know, it might."

He laughed. "You sure have big plans for such a little boy, Larry. Nobody is going to knock on your door, that's for sure. We're just plain, ordinary tourists, that's all. We have to make our own play, if we want to have some fun here."

"Well," I said, as nonchalantly as possible, "who knows? Maybe Suzanne will get bored with her day off and drop by. If she does, she won't be looking for you, though. She'll take Peggy out for the day. However... Peggy may have plans of her own, and then what?

You're the one with the grand imagination, Rodstein. How would it be if you came home after a day with your books, and found me in bed with Suzanne? What a laugh you and Bernie would have… but the laugh would be on you, wouldn't it?"

Rodstein snorted. "Don't make me laugh. You wouldn't stand a snowball's chance in Hell to even hold her hand, let alone take her to bed! Dream on, Larry!"

"Yeah," I said, "you're probably right, at that. But, never mind me… are you all ready for tonight? Remember what Suzanne said? She's taking us to the Pigalle, to meet a gal… tonight is not class, it'll just be ass, all ass, and Bernie and I are going to make sure you don't back out. We've already paid Suzanne to set us all up, you know. There's no way we can get our money back now, so we've gotta stick with Plan A.

"So, this is your big chance, Rodstein. You'll find out that not everything exists in books and theories. If you never come back to Paris, you'll never forget it either. All you need to do is take a bath when you get back from your library sightseeing trip today, and get ready for tonight. You agreed to do it, and you have to go through with it. We won't let you forget it if you back out, you know. So either way, it'll be a night to remember."

Figuring he would try to get out of it if he could, I badgered him quite a while about it, until he finally agreed, once and for all, he'd go through with it.

"Okay, fine," he said, "I'm game if you guys are." He was actually a bit impartial to the idea, but I knew he wouldn't want to face Bernie later on. I sensed his indifference, and told him…

"Look, it won't be so bad as you think. In fact, I'd be willing to bet you might even enjoy it. Why not? You can write home and say you had a prostitute in Paris, it'll be the scoop of the month, you'll be the envy of every kid in Toronto. It's part of the game, anyway… when in Paris, do as the Parisians do. Get laid once in awhile.

"You'll probably thank us later, too. You're acting like it's a crime, but it's legal here. It's taken for granted. It's no big deal. It's a bigger deal, in fact, if you don't go along with it. You're insulting the local customs. It's good for you, too… cleans out the body, relieves the tension, y'know? Every boy in the world wants it, and you're not *that* different! So, stop worrying and enjoy the ride...

"Think of it as ice cream, Rodstein. We just want you to get away from your books for an evening. They'll wait... an experience like this won't. Hey, don't miss Paris while you're here! Look, Bernie'll be back in a few minutes, so get yourself dressed and we'll all go our own ways today. But, be back by five o'clock, 'cause we leave at six with Suzanne. Okay? Okay."

He got the message. About 10:30 a.m., fifteen minutes later, Bernie knocked for Rodstein and after grunting "Hello" to me, he dragged him off into the streets. Thank God they were gone. Now I could have some peace.

I had plenty of time to kill, and turned on the radio, got my favourite outfit together... my "rocker" suit,charcoal with pink shirt, cufflinks, the whole thing... and laid it out on the bed. Then, with the radio belting out 'Johnny Be Good' in the background, I got into the shower and washed away the dust that seemed to have gathered while talking with stuffy Mr. Rodstein. I shaved, and laid out a bottle of aftershave ready to sprinkle over myself as I went out the door, like someone on a holy pilgrimage...

In reality, I figured the chances of Suzanne showing up were pretty slim. After all, it was her free day, too, and why would she want to spend it with the likes of me? She could earn some money, I imagined, by taking on another tour group... she said there was no lack of work for her at her agency... so why not? I'd be maybe a little annoyed, but I wouldn't blame her if she did that instead. Talk can be cheap, and maybe she'd just said it to pacify me and get my mind off those awful heights I'd been subjected to yesterday.

I got dressed and waited. And waited, and waited. By one p.m., I was beginning to think I was right, and that she wouldn't show up at all. Well, I'd been stood up before, and I'd survive this one. So, I decided to leave. I'd put on some old clothes and go out for a walk. maybe I'd find something else.

At one-twenty, though, there was a gentle knock on the door, and there she was, all dolled up and looking, in a way, like Audrey Hepburn. She'd managed to drop her business-like tour guide image for the day, and was wearing a very clingy sweater. I noticed right away how much better she looked when she let her figure show. Aside from the bumpy sweater, she was wearing a nice form-fitting skirt and flat shoes... a very simple, but sexy, outfit. As you can imagine, I immediately decided I liked it.

"Well, hello, Suzanne. I was beginning to think you weren't coming."

"I always do what I say, Larry. Now, why don't we go to my place? You'll like it there, and no one will interrupt us... they might here, you know..."

Yeah, I could just picture Saul dropping by, coming to ask how to get to the synagogues or something. I nodded, "Sounds good to me."

"We can listen to some music. I like jazz, but I have a lot of American Rock 'n Roll, too... Elvis Presley, Buddy Holly, Fabian, The Platters... and more. I have a whole load of them, all fresh from across the Channel in England. They're hard to get here, you know."

We went downstairs where she had her own car waiting outside. It was a Citroen, an expensive one. For a young single woman, I figured she must be getting some kind of a cut from the Madames of Pigalle on top of her tourist agency pay, for getting the male tourists past their front doors. Well, so what? Why not? Someone had to do it, and I couldn't think of a nicer person than Suzanne to be the one.

We climbed into the car and away we went. Suzanne spoke first.

"I guess you know what this is all about?"

"Well, I'd say... I think they call it a pick-up."

She laughed, and pressed her palm down onto my hand, and squeezed it.

We were at her place in about ten minutes. She lived in a friendly-looking brownstone in a definitely not-cheap neighbourhood. It looked quite a pricey place and not working class at all. Judging by this, too, she was doing all right indeed.

She lived at the top in a very congenial, roomy apartment. Lunch had already been set out on the table... egg salad sandwiches and cookies.

Suzanne took me by the hand and showed me around the apartment. The living room area was a bit on the small side, but you can't have everything. The bedroom was large, and so was the bathroom.

"A nice little playpen," I said, gesturing toward the bedroom.

Suzanne smiled. "Do you like playpens?" she asked.

"Only when it's playtime," I countered.

"Well, Larry, don't you worry about that. It will be playtime soon enough."

We ate in silence until she brought out a bottle of wine to loosen up the conversation chords, but we still didn't say much. Eating can always be a good excuse not to talk, when you don't know what to say.

When we finished, Suzanne got up and went into the living room, beckoning me to follow. She showed me her record collection and it was pretty impressive. She had material I'd never heard of before, and I selected a few and asked if she'd mind my playing some of them.

"Mais oui," she said, "please do! Larry, we'll do whatever you like today. But, listen. First, we have to forget who I am. Don't think of me as Suzanne, your tour guide. That would be a big mistake. This afternoon will never happen again, you know, so please, let us be at ease while we are here. And when we meet tonight again with the group, we must act as though we hadn't seen each other at all today. Do you agree?"

I had a sudden vision of her becoming indignant and asking me to leave right away if I said anything to the contrary, but who was I to argue?

"Well, sure, Suzanne, if that's how you want it? I see the point, don't worry. But let's forget about who I am, too, all right? Let Larry be *your* tour guide for the afternoon... how's that sound?"

"Marvellous!" she said, hugging my arm. I noticed a large world map on the living room wall, with pins stuck in it, seemingly at random. I asked her what it was for.

She laughed. "When I have a man from a certain country, I put a pin in that country. It's a kind of game I play with myself, that's all."

"I see," I said, a little disappointed at this turn of events. "So, I'm only another country to conquer on your war map, is that it?"

She said nothing, only snuggled closer to me, squeezing my waist. This only confirmed it to me, and I began to feel a little insulted, and like a dip-stick, I began to get angry with her. Here I was, thinking I only wanted to use her to get laid, but instead, she was using me to get laid! It wasn't supposed to work that way... this wasn't fair! Besides, I'd have lied about it, not told the other person up-front what my intentions or reasons were.

I still wanted her, though, so I managed to stifle my "anger" and decided to begin to do what I was here to do... used or not. A bit nervously, because she'd so easily turned the tables on me (now wherever did I get the feeling she was definitely laughing at me and not with me?)... a bit nervously, I reached out to touch her hand. As I did so, she stood up and headed for the bedroom. No warm-up needed with this one, I thought, and wanted to laugh out loud myself, because she was going to get the surprise of her life. Somehow, I'd gotten to thinking she looked at me like some inexperienced little boy from the land of snow and Eskimo pie. I'd show her pie!

I followed her into the bedroom, where she was very slow and relaxed, taking my clothing off, one piece at a time as if it was an everyday chore to her and not something to relish. By the time she got around to removing my shorts, I figured it was also time for me to begin doing something...

She was still clothed, and I was buck-naked, but what the Hell - I reached out and caught her shoulders, pulled her toward me, running my hands up beneath her sweater. Her body was small, but firm, and I rubbed it with the palms of my hands and slowly bent down to kiss her side, putting a hand behind her back where I could unhook her brassiere. I pulled both it and her sweater over her head. Her arms raised willingly into the air, and when this was done, she laid herself back on the bed, her head on the pillow, wondering, I suppose, what her Canadian novice would do next, and what movie he'd been to that showed him how to do what he'd just done...

The brassiere was a pale pink thing, lacy and ruffled. Her breasts were bared and ready for me.

"Suck them," she said. "Rub your hands over them, pinch the nipples a little. Put your lips on them and suck them, Larry, please!" There was an urgency in her voice I couldn't refuse. "Oh, I will," I replied. "Will I ever!" One hand was full of one of her tits, and the other found its way down her belly to the top of her skirt.

I unbuttoned it, and Suzanne wiggled, and it wound up on the floor with the rest of her clothes. So did the slip she was wearing, and as this came off, I realized she had nothing underneath it. Suzanne was definitely inspiring me.

She knew it, too. I was rock hard by now, and she began massaging my cock, but I pulled away from her. I was going to teach her a little lesson before she could have what she so badly wanted.

"No," I whispered, "not yet, baby. First, I have something else for you."

Starting at her neck, I began to lick her all over, working my way down and down, slowly driving her crazy with need. As I put my mouth on first one breast, then the other, at the same time my hands pushed her legs apart, so that they were spread as widely as possible. I brushed her pussy with my fingers, but didn't linger there... just to provide her with a little more desire than she'd bargained for.

I got onto my knees and heard her moan when I pulled my cock away, out of her reach... she wanted to hold it badly, I knew. "Sorry, honey," I said, coming up from her breast for a second, "but I have other plans for you. Don't worry, you'll like them!" I was on top of her now, my head face down between her tits, licking and gently biting at the nipples. Each time I did this, she moved her hips and groaned. I smiled, and lowered my face to her belly button, ran my tongue around inside it.

"No fluff on this girl, is there?" I said, and started up again. She was genuinely surprised at this new turn of events. She hadn't thought I'd know what to do to get a girl *really* horny.

"Larry, don't," she whispered.

She was losing the lead, and didn't like it. She loved it, and didn't like it. She grabbed my hair when I went down on the split between her legs. She pulled my head back, but weakly. Then, she pushed it down, giving up from frustration, giving in to the pleasure I was providing her with. Eating out was my favourite pastime. I'd thought about this, with her, back at the Eiffel Tower, and I had known exactly what I would want, the first time we were alone together... and this was it.

By the way she was acting, I got the impression no man had ever done this with her before, and when I was finished... but before she was finished!... I came up for air and looked up over her nipples, into her eyes. She ground her groin up toward me and whispered a single word: "More..."

My tongue did the rest then, and only then. It was the moment I'd been waiting for. I'd show her what a crazy Canuck could do to a gal, all right... And, I did; and she loved every minute of it, finally bursting into a marvellous orgasm that shook the entire bed and, I suspect, gave the downstairs neighbours something to talk about for the next month.

Having satisfied... and almost exhausted her... I raised myself to my knees, and snuggled up toward her breasts, her body between my legs. There was still something that needed doing, I told her. I lowered myself a little, until my balls rested neatly between her tits. "Now, you can have it," I said. "you can have it, but I think it wants something. A blowjob, maybe."

She took the situation well in hand, and said, "Yes. Maybe, baby, but first... first screw me, and then I'll do whatever you like, whatever you want, Larry."

"How do I know you're serious?" I asked. "What if you change your mind afterwards?"

She squeezed my cock with her fingers, and pulled it toward her. She kissed it, and ran her tongue down along its shaft, then back up again. Slowly. Then she put her lips around its head, and pushed her face forward a little, taking it into her mouth, ran her tongue over it, and pulled away again.

"It's sweet," she whispered, looking up over it at me with dreamy eyes. "I won't change my mind, don't worry."

Her doing this was too much. I had to get inside of her right away, and did... but as soon as I did, and she moved a couple of times, I came. Damn! Too soon! Too much anticipation, I guess, and that last bit, I shouldn't have done it, shouldn't have let her start kissing it.

It wasn't an entire flop, though. After all, *she'*d been satisfied... something I guessed wasn't always easily done. And, after a fashion, I'd been satisfied, too, although things should have gone on a while longer, and it would have been better. Well, you can't win 'em all...

When we were finished, Suzanne began to turn cold... she had done her self-imposed duty and knocked over her target; she'd had her fun (more than she'd expected to have, too!) - but now all she seemed to want to do was to get me the Hell out of her place, as if nothing had ever happened.

Strange.

There was no after-sex cosiness. She didn't offer me a drink, or put on any more music. I began to wonder what was with this girl, anyway? I did what I thought best, and turned the coldness back on her. I got up, went over to the desk, took a pin from a little box of odds and ends, walked to her man-conquest map and stuck that pin right in the heart of the dear old Canadian nation.

"So there you go, Suzanne. Eaten by Canada." I wanted her to remember I hadn't been the novice she'd expected to play teacher to. Her reply was equally as distant as her original idea.

"Please get dressed, and I'll drive you back to your hotel."

I picked up my clothes and started putting it on. "It's all right," I said. "I think I'll enjoy the walk."

She looked at me strangely, as if she didn't trust me, and blurted out in a half-afraid voice, "Remember, around your group, this didn't happen at all. *La, tout le parler est fini..* No talking. The party's over."

I nodded, and took my leave as gracefully as I could.

Slowly, I walked back along the Champs Elysees, looking into windows, feeling used and dumped on. I knew I'd turned the tables on Suzanne, upsetting her little plan, but still... for an egg sandwich, I'd been poorly treated. This was the first time I'd had this sort of cold treatment from a woman, and I didn't like it. It was a hard lesson to learn, and from now on, I told myself, things would be different. I wasn't going to be a sucker for anyone.

I chalked it up to "experience", though... what else could I do? I realized I'd done roughly the same thing to Martha. I'd slept with her on a Sunday, and left town on a Monday, without telling her a thing. After a relationship that had lasted over a year, one that everyone thought would end up in marriage, well... yeah, I'd been a heel, all right. Maybe I was getting my just desserts and fate had simply led me to a place where the same kind of thing would be dealt back to me. I'd had it coming.

I knew that with the next boatload of tourists, Suzanne's affair with me, such as it was, would be totally forgotten, that she'd find someone else to pin to her wall, that I was now history. That's what hurt the most, I guess… the fact I was nothing more to her than a quickie in the afternoon, and a way to fill a spot on a map. Who I was didn't matter at all.

When I got back to the hotel at about four p.m., Rodstein was lying on his bed, reading as usual. I was in a bad mood, and it showed, so he didn't bother saying much more than a short "Hello". the sight of him made everything seem worse than it really was. Of course, I had planned on telling him (in confidence, naturally) of my conquest of our beautiful tour guide. Now there didn't seem to be anything to say. She was only beautiful on the outside, and I didn't want to think about the inside part.

"Aw shut up, Rodstein. Why don't you go read a good dirty book instead of that tripe, and get a real education? Or do you think those thousand-page books on Troksky and Karl Marx are going to make you Prime Minister of Israel?"

Rodstein looked up and frowned. "Well, they won't make me Prime Minister, but they sure as Hell will make me smarter than the likes of you, Larry."

"I don't want to be smart," I told him.

He put his book down. This didn't sound like the Larry he knew, he said, adding, "So what is it you want?"

"I wouldn't mind going to bed with Suzanne," I replied, deciding to tell him nothing. A conquered woman was one thing… but a conquered man was another! "That would be something, wouldn't it? A true souvenir of Paris! It'd be something to write home about, for sure. My Mom told me to get a French girl while I'm here."

"Well, you can count Suzanne out. You'd never in a million years get to sleep with her."

"Yeah, well, I think I want to stay in Paris anyway. I don't want to be sent home by the Agency for trying something with our tour guide. Somehow, I doubt if they'd like the idea."

"Don't worry, Larry. It'll never happen. She's too good for you. She's a nice girl."

Yeah, sure. I knew I had to change the subject at this point, before I said something I'd regret later. in one way, I wanted everyone to know what a nice girl she *wasn't*, but on the other hand, I didn't want anyone to know what had happened between us, for a variety of reasons… my own pride being one of them, not to mention the danger to us both. I didn't really care about her, but I didn't want to jeopardize my position. Whatever awaited me there, I wanted to get to Israel… and not with a dark cloud hanging over my head.

"So, Rodstein," I said, shaking the thought of Suzanne out of my head, "what about tonight? You're still coming with us to the Pigalle, aren't you? You haven't changed your mind? I hope not. You'll get your money's worth… I'll see to that!"

"Uh, what happens, Larry, if I don't want to go?"

"I'll take your place, that's all. The worst that can happen is that I'll get laid twice to your not getting it at all. We paid for three, Bernie and I, so if you don't take your place, if you're not man enough that is… well, either myself or Bernie will have two turns.

"I think you'd better come along, though. We'll never let you live it down."

"I don't care about that," he said (this was a lie, though). "If you and Bernie have already paid, well, one of you can take a second turn. I don't think I'll go. I've been thinking it over, and I'm really not as interested as you are. I do want to see the sights of Pigalle, though… especially the Moulin Rouge. So, I'll be coming with you anyway."

"Okay," I shrugged, "if that's what you want. By the way, have you seen anything of Peggy lately? I haven't seen her all day. Come to think of it, I haven't seen her since we left the Eiffel Tower yesterday. Where is she?"

"Oh, she went off with Bernie, walking. She doesn't seem too happy about being here in Paris. For some reason, it isn't moving her the way it is the rest of us. I don't know why."

Peggy, I thought, was feeling odd about being in Paris. With a group of men, she felt a bit left out. It seemed like the famous City of Lovers was reminding her that she was utterly alone. She had no one… not that any of us did, really; but at least the rest of us were trying. She didn't even try.

She had expected to be excited by Paris and maybe even find a man and have a good time, be shown around the city by a genuine Frenchman. This, however, wasn't happening. I told Rodstein my thoughts about her, and he agreed. She wasn't enjoying herself at all. Our talk about visiting the whorehouses didn't help much, I guess.

We carried on our conversation for a while, Rodstein and I, discussing where we'd go that night, and what we'd do, imagining what the real Paris was like after dark, hoping we weren't simply having illusions about it all. I wasn't really interested in our conversation, but at least it got Suzanne off my mind for a while, and I felt a bit better for it.

There was a knock at the door, and in came Bernie and Peggy, back from their walk.

"You guys have a nice afternoon roaming the streets?" I asked. "Get into any trouble we should know about?"

Peggy answered, a bit morosely, "It was a bit dull, really, but pleasant. We passed by the Tower and the Arc again, just walking around. And we went into a little café for espresso. That was all. Then we headed back here."

"Exciting," commented Rodstein. "You sound like you're really enjoying yourself, Peg. Isn't Paris hitting you the way you thought it would? No loose Frenchmen running around?"

"Well," she said, "I did really think I'd have more fun here. The books all said to expect that. I thought I'd find those myths of excitement and romance here, but I just don't see it. It's like being in downtown Winnipeg, only everyone speaks French instead of English.

"And tonight will be 'Boys Night Out'… so what will I be doing? I'll be walking around the Pigalle with Suzanne, I suppose, waiting for you guys to finish…"

"Well, you can always drop in at a dance or something, can't you? There's bound to be plenty going on. Just tell Suzanne you want to go to a dance and maybe you'll meet someone there." This came from Bernie.

Peggy smiled back at him. "It's a thought, isn't it? Maybe... how long will you guys be, anyway?"

"A couple, three hours, who knows? Depends on how it goes, right?"

"Right... I guess," Peggy replied. "Well, okay. How about if we meet outside the Moulin Rouge after three hours. This'll give you enough time to finish doing whatever you'll be doing, I'm sure."

"Okay," said Bernie, "it's settled. We should all go and start getting ready, I think. Suzanne will be here to pick us up at six o'clock, and we don't have that much time. I'll see you later. Me, I'm going to go take a shower and get dressed."

Everyone thought this was a good idea, and we all went off to put ourselves together. At six o'clock sharp, we met again in the lobby. Suzanne was there, wearing a light blue suit, looking as cold as ice... all business, as if nothing at all had happened between us. That had been the plan, to pretend everything was "normal", but she looked like she really meant it. She wouldn't look at me at all, even when she asked a question.

"Has anyone seen Saul? What's he up to? Is he coming with us, or going off on his own?" She asked this as we piled into her little Citroen and drove off toward the Pigalle.

I wanted to tell her, "Oh, he knew you were coming, and so he climbed the Eiffel Tower to get away. If you ask him to come down, he'll jump." I didn't, though, and let Rodstein answer instead.

"Saul, he wants absolutely nothing to do with us... zilch. When he goes to bed at night, he doesn't have a thing to say, except goodnight. It's been like that all day today and all day yesterday. He's drifted away from us... not that he was ever overly involved. But since he signed that release form you gave him from your agency, Suzanne, he's been a different man. He's divorced himself from the rest of us."

"Well, if that's what he wants, it's fine with me," old cold-eyes said, "and we'll just have to go about our business without him. You want to enjoy Paris and have some good times, that's what you will do. He can do as he pleases.

"Speaking of tonight, we *are* going to enjoy ourselves, you know. I'll take Peggy to the Moulin Rouge while you men go and create some fond memories to write back home about if you like."

After a few minutes of driving, we pulled up in front of a little greystone house.

"All right, little boys. Here's where you turn into men. I've already set everything up for you, and now all you have to do is face up to the evening. It won't cost you a penny extra, remember. You gave me your money, and I've turned it over to girls I think you'll like. It's all been paid for, so... off you go! Follow me." She got out of the car and made her way across the sidewalk, motioning to us to come after her.

Bernie, Rodstein and I got out of the car and followed, like ducklings going to a slaughterhouse. I don't know why, but that was how I felt, anyway... I suppose it was because of the way Suzanne had treated me earlier. I still had a bitter taste in my mouth from that experience.

When we got to the door, Rodstein started to get cold feet. His eyes were flashing all around as if he expected the police to pull up at any moment and take us to jail. His lip trembled when he finally worked up the nerve to speak."I... I'm not going through with this. I can't. I'll pick up a disease."

Bernie stuck a finger in Rodstein's face. "Listen, you," he said, "we paid good money for this, and you're going through with it!"

Suzanne spoke up, too. "Mr. Rodstein, please. I set this up, you understand. Please don't make me look like a fool. You know, I don't do this for everyone. (I knew she was lying, but let it go).

"If you're afraid of catching a disease, why didn't you say so earlier? There's no disease here, not on the Pigalle. All of these women have been thoroughly checked by doctors, don't you know that? I wouldn't take you to someone you could get... sick from. Now, really! These ladies have their yellow cards stamped every week by the doctors who work with them. This is a legal, serious place of business. There's nothing wrong with this! You're imagining the wrong things, this is Paris, and these things are taken care of in a civilized way. There's nothing to be afraid of.

"Please, Mr. Rodstein. It's up to you, of course, to do as you see fit, but fear of disease is not a valid reason. The only risk of catching a disease from a prostitute here in Paris is perhaps if you have sex with a girl from the streets, one who doesn't work out of a clean house like this... someone who doesn't have her card up to date or someone who only goes to a doctor if she has to. But there's nothing to worry about here."

Rodstein pushed Bernie's finger to one side. "Well, I'm not going to take the chance. I'm just not going to."

I could see he felt he had to explain his decision to us. A bit of a lecture was coming.

"It isn't the disease," he said, making sure he looked at Suzanne and not us as he spoke. "What these guys want to do is their business, but I would be insulted, having an encounter with a prostitute. I don't believe I really need the blow to my dignity, to my self-respect. It just isn't my style.

"I need to find a different sort of woman... one who cares about me, not only the money. I have to know who she is, and she has to know who I am. Maybe you think I'm being old fashioned, but I don't care. This kind of a place is not for me, and that's all there is to it. So, if you girls don't mind, I think I'd like to accompany you to the Moulin Rouge, and leave Bernie and Larry here to indulge themselves if their other... er, pursuits."

I couldn't resist poking Bernie in the ribs with an elbow, and whispering, "I thought you said Saul didn't want to come with us. This sure sounds like him, doesn't it?"

Rodstein heard me, but ignored the remark, as did Suzanne, who seemed to be in a bit of a hurry.

"Fine," she said. "I'm not going to push you. You go back and wait in the car with Peggy. Tell her you've changed your mind... she'll be pleased with you."

Rodstein walked away from us, a smug little smile on his face, his dignity intact.

"Now," Suzanne sighed. "I'm glad that's over with. But you will have to decide between you who will have two girls or one of the girls twice, because at this stage, I can't get a refund, you know. They're expecting three men, not two, and I don't want to look foolish to them, so... and of course, if neither of you are *able*, then you'll lose your money as well."

Again, I almost made a sarcastic remark to her, but somehow refrained. It seemed to me she was much more worried about her "looking foolish" with the girls inside than she was about us losing our money.

"I'm good for once," Bernie blurted out, "but I don't know about twice. I'm not like Larry. Let him go for it."

If I hadn't known better, I'd say that it almost sounded like a compliment. I decided to let the idea sink in, as far as Suzanne was concerned.

"Yeah," I said, turning and looking at her straight in the eyes, "I think I can rise to the occasion. Some of us Canadians have been known to start where others finish. We won't lose any money, Suzanne, so don't worry about that."

"It'll be good for you, Larry," said Bernie. "You've never been laid in Paris, and you can write home about it."

"Sure. Remember that story we took in grade seven French - Le Petit Tailleur or whatever it was? The Little Tailor... the guy who killed seven flies in one swat? Thistle be me... seven in one night!"

"Two, Larry, just two."

Suzanne piped up, a bit slyly, "You don't think you will be too tired to go twice, Larry?"

"Not at all," I said, smiling sweetly at her. "I could stick a couple of pins in the centre of Paris, no trouble at all. I bet I could stick three, if I tried, eh?"

Suzanne's frosty glare turned a lot icier when I made that comment. Bernie just laughed, and probably went through the rest of his life thinking Paris prostitutes are known as "pins". Suzanne looked like she wanted to stick me... with a knife! Her imagination had taken my remark a step further, and I was sure she thought I'd told the others about my excursion to her apartment that afternoon, and what ensued.

I hadn't said a word to anyone, but she didn't know that, did she? So, I figured, why disillusion her now? I gave her a big, lopsided grin and raised my eyebrows, giving her a bit of a facial dig which she misinterpreted, thinking it meant everything was okay, and her glare relaxed somewhat. I'd meant to rub it in a bit. Well, you can't win 'em all.

So now she knew I hadn't spilled the beans. I'd honoured our agreement only because it was a private arrangement between two people. The fact one of us... me... was supposed to be some sort of prey, didn't mean I should betray her.

I was trying to come up with an appropriately cryptic comment to reassure her even more, but the door opened instead, revealing a heavyset woman in her mid-sixties with red, rosy cheeks and a broad let's-do-some-business kind of smile, who said, without further ado: "Hello, Suzanne. Dos iz di chevreh?" (These are the guys?)

Decidedly German-Jewish, I thought.

"Ya," Suzanne replied.

The older, larger woman slipped an arm around Suzanne's waist and pulled her forward, hugging her for what seemed like just a little instant too long.

Bernie's face turned toward me just as mine turned toward his, each of us surprised. It was quite obvious to us both that Suzanne and this woman knew each other very well indeed. I mean, here we were, two men and a good-looking woman, knocking at the door to a rather rundown-looking house where the two men are about to get laid by two strangers, the door opens and Suzanne gets a greeting like a long-lost sister. It just seemed to be a going a little too smoothly, like oil on a slippery surface.

Suzanne had connections to this house, all right. She got a cut for bringing her male tourists around. It was a quasi-pimping sideline, and a regular happening, by the looks of things. She was taking good advantage of her position at the tour guide agency, and I wondered what they'd say if they knew... or did they know? Maybe the whole thing was a front for all sorts of ventures. Well, it didn't matter to me, but all the same, I was surprised at how well she knew her way around the underside of the city. But, who cared?

Those were the things I was thinking while standing there waiting for Suzanne and the fat lady to say their Yiddish greetings... which seemed to go on forever. I didn't listen to the conversation, though. The beginning of it was too syrupy for my liking, so I shut the rest of it out. Finally, though, they quietened down and turned to us, as if they'd just realized that instant that they weren't alone on the doorstep.

Suzanne introduced us, then said, "I will be back for you in a couple of hours. Be sure you're ready when I arrive." Not a word of "enjoy yourselves", and I guessed she was hoping I wound up with the ugly one.

The Madame watched her go, then turned to us. "Come in, come in. Don't stand out here. Now, which one of you is the oldest?"

Bernie's finger went into the air again, turning in midflight and landing pointed at his own chest.

"I am," he said.

Not that she couldn't tell.

""I have a nice girl for you. She is about twenty years old, and I think you'll like her."

She dismissed Bernie with a flick of her wrist, and turned to me.

"How old are you?" she asked.

"Nineteen," I told her.

"Du bist noch alts a pisher!" (You're a young man).

"Yes, you're young, and I have a lovely young girl for you. She too is nineteen… just your age. She is very pretty, too, but new and inexperienced. She will like you, I think. You are young and she won't become frightened. You will be able to help one another along."

This kind and motherly Madame said the girl's name was Monique.

"Do you think I could meet her first? I mean, before we…"

"*Monique!!*"

Madame had a voice that would make a screech owl wonder, and when she yelled, it carved a new hole in my memory banks. It sounded like a drill made of fingernail filings, writing "EEEEEK" on a blackboard.

Monique entered the room right away. She must have been hiding behind the drapes, within earshot waiting; maybe peeking out at her new "customer".

Well, whether or not she was ready for me, here I was. I wasn't ready for her, though. I'd been thinking she'd be "just another girl" and wasn't prepared for the beauty who presented herself before us. She was lovely, beautiful in a very French way (mature and worldly, not like any North American girl I'd seen)… a real knockout with coal-black, wavy hair, and perfect teeth wrapped in an entirely seductive smile. Tall and lean, with an excellent carriage (I know, it sounds like I'm describing a new car… sorry!) - and a strong, clear voice, speaking as I stood there open-mouthed and gaping.

"Bonjour, M'sieur Blondie!"

"You like Monique, M'sieur Blondie?" Madame asked. (I never got her name, so I'll just call her Madame X. If you could have seen her, you'd know how well it fits.)

"Uh, well, yeah... yes, I sure do," I exclaimed. "I do... I do like Monique."

There didn't seem to be much else to say. Everything about her was incredibly sexy. She looked like a real feast, but seemed a bit modest about her beauty, as if she didn't know the impact it could have on someone like me. She was really quite elegant, and this scared me a little. I hadn't expected this from a prostitute. I'm not sure what I did expect, but it certainly wasn't a girl like her.

She was so very beautifully formed, so well spoken, so... everything!... I felt like I was the one who was being paid to perform for her, not the other way around. I knew I would never have this happen again. Once in a lifetime was enough, being with this amazing female. She really was a specimen to behold, a true piece of absolute biological perfection... a rare work of art.

"Well," said Madame X, "you have a choice... you can have an hour each with two different girls, or you can spend two hours with Monique here."

I told her I liked the sound of the latter proposition best. My equilibrium had been upset from the moment I'd first seen her. She really was something else. Madame X obviously noticed the urgent tone in my voice, and told us to go up to go upstairs to what she called the loving room.

Monique placed her hand in mine to put me at ease, and smilingly led me up the stairs. I let her go first, so I could watch her wonderful body moving. I was following her like a lovesick puppy, thinking about her most amply endowed chest, which was actually quite surprising to see on such an otherwise lean body. Man, I thought... if I could have those breasts between my ears and call Australia for help, I'd do it in a minute! Her figure and everything about her was simply astounding.

We arrived at the top of the stairs, and she led me to a doorway through which a dim light could be seen, revealing a large bed. The room itself had a New Orleans sort of feel to it, a bit gloomy with red and blue shades over lights that appeared to be old gas lights recently converted with electricity. In a way, it reminded me of a funeral parlour or the insides of a house from a 30s film, which gave it an overall eerie effect.

The neighbourhood was on the rundown side, but the house had one time been an expensive one, and it struck me that it had maybe belonged to a banker or someone like that in its prime, around the turn of the century. Then, Monique moved again and I forgot all about the room we were in.

"You're such a beautiful girl," I told her, a statement leading up to the obvious question, one she probably heard from all of her customers..."So why are you here? I mean, any restaurant would hire you on the spot, or a perfume store maybe, or... well, you could be a model if you wanted. So what are you doing here?"

"I want to make money," she said. "and the money is easy enough. Besides, I have protection here. No one will hurt me here. I simply take a man upstairs and do what he wants, and I get paid by Madame. Paid well, too."

"Well, what happens if one of the customers complains to the Madame, or tries to hit you... or worse? How are you protected? Couldn't Madame have you thrown out, too, or not pay you?"

Monique smiled at my naiveté. "No, the Madame always pays me. I'm not a decoy, but the real thing... I do whatever I have to do, that's the agreement. No one will hurt me. Madame has a way of knowing who is safe for us girls."

"It's a very strange way to make a living, if you ask me," I told her. "It's just that you're so young... and you just don't look the type to be prostituting yourself, selling your body to me for sex. It is, after all, a dirty business." I wanted to get straight to the heart of the matter.

"I have been doing it a long time, you know."

"But I thought you were new here?"

"I am new *here*, but not new to the profession. When I was twelve years old, I was very beautiful then, too. I have always been beautiful, and desirable to me. My family knew this even before I knew it. And, it is not such a dirty business... it depends on how you look at it. Maybe I enjoy it as much as the men, who knows? It may be that when my legs open, my heart opens, too…

"You see, when I was very young, I was raised by an uncle. He took advantage of me while his wife, my aunt, looked the other way. She knew, but did not wish to become involved in a family dispute. It would have ended their marriage, and, in other ways, she needed him. It was better that nothing was said. My uncle, of course, told me not to speak of our relationship, which went on for years. It is not as uncommon as you may think, this kind of thing.

"He drove a taxicab by night… he still does… and was home all day. He spent half his tip money buying me clothing he likes to see me wear, and he gave me other spending money, too. We had a very nice apartment, and I had a good life. I lived in comfort, and really didn't mind the sex. I was trading off what he wanted for what I wanted, and it worked. You see, I wasn't the innocent victim.

"As I got older, I realized that I could be independent and be paid much more for what I was doing. It was, as they say, a natural progression, from one to the other, from being an amateur to becoming a professional. Besides, at about this time, my aunt knew full well what was going on, and I had to leave. It was becoming too obvious. We got into an argument over my uncle, and in the end, she told me to get out.

"She said I would have to leave without my new clothes, though, that I would have to go the way I came… with only the clothes on my back. She said she didn't want a slut like me living under her roof. It was all right before, when she only guessed, but when I began dressing up, everything changed. The neighbours would notice, she said, and her reputation would be damaged. Imagine that! She was worried about *her* reputation! So, she didn't care about me after all. Not once did she tell me not to do what I was doing, oh no! She just wanted me to leave, because the people next door might talk.

"Anyway, I took my coat and left everything behind. I just walked out. I was sixteen years old, and everywhere I went, men would look at me as if I was twenty-one or twenty-two years old instead. I began to feel like a cake behind glass in a bakery shop. I had no protection of any sort then. I was walking the streets like a waif, without money, and I had nowhere to go. In those days, I didn't have a sou.

"After a while, I got a job in a café, but it didn't last very long. I tried factory work, store work, and so on. But these kinds of jobs never seemed to work out for me. I would always be let go soon after I started. So, I stopped looking for those kinds of jobs. There seemed to be no point, this working for a few days and then being let go.

"I wound up on the street, begging for a little bit of money just so that I could eat. I knew that with my looks men would be bound to give me something. But I needed shelter, too. I needed a bath and fresh clothing. Winter was also coming, and I was beginning to, how do you say... panic? Yes, panic... I couldn't even sell flowers in the streets, looking the way I did, and even if I did, I would make no more than a beggar out in the cold. I became very frightened, and concerned about what the future would bring.

"One afternoon, I watched a woman walking along the Champs-Elysées. She wore a large fur coat and looked very wealthy. I was standing on a corner, asking passersby for money. There were no gendarmes around to chase me off there, and I thought I might make something that day.

"The woman saw me and she stopped and stared for a moment, then approached. She looked me up and down, and asked me how old I was. I told her the truth, and I could see her eyes light up when I said, 'sixteen years'. She asked me when I had eaten a real meal last, and when I had taken a bath. I told her, and she said that she thought I would look very pretty if I were properly fed and cleaned up. I wondered what she was getting at.

"She asked me to come home with her where I could have a bath and something hot to eat. She said I could rest there, too... for as you might imagine, one does not get very much sleep when one is on the streets. Anyway, this woman got me to wondering about her, and I asked what she did. At first, I thought she was a member of one of the large, beautiful churches of Paris, or perhaps a social worker. But, no. She was neither of those, as I was to learn. At the time, though, she only smiled, and told me nothing of who or what she was. She just kept saying, you will see, you will see...

"I went with her. I thought that I had nothing to lose by doing so, since I had nothing to start with. At her house, she called for a girl who came running to her side. The lady told her to please bring the evening meal at once, and soon two plates appeared, one for each of us. I noticed there were other girls in the house, too, coming and going. Some of them were very scantily clad, and looked very comfortable, too, as if this was the normal way to live.

"I soon began to see what the set-up was, and realized they must be prostitutes. I knew, too, that before the meal was over, I would be offered a place there, and I knew I would have to reach the right decision. What should I say to the woman's offer, when it came? Well, you see… I really had little to lose, and if I turned her down, I would be back on the streets very quickly, and winter was still coming! I realized, too, that I could now be paid for what I had already been doing for four years, anyway.

"So, I asked her outright, not waiting for her to bring the subject up: Is this a house of ill repute? She smiled, and said that it was indeed, adding that I didn't have to go back out into the streets if I didn't want to. She said that if I wanted to stay, I would be well looked after, as long as I did my part and kept the men pleased. She said I would be protected, and that I would be in a position to make some very good money if I liked. What was offered was a nice room, comfort, and the company of the other girls. Everyone, of course, did the same thing…

"She told me that all I would ever have to do in order to get along would be to close my mind and think… "It isn't a man, it is a business." When you think like that, she said, you'd be fine. The rules were very simple, too. No robbing clients or asking them for extra money. Give the man exactly what he is paying for, nothing less, and nothing extra. And if a man gets too pushy or becomes angry for some reason, first, you try to talk to him, to persuade him to settle down. If that doesn't work, you call for help. However, you have to know how to protect yourself, too… just in case, because you never know when it comes to sex. At times, the sexual act can bring up other things, not so pleasant. It can be a frightening business, sometimes.

"But, if you know where to hurt a man, and how to do it quickly, you'll be all right. The woman told me all of this that first day, and she's right. She said that I would be protected for as long as I was here, and that she would give me one hundred francs a week. The other girls would show me anything I didn't already know... as she put it, the entire range of services we're expected to provide. She said I would be able to learn very quickly what sort of behaviour to use with whom. We must all put on an act, you see.

"Well, after a couple of weeks of observing, she said, I would then be ready to start working myself. I told her I'd already thought about it, and there was no need to wait for an answer, because I'd already decided I liked the idea. I told her it would be like going to school.

"Finally," I said, "I'll be getting an education!" And so, that's how I came to be here, how I began my apprenticeship. The lady was Madame, and to quote a phrase, she gave me to the 'hard cases' first. She sent all kinds to me, to see what I was best at, how I handled them. Some were very rough, and there were those who wanted nothing more than to talk. There were young ones, old ones, you name it, I've done it!"

Monique liked to talk, that was clear. It wasn't hard to believe she soon showed talented with younger, inexperienced men... first-timers. They were her age, and she genuinely liked them, she said, but also had the upper hand of experience on her side. So, she began to draw the business of fathers who wanted to introduce their sons to the world of sex, and Madame X acquired a reputation for offering young girls who were just starting out in the trade, learning the ropes.

Monique's reputation grew, too. She was a good draw for the wealthy youths of Paris. Families who provided their sons with access to a brothel were not unusual. It prevented the boys from turning up with trashy girlfriends, got them laid, and without danger of disease, being stripped blind of their money, and so forth. It also helped prevent unsuitable marriages. Having sex with a prostitute in a controlled atmosphere meant no unwanted children showing up later on. As the fathers often told their sons, "Keep your hands in your pockets, and your name in the blue book." And so word spread that Monique was becoming a good "teacher" for these youths.

"The only time I ever had an accident was when one boy, too scared to do anything, started to get a little rough. He was ashamed of himself, because he couldn't get it up. So he was going to get rid of his frustration by beating me around a little. Luckily, I was able to talk him out of it. I became very good at talking to customers, as I'm now doing with you... wasting your money!

"The other girls started to get jealous of me because of this... and because of my looks, too, and maybe because I was getting all the young ones, and enjoyed it. But I get all kinds of other types, too. Once or twice I've been slapped... hard! But, most men realize that Paris houses of prostitution are under police protection... we pay for it, of course, but it works. Besides, police like to have sex, too, and they also send their sons here, some of them."

"Well, I don't know what to say after all that," I told her. But, you're right... our time is being used up. We haven't gotten around to doing what I'm here for, but so far, the education I'm getting is worth it. What I've learned from you tonight, Monique, I'll never forget. If I ever get married and have a son, I'll bring him to someone like you. It's a good idea. But if I have a daughter, I'll keep a good eye on her, to make sure nothing happens to her that has happened to you. Her home will be safe, and I'll be good to her."

Our time was up, as it turned out, and nothing at all had happened... I surprised myself completely. She was so sweet, though, and needed to talk, and the time passed very quickly. She thanked me for being a good listener. I asked her for a kiss goodbye, just for memory's sake, and she complied. I told her I would be able to say I had been kissed by a very beautiful woman, and that it didn't matter if nothing had happened.

I left her sitting on her bed, probably wondering what was wrong with this young man from Canada who goes to prostitutes only to listen to their stories. I didn't care. I went down the stairs happily, smiled at Madame X, who was waiting by the door. She asked if I'd enjoyed myself, and I told her "immensely", and stepped out into the damp fog of an evening in Paris.

I walked aimlessly for a while, thinking about all she'd said to me, thinking how strange it was that, for all her beauty, I hadn't wanted to touch her. It was a puzzle I couldn't solve, though, and finally I gave it up and headed toward the Moulin Rouge to meet up with the others. It had begun to drizzle, and I passed by an old man with a four day growth of beard who was selling roasted chestnuts. The smell enticed me to buy some. Ahead, I could see a turning neon windmill, informing me I was approaching my destination.

I felt more intimidated by this place than I had back at the whorehouse. I thought I might be turned away from this enclave of the wealthy and aristocratic because I wasn't rich or famous enough, and felt very out of place walking in. No one turned me away, however.

Inside, it was ninety percent older men, ten percent young women who accompanied them. These were men who had made it... and their pets; men with one hundred pound bank notes in their hands... it was a temple of wealth. The smell of money hung in the air. The women laughed when the men did, they drank on cue, ate on cue. The women... all twenty-ish, too young for the diamonds and ballroom gowns they wore, played their parts perfectly. Though everything around them was far beyond their actual stations in life, this was their time in the limelight, false though it was, and they played up to it as much as they could. It was easy to see that these women were nothing more than playthings for the men.

Stepping into the atmosphere of the Moulin Rouge was like entering another world. The decor was lively, full of brass, polished like gold, with gold and red, very plush felt wallpaper everywhere, and a huge stage with coloured lights all along it and a large light hanging overhead. It was like being in a palace, and I felt like acting out a part in *Cabaret* or the Zigfield Follies of the twenties...

The outside world didn't laugh at this place, and only the Berlin of the 20s and 30s had cabarets to compare with this. The setting made me think of books like *The Great Gatsby* and *The Sun Also Rises*... the plush, the decadent, the total disregard for the outside world; you could never begin to count the famous who had passed through these doors.

A six piece band was playing the hits of the time, building up to the ten o'clock show when the Can-Can girls came on. I asked the maitre d' for the table booked by the Jewish Agency guide... Suzanne. This had been agreed upon beforehand. The man looked shocked when I held out an American dollar in his direction. (I later learned it was considered to be quite a lot... 650 francs at the time).

The maitre d' put his hand out for it a little too quick, I thought, and I gave him a dirty look. He was a fiftyish, greying man, probably there a number of years. He seemed very suave, but arrogant. I let him take the dollar anyway, though I immediately regretted it. Giving anything to a person so overtly greedy went against my grain, and it still does. Some people deserve nothing at all... but they always manage to make sure they get more than the next guy, don't they?

It was about nine thirty when I got to our table. Suzanne, Peggy, Bernie, Rodstein... and, surprisingly, Saul... were already there. Suzanne was the first to speak. She seemed to have calmed down since I saw her last.

"Well," she said, "it's certainly nice to have everyone together, isn't it? Now, since you will all be on your way tomorrow, the Jewish Agency wants you to have something to remember us by. We wanted to ensure you saw the real Paris, and this is it... the Moulin Rouge. Like any tourists, you've seen enough of stone walls and towers, so tonight is your sendoff, and the Agency, who considers you to be pioneers and therefore heroes of a sort, is paying for everything. Please feel free to order whatever you like, as often as you like."

Peggy ignored her, and asked me how my evening in the brothel went.

"Well," I said, "it was an experience, and a lesson that couldn't be bought. Someday, I'll tell you all about it." I turned to Bernie, and asked how *his* night had gone.

"It was a great experience!"

"You missed a good time, Rodstein," I said.

"Don't worry, Larry. I'm not going to regret what I didn't want to do in the first place."

"Well, it's too bad, really. You know, you could have played the end of Yom Kippur..."

"How do you mean?"

"You could have gotten your Shofar blown."

"Ten points for you, Larry. You scored a good one this time."

This was from Saul, who was actually smiling. As for Rodstein, his face had turned scarlet, and he was fidgeting.

Suzanne shook her head and said sourly, "They're right about you, Mr. Wiener. You *are* a real son of a bitch, aren't you?! You're full-fledged. But, you're right. He should have gone with you. It was paid for, and wouldn't have hurt. Larry here got your extra hour."

"Extra sextra," I said, making sure I had a large ear-to-ear grin on when I said it.

Bernie filled my glass with champagne from a bottle stuck in a silver bucket filled with ice which meant it was staying about as chilled as Suzanne's heart. He refilled the others' glasses, wanting to play leader again. He raised a toast "to Paris and Suzanne". We all raised our glasses, and I said, "Well, chaverim (friends), I guess we can call this a night to remember. So remember that Paris will be here tomorrow, and we won't be. People have spent a lifetime working just to come here to the Moulin Rouge, and we've done it on the backs of the Jewish Agency.

"We have been swayed and played but like all good times, we'll have to pay for it eventually. If you think this is a free ride, you're mistaken, brothers and sisters. We've had a good time here in Paris... thanks to our tour guide. Alone, we never could have done it, and you know that. Some of us may never come back, but the true person we have to thank is not the Jewish agency or the people who arranged our trip.

"All the credit belongs to our tour guide. Without Suzanne's car, our trip would have been wasted... we wouldn't have known how to get around. We would've been five jerks in Paris, but she made our stay something we'll remember for the rest of our lives. We've seen the real Paris, top to bottom... thanks to her." I smiled in her direction, hoping she'd interpret it as the mean-spirited, low-down, twisted fake smile that it was. I just had to turn her handle one more time... it's just the way I am.

The waiter approached the table then, bringing our dinner orders. They looked more like creations from the cover of *Gourmet Magazine*. It was all very nice, if a bit pretentious.

"More champagne?" he asked.

We responded by draining our glasses dry and nodding our heads like ducks on a shooting range. Well, what the Hell... the famous agency was paying, we weren't.

Suzanne raised her glass, and everyone toasted silently. When we put our glasses back on the table, she started talking.

"You know, group, it has really been a pleasure having you Canadians stay with us for a week. I can't think of a better bunch of people, honestly. When you first arrived, I suppose it hadn't struck me that you are going to a country that is only ten years old. That isn't much, is it? Your chances of getting back home are not very good, after all.

"They'll put you in some God-forsaken place or worse, God-forgotten, and the only people who even will know you're there will be your parents when you write home to Canada. I must admit one thing, and if I don't do this, I will always regret it. Because you are leaving tomorrow, and because I won't be able to live with myself otherwise, I want to apologize for something I did... something that I really had no right to do."

I wondered to myself if this was going to involve sticking pins in a map, and I raised my eyebrows in her direction.

"I think," she said, " I did what I did deliberately... to hurt the person involved. If I did, then I'm sorry, if only because he's honest and hasn't said anything about it to anyone else, and I respect that. Still, he had it coming, and it's true that he's a son of a bitch who received everything he asked for, even a little more. There's not much more I can say than this, but he'll know who he is. I just want him to know that while he deserved what happened, I might have treated him a little better. That's all."

The others were looking around the table at each other, and Peggy was the first to realize Suzanne was talking about yours truly. The others followed her gaze. I could feel my face turning red, and spoke up.

"All right, you've got me. Speaking as a son of a bitch or maybe a voodoo doll, Suzanne, as far as I'm concerned, I'm pinning it up as an experience, sweetie. You know... and I realize the others here don't know what we're talking about, though they can guess... you may never get another chance to pull that crazy stunt again. So, I would like to sincerely thank you for the time we spent together and the pleasure you provided.

"I'm quite sure, if I can speak for the whole group, we will never forget it... or you. From the streets to the whorehouses to the Kingpin of all Paris, the Moulin Rouge... we did it all, and we have nothing to regret. Nothing."

Rodstein tensed, and turned to Suzanne. "I never knew Larry would talk like this to you, I'm sorry we even brought him."

"You had no choice," I told him, "and now you're stuck with me."

Rodstein's fingers were holding his glass so tightly, I was waiting for it to break. Peggy saved the day, however, by putting a hand on his arm and saying, "Well, he certainly hasn't surprised me! I don't know what he did to Suzanne here, but I said he was a son of a bitch right from the beginning, didn't I? And, that's exactly what he is, isn't it? So, you know what, guys? Larry has screwed you all royally.

"He showed you up badly. None of you guys extended any kind of thanks to Suzanne, did you? But Larry did. You didn't even scrape together enough for a ten dollar gift. Think about what she's done for us, though... she was always right on time for everything on our agenda. When we needed cabs, she had them waiting. She helped order our food for us, and made sure we weren't treated as regular tourists. No one stole from us... thanks to Suzanne.

"You know, she could have given us a real snowjob if she'd wanted. She could have taken us to places and left us on our own, or given us ten minute tours of everything or allowed us to be taken advantage of... but she didn't. She looked after us like our mothers would have... God bless them, wherever they are! You just think! If I can be as crude as Larry, I'll say it... instead of snowjobs, she got you blowjobs, didn't she? Well? And for all of this, you couldn't even pick her up a little thank you gift. You guys are the living end, believe me! The cheap Jew legend will always survive as long as there are people like you around, believe me!"

At this point, I thought she was going to burst into tears, as she was really getting herself worked up. Everyone was sort of looking away, pretending she wasn't really including them in the "you guys" stuff, but she meant it all right, and just to prove it, she pulled out an envelope she'd had buried in her purse.

"So," she said, "let's see if you're as big hearted as you think you are. C'mon, dig into your pockets RIGHT NOW, and show that you're human beings after all."

"There's nothing to lose by being true Jews, eh?" I said as I passed the envelope over to Saul, whose conscience was first to be pricked. He'd had his wallet out before Peggy was done talking. He handed her an American twenty dollar bill.

"I don't need an envelope," he said. "Suzanne did very well by me. If it wasn't for her, I never would have seen the Jewish side of Paris. I never would have found a synagogue on my own, I know that. So, thank you, Suzanne, thank you. And you're right... I may never come back from Israel. So, please take this... I want to give it to you. It's yours, so spend it any way you like, and thank you for setting me free, and for telling me where to go, and... for everything else you've done for the group, too. I think you've helped them."

Rodstein and Bettle handed over a ten and a twenty, respectively; then all eyes, of course, were back on me. 'So, what are you going to give her, Larry?"

Suzanne didn't let me speak.

You know," she said, "I don't want to tell you what Larry gave me, because I don't think it's right I do. It's too personal, and just between the two of us. I would like to thank Peggy, though, for suggesting it. I'm just sorry that Paris did not really work out for her. I hope Israel does, I truly do.

"And now, group, remember... tomorrow I will meet you at eight o'clock in the morning and take you to the train station and see you off. From that point on, you'll be completely on your own. The agency in Italy will not take care of you the way we did. To them, you'll be nothing but so many lost waifs."

I was sure she could have gone on for some time about how wonderful she had been to us, pins and maps notwithstanding, but just then the lights began to grow dim and the MC's voice came across the PA system: "Messieurs 'Dames! Bienvenus au Moulin Rouge! The place the whole world comes to Paris to see! The show is about to begin, and you will see the most beautiful girls in the world dance for you the Cancan!"

Or some such rot...

I wasn't really impressed, as I was still a little pissed off with Suzanne for pointing me out the way she did. For a classy lady from a first-rate agency, the more she talked, the less I was impressed. But, the stagelights came on, making bright pools on the darkened theatre floor, the chatter of the crowd hushed, men with diamond stickpins lit up fat cigars, while hired girls rubbed their backs and picked their pockets. Or so I was beginning to assume. I pictured a roomful of men with their heads swollen like balloons, and all these painted up ladies of the night running around gleefully stabbing the air with their hatpins. I guess you could say I was becoming a little world-weary, despite the flash of it all.

The band struck up a Cancan song, twenty or so girls lined up on stage, filing in from both sides, and the place went up like a volcano with clapping, cheering, whistling while some of the more energetic (or stupid) men tossed money at their feet like so much confetti.

Suzanne's voice rose up above the din. "This is the real Paris! You know, this place hasn't changed since its inception in the gay nineties, and if you can afford an evening here, you aren't among the poor. I'm sure you'll remember it. Now, after the floor show, remember we'll have to leave and go back to the hotel to get ready for tomorrow morning. But, I must say this... I'll miss you all, every one of you... from the son of a bitch to the Russian General, and Mister Bettle and his Gestapo... you do run a tight ship, you know. And Saul, well, what is there to say? Everyone loves Saul! Peggy? I only wish you had a better time...

"But remember that human beings are like wild horses... if you let them run until they're tired, they will stop running. They will follow you that way. Just remember the old wisdom of your grandmother... you can lead a horse to water, but you can't force him to take a drink."

I was beginning to wonder how much champagne she'd had. Her advice didn't make much sense to me. If you drive a human being far enough, he's more likely to turn on you, and his following days will be over. I tried not to listen, to concentrate on the girls on the stage instead, but Peggy joined in with her high, squeaky voice, and I had to listen.

"So? He's lost the reigns already. Saul has his religion and Rodstein here is a paper Communist. Bernie thinks he's a big shot because he recruited us, and Larry's untouchable, like a leper. Bernie can't control any of us."

"Well, I will bet you that in the end," Suzanne said, "the son of a bitch beats you all. He'll take on the dirtiest job, and I don't mean the latrines, just to show you all that he can do it. I think that is what he is like."

"No," Rodstein said, "Larry's too lazy. He'd never take a job where he might get himself hurt. He's too careful for that... Larry, remember, loves nobody but Larry! He'll probably try to get a gardening job, something safe and secure, like in Mommy's arms."

I didn't even have to defend my good name... Bettle did it for me. "Now, wait a minute, Rodstein... you're stepping over the line here, and you'd better watch what you say. Not that I want to protect Larry, but because I want to protect you, so you can make the train tomorrow, at least to Italy. So leave it alone."

"That's right," Saul said. "You really have no right at all to say anything bad about Larry. He isn't knocking you. You're always berating him because he's the youngest in the group. Well, since I'm the oldest, I could have a few words to say, too, if I wanted."

"So go ahead," Rodstein challenged.

"If I did, you wouldn't like them."

"So, like I said... go right ahead. I don't care."

Saul gave Rodstein his best sad-eyed smile. "That's the thing, you *don't* care, so I wouldn't be so uppity, Mr. Rodstein. For a fellow who's come all the way from Toronto, Canada, now sitting here in the Moulin Rouge to be telling us what to do and how to do it, is, well... You know, you talk as if Larry is some kind of a disease that shouldn't be with us, a bubonic plague or something. But, I'll tell you what... you're the real plague among us. You should've stayed home. You sit there reading your books on Communism, dreaming that you're going to be another Lenin or Trotsky, the next revolutionary hero.

"I don't think so. I know you don't think much of me, but you were only three steps away from that whorehouse yourself, but did you have the guts to go in? Oh, no! A lot of talk about nothing, that's what fills your mouth, sir. I may talk about going to synagogues... but the difference is, I go. A person shouldn't say anything if they can't live up to what they say. The boys chipped in so you'd have something, at least, to write home about, maybe even to make you a man. I may not agree with the means, but I think if you say something, you should do it.

"Those books you read will never make anything out of you, except a slave. Those people killed nobody knows how many million people. The survivors eat black bread and borscht, but not you. No, you sit here drinking free champagne, eating the finest of foods. So what sort of a Communist are you, anyway? What place is there in Israel for someone like that? Are you dreaming of being the next David Ben Gurion or what? Because you'll never be that."

Our resident prophet paused for breath, and Bettle spoke up. "The rabbi's right, Rodstein. Israel isn't looking for fanatics who will try to impose a doctrine on their country. I'm sure they've got their own ideas. If you want to play Stalin, maybe you're going to the wrong country... you should try Russia instead. Israel is a country for people who can work and build."

"I'm sorry. I never should have spoken up," said Saul, "I went a little bit over the line maybe. But, I can't stand your arguing all the time over nothing. Manmade theories never work, that's a proven fact, if you know the history of your own people."

"You're right," Suzanne said, "new nations need workers, not dreamers. Reading all those books will never make anyone a hero. In fact, if you like, I can take you to a field where there are plenty of heroes, where the poppies grow, row on row."

"They're all dead," Rodstein said. That boy really had a habit of putting his foot into his mouth.

"Of course they're dead," Suzanne countered. "All the heroes are dead. Why don't you just take each day as it comes and leave it at that? The job they'll ask you to do will be as important as the President's. Every effort will count, you know. It isn't the job they ask you to do, it's the being a part of the whole. Every day that

Israel survives means that there will be a place for homeless Jews from around the world. That's what you're building... a refuge, a homeland, a place for people to go. That's what you'll be fighting for. Whether or not you personally live or die isn't important. Trying, that's what matters."

"Well put," Bettle nodded.

I was surprised at this outburst from Suzanne, and couldn't help wondering if there'd been a pin stuck somewhere in the middle of the Sinai Desert.

"Well," said Peggy, "I'll tell you one thing. This is a great show and you guys will hate yourselves when you wake up in the morning and realize you missed it."

It was time for me to jump in. I liked listening to them argue among themselves... it saved me the trouble.

"There's nothing like this anywhere on earth. Paris is my kind of city. It's everything I dreamed of, and I doubt I could ever earn the time I've spent here, or repay those who gave it to me, son of a bitch or not." I smiled in Suzanne's direction.

"You know, just to think of Paris when you're over there working on the kibbutz will make the time go faster."

"Life is not all that you want," said the rabbi in his wisdom. "Sometimes things go bad or turn sour as they say, but we all must make do with the time that we have allotted to us. As of now, I consider this to be a fantastic trip, one that I certainly never would have been able to afford on my own."

"And there's not much more," said Suzanne, "to add to that, is there? L'amour à Paris!"

As the lights dimmed, the curtain came down and someone said, "We'd better be going."

"It was a great finale," I said to Suzanne, "and if I had to do it over again, I'd live it exactly the same. I wouldn't change a thing... almost." I winked, and leaned toward her, and in the darkness provided by the newly fallen curtain, did what I'd been longing to do all evening: I kissed her goodbye, and gave her tit a squeeze, too. No-one could see us. She didn't say a word.

Then, it was over. The lights came up and we left the building, climbed into Suzanne's car, and she drove us back to the hotel. She didn't speak all the way back. I caught her reflection in the mirror, though, and she had a funny little half-smile on her lips. Maybe she wasn't as bad as I'd thought. Maybe, to her, it was all just a sad game, sleeping with people you'd never be with again.

By the time she let us out, everyone was yawning.

"So, I'll meet you at eight a.m., in the lobby," she told us, not looking at me. "It's over, and there are lots of ways to say goodbye, but I know none of them. We don't really say goodbye in Paris, we say "L'amour à Paris' instead."

Peggy went straight to her room, as did Saul. The rest of us decided to go out for a drink before retiring, and we did. On the way back to the hotel, Bettle, who was walking slightly behind us, was suddenly jumped by three street thugs and dragged into a laneway, presumably to be robbed… the predators were young men, all looking to be under fifteen years old, who targeted tourists. They were carrying knives. At Bettle's yelp of surprise, the rest of us turned around and I leaped into the fray without thinking of possible consequences. One of the kids grabbed me, but he was thin and not very strong, so I was able to shove him off fairly easily.

The one that had hold of Bettle, however, had him by the neck and Bernie's face was beginning to turn red. I was about to go behind them to pry the kid off, when Bernie twisted free, turned and lifted the boy up off the ground with his bare hands, both wrapped gripping tightly beneath the kid's chin. Bernie was only five foot eight, but chunky… he looked fat, but there was a lot of unused muscle there, too. He pushed the kid hard up against a building and held him there, kneeing him and shouting, "You little bastard, I should kill you right now!"

And, he did. When he finally let go, the boy crumpled to the alleyway like a sack of wet potatoes, dead of either strangulation or a broken neck. In the darkness, it was hard to tell if Bernie had known his big hands had cut off the air supply. He didn't care, either. The only comment he made about this incident was, "Maybe this is why we're here… to get rid of scum like this."

We got the Hell out of there, fast, following the example of the other two teenagers, who had fled when they realized Bernie wasn't alone. What else was there to do? Report it to the police?

Not when we were leaving the next morning. Our trip to Israel would be delayed, and well, who needed the trouble? The kid was dead, and nothing anyone could say was going to bring him back. Besides, it was done in self-defence, and how were we supposed to prove that?

So, tomorrow morning came and everyone gathered in the lobby, excited about getting onto the train we'd be taking to Italy. Peggy was the first to speak.

"So, another Bon Voyage. I've studied a little about Italy, you know, though not a lot. Enough, though, to get me by. It should be an exciting part of our trip."

Bettle smiled sourly, "I hope it'll be as exciting as our stay in Gay Paree."

"Paris to me was a flop, like wet crackers. I didn't get anything out of the tour except a bit of sightseeing. Paris? It's for men."

"Well," Rodstein said, "you know who got the best out of Paris? Larry did. He got Suzanne, he got a double shot with a prostitute, he got it all. The rest of us didn't have such a great time here either, Peggy. I want you to know that. But, you know why Larry got all the goodies? Because he's the youngest, and doesn't have any sense."

No matter what he said about me, he had to add something of his own. If I'd saved them all from drowning, he'd say it was simply because I liked swimming. Christ, couldn't he say anything positive at all? I didn't think he'd be smart enough to pick up on my having slept with Suzanne, though. Maybe it was just a guess on his part, so I just grinned in response and he turned to Peggy.

"At least, though, the rest of us can say we were here, Peggy. It wasn't so bad, everything considered."

"Well, I'm not going to worry about it. Italy's a man's country, too. If I find one there, you won't see me for dust until the boat leaves. I'm not coming out of this trip with nothing, you know. Here in Paris, our guide was best at looking after men, I think, and where did that leave me? Holding the wrong end of the stick, that's where. But in Italy, who knows? It's a country ruled by men, not by prostitutes."

Ouch.

"But all I have to say is that they don't exactly make whorehouses that cater to ladies." Peggy's face began to redden as she saw our eyebrows raise a little. It was hard to imagine our little Winnipeg girl in heat, and she knew it. "Well," she added, giggling, "I got stuck walking around with a guide who acted like a nun… see none, get none."

Bernie, whose killing of the boy hadn't affected him at all, piped up, "Men are the same everywhere, Peggy. They never change a bit. If you would have actually looked, you would have found someone in a nightclub or somewhere. You're a tourist, you're not broke, you're… attractive. Don't put all the blame on Suzanne. There are a million Jewish men in France, isn't that enough? Stop bad-mouthing Paris, when you're the one who didn't go out there to get your share of it."

"That's right," Rodstein said. "I wanted to see Paris, and so I saw it. Nobody stopped me from doing what I liked. Even Saul went off on his own, to commune with the prophets. You talk like you were in a prison, Peggy, but you had your chance. Don't blame the French. If you'd found a guy and spent a night with him out on your own, well, so what? It's your life. But you didn't… you didn't even try. It's not such a big deal already. But I don't want to hear the same thing from you when we're done with Italy, please. If you complain then, what are you going to do, ask for your money back? Christ!"

Go, Roddy, go. He always had to try to get the last word in, and it always had to be a dig of some kind. The master speaketh…

Peggy gave him a downturned thumb. "Up yours," she said.

This was a cause of inspiration to Bernie, who'd been off to one side watching her. He stepped in front of her, grinned like a lovesick bull, and stuck two fingers in front of her face. "Hey Peggy, how about if I…?"

I thought she was going to deck him on the spot. Instead, she muttered something beneath her breath and stomped away, headed for the other side of the lobby.

Just then, Suzanne reappeared from outside. "You have a train to catch in an hour," she said. "We'd better be going."

We piled into her little Citroen and took our final look at the Champs-Elysées… and the City of Love. It was a ten minute drive to the station, going along the West Bank of the Seine. The artists were out in full profusion on the street, painting up a storm for the tourists. Couples were cuddling on the benches, and I was missing the place already.

"I, for one, am truly sorry I have to leave," I said to no one in particular. "Look at this place… it's beautiful. I'll never forget the sights and sounds of Paris, that's for sure."

No one answered. My remark hung in the air like smoke. Well, to each his own, and the Hell with them anyway.

As we were approaching the train station, Suzanne handed us our tickets. "I'll take you right to the platform and see you off. Then I have a new group to meet."

"It's really been a pleasure," I said. "You taught us something we'll never forget, and you showed us the real Paris. I learned a lesson, too… never be a pin on anyone's map." I could see her face in the mirror, her cold straight-ahead look saying, "Fuck you, Larry. Fuck you."

Her mouth, though, said something else. "My only regret is that Peggy didn't have such a good time."

She handed back an envelope to Saul. "Open it," she said.

He did, and found the release form she had never handed in to the agency.

"Why are you giving me this?" he asked.

"Call it a souvenir, Saul. If I had turned it in to the agency, it would have been a black mark against me for not being able to control the group. So, I just never gave it to them. It worked out anyway, didn't it? You got to see your holy sites and the Jewish side of the city. You're happy, and I'm happy."

I was willing to bet they'd both like to be a whole lot happier, but I said nothing. We got to the station at about 8:30, Suzanne walked us to our platform, and said a final goodbye by kissing everyone on the cheek. When it was my turn, she bit me, lightly. "You're still a son of a bitch, you know, but I enjoyed it."

Then she walked away, turned once, said "Au revoir", and that was the end of her.

Italy

The platform was crowded with people, all waiting to board a beautiful old train that made me think of the battered elegance of the "Orient Express", except that it was electrically powered... something America hadn't seen yet. We were supposed to get into Switzerland by four p.m. where we would stay for twenty-four hours, doing what, no one knew.

The train trip was essentially pretty boring, except for the view from the window. At our destination, we unloaded and checked into our hotel, an Old World affair built in the "gay nineties". It was much too old to be its former self... a rich man's playground, and was now turned into affordable middle class vacation lodgings. After getting settled, we found a restaurant that served up good food at good prices, and then decided to take a look around.

The Swiss we saw out walking were very friendly for the most part, and the legendary "Swiss rich" were unseen. It wasn't too hard to spot the tourists... aside from their dress, which was quite different from that of the locals, everyone from out of the country had their heads thrown back, gazing in amazement at the huge mountaintops looming around us everywhere.

We were tired from our trip, and decided to forsake whatever nightlife Switzerland had to offer, and so we all retired early. In the morning, we'd be heading out again. Our train left at 9:30.

It wasn't much of a train. There was no seating arrangement... first come, first served. There was an air of something chaotic about being on it, like we'd stepped into a cheap grade B movie with nobody special as the star. The inside smelled like a garlic factory.

The train contained the young, the old, the fat, the thin, the primitive... mothers nursing squealing babies, workmen returning to their families after an unsuccessful job hunt, transient young men... rapid-fire yapping and shouting in Italian, which sounded like so much loud babble to me, ignorant young Canadian that I was. *Journey with the Uncouth*, I dubbed the imaginary film. It was a pretty sad, rough-hewn crew, all in all. Maybe the sub-title could have been *In the Sweat and the Heat*.

The trip seemed never-ending a the train lurched its way along... talk about Rock 'n Roll! Bang! Crash! Luggage fell from above us. A bleak-eyed young man threw up behind me, by the door. Our group was scattered throughout the train and the only one I could see was Rodstein, seemingly oblivious to it all, reading one of his books. Oh, it was a fun ride, I'll tell you!

Actually, if not for the passengers and the way they carried on, the train would have been pretty clean, I think... but what an atmosphere! Italy was supposed to be the land of art, wasn't it? At that point, you certainly could've fooled me. The train belched out bellows of greasy, dark smoke, which flew past the windows with a vengeance. There was no running water in the washroom, and the lineup to get in there, anyway, was always six or seven deep. When I finally got in there, what a mess! The floor was drenched, the walls were filthy, and someone kept banging on the door to get in. It just went on and on.

Travelling through Italy, I was constantly reminded of the war... we passed places bombed by the Allies, still not rebuilt or restored... even the rubble remained to serve as gravestones, maybe... reminders of what can happen anywhere, anytime. Rather nasty memorabilia, but there it was in all its horror, popping by like lamp posts through the window.

Peasants in the fields would wave at the train they might never board. The tumbledown farmhouses, the conductor told me, were built in the 1700s, and the churches were from the 1600s and earlier. Later on, we moved into the lush vineyard country, wine-making being the ancient trade of Italy. I couldn't help being impressed by some of the old world elegance, mixed as it was with the devastation of war... welcome to the twentieth century!

"Nexta stoppa Roma!" bellowed the conductor and sure enough, the sight of modern suburbs of a city built on money was coming into view, with all its fifties' shoebox architecture, little pock-marked office buildings which were all in the Bauhaus style, which meant (to me) they were simply plain, nothing-shape erections.

Our group had been split up during the train ride, and I hadn't spoken a word the entire trip, except briefly to the conductor. I'd just sat there, fascinated by the people and the strangeness of the landscape we were travelling through. After a while, I began to realize I was the strange one... I was the foreigner, the alien who didn't speak or understand the language, the one who was out of place.

Arriving at the train station and being met by the Italian Jewish Agency was something else... the term is "gurnish" in Yiddish, which means "nothing". We were herded to a waterfront train station and given 9000 lire each (about $10). The station had a beautiful old clock, twelve feet wide with bronze animals surrounding its face, a Swiss mechanism. Everything danced whenever the hour was struck... an intriguing affair indeed, and much more impressive than the rundown hotel we were put up in for the night.

Next morning, the train left early, travelling through a countryside that offered little to whet the imagination of the tourist. The only time I spoke on that journey was to a young American university student who was spending his summer in Italy at his family's expense. He was an Italian New Yorker (Little Italy type) and possibly the most boring person I've ever met It was a three to four hour trip, uneventful and bland. I was glad to lose him as the train pulled into Genoa, where a guide waited for us on the platform, holding up a sign "JEWISH AGENCY". Like, let's tell the world we're the suckers are here.

The group formed a circle around our new guide who had a list of our names and was calling them out one by one to ensure everyone was present. He was a suave young man, an Italian Jew with an interesting accent and full of professional courtesy. However, he turned out to not be of much help to us. He took Bernie, our designated leader, aside and gave him an envelope for each of us containing enough Italian lire to feed us for three days and give us a day tour. He told Bernie he would take us to our hotel and then we'd be on our own.

"Well, what about a guide to show us around?" Bernie asked.

"But that has not been paid for. You must take the tour bus."

"Welcome to the land of Il Duce, everyone!" Bernie shouted, obviously expecting that someone of his importance should get the keys to the city and a grand tour.

The guide frowned. "That-a no way to talka 'bout Roma," he said, then proceeded to take us silently to our hotel. He brought three keys from the desk after checking us in, explaining to the clerk, "these people have already been paid for by the Jewish Agency." The way he said it made me wonder if he thought we were Arabs in disguise. Bernie's blurting out his expectations hadn't helped to enhance the guide's perception of foreign Jews. Neither did Rodstein, who mumbled, "Arrividerci, fongula-la" behind the guide's back, causing him to turn around to see who'd said something derogatory. We all just grinned in return.

The hotel, called the St. George, was a real dump... a flophouse with an air of New York East Side seediness hanging over it. The guide explained that it was no great shakes. He also warned us of what we might encounter, once we got to our final destination. He knew there was trouble brewing in the Middle East, he said. He'd been educated in New York and was halfway through a political science degree back in the States, and well aware of what was happening in Israel.

He said there were a lot of problems in the Mediterranean. He kept saying, "You'll see, you'll see. You'll remember what I told you!" He said he wanted us to be prepared for a possible delay or some other aggravation, but wouldn't be specific about it. Well, we'd deal with that when we came to it. Meanwhile, here we were, stuck in the beautiful St. George Hotel, which had once probably been quite the place to be... but not any more.

It's glory days ended, it was still the kind of old world place sought out by the knowledgeable traveller who looked for the best of what a culture had to offer, rather than staying in some Americanized, sanitized, overpriced, vertical shoebox. The St. George was affordable but elegant in its way, a charmingly run-down version of its former greatness.

We were left in the lobby with our three keys and our baggage.

Bernie asked what we were going to do next. I suddenly realized he was afraid to be on his own, that he expected a guide everywhere he went. His image of "leader" dropped to the floor with a crash when he said that, the expression on his face telling all.

"Don't worry," Peggy laughed, "Mommy's here. You'll see Rome tomorrow. I haven't told you any of you before, but I can speak enough Italian to get around easily."

I liked the St. George, despite its grunginess, but I knew why we'd been booked there… it was cheap, and we were young, and the bottom of the line shouldn't matter to us. Also, we'd been told we'd be there three days, and, unlike when we'd been in Paris, there was no prearranged tour programme at all. The only other thing besides the hotel keys we'd been given… was the name of the boat we were to board at 7 a.m. in the morning… the *Gramani*.

After telling us quite frankly to expect a rough voyage on "an old utility tub", our suave young Yankee "guide" made his exit.

I didn't feel like going out that night, not by myself. Unlike Peggy, I didn't know enough of the language to say "Hello, where's the local wine shop?" So, I simply took a walk around the block, in search of a good, cheap dinner of spaghetti and meat balls, which was about all I knew to ask for. When in Rome, eat as the Romans was my philosophy. I just couldn't get excited about the place.

It wasn't the place, though… it was me. As the others went out on the city that night (without inviting me to go along), I realized again how utterly alone I was on this trip, and began to get home-sick. I hadn't had a good homecooked meal, it seemed, in weeks. I wouldn't have one for nearly a year to come, either, though I didn't know it at the time. My Mother and anyone else who cared about me had been left behind. I'd shafted Martha and wouldn't be able to go back to her. The year ahead looked dismal from that point of view… it would be spent with people who didn't give a shit about me, who resented my being there to start with, because I didn't share their "sense of mission". I'd conned my way into the trip, and now I realized it might have been a mistake… a lonely mistake.

In the midst of all this melancholy, I wrote home to Mother, telling her I was having a wonderful time, that everything was great, we'd reached Rome and were enjoying it. I ended the note

with the old adage, "When in Rome, do as the Romans do"… but
neglected to tell her that one of the things I noticed about the
Romans was, they despaired a lot. I didn't want her to think her little boy was having a bad time. Besides, I figured, my feelings were
probably only temporary.

I wrote the same cheerful lies to my brother David, to Bubby
(Granny) Wiener and Buddy Altman. It warmed me to know that
people who did care about me would soon have my letters and
would tell one another I was halfway to Israel and still safe and
happy. I decided not to worry them with my darker feelings. Eased
by the release of writing, I soon fell asleep.

At eight the next morning, we all met in the hotel dining room,
where Peggy announced she had good news for us."Okay, fellas, I
did what I had to do. I promised you'd see Rome, and you will. You
owe me 150 lire each, so hand it over."

"What did you get us?" Rodstein asked.

"Don't be a schmuck," she said, "we're not even going to have
to walk. You'll see when you get there. You'll get your precious
money's worth. You're in Rome… you're going to see Rome. You'll
be able to throw your three coins into the fountain… that is, if
you're not too cheap… the money goes to help the needy, you
know… and I'm told there's plenty of them around!"

Saul, of course, wanted to know about the synagogues.

"You don't need a synagogue," I told him, winking. "You can
pray at the Vatican." He immediately got his hackles up.

"What's the matter with you, Larry? Are you a non-believer?
Aren't you Jewish? What do you mean, at the Vatican?"

"Good grief, Saul, give it up already. It's not what's the matter
with me… how about you? Isn't the Pope high enough for you?
Jews don't have a Pope… all we've got is Moses and a bunch of
funny hats. The pope is God's representative, the Vatican is a high
and holy place. How you behave there will reflect on you later on."

I had no idea what I was telling him, or why. I just liked
getting his goat… someone had to get it, or it might run start
running wild.

Peggy intervened at this point, informing us there was no need
to argue, and that a bus would pick us up at 9:30.

"So, because we don't have a whole lot of time here, we should enjoy the day tour... it's all I was able to arrange."

We finished breakfast and got ourselves ready to meet the bus. We were going to see Venice. We went, but it wasn't really much of a trip... we saw a wedding and a funeral, almost at the same time, both on the water. Somehow, the place didn't excite us. Too much water, maybe, and nowhere much to walk. It's not a fair judgement, though, because, after all, it was a "tour", and like most tours, probably missed all the really interesting spots.

Back in Rome, things were more exciting... Bettle and I got into a rip-roaring argument which led to him saying (for the hundredth time?) that I should pack up my stuff and go home. He yelled about how my Mother had gotten me on the trip to start with, and that if I had any sense I'd call it a day and phone her and say her little boy missed her and could he come home please. He was unrelenting, and I told him to stop before he got me going... I was ready to sock him. "I'll give you a free ride," I said, indicating he'd land right in the gutter if he kept it up. He backed off a bit then, because neither of us wanted to fight and Peggy got into the middle of it and started calming us down.

I agreed with one thing, which infuriated them both... I was getting a free ride out of it, and I didn't have the same ideas and ideals or whatever naiveté it was they thought they had that qualified them for the trip but not me. They didn't like my saying that, because of course it made them question their own reasons for going... something none of them liked looking at, I figured. But after a while, everyone shut up and we drifted off in different directions to cool down. Bettle and I came very close that day to being physical with one another.

From Rome we returned to Genoa, where nothing much happened. We gawked at the tourists, who gawked back at us, and we strolled the ancient streets for a while. We were supposed to head off for the boat which would take us across the Mediterranean to the Promised Land, but we were told the trip had been delayed due to fighting breaking out between Egypt and Israel, and we'd have to wait at least three days before it was considered safe to sail. (How they figured that out, no one knows... maybe they had a seer on board).

The representative from the Jewish Agency gave us this news, and to me it came as a sort of warning of what to expect in the days ahead. Rodstein queried the man about it.

"Well, you see," the agent said, smiling sadly, "it is for safety reasons, and that is all I am able to tell you. We are willing to help with your additional stay in Italy, as this is an unavoidable hazard in these times. So, we'll pay for a two-day trip to Florence, if you'd like to go there."

"What are we supposed to do when we get there?" Bernie wanted to know. "Study art?"

The representative looked Bernie up and down and, probably wondering why he had to deal with schmucks like us, said in a sweet voice: "Don't worry about that. You haven't seen all of Italy yet. You'll be grateful to us later, I am sure. However, if you prefer to sit here for three days doing nothing, well... that can also be arranged. It is up to you. What would you like?"

No one said a word.

"Fine," he continued. "We will pick you up at 6 a.m. at the train station. Here are some stickers. Please put them on your clothing, and when you arrive in Florence, our representative will be able to find you easily. She will be holding a sign that will read 'JEWISH AGENCY'. Is that all right with everyone?"

It was. The stickers, by the way, simply read 'JA'. Saul noted that if there had been an H. at the end of it, we'd be better looked after, because they'd realize we were on a religious mission. His head really was up in the clouds. We were, with the exception of Saul himself, perhaps the most irreligious bunch of young people the Jewish Agency had ever dealt with. It was at about this point I began calling Saul "Reb", a common term for "rabbi", stating that if he was the "Reb" of the group, I must be the "rebel". Nobody laughed, mainly because it was the truth. Only Saul seemed to get the joke, because he smiled and said, "Larry, you shouldn't make light of the truth, because one day the truth might make light of you."

The representative bid us "Arrividerci", saying he'd see us in the morning. He left us with a word we would hear often once we got to Israel... "Shalom".

Peggy grinned at us with a Cheshire Cat look, "I just can't

believe this is happening. In a hundred years a chance like this comes along. You maybe see it in the movies, or read it in a book. I've taught about Florence in school, to my kids, but I never dreamed I'd be actually going there to see it for myself!

"Well... life is stranger than fiction, isn't it? So, look at it this way: two weeks ago, we were on a hachsharah in New Jersey picking eggs and apples, and now we've seen half of France, half of Italy and now we're on a trip to Florence. I hope it will be as exciting as you seem to think."

Bernie started talking about how we were almost at our destination, how none of really believed it possible in the beginning, how reality has a way of coming around every once in a while for a visit, and God knows when he would've stopped, or how he even got started, but finally Peggy shut him up by saying we should all go back to our rooms and get to bed early, be up at five a.m., be ready to meet the agent at six at the train station and how everyone should have pleasant dreams about the morrow... or some such stuff. Anyway, it stopped Bernie's babbling, and we did as she suggested, and in the morning the hotel staff woke us up as prearranged and off we went.

The representative met us at the train station, a cheroot stuck in his mouth, which made him look a bit like Doc Holliday... all he needed was a medicine bag and a gun. He wore a large black hat, which, although Jewish by design and make, could easily have been flattened out to create the American western look. I wanted to ask him where his horse was, but it was too early in the day to ask silly questions. Besides, the train left at 6:30 and we had to get our baggage checked and so forth.

We went with the agent to the ticket wicket where he handed in an envelope and had a brief exchange in Italian, and were given in return a package that contained our passes. This done, he then led us to the Florence track and put us on board, wishing us a good trip. I imagine he was glad to see us go... we weren't the friendliest group he'd ever dealt with, I was sure of that.

On board, the seats were arranged so that one of us would have to sit apart from the others, and I jumped at the opportunity... anything to avoid my reluctant companions! A girl of about seventeen or eighteen sat down beside me. She was wearing what looked like a school uniform, and she filled it very well. Of course, I was delighted at my good fortune. This beat arguing with Bernie any day.

Once the train got going, I introduced myself to her and she asked, in broken English, if I was from America. "No," I told her, "I'm from Canada"... whereupon she shrugged, unimpressed, as if to say she'd never heard of the place.

"I'm on my way to Israel," I said, determined to strike up a conversation. She shrugged again, looking puzzled. "America?" she asked again. After a while I gave up trying to talk to her and concentrated on falling asleep.

I might as well have slept all through our tour of Florence, too, although I must say some of the art we saw was world famous. Peggy was delighted, acting as if she'd landed in Heaven... She "Oohed" and "Aahed" her way through, like a kid at a circus. Most of our time there we spent arguing. If you could speed up time and watch the years pass, eroding the statues of Florence, our group still would have been falling apart faster!

The art galleries and museums were impressive on their own, I suppose, but we were so busy cutting each other up, the guide must have thought our tour would end in a multiple murder. Even Saul got in on it here and there, whenever our cursing touched a religious nerve.

There seemed to be no apparent reason for Peggy's behaviour... she was part of the arguing, too, but it didn't seem to affect her. Maybe she was trying to save face or something as she really had been hot on the idea. Maybe she tricked herself into thinking she was seeing "the real Italy", with or without the rest of us. It was intriguing, trying to fathom her thinking, and somehow she reminded me of that schoolgirl... her mind was made up and that was that. Of course, I might have been a little prejudiced, because at the time, my idea of good artwork was a *Playboy* centerfold.

After a couple of uneventful, and (to me) boring days in Florence, we left that fabled place and were shuffled off back to Genoa. Four days after we left Florence, there was an earthquake there, causing Reb Saul to explain how God was leading us away from disaster. That made me wonder if it wasn't the other way around... not God, maybe... but something seemed hell-bent on leading us *into*... not out of disaster!

The next day, our last day at the hotel... we woke up early, everyone filled with excitement because it would be our final day in Europe. All we had to do was get breakfast, gather up our belongings and set off to meet our Jewish guide who was to get us to the boat going to Israel. Looking back, the European part of our journey was fantastic in many ways, though we argued all through it.

Not knowing what this last day would entail, we gathered in the St. George Hotel lobby and went off together to the dining room. It was nice to think someone else was paying for all of this, and the thought seemed to make me hungrier than usual, so I ordered the best the place had to offer, while the others gawked at me and mumbled to themselves, something about me being an "ungrateful wretch"... and worse! I couldn't have agreed more, and made sure they watched my every gleeful bite, just to rub it in a bit. If these people were dumb enough to send a jerk like me on a year's trip, I was going to make the best of it. Besides, I had no idea what was in store for us once we reached our destination. For all I knew, life on the kibbutz might mean a steady diet of grasshoppers and honey!

Being just a teenager still, I was in a constant state of wonder at the good fortune I'd had to even get to go on the trip. My family was well respected, and here I was, pulling off a trick like this, everyone knew what I was up to, or had their suspicions, and there was nothing anyone could do about it. So many people don't even come close to having an opportunity like I had, and while it may seem to the reader that I didn't appreciate it, let me assure you I most certainly did, in many ways. I just didn't believe in the cause, in the reason we were being sent there to start with.

Meanwhile, the rest of the group, by this time, had settled into getting themselves mentally ready for Israel. They were really excited. In the dining room, Saul was poring over his holy books, Peggy was talking enthusiastically about how soon we'd be serving the Motherland, and in the midst of this Irving (as usual, as he had never liked me from the beginning) took it upon himself to announce yet again how he couldn't figure out why I'd been able to last as long as I had.

"You should've jumped ship in France," he said, and plowed into a repeat of everything else he'd ever said about me. I ignored him, which made him angrier than ever, and kept on piling food into my mouth, grinning at the thought of his mounting frustration. I wasn't about to let him bother me too much... to Hell with him, anyway.

After breakfast, we went off to meet with our Jewish Agency man who would be taking us out to the boat that would get us across the Mediterranean... which is just as beautiful, by the way, as it was advertised to be. The Agency, maybe wanting to make sure we left the country, sent two people out to meet us instead of the usual one. The new one was interested in the idea of our going to the Holy Land. The fact that we were the first contingency group headed for Israel to work in the fields really seemed to appeal to him, though he never explained why.

He told us we would be leaving at 8 p.m. that evening on board the *Gramani*. We'd been told already not to expect too much... this would be no *Queen Mary*... so, we were all a bit anxious to see it. He informed us we might be surprised, and again, didn't explain why. He then said that as we had to vacate the hotel rooms that morning, we might as well finish packing up. We could leave our bags in the lobby where they would be safe, and then go walking around Genoa for the last time. It would give us, he said, a chance to absorb more of the Italian atmosphere, and we could think about the time we'd spent in Rome, Napoli, Venice and Nice. Why he thought this would be of any benefit, none of us knew, but possibly he was aware of our differences and figured to try to get our minds off each other for a time.

We knew he was probably right, though, as this would be a lifetime memory, and something we could tell our grandchildren about in our declining years... if we ever had them. I thought, yeah, well, let them go ahead and soak up the atmosphere, maybe it'll do them some good after all... and left them, going off in my own direction. I decided to take a walk by myself, and see the beautiful if quaint little stores on the hilly streets and get a final look at Italy without having to listen to snide remarks from my so-called compatriots.

It was something else, this place... there was music everywhere, coming from old men with organ grinders. They had it down pat, though I wondered where the monkeys were. So, there I was for a time, wandering among the locals, in a little cosmos all my own, watching people who didn't seem to have a care in this or any other world. I'm sure they did, as they probably didn't have any other income... but I joined in the fantasy.

It was so pleasing to me, to be able to feel at such peace, being a part of the easiness of the people there. The humdrum of humanity as I knew it was absolutely missing, as if it had never existed at all. No rushing cars, no speeding subways, no one in a hurry. Clothes lines were strung out across the old, cobblestone streets and back alleys, from balcony to balcony; women were calling to one another like birds perched in their nests; from somewhere, I could hear the sounds of young children playing happily together...

Here, there was something I'd never seen back home in Toronto... the camaraderie of the working classes. The live-and-let-live (and enjoy it as best you can!) feeling impregnating the city streets. Of course, these people were mostly poverty-stricken, but they seemed to refuse to acknowledge it, or let it become a big deal. They'd been born to it, and they looked out for each other. It occurred to me they had something North Americans kept to themselves - love.

The children had no idea of what might be ahead for them... the hard life. A life, maybe, of living hand to mouth, of hoping for a bit of money in exchange for a happy tune, or menial labour, or, possibly, having to rely on tourists for a living. From what I gathered, certainly the Italian government didn't give a damn about these people. If live-and-let-live was the philosophy of the common people, live-and-let-die seemed to be the attitude of those above them. A little reading of history will prove that out.

The aroma of fresh baked bread filled the air, and I decided to find one of the sources of this... a little bake shop. I went inside and purchased a hot loaf of Italian bread and proceeded on my walk, eating broken off chunks of it as I went along. I stopped in a coffee shop and ordered what any Italian would... cappuccino. While sitting in the restaurant, I saw that people were staring at me as if I was stranger in a strange land, which of course I was. The owner came over and asked if I was an American (the whole world at that time had a fixation with America, as if nothing bad could ever come out of it).

I told him, "No, I come from next door, from Canada, I'm a Canadian." I told him I would be leaving Italy that night, and wanted to have a final look at the streets of Italy before I went. People had begun to drift into the shop, and were sitting at the tables around me, watching out of idle curiosity. I turned up the B.S.

"You see, I saw this wonderful little shop of yours, and decided to venture in. It looks so nice from outside, and I want to remember it when I get back home." The patrons were all ears, and seemed to want to talk, but I wasn't sure they could understand English, which most of them didn't. One girl, however, had a fair command of the language. She spoke up, telling me this, adding that she was very proud of the fact she'd been able to go to a school that taught English. She wanted to know if I was really from Canada, as if it was some fabled land next to America, but not America... as if she didn't really believe such a place existed. I informed her it was actually quite a lot larger than the United States, and she laughed, probably sure now that there was indeed no such place.

Well, I didn't know much about Italy, either, I told her, but at least I had known it existed. "Italy is famous, even in Canada," I said. "In Toronto, we have a large Italian population." She said that was very nice. I have no idea how much of what I was saying she actually understood. English can be a funny language, if it's not your native tongue. She wanted me to tell her more about "Canada". I did...

"In Canada, there are lots of people with big cars. The buildings, too, are large, but mostly, they're ugly, except for the older ones. The age of everything built in Canada can be figured out by the architecture. It's very trendy there, to put up buildings that all look the same for ten years, and then, when people get tired of them, to build something different. The older the building, the more interesting. Hospitals, churches and jails sometimes all look the same... depending on their age. The older they are, the more the same they seem to be, as if one person built them all.

"But never mind that. In Canada, people have freedom. You can work and make something of yourself. There's employment enough for almost everyone, from one coast to the other. Toronto is the centre of commerce, a very large city full of people from just about everywhere. It isn't like cities in the United States, not yet, though we're heading in that direction. In Canada, money rules everything. If you look at who owns what, you'll find some foreign ownership, but then you'll find some very rich and powerful families who run most everything, build most everything, and control the economy."

What the Hell did I know about it? But I went on anyway. It's always nice to have the opportunity to spout off to people who can't argue with what you're saying, who may not even know what it is you're saying. I felt like a king with his subjects at his feet, eating up every word (all wise, naturally) that came from my mouth.

"Where I come from, you can work and become as rich as you like. If you know someone in business, all the better, you can become richer quicker. There's so much land in Canada... so many untouched resources. The country stretches for thousands of miles! There's fishing, logging, mining, you name it... we've got it. Everyone is Canada has opportunity... we have plenty of gold, plenty of coal, nickel... billions and billions of acres of forests, and on the prairies, there's wheat... the breadbasket of the world, that's us! And the fish, why, there's tons of offshore fish just waiting to be caught. We have everything!"

The girl asked, very politely, if things were so good in Canada, why was I in Italy?

"Oh, I'm not here for long," I told her. "My friends and I are going to start a revolution in the Middle East. Our ship leaves at eight o'clock tonight. I have to pick up my luggage first and then we set sail. We are Canadian Jews, and we've had a calling from God to go to the Holy Land and help rescue it from its enemies. We're going to raise up an army of farmers, and beat back the desert. We'll plant crops and grass and even flowers... we'll make it look like, well... just like Canada!"

"You are making fun for me," she said. "Flowers will not grow in the desert," she said. Little did she know how right she was, and the remark never left me. It's strange how things work, isn't it? I'm using her words for the title of this book, and I never even got her name. Maybe I should have dedicated it to nameless but very wise Italian girls everywhere?

After laying on a bit more B.S. about how wonderful our little group of pioneers was, I finally said goodbye, telling them how nice it was to sit and talk with such friendly people as they were, and left them to discuss crazy Canadian Jews. As I left the little restaurant, I had the same feeling that had cropped up in me when we were leaving Paris - I'd never again experience such places, because I was heading off into my own real world. Leaving Italy was like finishing off the dessert before the main course came.

I walked slowly up the street, back to the hotel. At the St. George, the revolutionaries were sitting around talking about what they expected to encounter once we got across the Mediterranean. The tourist guide was there, too, waiting to take us to the boat. He told us to collect our luggage and take them outside where there would be a couple of cabs to take us to the docks. Our luggage was already downstairs, we reminded him, stashed away in the cloakroom, so there was nothing to do but wait for the cabs to show up.

Bernie spoke up, saying how much he enjoyed being in Italy. He was looking forward to the boat trip, as were we all, especially Peggy. He didn't explain further, and there was no need to. He just liked being the centre of attention, whether there was anything much to say or not. He reminded me of Mark Anthony who said, "lend me your ears", except Bernie would never have used the word "lend"... he'd have wanted to keep them listening!

Irving, too, said he was glad to be leaving Italy, because the time spent there was not so good. All the arguing, I guess, had gotten to him, and he hadn't enjoyed it. Well, good for him, I thought. He told us that Italy hadn't fulfilled his dreams as he had thought it would. I wanted to tell him it might have, if he hadn't been so disagreeable about everything, and had taken the time to explore and enjoy, like I had.

He really had been having a bad time in Europe, though. Things just didn't seem to be working out for him, no matter where he went. His time in Paris had backfired on him and Rome wasn't his cup of tea, either. He had trouble grasping the meaning of the Christian side of Italy. There were crosses everywhere, and statues of Christ and the Virgin Mother... you might have thought you were in Quebec!... anyway, I guess he hadn't realized what an extremely religious place Italy was. The odd part was, he enjoyed visiting the Vatican, though he looked at it as simply a bit of history, instead of the seat of worldwide money and power it really was.

Bernie had a better time. He enjoyed sampling the food, the coffee, and looking at the pretty girls... he lost no time there. He'd return home with the feeling that Europe had been good to him. None of us, though, knew what lay ahead on the last part of this trip. The common train of thought was that it would be Paradise on earth, that everyone would be happy ever after. I didn't think so, but then, I didn't have their "vision", either. As things eventually turned out, maybe I was lucky.

Every day we'd spent in Italy, though, had been a twenty-four hour learning experience. We were all young, and we treated it that way. It was good in the respect that while none of our guides would ever think of suggesting to us where the raunchier side of town was, they deferred to us in every other way, doing all they could to help us feel comfortable and at home. While I was thinking about this, the cabs arrived and we were hustled outside, where we were immediately asked if we'd like some ice cream... there was an ice cream cart parked at the entrance of the hotel. The owner was the epitome of a vendor, with a short silver-grey moustache and white outfit. He looked as if he'd escaped from a Walt Disney cartoon. Unable to speak English, he began pointing to the cart, then to us, stretching his fingers out one by one, asking in sign language how many ice creams we wanted... whether we wanted them or not, mind you. Our guide interpreted for us, though there was no need to... the gestures had been perfectly performed.

One by one, we nodded our heads, "Yes"... we'd just eaten breakfast, but it was getting warm out and a bit of dessert sounded good to us. The vendor gave a wide grin, revealing a couple of gaps between the rest of his teeth, and began scooping away happily, saying, over and over..."Buon gelato, buon gelato... (good ice cream)."

We had a ten minute wait while the cabbies engaged themselves in an exchange of loud conversation... at first we thought they were arguing, but realized when they began to laugh that this was simply the way they expressed themselves. I'd often had the same experience back home in Toronto... watching a couple of Italian-speaking men seemingly arguing on a street corner, only to break into friendly laughter after a minute or so. It was just the way it was... let outsiders think what they liked, and maybe that was the joke.

Finally, the ice cream was gone, and the cabbies' laughter stopped. One of them approached us and smiled... a very smiley people, these Italians. He asked, in broken, but good English if we were the ones heading over to the docks, the "Canadians going to get on the boat". We answered yes, and the big, checkered cab doors were opened and in we piled, bound for dock number three. The guide paid the cabbies, said "Arrividerci" and we were off.

My thought was that the guide was saying to himself, "Thank God they're finally out of here!" and I sort of shared the same opinion. Not that I didn't like being in Italy, but I had mixed feelings about it, because of the attitude of the others. I hoped I'd remember more than just our constant bickering... it really was depressing, which was why I was always happy to get away from the others. I also wanted to get on with the trip. I'd seen enough of Italy, and if anyone had asked when I wanted to leave, I'd have replied, "Well now there then, just about as soon as humanly possible!"

Of course, if Saul had been the one hearing my reply, he'd have informed me that nothing, absolutely nothing was humanly possible, and that I should pray for guidance. I had a funny feeling in my gut he might be right, too... that the upcoming portion of our journey was going to somehow turn into a disaster... the way I was getting along with the group was not good at all. I didn't want to argue with anyone, though, so kept my thoughts to myself. I felt it was going to be the beginning of the end for all of us. I had no idea what our boat was going to be like, but I gathered it wasn't going to be the best thing afloat, but hopefully, it would stay afloat, at least until we got to the other side of the ocean.

I'd had enough of the group, though. Europe had taught me we just weren't compatible, and I wanted nothing to do with them. I was stuck with them, of course, but still... they disliked me and I began to dislike them immensely. If we never had to talk again, it would have been fine by me. So, whatever they wanted to do on this trip, they could count me out. I'd go my own way. I was determined to have a good time despite them.

The cab we were in was slow, made slower due to the fact no one but the cabbie spoke and even he backed off after a while, once he realized what a sour group he was carrying, but it finally arrived at the docks. There were all kinds of vessels in the water, all sizes and in varying condition. I wondered which one was ours. That dirty old scow over there, or that big, white tourist boat next to it… or was it one of the smaller ones that looked like they'd only that morning been dredged up from the bottom?

The cab stopped, we got out and retrieved our luggage, and for once did something together spontaneously - pooled our coins together to give to the cabbies as a tip. He accepted it, saying, "Gracias, gracias," several times, then sped off to look for his next victim. As he left, he pointed to the wooden planking that led to the docks themselves, and said, "The *Gramani*, the *Gramani*!"… I guess he wanted to make sure we got on the boat and out of Italy, too!

We walked along, dragging luggage behind us, searching for some sign of our boat. We passed an ugly old vessel that looked like it should have sunk years ago, and as we passed its bow, Saul called out, "Fellas, I think this is the one we're supposed to be on!" And he was right.

What a disaster it was! A rusted old tub that had to have been at least fifty years old, looking like its last trip might have been hauling garbage. It looked like it had been left over from the days of Christopher Columbus!

Bernie was the first to go up the plank. He found the purser at the top of it and asked if this was supposed to be the ship we were going to cross the Mediterranean on, explaining in a voice loud enough for us all to hear that we were the Jewish group from Canada. The purser smiled, and nodded his head. We all climbed up the plank, struggling with our luggage (very carefully, too, as it wasn't very wide) and that was it… we were on board. The purser bid us a smiley welcome and asked for our passports, and one by one we handed them in. When we'd complied with all of the desired little formalities and so forth, we were told someone would come and lead us to the quarters we'd been assigned to. Then, he spread out his arms, bowed slightly, and said, "Welcome aboard the *Gramani!*" I swear his grin widened at the way Peggy and Rodstein were scowling as they looked around the deck, which was in dire need of a paint job.

The purser continued,"I will now give you your cabin numbers, and you will find out who is with who, and where." I wound up with the religious member of our gang, and we went off to find our room. It turned out to be every bit as in need of paint as the rest of the tub. There were two bunks on the floor, which needed cleaning... and that was about it.

"So what do you think of this?" Saul asked.

"It's like having to live in a jail cell," I said. "The only difference being I can walk out on the deck and wait for the thing to sink. But, the air will be salty out there, and maybe it'll make it across, who knows? Maybe. If we're lucky."

The others had settled in as best they could, and we all met on the deck where the purser was waiting for us. He had a little speech to make about the boat, informing us regrettably that "its condition is not the best." Wonderful. We never would have guessed. It was the understatement of the year, but what could we do?

The food, however, turned out to be very good, and passengers could eat as much as they liked. There was also plenty of liquor, and we were told we would enjoy our stay on the vessel if we would give it a chance. "There is always fun to be had on the *Gramani,*" he said. "You are young, and so there is a good chance of meeting someone your age. There is nothing like a shipboard romance, you know. You will find it very adventurous, like in a romance novel." Then his smile faded, as he reminded us gravely that we set sail at eight o'clock sharp, "So please make certain you are on board the ship before that time if you want to get to your destination."

The guy reminded me of Jack Benny in the movie *The Horn Blows At Midnight.* He told us we should get together and take a walk along the shore before setting out (it might be our last look at it... or any shore?)... He pointed out that there was a good restaurant where we could eat seafood not far away, that we should look for a place called the Pilot and Anchor, and there we would find a good meal for not much money. He also said we could, if we wanted, pay for an entire full course dinner, which included lobster, scallops, fresh fish, shrimps, salad and "free drinks, exquisite wines and champagne", but that beer was extra. We decided to take him up on the idea.

The restaurant trappings included wooden tables by candle-light, settings perfect for lovers. We had time to eat and get back to the boat by seven p.m.... this gave us two hours to mosey about. We were warned specifically to not be late, and told to have a good time. The food was served one portion at a time, and the waiter, overhearing us talk about the ship, said, "Be careful to take your drinks very slowly. You have a long and bumpy night ahead of you." Just what we needed to hear, even if the last part of his warning was, as Peggy pointed out, a quote from a Bette Davis movie.

Irving, always difficult, didn't want any seafood. The rest of us did. Peggy told him he could always find some other place to eat if he didn't want to sit with us, and he in turn gave her a nice dirty look. What a bunch of losers we were! He tried to get the rest of us to go with him, but nobody was moving, and finally, he left the restaurant, headed God knows where, and who cared anyway! Couldn't we even eat in peace?

The purser was right... this was a beauty of a restaurant. The waiters and waitresses were dressed up like pirates, complete with a patch over one eye and headbands with a skull and crossbones print-ed on them. They wore knee-high boots, and spoke to us in broken English. Bernie said he was as hungry as a horse and I told him that wasn't exactly a kosher meal here. Peggy added that we weren't going to find a kosher restaurant on the Mediterranean, anyway.

I began talking about how maybe Irving wouldn't be coming with us, because he might get lost trying to find a Nathan's Hot Dog stand on a street corner somewhere, and this got Peggy riled up again. "He'd better show up. There's no safety for us unless we're together. Imagine how dumb it'd make the rest of us look, too, if he didn't make it back to the ship! Why can't he eat with us and at least be sociable? He's just a snob, that's what I think! Well, let him get lost! Who needs him, anyway?"

The essence of sociability, that was us.

Right in the middle of chewing on a lobster claw, Saul suddenly decided to share his insight into what was wrong with us, and began to tell us, "You know, it really would be for the best," he pointed out, if "the rest of you" resolved our differences before we set foot in the Holy Land, because, he said, God didn't want disagreeing factions building His country… He wanted a unified people.

Yeah, sure, Saul. Unified, that would be us. I could see us now, all smiling, digging trenches and waving a big banner together. My private vision of what would happen if we kept on the road we were going… from bad to worse… was that if we didn't wind up shooting ourselves, the Israelis themselves might save us the trouble. We were just what they needed, a bunch of would-be zealots and klutzes who didn't have a clue about what they were doing or where they were going, plus one disbelieving drifter by the name of Larry.

We left the pirate restaurant and headed back to the dock to catch the *Gramani* to take us on our last leg of our journey to the homeland. We walked like a line of ducks down along the seashore and as we were about to board our vessel, the purser, standing at the top of the gangplank, spotted us coming. He wanted to know if we had enjoyed our four hour wait. We told him we liked the restaurant well enough. Debbie mentioned how much she enjoyed her meal, saying that it made "just the perfect start" to the four day voyage through the Mediterranean ahead of us.

The purser smiled, and asked for our boarding passes. "Your friend," he said, "arrived a few moments ago." He meant Irving. As we already knew where our quarters were, we headed for them. We were to set sail in ten minutes. The rooms were despicable, to put it mildly. My old mother always said, "Larry, in life you get what you pay for," and in this case she was right. We paid nothing, and that's what we got. And as life would have it, I was bunked with Irving again. If two people on the face of the earth were ever mismatched, it was Larry and Irving. I had been bunked with him in New York, on the *Queen Mary,* in Paris, it seemed forever. I'm convinced that our little group was sure one of us wouldn't survive the trip, and they were all hoping it would be me.

I remember Bernie walking into our quarters and saying in his first line, "I see they've managed to get you two schmucks together again." Bernie, being a large and pushy individual, wanted to make sure everyone was abiding by all of the rules and regulations. This included such things as… meals on time; no switching tables; follow the fire drills (usually at least once a day). His last words were, "So, I guess I'll see you schmucks at breakfast if you're still alive."

As he was leaving, Irving turned to me and asked, "How the Hell have you survived this far, Larry? You conned the Salvation Army. You conned every Jewish agency we came across. You always had money in your pocket, even when it didn't belong to you, plus your uncle gives you an American hundred dollar bill to help get you on your way. You're one lucky son of a bitch, aren't you? Probably you think you're the favoured son of Judaism, too. You really are something else!"

Tired of hearing this sort of stuff over and over, I blew it back at him, "So, what's wrong with you, Irving, you're so goddam jealous? My mother was sick and my Uncle George was a millionaire! What's it to you? You just wish it had happened to you, that's it, right? Well, it happened to me, didn't it? So leave it alone before you push it too far. I mean, you had a chance for a free trip, too, and you took it, didn't you? So what's the big deal, anyway?"

Irving wasn't going to give up so easily. "But Larry! You're not even religious! All you wanted was a free ride. It could've been to Outer Mongolia for all you cared. This is serious business. It's not some kind of a joke, you know."

"Yeah, well, they can't send me back, can they? So you're stuck with me. The trick to this whole thing is that my Mother knows how to talk. She talked them into accepting me. I realize she didn't talk to you, or you might have seen the light, too. But win or lose, you're all stuck with me now, and that's the way it is, so you'd better get used to it…"

His reply to this was, "I don't see how she could have managed to talk them into taking you. You never went very far in school, and you never worked for anyone in your life except your uncle. You don't care about synagogue. The only thing you had going for you, really, was the fact that your mother threw a lot of big parties, and had the right connections. Your Uncle George donated plenty of cash to the Jewish agencies around the country, so I guess they were a little hesitant about not letting you go. You had pull, Larry. That's the only reason you're here.

"They didn't want a man of your uncle's stature to quit contributing to the cause, that's all!"

"Well, Mr. Know-It-All, I think you'd better leave my family out of it. You've managed to bring them down to your level. No matter what your dirty little mind thinks, Irving, one fact remains. I'm here, and I'm not going away. You have to learn to live with that. At least I made it on my own. You used your education and your religious pride, if you can call it that... but Larry got the free ride by just using his wits... something you don't have.

"So, never mind all that. Listen to me for a change. Here we are, on our last step of the journey, and we have to at least try to tolerate each other until the boat docks in Israel. Then, you're home free, Irving. You can kneel down and kiss the soil of the Motherland, like the millions of Jews that came before you. As for me, right now I've had enough of this talk. It reminds me of two little kids fighting over a ball neither of them owns. I'm going out for some fresh ocean air... the air in here, Irving, is getting very stale."

I left the room, closing the door behind me, saying, "See you later, Oh Holy One." I could hear him muttering as I walked away. Deliberately, just to make him mad, I turned back and opened the door a few inches. "Irving? I still love you, Irving!" I made good and sure to say it loud enough for those in the next room to hear. To Hell with him, anyway, the jerk.

I imagined him sitting there red-faced with a dumbfounded look, which, for Irving, was about his speed. Leaving the quarters, I proceeded upstairs because the boat was ready to set off in a few minutes, and I didn't want to miss it. I wanted to hear the horn blow at midnight, like in the old Jack Benny film. As I walked along toward the railing, I thought to myself, Larry, you really are a bastard. You made it, after all!

Looking out over the rickety railing of the good ship Gramani, I spat into the sea. Maybe it would help get rid of the sour taste the trip at this point was giving us all. We didn't even get to see Naples. I would have liked to have left a leak in front of the Royal Palace...

Between my gazes out over the water, I happened to notice a gorgeous looking girl doing the same thing. The water was so calm and peaceful, you were able to see your reflection in it. I wasn't interested in seeing my own reflection, though… this girl really was beautiful! Just looking at her made me feel like "Rick" in the movie *Casablanca*. She reminded me of my favourite actress of all time… Ingrid Bergman.

One thing kept going through my mind… whether or not I could work up enough nerve to approach this beauty and say hello. All I could see was her gorgeous face and long cascading red hair. I came to the conclusion that she couldn't help seeing me, and really only had two choices if I approached her - she could go back to her cabin or stay and talk with me. What the Hell, I thought, there's no harm in trying. Always the dreamer, I figured it might turn out like the end of *Casablanca*… the start of a beautiful friendship.

Slowly, I worked my way along the railing, pretending to be following the trail of a swooping seagull. As I drew closer and closer, I somehow got up the courage to introduce myself. "Hello there," I said, "my name is Larry. How are you today?"

She surprised me by turning toward me and looking me up and down, as if I was a new dress hanging in a storefront window. "My name is Saundra," she said sweetly. "Where are you going?" I told her about the trip to Israel, forgetting about my real reason for a moment and adding that I was on my way to become a border guard there. I asked about her destination, and she replied in the same sweet tone that she was headed for Israel, too, but to visit an ailing uncle. There was a bit more small talk, and suddenly, I felt very comfortable with her, and warm inside my heart, knowing I would have company, at least on the trip across the water.

I told her I was sorry she had to be visiting Israel under such circumstances. She mentioned that she didn't think her English was particularly good, and that she was of Jewish-Spanish descent. She said she would be happy to be able to learn as much English as I could teach her during our four days on the boat. Of course, I had other thoughts as well… there were other things I'd like to teach her, too! The picture that stood out in my mind most was one of her lying beneath me. In reality, though, I was only too pleased to be able to help her in any way I could, whatever my ulterior motives might have been. She was simply too beautiful to let go.

Somewhere in the back of my mind, I had a feeling that the relationship might just work out. I reasoned it this way - she was heading to Israel with the same intention I had... to help her family. I was supposedly going there to stand up for my country. To my twisted way of thinking, it was all one and the same. Family is family. Jews are Jews everywhere, whoever they are, whatever the circumstances. Somehow, I was able to see all of this very clearly, while staring into her big, beautiful soulful eyes.

So here I am, I thought, just a kid from Toronto... from nowhere, really, yet I'm standing on the deck of a boat bound for the Promised Land with the most stunning girl in the world. To me, it was like being in the movie, *When Worlds Collide*. I could see by the moon that everything was flashing by me, like time had stopped, and anything was possible. I had an intense feeling that this trip was meant to be, that this was all a part of my destiny. I was on the highway to life, and Saundra and I had been meant to collide, or at least bump together, if you know what I mean.

Saundra asked what I did back in my own country. I told her that there were recruitments for Americans and Canadians to go and work in the kibbutzim. I went on to tell her that I had jokingly enlisted, with no real intention of ever being chosen to go. "But here I am on board the *Gramani* with you, heading for Israel, Land of Hope and Promise. I'm also hoping for pleasant relationships and friendships, too, with new people... new people like you, Saundra."

Thinking it best to get straight to the most interesting point (in a roundabout way, of course) I then asked her if she had a boyfriend. She told me, yes, there was such a person, but that her mother did not approve of the relationship between them. He wanted this and that, wanted to marry himself into the family at all cost, and her mother would have nothing to do with it.

"This is where the part of my going off to Israel comes into play," she said. "My mother thought it would be best for me, to get away from him for awhile." I mentioned to her that this trip must have been a big financial burden on the family. I was a little surprised when she smiled and said that it wasn't at all, that her family was really quite wealthy… her father was in the cattle business. Her mother had received a letter, she said, from her Aunt Malka, saying her uncle was very ill. Saundra wanted very much for her mother to accompany her on the trip, she said. No-one could replace her mother, and that was that.

Immediately following the news of her uncle's illness, her mother had purchased her a ticket and Saundra was on her way. I asked her if she had stopped anywhere along the way, and was not very impressed with her sense of adventure upon learning she'd missed seeing anything of Europe. Snob that I was, I couldn't help but casually mention that I'd been "travelling extensively" in both France and Italy. I was a seasoned tourist, having spent time in Paris and in Rome, I told her. Of course, I threw in a little about my trip across the great Atlantic on the *Queen Mary*, too. I couldn't let that one slide.

I told her I was very surprised that a young lady as beautiful as she hadn't yet been to Paris. Her reaction to this caught me completely off guard. She asked if I'd visited the "red light" district, and seemed genuinely curious to know the answer. For a moment, I didn't know what to say. How should I reply to a question like that? If I said the wrong thing, she might not want to continue the discussion. On the other hand…

It seemed I was always having to weigh things… maybe in a previous life, I'd been a Libran! At first, I put on what I thought was a puzzled expression, and said nothing, just to see if she'd pursue it. She did, by asking again. "Well? Did you or didn't you? If you did, did you enjoy yourself?"

It's funny how a person can be embarrassed in the presence of what one thinks is innocence, even if it really isn't. I felt my face beginning to blush a little, and blurted out something along the lines of, "Well, if I enjoyed it, I paid for it." I went on to explain how it's a sort of tradition for North Americans when they first come to Paris, to "liberate" themselves from the sexual shackles of the New World or some such thing. I didn't think she'd fall for that, but I had to say something.

"So what's a red-blooded Canadian boy supposed to do in the City of Light, anyway? Stay holed up in a hotel and watch the world pass by? As a matter of fact, I wrote to my mother and told her I'd visited some of the girls of Paris. I don't know what she thought of that, though. " My defences were coming up at this point, and I've always found that when that happens, it's better to take another step ahead, instead of turning back with your tail between your legs... so to speak. So, I asked her jokingly if she would like to visit the famous area.

"A pretty young lady like you would be able to make quite a pile of money there, you know." She just laughed this off, and I felt I wanted to change the subject and get back to her life at home. What was she really like? I asked about her schooling and things of that nature. Her sense of humour surprised me. I still can remember the joke she told me about the nun:

"A nun has none, wants none, and gives none... and that's why she gets none." Well, it sounded funny at the time!

I told her a joke or two in return, probably just as dumb, and then we got back to more serious topics. Saundra was not doing very well in school, she told me. She felt she didn't deserve to go on the trip. She said she felt unduly rewarded and it was simply good fortune that put her on board the *Gramani*. (I often wondered if her sick uncle felt the same about it!) But, she said, her mother was worried that she had nothing but boys, boys, boys on her mind, and that a trip would do her good.

She mentioned she wanted to become a lawyer more than anything else in life, and I've often wondered if she did. In the meantime, though, all she wanted to do was make sure she had a good time during her stay in Israel. She said she hoped everything would turn out all right regarding her uncle, but didn't seem overly concerned with it. Inside, she said, she knew he was going to die, that the end was near. He had some kind of incurable disease, and she was mostly going to see him to offer some moral support... maybe for her mother as well, who would feel better knowing her brother wouldn't die unrepresented by his family.

Saundra said she felt very privileged to have met a young Jewish man she could have a pleasant relationship with so soon in her journey, someone who showed some compassion towards the situation with her uncle. I've always been a good listener, and still am, even though three quarters of what you hear is BS, especially today. When I was younger, though, especially around pretty girls like Saundra, my ears were so open, you could probably have shone a flashlight beam in one and get light coming out the other!

The conversation turned to her life at home again, and she informed me her family's land holdings were huge indeed. She made me laugh by saying when it came to cattle, she'd done it all, and had even rustled cows. She'd been a kind of tomboy, she told me, ever since she could remember. Maybe the way she'd grown up had something to do with that... from an early age, she said, she'd known how to ride, how to brand cattle; and she'd even worked with the guys on the cattle drives. That, she said, was the hardest work of all. They used to bring the cattle in to market once or twice a year and she made the farmers who noticed her on the drives respect her. It meant doing all of the things everyone else did, though, and that wasn't easy for a young girl, but she'd done it anyway.

Going on a cattle drive was the only time she'd ever left home. These were times she was on her own, but she enjoyed it, she said. It showed how she was able to work alongside the best of them and do a good job. She could do a good job on me anytime, I thought... she didn't look much like a tomboy to my way of thinking!

I asked her how long she would be staying in Israel, and she said probably until her uncle passed away, whenever that would be. Her mother wouldn't be able to get there under any circumstances, and someone had to stay to represent the family. She was quite at peace with the fact her mother had supplied her with enough money to get by comfortably, so she wouldn't have to live off the goodness of her dying uncle... he had enough troubles as it was, and didn't need to worry about her!

Deep inside, I had the strange feeling I wouldn't be seeing her again once we got off the *Gramani*. I kept thinking in my mind that I should ask her if we shouldn't become sort of partners or friends while we were on the boat Since she'd so openly given me her name when I'd first approached her, I figured there couldn't be any harm in trying. So, I did.

She replied that she thought it would be good to have a friend on board, someone she could spend some time with and talk to or confide in. At this point, I decided I'd said enough for a first encounter, and it was time to say goodnight. We'd been talking since the boat had left port, and now it was well after midnight. Funny how time flies when you're with a pretty girl! I didn't want to give her the impression that I was the pushy sort, though, and was about to say goodnight when she surprised me again by asking if I would meet her the next day and give her a first English lesson. Of course, I agreed. We decided to meet on the deck after breakfast in the morning.

To be quite frank (or better yet, quite Larry!), I had other things on my mind than English lessons. I'd just met her though, and figured a simple handshake would suffice until the morrow, and a good night, world, it would be. But, I soon realized she was more in the mood for a shipboard romance. She looked up at me, smiling, lips puckered slightly. Slow as I was to recognize her immediate need, it finally dawned on me that she wanted to be kissed! Well, mazel tov, I said to myself (congratulations), you've got a live one here, Larry.

Now, be assured I would not resist an advance like this from such a young goddess as Saundra. It was getting late, though, and I seemed to be taking an extraordinarily long time to get with it, as they say. I was thinking a little peck on the cheek would be enough for the night, and I could go home and dream... but it was becoming evident that she wanted nothing less than a full kiss on the lips, and that's what ensued.

Breaking off for a moment, I whispered softly, "So, what is this all about?" She simply replied she thought I was a "nice young man", and things of that sort. She also said she thought it was great, seeing someone stand up for his country. Boy, if she only knew! Something was beginning to stand up, all right... but it wasn't a young man for his homeland! As the evening slowly wound down to a close, I said, "Saundra, I'll see you after breakfast, okay. We'd better get some sleep before we don't get any at all!"

She thought that was funny. So there was something likeable about me, after all, despite what the rest of my gang thought. I chuckled inwardly at them, wishing they could have visions of me and Saundra, kissing while they snored away in their save-the-homeland fantasies. Smiling at my own thoughts, I walked Saundra to her cabin and there we kissed again and she whispered good-night into my ear, wetting it a little with her tongue... a promise of things to come. Floating, I headed back to my own cabin, my head spinning with crazy ideas. I knew Irving would hear me come in, and that he would be a real question box. After all, I'd been gone for over four hours. Probably, he'd been hoping I'd fallen overboard, but I had a surprise for him. I knocked on the door (just to make sure he was awake, miserable roommate that I was); besides, he had a habit of locking every door he was behind. The fact that someone else might have a legitimate reason to get in didn't matter to him. He answered the knock, and opened the door, grumbling something about my being back already.

I told him I was sorry, really sorry I hadn't jumped into the sea for him, but that was life. He started asking his stupid questions... where had I been, why had I been gone so long, who was I with, and so on until finally I'd heard enough and replied, "Irving, I was just out talking to a sea monster. Everything's all right now, because I talked it out of eating the boat, so you can go back to sleep now, okay?"

I didn't really feel it was necessary to discuss my private matters with him at this... or any other time. He persisted, though, so I told him I simply wanted to get a good night's sleep, and didn't want to get into any personal discussions with him at this time just so he could relay all the information to the group in the morning over breakfast. I decided to let him go back to sleep with a puzzle - "I've got something very special to do tomorrow morning, by the way, so if it appears I'm not being too sociable, don't worry about it. We're not in the army yet, you know, and I figure to spend some time on my own tomorrow. So goodnight."

Bearing that in mind, whether Irving got back to sleep or not, I couldn't say, but I remember falling asleep very quickly, with Saundra central to my thoughts. The waters seemed very peaceful indeed, that first night out. Things couldn't have been working out any better if I'd planned them.

The next morning, it came as a surprise when, at the breakfast table, Bernie mentioned he'd seen me on the deck with a "beautiful young thing" the evening before. He said he'd bumped into her earlier, and had noticed how beautiful she was, but didn't have the nerve to say hello to her. Never one to let a chance at a dig go by, I told him (and everyone else) it wouldn't have mattered if he did have the nerve, because he didn't know the language, anyway.

"What language, Wiener? What are you talking about?"

"The language of love, Bernie. She wouldn't have understood a word you said."

God, how I loved hating that man! Debbie saw a fight brewing, and quenched it by jokingly saying, "Don't get upset, Bernie. So you didn't have the nerve to meet the girl, and Larry did? So, Larry, tell us... what's wrong with her? Bernie probably knew it instinctively, and stayed clear of her. Larry, let us in on her secret... what's she got that attracted you? Money? Jewels? A rich uncle?" She winked at me, letting me know why she was saying these things. Otherwise, I might've taken it the wrong way. One thing I was learning on this trip, though, was that Debbie was the peacemaker of the group. It was a good thing someone was. She was pretty good, too... she even had Bernie half smiling!

Religious Irving brought us back to the serious side of reality by asking, "Is she kosher, Larry?" There were no scriptures he could find to reply to my answer, though: "Well, Irving, I'm not sure about that. I haven't eaten her yet."

"You're nothing but a pig, Larry, a real animal!" Thus spake Debbie, her peacemaking persona rapidly disintegrating. I didn't care. I said, "Debbie, if what is going to happen to this girl happened to you, you'd be the happiest girl in the world. You'd rise up and float right above Irving's seventh heaven or wherever he thinks he's heading."

Irving, looking sombre, had finally found something to say, "Well, Debbie, I hate to say it, but you know, whatever Larry says, whether you like it or not, it's the truth. I've known him for a long time. I remember how he was in school, and how he acted in the YMHA. At those dances, he was the wildest and most uninhibited person imaginable. The other people would gather and surround him when he got up to dance. They thought he was crazy, and you know how people are... they love to watch someone else go meshuga. Mostly all of the girls he danced with were very good looking, and when they played Bill Haley's 'Rock around the Clock', sometimes more than one girl would dance with him, just for fun.

"He was a real live rocker, I mean, he really would go nuts. When he hit the dance floor, it was as though he'd invented it. Maybe it doesn't make much sense, but whatever Larry said happened, it happened. Don't make the mistake of underestimating him. If he says he'll do something, he'll do it. Win or lose, he doesn't care. I remember him always saying, 'Whale it or jail it!' So if you don't want to hear what he has to say, all right. But, he won't be making it up."

Debbie looked exasperated after this. It seemed Irving was taking over her role, and she didn't know how to handle it. Instead of backing out of the conversation, she pursued it, "So, Irving. Exactly how long was Larry on deck with that girl last night?"

"He didn't come back to the cabin until one o'clock," Irving replied.

Bernie wanted to know what her name was, but I'd had just about enough of this conversation. "Well now then there, old buddy, I'll tell you. It's none of your business, and if you think it is, I suggest you should go and find her and ask her what her name is. Because I'm not going to tell you. You, Bernie, had the same chance I did to walk over to her and say hello in there, but you apparently couldn't work up the nerve. So don't expect me to do your work for you. I'm working for myself these days, don't forget that. If you snooze, you lose, pal."

I was annoyed with Bernie anyway, for always asking me personal questions, like he felt he was my rabbi father confessor or something. He just wouldn't let up, wanting to know Saundra's name, her cabin number and if her breasts were real.

"Don't try and hustle me, Bernie. It won't work. If you want a girl to bother, go find one. Put an ad in the newspaper. Scratch your number in a telephone booth for all I care. But, don't bother me about it. There are three decks on this tub. You're such a schmuck… why don't you take a look around for yourself? But this girl is my friend, not yours. Go hustle your own, okay?"

Debbie, finding her pace again, intervened. "Bernie, maybe this time Larry is right, like Irving says. You have no right to question him. You're not his father. He's on this trip just like you are, and you really don't have the right to inquisition him or try to cut in on his business."

"Listen, Bernie," I said, "if you want to meet her, go and meet her. Find her and talk to her if you like. It's all right by me if you do, but don't expect anything to develop. She's just a girl on a boat, trying to get someplace, headed for dry land like the rest of us, going to the land of sand. So, do what you want. I don't care." I said this, but didn't really mean it. However, I figured it had been pretty dark when he'd seen her, and probably wouldn't recognize her anyway, so what the Hell.

Aside from all the pettiness, glares and silly bickering between and among us, breakfast was a beautiful meal. You could consume all you wanted, and then some if you liked. But I remember Rabbi Irving wouldn't eat anything except the eggs, which I guess he must have blessed himself. He drank his coffee and said he was going to his quarters to daven, I asked, "It's a beautiful day out there, Irving. What are you going to daven for? Are you afraid the boat will sink?"

He replied that he thought I was just a smart ass, and that a bit of davening wouldn't hurt the likes of me. "I daven every morning and every meal," he said, "and also at night. How often do you daven, Larry? My parents were very religious, and so am I. On the other hand, you are probably a thinking Nazi."

Irving could be very blunt in his thinking. I laughed, asking what in Hell a thinking Nazi was. "It sounds like a disease, Irving! But whatever it is, I'm not one of them, so don't worry about that. Maybe I'm close, though. When you get to Israel, you'll be going into a religious kibbutz where you can daven all day long, and all night too if you like, and they'll feed you and pamper you and treat you like the Jewish saint you think you are. You'll be able to levitate by the time they're through with you! You'll have to be careful you don't float off into the heavens, Irving! What's that passing overhead? Oh, don't worry, it's just Irving again, going to Jerusalem...

"Okay, so I'm not the religious type, so what? Neither was Moses, until the thunderbolts started flying around his feet. Go ahead, continue in your training, be whatever you think you're meant to be... it's a free world, we're told. You can do whatever you like. You'll be happiest in a kibbutz of that nature, make sure they don't stick you in the fields, digging for your supper like the rest of us!"

That shut him up, and he arose and left the room, to daven twice as hard, I supposed. Well, good for him. When our group exposed its wilder side, he always felt uncomfortable and went off by himself. Actually, I felt a little bit sorry for him, but everyone builds their own bees' nest and if you get stung, you get stung; if you want to enjoy the honey, enjoy it. The group was relieved to see him go to his room. We constantly had to wait for him, as he had to do his prayers before each meal, as if his mumbling would change the flavour or increase the portions.

I always thought that others on the boat would make fun of him, that they'd be laughing behind his back. The other Irving, the one who was sharing my quarters, he thought Rabbi Irving was doing the right thing. Maybe he was davening for all of us. In a way, I agreed... after all, at the rate we were going we needed some prayers said! Anyway, it was only for another four days. The group could understand what he was doing... we were all Jewish. We'd seen this type of behaviour before. There was nothing unfamiliar or strange about it. We weren't about to question someone's religion... he had as much right to devote his time to God as he wanted.

Rabbi Irving was, in a way, a martyr. He thought that only God could reside in Israel. His father was a poor tailor who worked down on Spadina Avenue with the rest of the rag trade people, and his mother did housekeeping for European Jews. They put all of their extra earnings into Irving's education, but what he really wanted was religion. Ever since his Bar Mitzvah, he'd wanted to be able to go to Israel, so, his parents saved their money, what little they were able, to send him there. God had a better idea, I guess... He must have shone a light on Irving, because they were looking for people like him to send free of charge to the country of his dreams to help rebuild the faith, and so his dream was coming true. Here he was, with the rest of us on the boat.

It's true, life works in mysterious ways. They even accepted a wretch like me! Bernie mentioned, though, that he was too proud to have a person like Rabbi Irving come along with us, but he was the one who recruited him. He recruited all of our group, with the exception of Debbie, who came from Manitoba. The other Irving was of a different cloth altogether... he was the studious type, always with a book in his hand. He liked reading "deep" tomes, the works of Karl Marx, Lenin, etc. and once I even saw him putting away a book I never dreamed he'd want to read. It was Hitler's *Mein Kampf*.

I asked him why he would want to read such a thing and he replied, "I want to learn about the German way of life."

I asked, "Why, do you want to become a Nazi, or what? They killed six million Jews, which, in case you've forgotten, are our own people, you know? What can this book possibly do for you? You're on your way to the Promised Land, not the Despised Land! You're not going to a concentration camp."

I told him the rest of the group would communally turn against him if they knew the kind of garbage he was reading, that he was busying himself by studying the words of Mr. Hitler. I told him he should throw the book into the ocean, it might kill off a few sharks. Besides, wouldn't it look good if, at the end of our journey, someone goes through our luggage at the point of entry and discovers they have a Nazi in their midst. A Jewish Nazi, at that... wouldn't that be cute! He'd be prison bound, or maybe worse, who knows? There might be questions later, but before they came about, I imagined it would be mighty unpleasant for good old Irving... and maybe for the rest of us, too. So, I spoke my mind to him.

"Irving," I said, "I'm going to go up on deck for awhile. I can't tolerate what I've just witnessed... your choice of reading material. It's not exactly a *Reader's Digest* book-of-the-month club choice, is it? Your stupid communist books, I can put up with, but not this. You've stepped over the edge this time. I hope when I return, you'll have seen the light and gotten rid of the damned thing."

I left, and made my way upstairs, and who should I bump into, but Saundra. It was as though she had been there since the previous night, waiting for me. She was wearing a pair of deliciously tight white shorts, sitting nice and high up on her legs. These, along with an equally tight red halter top, almost matching the colour of her hair, made me glad to be alive, and I forgot all about Hitler.

"Hello, Larry," she said. I immediately noticed a different tone to her voice. If anything, it was more musical, sexier, more full of an unspoken promise.

"Are you ready for your first lesson, Larry?" I asked myself, "first lesson?" - if only she knew what she could teach me! Right now! Anytime at all! Anywhere! I was glad at that moment that Saundra's mother could not see what was running through my mind, because if she'd been able to, if she'd even come close in a wild guess... boy, there'd be trouble... big, big trouble! All I could visualize at that moment was having this gorgeous woman alone with no clothes on or, better yet, with me slowly peeling them off, layer by layer.

The only English I wanted to teach her was two words, consisting of three little letters each: S E X... and Y E S. I was hoping in the back (or the front?) of my mind that my dream would come true, and my hands would wander carefully and lovingly over her luscious young curvaceous body, and Rabbi Irving saying his prayers came to mind. Yes, Irving, the delicious dish in front of me now was most definitely a kosher meal!

I realized things were proceeding at too fast a pace. It was still morning, and we had an English lesson to get through. Back to reality, Larry! I asked her if she'd brought her English phrase book, and she pulled it out of her purse to show me. I nodded, and asked where she would like to start the lesson. In my mind, the best place I could think of to be with her was in her quarters, with no one to disturb us, and the only thing I wanted to study was anatomy... hers, and in depth!

She succeeded in bringing me back to earth by saying we should get a table on the third deck, where we could get some sun at the same time. I vaguely wondered if she'd ever considered sunbathing in the nude, but stopped myself from inquiring. We went up the stairs and sat down next to a table. She laid the book on it, and I heard a familiar but unwanted voice say, "Oh, hi Larry! Fancy meeting you here."

Damn! It was Bernie, effectively putting the lesson on hold, at least until he went away again, which I hoped he'd do right away, but knew he wouldn't. Right away, he started to hustle Saundra, asking her the same questions I'd asked the night before. After he'd exhausted these to his satisfaction, he started in on me.

"So, where'd you meet this blond jerk?" Jealousy is a wonderful thing at times. Bernie had gone beyond himself by asking this question, and Saundra let him know.

"Well, I think you're the jerk," she said. "I don't even know your name. Why don't you just leave us alone, and go about your business. We aren't bothering you, so please don't bother us." It was hard to believe, but Bernie had put his foot right in his mouth and defeated his own purpose, which had been to get rid of me so he could have Saundra to himself. Instead, he got rid of himself so I could have her! Now, that's my kind of justice. He gave us a dirty look, and disappeared down the stairway, mumbling to himself.

Turning back to the book, Saundra told me that she didn't want too involved in the language, but was more interested in basic aspects of it, so she would be able to meet and get along with people. She spoke Hebrew and Spanish well enough, but knew almost no English. We studied for two hours or so until Saundra finally said she'd had enough. She was smart, and after questioning her on what we'd been studying, if she was able to remember what she'd learned, it seemed she knew enough to be able to communicate.

She then asked if I'd be interested in a game of shuffleboard on the main deck. I'd never played shuffleboard before, but had heard it was interesting and fun. We saw the sticks hanging on the wall, so we asked the deck hand for the puck. Saundra looked absolutely beautiful playing this game, especially when she leaned over to push the puck along with her stick. The people watching us were really watching her tush, I decided, but that was all right. She either didn't notice or didn't mind.

We played for an hour or so, and after beating me, Saundra said we should go up to the top deck and have a talk, to see if she'd remembered her English well enough. She said she thought it would be a big asset to her when she returned to her native country as English was becoming used in business more and more commonly. Many people of different cultures went to the cattle exchange, and she had never been able to understand the English a lot of them spoke.

We went upstairs, found a table and set up our chairs and asked the deck hand for some croissants and a couple of cups of cappuccino. I realized that I really did not want to sit and talk with her for hours.. My intentions were quite different, and looking at her, I wondered what she would think if she knew. I also wondered how to get off the topic of language, and break the ice a bit more. What if I reached out and held her hand? The feeling I had probably wasn't appropriate to the time of day and the setting, but for me it was just right. I was thinking that if we could talk more about each other, sooner or later we'd wind up in bed together, and then even if we never saw each other again, we'd have some pleasant memories to carry with us.

Then, to my utter amazement, as if she'd been thinking along the same lines, she offered me her hand to hold, and began asking about life in Canada. She had a keen interest in this, and wanted to know all about school, family, friends, what Toronto was like and so on. I mentioned to her that my father had passed away in 1950 at forty-two years of age, of heart failure. He'd been a musician with dance bands. My mother was a bookkeeper for fashion houses. She always made sure the family was well kept. She bought mortgages on buildings which eventually made her wealthy.

I was never very good at school, always busy looking out of the window, or at the girls. I remember a teacher finally commenting, "Where do you think you're drifting off to, Larry?" I told her that some day I would travel... "further than any high school will ever take me." Eventually, I quit school and went to work as an usher in Lowe's Theatre. I then went to work for my Uncle George's film company. I also kept my night job as an usher at the theatre.

I mentioned to Saundra one incident I will never forget. One night, a wallet went missing, and I was accused of being responsible for the theft. In the morning, my uncle confronted me, and asked straightforwardly if I took it or not. He knew me quite well, and when I told him I didn't, he said not to worry about a thing, he'd take care of it, he'd straighten the matter out. By noon, everything had been smoothed over. My uncle told the manager that if they were not sure someone had done something, if they had no proof, then they had no right accusing anyone. He said he thought it was a miserable thing to do, to try and lay the blame on one of the ushers, when it was more likely a member of the audience who had taken it.

Uncle George was quite the guy… he told them they had only a few hours to settle the matter with me, that if they didn't, he wouldn't provide their film for that evening. "That means you will be officially closed," he told them, "and you can't afford to be closed." About an hour later, Uncle George received a telephone call from them stating that they had found the wallet underneath one of the seats. The money had disappeared from it, but the identification papers and the rest of its contents were still intact. "You can tell Larry he can come back to work tonight. Please tell him there will be a small gift waiting for him which he should accept as an apology for being falsely accused of the theft. He will also receive full pay for the time he was off." They had, of course, fired me on the spot. Uncle George immediately dispatched a special truck to hurry to the theatre with their film for the day. I told Saundra this story because I wanted her to know I was an honest person.

Saundra then asked, "Tell me, Larry, what really made you come on this trip?" I explained to her as best I could that the main reason was because the teacher had made fun of me and said that I was "going nowhere fast", that I would never even get out of Toronto.

"So, you see, when this opportunity arose, I did not hesitate for a moment. My mother said she would hold a big party for the entire family, and the group from Toronto. We were living on Overbrook Place at the time, which is known as the Jewish community of the north. My mother mentioned that if I had the nerve to scorn the trip, I deserved to be on it. She knew me well. I waited about a month after saying I'd go, and then received a letter to come to the office of a coffee company called Blue Ribbon. It was on Spadina Avenue. I came to the conclusion I was not going to make it on my own, so I brought my mother along.

"We went to the office, and to my surprise, my mother knew the man I was supposed to see. He was asking me all sorts of questions about my education, why I wanted to go to Israel, and so forth. He even went so far as to get personal, wanting to know about my religious beliefs. I replied to these questions as best I could, then came the bombshell. He said, 'Mrs Wiener, your son here is really not qualified to go on this trip.'

"My heart skipped a beat or two, hearing this news, but everything worked out all right. My mother must have talked some sense into him... made him an offer he couldn't refuse, that is. He would need a couple of weeks to get his okay, but he would see that I got to go along. Mother said she'd had a feeling that this wouldn't be enough to get me on board the boat. The reason she had gone to see him in person was to make sure he knew that Uncle George was quite a supporter, and it would be a shame if his own nephew wasn't among the chosen.

"She must have explained to this man that I was not your typical Jewish boy, that I wasn't very religious, I did things my own way, and that as far as Israel was concerned, all I knew about the place was that it was somewhere on the map, that the flag had gone up ten years previously and that was about it. Mother wouldn't have told him anything but the truth. She probably said something like, 'We want the best for our boy,' but no doubt mentioned Uncle George's generosity more than once. Like they say, money talks...

"When she came out of that room, she had put a very straight face on. I was waiting outside for her, and when I saw her, I didn't know what to think. I couldn't read anything at all in her expression... no smile, no frown, nothing to let me even guess what had happened. Finally, she said, 'Well, Larry, we'll have to wait.' I wasn't sure what she meant by that, and started to explain that all of the other boys had been accepted without any rigmarole. They came, they were seen, they were accepted. They already had their letters to start packing.

"We went to the Varsity Restaurant and she bought me a chocolate sundae in an attempt to mollify my nervousness and disappointment. Would I be going, or not? That was the burning question of the day. For the next week, I was listless and half-convinced myself I was going to be rejected. Then one day the postman brought a Special Delivery letter addressed to my mother. It was from the Jewish Agency.

"It was very formal, and read something to the effect that Larry

Wiener had been accepted to volunteer for a period of one year in the state of Israel. The trip would begin on September 2nd 1957. It mentioned that I would be receiving another letter stating what the proper apparel to bring would be, etc. It said not to take a radio or any other electrical product, as the overseas electrical system was different from that in North America.

"I was ecstatic. I was officially going to be on my way. I'd beaten the system, thanks to Mother and Uncle George. When I blurted this out in front of Mother, she just smiled and said cryptically, 'Well, maybe you did, maybe you didn't.' I never did find out exactly why I was accepted, but it didn't matter. In the back of my mind, I've always thought that Mother and Uncle George were the main influences, because inside, I knew I really didn't fit in to the group. Going to Israel meant something to the others, but to me, it was mostly a lark. The rest of the group were almost bloodthirsty to go and 'build a country', but to me it was just a joke.

"The joke backfired, though, because in the end I, too, was chosen to go and be a part of whatever it was we were to be doing. Maybe Uncle George, in his wisdom, told the Jewish Agency it would be good for me to go, that it would work the wildness out of my system. There had been a day he told me he no longer wanted me around, and Mother would have seen things a bit differently. But, Uncle George had a lot of influence, and maybe Mother went along with him. The same argument, that a year away would be good for me, a year of army-style life, was probably the argument, aside from money, Uncle George used with the agency. I told Saundra the truth, that my reason for going was really to enjoy a one year excursion, and to see a bit of the world. I didn't think there was anything wrong with that. I was going under false pretences, but so what? Some of the reasons of the others weren't so altruistic, either... although I wouldn't even have known what that word meant in those days.

"Mother began packing my clothing and getting my things in order, so I'd be ready to leave in September. I telephoned Bernie to let him know that I had been accepted, and had received my letter to prove it. Boy, was he upset! He didn't believe it at first. In his wildest dreams, he never thought I'd be going with them. He'd intended to say goodbye to me and rub my failure in my face. He was not at all happy that I would be going, and this was in itself ironic, as he'd been the one who had originally approached me about the trip. I guess he never thought I'd want to go, and the offer had been made without thinking of the consequences. I bet he kicked himself all the way up Yonge Street that day. A couple of days earlier, he'd laughed at me and said, "I'd bet my life on it, that you'll never get a letter from them!" I told him later, it was a good thing I hadn't taken him up on that bet. He didn't even smile. Once he realized he was stuck with me, he really began to dislike me in earnest.

"Irving, too, was aghast at the prospect. I phoned him and said, 'Hello, it's me, Larry! Hey, guess what?' He just said, 'Oh, no! Not you! You're not going with us, are you? You little bastard!' I laughed into the mouthpiece, 'That's right, I'm going to be your mascot, the most important member of all!' His response was to say in a very flat voice, 'Your mother paid to get rid of you, didn't she?' Oh, these were very nice, understanding people, this gang I was joining.

"My mother made all the arrangements for her dinner party. Everyone would be there to see me off, to wish me a safe and happy journey… or maybe they were just glad to see me go. I couldn't have cared less… I was totally excited at the prospect of leaving for foreign shores.

"About fifteen people showed up at the party. Some of them might not have liked me, but it was a free meal, and they had to try to be polite. I enjoyed watching them squirm. I remember Uncle George making a big production out of giving me an Italian suit, saying, 'I want you to wear it when you get to Tel Aviv, and when you get there, check for holes in the pockets.' He might have said, 'When you get to the moon!' for all I knew about Tel Aviv. It sounded like a city built out of TV sets. The crack about holes in the pockets meant there was something in one of the pockets for me… money. He may have been glad to see me go, but he had always been very good to me.

"The party was a great success, especially as far as I was concerned. Aunt Shirley turned up, and gave me an envelope, as did Uncle Allen. My grandfather and grandmother shook my hand and when they were through, I found a hundred dollar bill in it. Uncle

George said to me, "Larry I don't know how you did it, but mazel tov (congratulations)! It's a good thing, so don't mess it up. Mother motioned to Irving and Bernie (who had shown up against their will, but of course they had to be polite). She drew them aside and told them since I was the youngest, they should keep an eye out for me, make sure I didn't get separated from the group, etc.

"Bernie smiled sweetly at her and replied, 'Larry was able to get to go on this trip. I think he knows how to look after himself, Mrs. Wiener. He'll be all right, don't worry.' The party eventually wound down to an end, and Mom kissed them all goodbye. Then, she handed everyone a twenty dollar bill, saying, 'It's just a little something for you gentle young men going on such an adventurous, brave journey.' I've never been sure if she actually meant that, or if it was offered as a sort of bribe to keep good old Larry out of trouble.

"And so, Saundra, that's how it all began. You know as much about me now as anyone on board. Now, I'd like to know more about you, because… if you haven't guessed… I think you're someone very special. Say, just for luck, how about if I give you a kiss?"

I figured it was about time to get down to brass tacks, to think about doing some serious loving. I was a little surprised at her reaction to this. "Why, Larry, I'd be pleased to accept a kiss from you, especially a lucky kiss." And she turned her face toward me. I kissed her on both cheeks, and then on the lips.

"Not too bad for a Canadian," she laughed. "Would you like to do a retake," I asked, "just to make sure?" She shook her head, "Not here. Let's go to my quarters." I could hardly believe my ears. When she got up and beckoned to me, I would have followed her anywhere.

As soon as the door to her room closed behind us, I froze up. She looked at me and shrugged, smiling, and that melted any icy fear I might have had that it was all a joke. Teenage insecurity hits the best of us, I reasoned, and tossed the momentary feeling aside. We kissed, softly at first. My arms went about her and we waltzed toward the bed. Pulling me down on top of her, she looked up at me with her big, beautiful eyes and whispered, "Well, Larry? Why didn't you do this the first night we met?" I didn't know what to say, except that I'd wanted to, but thought she wouldn't want to, because at that point we were strangers. "I wanted to know you as a friend, not an enemy, Saundra. It's not that I didn't think about it, but my mother always said to be respectful. If something's going to happen, it will, but you have to give it a little time."

"I thought maybe it would have happened sooner," she said. I didn't know what to say to that, but she went on to explain. She'd always had a problem this way. Boys always thought she was so pretty, she said, but they were afraid to make an advance. I told her that all beautiful women felt the same way. "People are afraid they'll be refused. No one likes to be rejected, so, thinking they might be, they don't bother trying."

"How about you, Larry? If you refuse me, I get nothing. If you didn't approach me, I'd be left out on a limb, too. It's not a one-way street."

Not a lot happened then… we didn't have sex, if that's what you're wondering. We fooled around awhile, and then went to lunch. There would be time for making love afterwards. We'd make sure of it. Probably, we'd never see each other again, except in memories.

We went up and had lunch. The gang was there, and I expected a bit of static because I hadn't spent any time at all with them, and they weren't very happy with me anyway. To them, I was the fifth wheel that just couldn't fall into sync with whatever was supposed to be going on. A tight knit group isn't the best place in the world for anyone who just wants to be himself.

So the first comment came via Debbie, "What's the matter, Larry? You think you're too good for us or what?" I shook my head, "No, it's just that my parents came from better stock. I mean, if you want to sit here and trade insults, we can do that, but I don't have time for it. You're blaming me for being unfriendly, but listen to how you start off a conversation. Why should I lower myself to that kind of talk? I can, but why should I?"

I went on to say I wasn't very interested, if at all, in their little group meetings. "You discuss your plans over and over and over. What will we be doing when we get to Israel? Where will we sleep, what will we eat, what kind of work is there to do, how will we like it? I'm sorry, but I'm just not interested. I want to take things as they come, live life as it happens. I don't want everything all mapped out for me. If I wanted to do that, I'd sit at home and dream, start writing poetry or something. If you don't like the way I do things, well... there's nothing to be done about it.

"So, I beat the system. My motives are different from yours. Why not just leave it at that? You go about your business, and let me tend to mine. I don't interfere with you, why are you always bothering me? Live and let live... ever heard of that saying? I suppose not. They didn't tell you that in synagogue. I don't care about your plans. We'll all go to Israel on the same boat, but that's it, okay?"

The more I talked, the angrier I became. I'd been storing it up, and now it was coming out. Well, she shouldn't have pushed me. Couldn't they just be friendly? Hadn't they ever heard of co-existence? Rabbi Irving piped up then, saying to the group, "Well, you know, Larry may be beating you at your own game. You see, Bernie, you offered him a deal to have an expense paid vacation in Israel, and I think you didn't really mean it. You didn't ever expect him to go, but here he is, isn't he? Mark my words, Bernie - I have a real feeling about this. Larry will do his job, and he will do it very well.

"You may be against him and everything he stands for, but this is because of jealousy. He, you see, gambled the same as you did, but he won. Leave it at that, or no good will ever come out of it, wait and see."

It was nice to see someone agreed with me. Maybe he'd had a revelation from God, and was sharing the wisdom. It made sense to me. Of course the others didn't quite see it that way.

"He didn't gamble much," the other Irving muttered. "He held all the high cards from the beginning. When you have the money, you can't lose. So, he didn't lose."

This being their favourite note, they all started in on me. I said nothing to defend myself, though I could have. I might have mentioned that Bernie was no more than a big bully, pushing his weight around wherever he went, to get his way, or that our wonderful Jewish pilgrim Irving was studying how to be a good little Marxist. I might have talked about Debbie's moodiness when she didn't have her way, too, for that matter. And, even if he sometimes did side with me, it would have been easy to point out the Rabbi's nutty religious habits... I mean, weren't they a bit extreme? But I didn't like hurting people's feelings.

Privately, I thought we were the motliest crew of pilgrims ever invented, and if this was typical of groups coming from America to help build Israel, the country would be in a shambles long before we left. Collectively, about all we were good at was fighting. But even if we were put in that position, we'd be so busy fighting each other, we'd still be useless to "the cause". In a way, I hoped the whole thing would fall apart, that we'd be sent back... but not before I got some more travelling in! It was obvious, the group and I were worlds apart, in almost every way imaginable... why waste time arguing with them? It didn't do any good.

I decided that when we arrived at our destination, I might be able to lay down a few ground rules of my own. Knowing Bernie, he'd never let me, he was just too regimentally-minded. He was like a straight peg in a straight-peg world, and refused to see that there might be other worlds. He'd never allow anyone near him to be anything else than what he thought they should be, and in a way, I felt sorry for him. I had my own ideas, though, about what life in a kibbutz might be like. Maybe the people there would live like monks in a monastery, everything done to a daily routine. Bernie would like that, but he'd like a militia-style kibbutz better. Hell, he'd probably like living in a bunker, with barbed wire surrounding everyone so no one could move.

The Rabbi burped, snapping me out of my thoughts. The group was staring at me, as if expecting some sort of reply. Maybe one of them had said something I hadn't heard. I thought we should change the subject, though, because we were getting nowhere. I didn't want to turn the group completely against me. Things were bad enough as they were, and I still had to be with them.

The Rabbi burped again, and excused himself, adding, "Larry, I can see your girl over there having her lunch, and she really is gorgeous." I didn't think he'd notice such things, but he did. "I don't know how you do it, Larry, but I noticed she was talking with you, and seems to like you."

"Maybe I'm just lucky, Irving, but I think we should enjoy ourselves while we can. She's just a friend, you know... someone to talk to." I tried to say it in such a way they'd get the message, there's nobody in this crowd I can talk to!... but I imagine it went right over their heads. Irving asked a few more questions about Saundra... where she was from, what her parents did, where she was going, why and for how long, etc. I was glad to tell him, to talk about something else for a change.

I said she was from Argentina and that she was going to visit her uncle. Then she'd be heading back home. This seemed to satisfy everyone, though I don't know why they were so curious. I knew what the others were dying to ask, but didn't have the nerve to... had we slept together yet? In my mind, I had a flash of them all, fifty years later, sitting around gossiping about their neighbours. They were getting a good head start.

Having heard enough about Saundra, Debbie asked what was on the agenda for the rest of the day. Bernie replied there wasn't any agenda, but mentioned there'd be a fire drill between one and two o'clock in the afternoon. "They want everyone to be sure of what to do, in case of an emergency. We have to be ready to face anything." He seemed to be taking it very seriously, so I remarked that the *Gramani* would probably sink if it accidentally ran into a sardine. It was funny, but no one laughed.

A short discussion about life in Israel broke out. Debbie was curious to know what the men were like there. Being my usual somewhat saucy self, I told her I had no idea, as I'd never been there. Rabbi Irving wondered aloud what life in a religious kibbutz would hold for him. He had heard about them when he had first been recruited and the idea had stuck. He wasn't very fussy about having to go to an ordinary kibbutz, but the Jewish Agency had explained to him that, really, there was no way they could directly place him in a religious one. When he had been on a regular kibbutz awhile, they said, he could then apply for a transfer. If there was an opening, there was a chance he would be moved. That was all they could tell him about it.

As the Rabbi was telling us (for the fiftieth time), Irving spoke up: "So, what's the big attraction at a religious kibbutz? Do you expect Moses himself to come and visit every three days?"

The Rabbi's brow began to knit as he thought of an answer to this. Would these idiots never understand? He was saved by the bell just then, as it rang over our heads, meaning it was time to go and get our life jackets and put them on... another drill. The only way you could avoid taking part in this was if you were in the infirmary. You had to put your life jacket on, and you had to put it on the right way, and all done up. No half measures here. Then, you proceeded to the main deck and lined up with all of the other passengers, and stepped out when your name was called. They used the "buddy system"... each person paired with another, so that in the event of our actually having to vacate the boat, no one would turn up missing afterwards.

It was a good enough system and privately I was glad we had to rehearse it every day. The *Gramani* looked ready to go down anytime. I imagine the insurance company demanded these safety rehearsals, which took about twenty minutes to run through. Nobody seemed to mind. I think everyone was secretly glad, due to the terrible condition of our well-aged ship.

Afterwards, I came to realize I'd been spending enough time with Saundra, and that it might be best if I just let things between us slide for the time being. We had all been given a small book about the Holy Land, called *This is Israel*, and I figured maybe it was time I took a look at it, seeing as how we would soon be there. It would be a bit of a chance to learn a little about the country beforehand... which was, of course, why we'd been given the book. If there were customs I didn't know about, now was a good time to learn, before I got myself into trouble due to simple ignorance of what might be expected. I mean, did people bow to each other when meeting, should pilgrims (like our group) kiss the sand upon arrival, look for signs in the skies, or what?

So, I went to my room and found the book, laid down on my bunk with it, and started to read. To my complete amazement, I discovered there was absolutely no means of transportation anywhere between sundown Friday to sundown Saturday. If you wanted to go anywhere, you'd have to hoof it! Incredible, I thought. I read on. You might be able to take a taxi, if you could find one, and there was ambulance service if you happened to become sick enough to need hospitalization, or were in an accident. I shook my head, and read on.

The foods available included many small portions of meat, but vegetables and fruit seemed to be plentiful. There were the native foods such as falafel, chumus and pita bread. There was also halvah, and what there seemed to be the most of was sunflower seeds. Wonderful, I thought. I'll have a sunflower seed steak, please make it rare, and some sunflower seed pie for dessert!

The way of life in Israel was hard, but the people had found ways of balancing their time well. Most people seemed to think at that time that Israel was a closed-minded society, because of the religious connotations. Probably, people think that today, too. It isn't true, though. Even when I was there, in the late fifties, you could go to a movie theatre, and anything might be playing. There were dining halls, dance clubs... you name it. So, contrary to what others thought, Israel was pretty much on a par with other countries.

The hardest job to be found anywhere in Israel (and it stated this right there in black and white, in the little book I was reading)... was working on a kibbutz. It was described as being one step below army life. "Just what I needed to hear," I thought. That was about the time it began to dawn on me that maybe I'd let this thing go too far, but it was too late to do anything about it now. Having come this far, there was no backing out. Once I'd stepped on board the *Gramani*, I'd signed my year away. I felt like I'd joined the foreign legion.

Something fell out of the book... a little game to while away the time with. There was also a bit of money stuffed away in the back of the book. I flipped through it, to empty it, and noticed the pictures. The scenery was described as being very beautiful, breathtakingly so. The hotels were also supposed to be quite elegant. According to the book, Greece and Israel could stand together in their claim of being the most historical sites in the world. I read on and on, marvelling at some of the things it said about my destination. After an hour or so of browsing in the book, reading a bit here, a bit there, I suddenly felt very tired, laid the book down and fell asleep.

I awoke to the ringing of the supper bell. It was five o'clock. I felt like I'd slept for a week. I was hungry, and hurried up to the dinner table, thinking to myself that I didn't want to start in arguing again with the group as had happened at noontime. When you're busy arguing, thinking of ways to attack others or defend yourself, you simply don't enjoy your food. So I thought I'd just sit down, mind my own business and eat my bagels and whatever else was on the menu.

In the middle of the first bite, Debbie caught my eye and said, "Larry, why are you so quiet? Aren't you feeling well?"

I told her the truth, saying I'd had enough of arguing for the day. I figured if I said nothing, they'd have nothing to say, either. "I'm not trying to be anti-social. I don't mind talking, but I hate this constant bickering that's going on." She looked puzzled, as if I'd said I'd just returned from Mars.

As if on cue, Rabbi Irving nodded to me and said he'd heard that our boat would be making a stop in Sardinia for a few hours, if everything went smoothly. I asked what he meant by everything going smoothly.

"Well," he said, delighted to be the one bearing news, "there seem to be some rumblings around the ship that something big is happening in Israel." I asked him, "Like what?" but that was all he could tell us. I wondered if it would affect the people on the *Gramani*. As we found out an hour or so later, there had been some strange activities on the mainland. Every boat on the Mediterranean heading toward Israel was notified and told to halt. This was relayed to us over the loudspeaker system, saying that the vessel would only be going as far as the island of Sardinia.

They gave us no reason for this procedure, however, and we were left to wonder what was going on. We were only told that we would be docked on the island "for as long as the Israeli docks are closed". One of the passengers had a small portable radio, and we heard on a news broadcast that Israel was being attacked. I went searching for Saundra, wondering if she had heard this yet. I figured she had, because the whole ship was abuzz, with little pockets of people scattered here and there, talking it up, wondering what would become of us.

I met Saundra coming down the stairway on her way to look for me, just as I had been looking for her. "Great minds must think alike," I told her. We went out onto the main deck where a genuine Rabbi was urging people to go on a hunger strike if the boat didn't proceed on to Israel. We thought this was taking things a little too far, and went off in the other direction, away from him.

It was a nice day, and so we stayed out on the deck for quite awhile. Then, there was another announcement: the island of Sardinia was only twenty-five minutes away, and the boat would be docking there. No-one knew for how long, though. We were given new rules to abide by. No passenger would be able to leave the ship when we docked. When this was announced, the Rabbi showed up again. He had been pacing back and forth along the deck mumbling away to himself (or to his God, perhaps) for all he was worth. Now, he became more animated... and loudly proclaimed that we must begin our hunger strike immediately. No one had any idea how long we might be stuck in port, though, and I had other ideas!

A certain passenger that I had met was there, with a full regular salami and a loaf of bread. He asked if I would like to have some of his food. The rest of our group, urged on by the zealous Rabbi, had decided to join in the hunger strike, but I wasn't about to. What was the good of that, anyway? We'd all just wind up hungry and weak. So, I obliged my friend, and accepted his offer of something to eat, and shared half of what he gave me with Saundra.

Someone in the control room must have called the local radio station, as I noticed a small motorboat approaching the ship, carrying a man with a camera slung around his shoulder. We had finished eating, and Irving and Bernie came over to razz me about not joining in the strike. The boat pulled closer to the *Gramani*, and the man started to climb aboard. As we were hanging over the railing watching, as soon as he hit deck level, he made his way toward us.

"Can I have a word with you folks?" he asked, looking us over carefully. "Are you with the group of five Canadians going to Israel?" Bernie, always on the lookout for publicity, spoke up, "Yes, we are. What would you like to know?" You'd have thought we were heroes, the way the reporter/photographer looked at us.

"Well," he said, "I'd like to take your picture, and ask you a few questions, if that's all right with you." He reminded us that the world was already aware that the boat had been ordered stopped. He then asked if we'd read the morning paper. None of us had. He informed us then that our picture was on the front page. We, of course, were delighted to hear this... everyone, that is, except Rabbi

Irving, who thought it was an invasion of the group's privacy.

The reporter asked again if he could take five or six pho-tographs, and asked the usual questions… how we had been cho-sen, why we were going, and what we thought we'd be doing once we got there. He didn't seem to know where Toronto was, though he'd heard of it. When we explained the geography of Canada, he'd never heard of the province of Ontario. He'd never heard of any of the provinces. He snapped a few more pictures, making sure every-one showed a lot of teeth, and asked what we thought of the hunger strike. Seeing that Bernie and I were going to begin arguing about whether or not we wanted to fill our bellies, the reporter smiled and said, "Forget it. What I really wanted was the pictures. What you think isn't important."

He shook our hands, and headed off to another deck. I was so pleased with this turn of events, I couldn't keep the news to myself, and went off in search of Saundra. I found her in her cabin, sitting and reading.

"Saundra," I said, "I'm famous! This time tomorrow, my picture will be on the front pages of newspapers all around the world! What do you think of that?" She said she though it was great. We talked for a while, and then I kissed her goodnight and said I'd see her in the morning.

I went to our cabin, and said goodnight to Irving. The night passed quietly and without further incident after that, although none of us knew what would happen. There we were, stuck. We were just sitting in the water, waiting for further instructions and there was nothing to be done about it. Not even the captain could do anything. If he made a decision on his own, like deciding to go ahead with the trip and hang the consequences, we'd all be in trouble, possibly big trouble. So, we waited. It was completely out of our hands.

I had an urge again to eat something. That salami simply was-n't enough to hold a growing boy like me. Looking over at the other bunk, I saw that Irving was in the land of dreams, and I crept out of the cabin. I went up onto the main deck, where I saw the purs-er. I told him I was hungry.

He was very accommodating, saying not to worry, he'd fix me up with some food. What would I like? I told him it didn't matter,

I'd leave it up to him. He told me to stay where I was, and he'd be back in a couple of minutes. He returned carrying a plate of roast chicken, potatoes, corn and gravy in one hand, and in the other, he balanced a dish of ice cream and a bottle of Brio. I thanked him and sat down and started in on the meal.

So here I was again, in my usual position: while the others starved, I feasted. Well, that was their problem. If they were stupid enough to think a hunger strike was going to change anything… let them. When I finished my meal, I headed back to our quarters and, with a full belly, fell asleep almost instantly.

At about five in the morning, I was awakened by the steady chuga-chuga-chuga of our engines. We were underway again. Still feeling the effects of the chicken, I smiled and drifted off to sleep again.

When I next awoke, I was thinking that with the ship on its way again, there would be no more outside friends after we hit port, that my little romance with Saundra would be over and I'd be in the salt mines or wherever we were all headed. What did I know about kibbutz life, anyway? Maybe all it meant was we were going to be the ones to provide the cheap labour. Why not? They've been doing it on Spadina Avenue for years, haven't they? I knew I'd have to pay for my good times, one way or another. It's a terrible thing to think of though, first thing in the morning, before you even get out of bed!

After getting dressed, I headed down to the dining area for breakfast. Despite the forlorn appearance of the vessel, the trip aboard the *Gramani* hadn't been a bad one, and was actually much better than we'd expected. We hadn't encountered any heavy seas, and I was thankful for that, but everything else went very well. The meals were good, the staff was friendly. It wasn't the *Queen Mary*, but we knew it wouldn't be. Even the group I was with weren't so bad, if I thought about it. After all, we were just kids really. None of us had any real life experience behind us… we were on our way to get some!

I caught myself thinking these things because I was trying to avoid thinking about Saundra. I really didn't want to say goodbye to her, but knew I would have to… and soon. Within the day, we would be seeing the shoreline of Haifa, and what we had started off to do seemingly so long ago back in Canada would soon enough have become a reality. In a way, I looked forward to it, and in another way, I didn't.

After breakfast, I went out on deck where the rest of the group had already gathered. They were clearly starting to get excited about the prospect of landfall. "Homelandfall," as Bernie put it, pointing into the distance when he saw me approaching. "This is a special time for us," he went on, "a day to remember. We'll have something to tell our parents about and our children later in life. Future generations will look back on us and remember what we're doing."

"And with a free tour of Europe and the Mediterranean, as well," piped up Peggy,"Winnipeg will never look the same to me again. I never did like living on the edge of the prairies, anyway."

Nodding my agreement, I started to tell them that I, too, had had a pretty good trip so far. Then, I spotted Saundra heading for the bow of the boat. Being my usual congenial self, I excused myself and left them.

It was a beautiful day, and seeing Saundra made it even better, even if I was feeling a bit melancholy. I sidled up to her and surprised her from behind, slipping my arm around her shoulders. She turned and smiled, a sweet, sad smile. She, too, knew we were coming to the end of our little affair... if you could even call it that. I told her I thought we had been meant to meet and spend time together, and that without her, the trip for me would have been a complete bore. That probably wasn't true, as I seemed to have a knack for meeting new people when no one else did, but still, it was the right thing to say to her.

She told me the same applied to her. She had always wanted to meet a North American, preferably male, preferably young. I fit the bill perfectly, she said. I asked how we might be able to get in touch with one another once we landed in Israel, but she didn't want that. "I'm happy the way things are, Larry. It's been a simple shipboard romance, the best. Let's not push for more. This way, we'll both remember it for the rest of our lives. We've had our fling and it's been great. We should leave it like that."

Once she disembarked from the boat, she said, it would be strictly business... she'd be busy with her family affairs, and wouldn't have time for much else. Eventually, she'd have to return home, and that would be the end of her travelling for a while. Once we got off the boat, it would be the same for me... strictly business. There was a nation to build, or so I'd been told, and I was to be one of the builders. We'd never see each other again, so why try to carry something on that could never be? So, I thought, this is it. I'd better make a play now, or forget it! I still wanted to get her into bed. I didn't know why, but I needed another conquest. I didn't want to forget her. I didn't want her to forget me.

I put my head down next to hers and whispered a suggestion into her ear, something I thought we'd both enjoy... sort of a parting gift to and from each of us. She laughed and said, "Sure, Larry, I'll give you a goodbye kiss, if you like. You've been a good companion on this trip, and I appreciated your company." She kissed me, giving me a little hug to boot. She had to go to her quarters and pack her things, she said. And with that, without another word, she traipsed off toward the stairway leading to her cabin. I stood watching her go, out of my life forever.

As she disappeared down the stairs, my room-mate Irving was coming up. Spotting me, he waved and came toward me. Neither of us said anything for a moment, but just stood there, staring over the bow at the water beneath us. Finally, he asked what I'd thought of the whole trip, now that it was drawing to a close. He, too, seemed a little sad. I told him I hadn't dreamed it would ever turn out the way it did. We'd been in four countries, and been treated like royalty. And now it was over and the work would begin.

Originally, we'd thought the trip would be a simple matter of jumping on a boat and winding up in Israel, just like that. Splash splash and bingo, we'd be there. We hadn't realized the effort that had been put into it, to keep us happy and occupied along the way. They might be recruiting slaves, but the Jewish Agency wasn't all that bad. They'd treated us pretty good, all in all. We couldn't argue about that. What we had signed up for wasn't exactly what we'd been given. We got more than we'd bargained for, and for a moment, I was almost thankful. We'd been given a crash tour of Europe, with a few days in each place completely free of charge. For someone like me, who'd signed up as a sort of joke, it was beyond belief.

I'd written to Mother every few days, and asked Irving if he'd written to his mother also. He said he had, right from the start, just to let her know how things were going, so she wouldn't worry. I never met a Jewish mother who didn't worry, though, so the letters we sent probably helped.

"Well," Irving said suddenly, as if remembering he really wasn't supposed to be a friend of mine, "enough of this talk. I'm going downstairs for awhile."

His saying this made me remember there was a gift shop on the next level. I thought maybe I should go down there and pick up a little something for Saundra as a goodbye gift.

"Wait up," I said to Irving. "I'll go with you." I told him what I'd been thinking, and he, too, thought it would be a good idea.

"You spent four days with her, Larry. I don't know what she could have seen in you, but women are a mystery, and they say love is blind. It would be nice, though, if you gave her something in appreciation."

He was right. At the gift shop, I couldn't see much in the way of jewellery or trinkets she might like, and so bought her a box of chocolates for her to take to her aunt and uncle. I picked up a couple of cards to go along with it... one from me to her, and one for her to give to her relatives, and headed off to her cabin. I knocked, telling her who it was, and she opened the door. Handing her the chocolates, which I'd had wrapped, I told her she could do what she wanted with them, but that I thought it would be nice if she passed them on, and gave her the cards.

As she took them, she leaned over and kissed me, saying she'd never forget me. "Thank you, Larry. You're very sweet." And she closed the door, slowly. I knew then that this was it, I'd never see her again, and walked slowly back to the stairway and up onto the deck again...and who was there waiting for me, but Bernie, standing by the railing.

As soon as he saw me, he called out, waving me over. "Hey, Larry! So you're still on board! I don't know how you made it this far on your own!"

I said, "Well, Bernie, it wasn't hard. It was free, and for free, you can do anything. But we'll have to start work soon, too. Are you ready for that? I am. But, listen Bernie… how about doing every-one a favour and knock it off, will you? We don't have much free time left, so let's at least pretend to be friendly, eh? I mean, the first thing you said to me today, just now, was to razz me. Just drop it, okay. Because I'm not going to respond. Or, if you push it, and I do respond, we'll both be sorry. I'd sooner we got along. What do you think of that idea?"

He nodded. "You're right, Larry. When we get to Israel, it'll be their show, not ours. We'll just be the players, doing the dirty work. Yeah, you're right. We might as well try to get along."

He shook my hand, probably against his will. But he did it, most likely not for my sake, but for the sake of the group. I thanked him, and said I had to leave. There were a couple of people I'd met on board, like the fellow who'd shared his salami with me and I want-ed to say goodbye to them. I wanted to try to find the Rabbi who had been so instrumental in forming the short-lived hunger strike, too. Just for the fun of it, I wanted to ask if the first thing he'd eaten when it was over had been kosherized! I thought I'd better not get him going again, though, and went looking for some of the others.

Over the intercom, we could hear the purser telling us to go to our quarters to get our things in order, and to have our passports ready because we would be disembarking shortly. All I had was just a small bag, so it wasn't long before I was back on deck, all set to do whatever came next. The purser's voice came over the speaker sys-tem again, informing us that within twenty minutes, we would be docking at Haifa.

In a way, I felt a little disappointed that the trip was over, and slightly sorry because of the way I had acted (or reacted) toward some of our group, but the excitement of not knowing what might be coming next quickly overcame any sense of loss or remorse. I began to wonder what they were going to do with us now that we were there. Really, I didn't care, because after all, I would have a year to think about it. We would go wherever they sent us, and that would be that. There wasn't any use in worrying over it. Quite lit-erally, we were all in the same boat. I remember thinking, "Well, at least we'll have our feet on solid ground for a change."

Then the whistle was blowing and the ship's engines stopped. The loudspeaker system squealed as if in pain, and the voice of the purser was telling all and sundry how the captain and crew hoped we all had an enjoyable voyage aboard the *Gramani*, reminding us to have our passports ready. We were to line up by the landing board. It would take roughly an hour, he said, for us to claim whatever other baggage we had on board. The loudspeaker squealed again, and it shut off.

The purser came down to the gangway to check our passports and to see us off. I could see the luggage coming down a slide from out of the side of the ship, and once it was all down, searched for my old brown suitcase. I couldn't see it, and looked more closely. All of the baggage had come down, because they were taking the slide away, but mine just wasn't there. I made my way toward the purser, and told him I couldn't see it.

"I'm in a foreign land," I said, "and everything I own is in that bag. I can't claim anything if I don't have it. Where is it?" I was upset, obviously.

I think the purser's intent was to try to calm me down, but his words weren't very reassuring. "If you give me your baggage ticket, we'll check it out for you. I'll have the crew members try and track it down for you, but you know, from time to time, things are taken right from the docks. If that's the case, you'll most likely never see your baggage again. We'll do our best, though, to get it back for you. There's a slight chance it may have been left in the ship's baggage room, or otherwise misplaced."

That wasn't much help, but there was nothing I could do. The way I looked at it, if worst came to worst, I would have to start collecting odd pieces of clothing here and there. I wondered what the shopping was like in Israel. Bernie, enjoying my discomfort, whispered to me something like, "So, you lost your clothes, Larry. Well, there's no need to fret, is there? They say the desert gets very hot, so you won't need much, anyway." It was so nice to know that he sympathized with me... a true friend.

Our group was together now, and before I could tell Bernie where he could stick his desert and everything that was in it, one of us spotted a man standing on the dock holding up a big hand-drawn sign, "Looking for Canadian Jewish group". Peggy, revealing her nervousness and excitement at the prospect of finally being where we were supposed to be, slapped Irving soundly on the back and shouted in a voice loud enough for everyone to hear, "Hey, he must mean us!" Very astute, Peg, we never would have guessed.

With our hands raised in the air, as if he hadn't already heard us, we made our way toward the man like a group of trained seals. After a short introduction, he told us he would give us a little time to get our things together and "get the feeling of being on land back into our legs." I was just beginning to do that, when all of a sudden who should I see in the distance but Saundra. She was looking furtively around, and then I heard a rather high-pitched voice calling her. "Saundra, Saundra!!"

"Here I am," she cried. It must have been her aunt. I was going to go over and say yet another goodbye to her, but just then the Jewish Agency man told us to pick up our things and get ready to take a "Sherut", which is a large taxi. I took one final look in Saundra's direction, then at the boat. It really did look unseaworthy on the outside, but I had to admit, it hadn't been bad on board. It had been a pretty good trip. We piled into the oversized cab and it pulled away, the driver making sure our introduction to the Land of Milk and Money was an exciting one, by passing everything that got in his way, horn blowing like he was heralding in the arrival of the new Messiah.

And so, the final leg of the journey was over. This was it… there'd be no turning back from this point on. If anyone had any thoughts of backing out, it was too late to do anything about it now. I felt good about myself, and the taxi driver must have sensed this… when we suddenly came to a shrieking halt, he turned around and winked at me… probably because I was obviously the youngest member of the group… and said, in impeccable English, "So, welcome to Israel, kid. This is where it all begins."

PART FIVE

Israel

...We Made It

As we wound our way through the crooked streets, Rabbi Irving spoke up, as if waking from a deep trance,"Well, gang, we made it. We're here." He had a habit of doing that, and unless you knew him, he gave the impression of being about to say something momentous. I turned to the driver and asked, "Where are we headed, anyway?"

He said that we were going to stop over in a place called Beer-Sheva for lunch, adding that the food might seem somewhat different to us from what we'd been used to. He told us that he would do the ordering, and we should enjoy the result. Irving, always conscious of the almighty dollar, asked how much this was going to cost us. We were told not to worry about that, as everything was being paid for by the Jewish Agency.

We weren't accustomed to using Israeli currency, and besides, we had none. The driver explained it would be best to go slowly, to take things in one at a time, and again, not to worry about anything. We were in the Promised Land, weren't we?

In the cab on the way in to Beer-Sheva, I had been sitting next to the window, and the scenery was quite different from anything I'd ever seen before, kind of unrelentingly the same, but very beautiful in its own way. My thoughts were interrupted by the driver asking where we'd come from. Bernie told him that three of us were from Toronto, Canada, and that the young lady was from Winnipeg, Canada.

The driver scratched his head, as if trying to remember where Canada was, then nodded his head as if suddenly seeing a map inside his head. He seemed to know all about us anyway, and was probably asking only to be polite, but he was curious, he said, as to why such a group of young people would come to a land so far away from their home. Bernie, of course, told him we had come to do service for the Israeli government for the period of one year. The cab driver was impressed, saying that we must be very strong-willed individuals to decide to do such a thing. I distinctly got the impression he would never dream of leaving home and country to go anywhere, unless it was under the instructions of a fare.

Rabbi Irving made us sound even better, stating that he felt it was the duty of every young Jew to come to the homeland and work as best they were able to help build it up. He added that he thought a year in a religious kibbutz would be the best idea, and that this was his plan, while the rest of us would simply be working in the fields. "It'll be good discipline for all of us," he added.

Discipline, I thought. Just what I wanted. The cab driver nodded his head in agreement. "You are smart. Young people need discipline these days. I admire you, all of you, for what you are doing."

I asked him where exactly we were going, but he would only tell us, "to have lunch in Beer-Sheva." That wasn't what I meant, I explained. "Well," he said, "we will see. In about five minutes, we will be stopping to eat your first Israeli meal, and then you will be going to where you will be living for the next year."

We were approaching a road sign, which was printed in both Hebrew and English. "We have arrived," our driver said. "There is a small restaurant just along this road, where we will stop. The owner knows of the Jewish Agency and so he will treat you very well. He will feed you, but ask for no money. So, choose whatever you like, and enjoy your meal. When you are finished, simply tell him to thank him for being such a good host, and he will be pleased. That is all you have to do."

We stopped and got out of the cab and stretched, then went inside the restaurant or café as it was called. A man came over to our table and said, "Shalom!" Our driver, who had taken it upon himself to accompany us, spoke to the proprietor, asking him to please speak in English, as we didn't know Hebrew well enough to converse in it.

"Of course!" the owner said, smiling. He spread his arms out and shrugged. "We will speak in English, then. And what would our young friends like to have to eat?"

We didn't have a clue what to order, since we couldn't understand a word of the menu. The cab driver, however, came to our rescue, and made choices for us. "Give them falafel, chumus, and pita... oh, and four gazoz (soda pop).

The owner thanked us and went off to get our food. A few minutes later, he was back. Everything was ready for us. We really enjoyed the pita, as it was about as fresh as it could be... still warm from the oven. The owned stood by, watching us eat, as if it gave him great satisfaction. "You should eat sparingly," he said, "because your stomachs may become upset owing to of the heat."

We thought that over for a moment... it was very hot... and ate slowly. The food was excellent, and when the proprietor saw that we had finished, he brought us dishes of ice cream for dessert. "This is help for the heat," he said. It was a little different, being slightly richer than what we were used to, but very good.

Again, I asked the driver the exact location of our destination, but he only shrugged and said, "You will see, soon enough."

"Why won't you tell us? What's the big secret?"

"Well," he said, "all I have been given is a note. When you have finished eating, we will return to the taxi and be on our way."

It seemed a very mysterious way to act toward us, but we supposed the driver had his reasons. Maybe it was a secret location or something... maybe it was near a military site. Still, it didn't make much sense to me, why he couldn't tell us. There was no one else to hear, except the owner of the café, and he was obviously a sympathizer, at least with the aims of the Jewish Agency. But, there was nothing to do except trust that the cab driver knew what he was doing.

After thanking the owner for his fine food and hospitality, we piled back into the taxi and were soon underway again. The scenery changed... wherever we were headed, now all that could be seen was highway and desert. There were no buildings, or any other sign of life… which was a trifle disconcerting. The driver mentioned that we might find our destination strange at first, but added that we would enjoy it. We only had a short way left to go, he said, and now he felt it would be all right to let us in on what our destination was.

"Do you know where you are now?" he asked.

"Of course we don't," I replied. "How could we? We've never been here before!" I was getting a little tired of the secrecy game. "You can tell us any time, you know. We're not going to jump out of the cab and run away."

"We are in the land of God," the rabbi said, not seeming to care what the taxi driver had to say.

"Irving!" Debbie hushed him. "Let the man tell us himself!"

The cab driver, whose name, it turned out, was Abram, had kept the secret to himself long enough. "Have you heard of the Gaza Strip? It is better known to the rest of the world, perhaps, as the Negev. We have entered the most dangerous part of the land of Israel. There is but one thing to say about this place, and that is, you stay here only as long as you have to. You leave this place as quickly as you can, before you are killed. More people, you see, are slaughtered here on the Gaza Strip than in any other place in the country. So this is where we are. The reason I didn't tell you before now was because I did not want to frighten you. But, to get to your destination, we must take this road. There can be no avoiding it."

Fearless Bernie wanted to know why, of all places, we had been placed in such a dangerous location. "I've read plenty about this area, it's a desert Hell! Why would they send us to this kibbutz, anyway? There must be safer ones. I don't understand this!"

I wanted to tell him that maybe our reputation had preceded us, but figured he was upset enough already. I didn't know if I should be scared or not. Looking out through the windows of the cab, there was no sign of anything dangerous, unless you count sun and sand. I'd heard about the Gaza Strip, too, though. There was always some kind of trouble here.

Abram tried to make us feel better by saying that out of all the kibbutzim in Israel, this particular one… Nachal Oz… was reputedly the strongest. "Those who come here are hand-picked. They do not know what fear is. To them, it's a business, a work to be done. If they have to kill, they do so without worrying about it. Killing means nothing to any of them. It is really their purpose in being here, you see..."

What? So why were five unknown Canadians being picked for a year's duty in this place? It didn't make any sense to any of us, and we said so.

Abram replied that he didn't know, either. His orders were simply to get us there safely and to go home again. He was unable... or unwilling... to explain anything more than this to us. Fear can do wonders when it comes to uniting people. For the first time in a long time, our group acted as an actual group, debating back and forth, trying to come up with some sort of reason that made sense, why we would be stationed in a place like this. We didn't come up with much, except Bernie's notion that it may have been some kind of political thing... killing young innocent Canadians might not work to the best interests of anyone...

"Except, of course, the Israelis," I said.

The Rabbi had his own idea about why we were here... it wasn't the Israelis who wanted us, it was God. This was a test, and if we had faith like Moses, everything would work out. There's one thing to be said for being overly religious... you can talk yourself into anything. All you have to do is believe Something is making you do it.

In the Fields of Nachal Oz

Up ahead of us, off to the right, we could see a fenced off area that looked suspiciously like a military compound, with rolls of barbed wire heading off in almost every direction, and buildings set back from the road. We pulled up alongside the front gates, and Abram said, "Welcome to your new home. Come with me. Have your passports ready. We must meet briefly with the leader of the kibbutz, and then I will be on my way."

We piled out of the car and headed toward the gates, which opened at our approach. A giant of a man came out and shook Abram's hand. Then he turned, looked down, and greeted us. He really was huge, just an immense man.

He looked us over, grinning. "Abram, my friend," he said, "what is this? Are they sending children to us now? A child will have to do a man's work. Well, well…"

He introduced himself as Moshe, extending an enormous hand, which, one by one, we accepted (hoping he wouldn't squeeze too hard!) as he asked us our names, explaining that he was the leader of the kibbutz. He was in charge of assigning people to various duties. Looking at Debbie, he said, "I think you will do well working in the laundry room." She could also help with taking care of the children, he said.

The women of the kibbutz, he said, carried guns with them "to protect the land". He wanted to know which of us was the leader of our group, and Bernie made sure everyone knew it was him. His few seconds of glory were just that. Moshe's smile disappeared as he said, "Well, son, you may be the leader of your little group here, but as long as you are in my kibbutz, the individuals in your group will listen, obey and answer to no one else but me. We do not allow contradictory orders or dissension here, and it is well you should know this at the outset."

I wanted to ask this Moshe monster of a man what he weighed, but decided against it. He had laughed when he first saw us, but his sense of humour might only apply to others, and not himself. He didn't look like the type you could mess around with. You'd better do what he said, when he said it.

"Passports, please! I will have to keep them for our records, in the event anything should happen to any of you."

I asked him what could possibly happen to us? Weren't we safe here? His response wasn't the one I'd wanted. He stared at us for a moment, taking in a picture of what could only seem to him to be a bunch of frightened kids, far from home and everything familiar.

"I suppose you don't know what this kibbutz is. Well, let me tell you, just in case you decide to go back with Abram here. We are in the very worst part of Israel, and this kibbutz is well known as the one our enemies would like to see destroyed most of all. Why? Because it is the toughest of all the kibbutzim in Israel. We are right on the border here.

"Everyone here knows his or her job, and does it well. It must be this way, otherwise we would not be able to survive. Those who live and work here do it from their hearts, and they will not be pleased to see a group of, how do you call it, greenhorns… running loose without any discipline. That would be a serious breach of security, and must not be permitted. The people here work fifteen hours a day, just to keep the kibbutz in operation. This also must be.

"With those who are already here, who perform their duties faithfully, there is no turning back. While they are here, in fact, they are dedicated to only one thing, and that is keeping me satisfied that we are doing our job. Your people most likely never did a hard day's work in their lives. That will change, because I will ensure that you do, yes, for as long as you are here with us. We must function as a single unit, like a family. There can be no other way, else we cease to exist. It is an important work, this, and everyone must play a role. Everyone must work hard.

"Some of the people here are the children of very well-known families. They are here only to do one thing, and that is to work for their country. We have never had a group like yours before. You know little or nothing about the land of Israel, and less about living the kibbutz life. It can be very difficult, but I am willing to give you the opportunity to prove yourselves. If you are wondering why you would be sent to such a place as this, and believe me... it can be very dangerous here... I am unable to provide you with an answer. I am asking myself the same question...

"However, here you are. When you leave this place, you will be the better for it. I intend to see that this is so. You will receive no special treatment here, and much will be expected of you. This is essentially a farm, but farming life in the middle of the desert is by no means easy. But, you will learn, and if you do not learn... there is only one place for you to go. You will be buried beneath the sands of the desert. This is why I must keep your passports, for our records. I hope it will not come to that, but life is unpredictable here in what you westerners call the Middle East. It is an irony that while what we are doing is in one sense fulfilling prophecy, in another sense everything we do can take a turn that has not been foreseen at all. Therefore, anything can happen here, and often does."

So, Moshe would be our teacher, he said, albeit in a reasonable manner. Because we were foreigners, he said he didn't want to go overboard with us. I mentioned to him that all of my clothing had gone missing from the ship we had come on, but he said not to worry, clothing would be provided for all of us. "Work clothes," he added. I stupidly asked what they would look like, drawing a bit of a sarcastic reply.

"Your new clothes? They will have a few holes in them, because we do not throw anything away here, and because they will have belonged to someone who has already been shot. I am told he has no further use for them."

I wanted to let him know I had a sense of humour, too, and asked if the bullet holes were still in the jacket. "They are," he said. "See that you take better care of them."

Moshe then gave me a disengaging nod, as if to say, "Beat it, kid, you talk too much"... and walked off. About fifteen feet away, he turned, and said, "Get yourselves settled in. That's the first step. You might do, after all."

Irving remarked, but in a low voice, "Well, I signed up to join a farming venture, not the foreign legion." If Moshe heard him, he ignored the comment. Instead, he called out, "Deborah, come with me, please."

Debbie was to be the first to be shown her cabin. She followed him and was introduced to the family she'd be staying with. Moshe told her they worked in the gardens every day, and that her job would be to mind their children and keep the cabin clean. If either the man or the woman happened to get sick, or otherwise couldn't work, she was to replace them and take up their duties in the garden.

There was no such thing as a holiday from the garden. The vegetables that were planted, tended and picked were said to keep the kibbutz going. When asked for more details, Moshe simply explained to Debbie that she should follow the woman's orders. She would discover her new lifestyle by living it. Her duties included doing laundry for the entire kibbutz. He left her in the cabin, no wiser than when she had entered, to await the coming of the "cabin master," whose name was Sara.

While this was going on, the rest of our crew had been standing around outside looking things over. What a barren looking spot! I wondered at the lack of fencing and barbed wire at the front of the compound, near the housing. Apparently, it was more important to protect the land than the people. I thought about it for a minute, and decided it had always been this way. Viva the land of Israel, who cares about the people? If I was wrong, it didn't seem so. The whole front of the compound was as wide open as could be. I was just about to say something about this, when Moshe reappeared, headed our way in a half-march. He reminded me of Fidel Castro... all he needed was the cigar.

Moshe made off with Rabbi Irving and Bernie across a field to cabin number six. He told them that it would be their "place of habitation", and they must keep it clean at all times. They would share the cabin with two other Israelis, as each "home" held four people.

Not to my surprise, I wound up once again in the company of Irving. Moshe took us to cabin number one. He told us it would be the best place for us to be, because he wanted to keep an eye on us. I don't know how he found out, but he seemed to know that Irving and I weren't exactly the best of friends. He said he figured we needed some supervision, so he'd placed us closer to the centre of activity, where we wouldn't be able to kill each other without some-one noticing.

I asked Moshe about this. He shrugged, saying, "News travels." Irving wanted to know how we had ended up at this particular kib-butz. Moshe told us that back in Canada things had been set up in such a way that the five new people (us) would be sent to "a place that was real", because they hadn't wanted to give the impression that anyone was getting a free vacation out of the deal. They were very serious about rebuilding Israel. There had been cream puff people picked before, and they hadn't worked out well, so this time it was thought our group should be treated differently.

"You will have the first four days free, to look the place over, to meet people and to acquaint yourselves with your new surround-ings. After that, you'll be put to work. I expect you to do as the others do, so watch them, learn from them, and try to get along with each other. This isn't a game or a vacation. You indicated you wanted to do something for your mother country, and this is your chance. Whatever you are told by the people here will be true, so listen to them, and understand what they tell you. If you are told not to go into a certain sector or not to venture too close to one part of the fencing, do as you are told, because otherwise it might be very dangerous. These people live here, and they know. It isn't a picnic you're on.

"In the meantime, enjoy your free time, get to know the people. This is Israel. We are friendly, but we can't allow friendship to get in the way of business. Remember that."

Irving and I looked at each other and shrugged. Moshe asked if any of us had any medical needs, adding that the kibbutz had "absolutely the best" care available, and that we needn't worry, we'd be well looked after if anything happened to us. The working con-ditions, however, weren't so easy... you were out in the fields from very early in the morning until noon, when it would become very hot. The second shift would take your place. The only real "job", he informed us, was that of doing guard duty. I wasn't sure what he meant by that, so I asked. He told us that was one thing we wouldn't be required to do. Our main detail would be getting down and dirty, becoming one with the soil, as he put it. I hoped he didn't mean that too literally... given the circumstances, though, maybe he meant it as a kind of joke... dark humour or something.

The kibbutz farmed vegetables, but nothing very exciting; basically, we grew carrots, carrots, potatoes and potatoes. Moshe told us to expect to have sore backs, and he was right. Carrots and potatoes don't hang from trees, and the soil must be tended. In the beginning, we wouldn't have to put in a full day's work... we were too young and tender for that, he said. He was insulting us, but giving us a break at the same time. He was such a huge man, I wanted to ask him if he was sure he wasn't descended from Goliath instead of David.

The other workers knew we would be slowly broken in, he said, and they'd be watching us. "Within a week or so, your body will become accustomed to the schedule here. It won't be easy, but of course you knew that when you signed up. There are no Saturdays or Sundays here, no let-up in the work. The sun does not recognize weekends. Every day is a working day, but you'll get used to it. This isn't a religious kibbutz, remember. You will be paid once a week, on Sunday, the amount of five pounds. Cigarettes are free. Simply tell us how many you need, and you'll get them, starting at the rate of a carton a week. You'll receive these once a month, and what you take will have to do. There's a limit of five cartons a month, which should be enough for even the busiest of smokestacks.

"I know that your possessions have been stolen or at best, misplaced. I doubt you'll ever see them again, so if you're wondering what you will wear, the answer is simple. You will go to the clothing cabin and pick out what you need. If there are any problems that can't be resolved, come and see me. But, please don't bother me with unimportant issues. We have many capable people here who can help you, so please ask someone first. My duties do not include babysitting." When he said this, he laughed, a great, booming roar that almost shook the ground we were standing on. He may have thought it funny, but we understood what he was saying all right. Somehow, we knew that this was not a man whose path was to be crossed more than once or twice, and then for the right reasons. He didn't like pettiness… a field we were experts in. We'd have to be careful.

When he stopped laughing, he became serious again. "Of course, you will all have to take Hebrew lessons. There is a small school here which should satisfy your western lust for knowledge. Then, you'll be able to converse with the rest of the people here. There is entertainment, too. We show movie films every second week, on a Sunday. These are American films, so you should feel right at home.

"There are other activities, too, designed to help get your mind away from your work and its inherent dangers. We have folk dances and singalongs. After your workday is finished, if your fingers are not too sore, you may play checkers, chess and cards. We do our best, you see, to keep our people amused. This kibbutz is not well known in Israel. In fact, it is closed to the public, and there are no visitors, except those on official business. We do not need the publicity.

"Two things, however, are well known about this kibbutz. They are work, and death. Once you have completed your stay here and leave this kibbutz, no one will know you were here, not officially, at any rate. What you did while you were here is nobody's business, either… there is no way of finding out. This is a private place, and we do not reveal our secrets. You are young, but even if your parents were to call, nothing may be disclosed. Is that clear?"

It was clear enough, but the more Moshe told us, the more confusing it all seemed. My first impressions weren't particularly pleasant ones… the place was more like an armed camp, or some kind of prison than anything I had expected. Why all the secrecy? What would happen if we did say something? Mother would have seven fits if she knew where her little Larry was being placed… in the middle of a war zone! I felt we'd been misled, but kept my peace. Moshe didn't look like the type to listen to complaints.

"Well," he continued, "Now that you know a bit more about your new home, you should take a look around, get to know the locals, as they say in America. Or, go to your cabins and start settling in. Your stay will be made as pleasant as possible, under the circumstances." He paused, looked at the sky, and then down to our feet.

"There is just one more thing," he said, "something that is very important." He looked up, his big brown eyes searching our faces.

"When you go to sleep at night, never jump onto your bed. If you do, it may turn out to be the last sleep you will ever have. I know it will sound strange to you, but there is a very good reason. There are poisonous snakes in this region, and they have been known to bite. They have also been known to crawl in between the covers of freshly made beds. This is one reason why there is a dog assigned to every cabin, as a precaution. These snakes come in from the heat of the desert. Be careful. Examine everything, and you will be all right. I do not want to have to write your parents and tell them what has sadly become of you. I am not good at letter writing.

"This is all I have to say to you at present. You will have until the coming Monday to decide whether or not you wish to remain here. It is a good life, but not an easy one. Living and working here will build your character, and you will be doing your homeland a great service. But we do not want unhappy people here… they tend to work against our purposes. If you do not want to stay, let me know, and we will see what can be done with you. Now, you may go your way. Enjoy yourselves. Shalom."

He was chuckling as he walked away, as if there was something he knew that we didn't, and he wasn't about to let us in on it. We were all very quiet for a few moments, then I asked Irving what he thought of all of this. He said he thought it was great. He was thrilled with the whole thing, and wondered if he would be allowed to choose his own detail. Obviously, he wasn't very impressed with being told to work with the irrigation crew… he wanted something better, something easier, maybe a job that wouldn't have anything to do with working in the fields… something, he said, that would match his intellect and education. Maybe he didn't realize what a kibbutz was.

"This is a farm," I told him, "not a university. Farms need farmers, not geniuses. What you're given to do, you have to do. It's like everything else, Irving, you have to start at the bottom, not the top."

"But, I don't want a dirty little job like that. I didn't go to college so I could pick potatoes."

"So, pick carrots. Of course, if you're not happy, you can always tell Moshe. I'm sure he'd love to listen to you. You know, you're the reason I'm here, Irving. You asked if I wanted to come here and work on a farm, remember? You didn't say then that you would be running the place, and if you think that now, you're going to get yourself in trouble. Even the Israelis who work here don't question things. I bet they don't complain, either. They just do their work, because it's what they're here for. You know what Moshe said, a lot of them come from very well-to-do families. They don't have to be here, but they believe in something. You're supposed to believe in it, too. You said you did, anyway, back in Toronto before we left. So, here we are, and we have to make the best of it."

I was thinking to myself that he was just lazy. Some people are very good at telling others what needs to be done, but they won't do it themselves. They must be the people who run the world. They're smart, but they really just want everyone else to do the work for them. Then when the ordinary people have driven themselves into the ground, the "thinkers" can take all the credit. It doesn't make them any better in my books, though. It makes them worse. They're nothing but opportunists who take advantage of others. Irving would have loved to be in that position... what he was seeking was power, but real power comes with learning the ropes all the way up from the bottom. Even I knew that... but I didn't tell him what I was thinking. Who needed the argument we were sure to get into? Moshe didn't, and there was something about him that frightened us all. Maybe it was the way he laughed, like the laugh was just a facade, something to hide behind. I thought we'd better change the subject before our conversation took its usual route, and got out of hand.

"So, Irving," I said, "why don't we take a walk around and give this place the once over? We may as well see for ourselves what we've gotten ourselves into."

Irving grunted in reluctant agreement. Moshe would be happy to know we used our time investigating the kibbutz. We headed for the dining hall, where we spotted a pretty Israeli girl. Oddly enough, she spoke English and said, "Hello. You must be the new arrivals from North America." We told her we were, and she said she'd show us around the building.

As we walked, she talked. She said there was one good thing about the kitchen. Anyone could eat as much as they liked, because there was always plenty of food. This kibbutz was considered to be a "war kibbutz" which meant there were no rules or regulations to anything except during working hours. As long as you performed your duties, no-one would bother you, whatever you might be doing. That came as welcome news. I had pictured it as a sort of slave camp, but things weren't as bad as all that.

I asked her about the food. She said, "We have no cattle here, so this is not what is called a meat camp. The only kibbutz' where meat is eaten are those that raise their own livestock. There are not many cows or horses in Israel, though there is plenty of lamb, which is the main meat eaten here. There are other foods that can take the place of meat, though. You will notice that after you have dined a few times, you will come to realize what you like and dislike, as all of the food will be new to you."

She let us know that if we got hungry during the night, or after guard duty, we were allowed to eat anything that was available. That was nice to know… a little consideration for the troops to help keep up morale. We thanked her for her time and the information about how the kitchen was run, and went our way, in search of the clothing cabin.

When we got there, we met another girl. She was in charge of the distribution of clothing. It was becoming apparent that all of the cabins were run by females. Perhaps they were considered to be more organized than males. Upon entering and seeing her, we said "hello" and she replied, "Shalom. You must be the Canadian tourists who have come to work here. I guess you're here to find clothes to work in. Come and follow me."

She led us into a small room where we could pick out our own clothing, whatever we liked. I told her I had to start from scratch, as I had nothing at all to wear. She smiled and said not to worry, that there was plenty to choose from, and they had all sizes. I began by picking out some jeans, shirts, socks and underwear, thinking to myself that I wasn't going to hang around for the next four days doing nothing. I was eager to get started. There was nothing much to see, so I might as well be doing something, I reasoned.

I figured I'd take my new clothing back to our cabin and prepare myself to go and see Moshe and tell him what I wanted to do.
I really didn't care what kind of work they gave me to do, as long as
it was something. I just wanted to get on with it. Around suppertime, I went into the dining hall, and there was Moshe, sitting at a
table by himself. I went over and asked if I could join him. He
motioned to me that by all means I should sit down.

After answering his introductory, "Well, what do you think of
our little compound?" questions, I finally blurted out my reason for
seeing him. "I'm ready to go to work," I said, "I'd like to start tomorrow, if you'll tell me where and what I can do."

Moshe showed surprise at the fact that I was willing to start
working right away, so soon after my arrival. I think he thought that
I was simply trying to show off, to put myself above the rest of our
group. I wasn't, though. I genuinely meant it. I didn't want to just
sit around waiting for the next few days. It would be too boring.
Moshe told me that the only thing that was open at present was
helping to carry the irrigation equipment out to the fields. He mentioned that this was not too heavy, and that I would only be working half a day for one week. This was in order for my body to get
used to the climate, as the daytime temperatures were very high.

"What your mind wants to do, and what it is possible for your
body to do, may be two different things," he said. "It may be quite
cold early in the morning, but by noon it will be extremely hot."

Moshe made a sensible suggestion then, by telling me it would
be wise to get to bed early and to have a little snack before retiring.

"I will leave a message for you in the kitchen which will allow
you to eat whatever you like from what is available. You will then
be awakened at five o'clock in the morning. This is a half an hour
before the rest of the workers head out into the fields."

I thanked him, and left the table. The only thing left to do during the remaining hours was to find some way to help kill the time.
I was young and restless, remember, and didn't like the thought of
having nothing to do. I liked to keep busy. As I was leaving, the
grays, as everyone called them, started coming into the dining
room, Irving trailing in after them. He wanted to know if I'd picked
up my work gear, and I told him I'd been given all I needed, includ-

ing toothpaste and a new toothbrush. All of our needs were looked after, everything. They'd even given me a comb.

Irving said, "So, we have four days of rest ahead of us, Larry. What will we do to pass the time?" I said I had a surprise for him... I was going to start work the following day. Cynical as ever, he asked if I was looking for extra points. I told him he could think whatever he wanted, it didn't bother me. I just didn't want to sit around and be bored..

I would start working on the piping equipment for the irrigation, a half day at a time. At least it gave me something to do. Irving was about to make some new wisecrack, when the rest of the group entered the room. We followed them to a table and sat down. The meal was surprisingly good... roast chicken, to everyone's surprise.

Rabbi Irving didn't seem very happy about it, though, and sat there staring at the food morosely. I asked what was the matter.

He looked up at me with his big, sad eyes, and said slowly, "Well, Larry, I don't think this food is kosher, and also, they say very few prayers here." He didn't like the setup at all. It wasn't what he had been expecting.

"So where did you think we'd end up?" the other Irving asked, "in a temple? This is a farm. We signed up to go farming, not praying, you know. You have to accept that."

I think our rabbi actually wanted out of the whole deal. He just wasn't happy, and didn't want to cooperate with the system that was in place. He was ready to leave, if he could. If he wanted to daven or pray, he would have to do it on his own time, in privacy. This was definitely not a religious commune. It was anything but. He'd have to abide by the rules and regulations, though, and do whatever he was given to do, whether he liked it or not.

Bernie asked what type of work he'd like to do. Irving's face lit up in a strange grin, and he said he wanted to work with the children, teaching them religion. Bernie explained to him that since this was a working kibbutz, he simply had to be accepting of what fate had sent his way. He could put his name in, though, and apply for a transfer to a religious kibbutz, and he probably would be accepted when there was an opening for him. That was all Bernie had to say about it. He didn't want to probe any deeper and start an argument. "When you see one coming, change the subject"... we were slowly learning this was the best course, since it was evident that none of us would ever see eye to eye on much of anything.

We asked Debbie what she thought of her new position, as she seemed extraordinarily quiet. I thought she was in one of her sulky moods, but she said she thought it was a great setup. She had a well worked out schedule, and said it was even better than being at home.

"I get up early in the morning, feed the children, do the laundry, clean the house, and then I can relax until someone asks me to do something else. It's really very easy. Some days I work only a half day, and once in a while a full day. In a way, I'm glad to be away from the rest of you. No hard feelings intended, but I'm sure you know what I mean. I like being by myself at times." I knew exactly what she meant.

After supper was over, I went back to our cabin and wrote my mother a few lines. I wanted to let her know that I was beginning to settle down, and was getting ready to take up my duties at the kibbutz. I'd start working first thing in the morning. I mentioned a couple of other things as well, like the wonderful girl I'd met on the boat, and the fact my clothing had gone missing. I told Mother I would write her once a week to let her know how things were coming along.

After signing off, I put my pen down and glanced out through the window. The front of the cabin was facing the fields, and the Gaza Strip was at our back. I wasn't sure if I should try to go to sleep right away, or if I should read for a while first. It was only eight p.m., which seemed rather early to me, and I wasn't very tired to begin with. I decided to stay up for a while. I'd wait for Irving to come in, and see what he was up to.

When he arrived a short while later, he was clearly upset. I asked him what was wrong, and he told me he wasn't at all happy about the fact that he had gotten stuck having to stay with me again. He said he was going to ask Moshe if he could be moved. I knew that would be fruitless, the main reason being that all the other cabins spoke nothing but Hebrew. To Moshe's way of thinking, pairing the English-speaking people with each other made for better communication all the way around.

I told him we were stuck together, and we'd have to make the best of it, that was all there was to it. We'd been closer than brothers since leaving home, so we may as well just accept it as our fate. "Just think of it, Irving," I said, "if we get ourselves killed here, we will be buried together. Won't that be fun? Then we'll be together for eternity."

He replied by asking if anyone ever told me what a smartass I was. I said I thought I'd heard the rumour before someplace. "Well, Irving, look at it this way… it's only going to be for a year. Just pretend we're in a jail. The only way to get out of this place is to try running across the desert. If you really can't handle doing time with me, that's your alternative. Take a look out the back window there, and make up your mind."

He gave up his complaining then, and asked why I had picked the next day to start in working, instead of waiting like everyone else. I explained that I had landed with absolutely nothing, not even an extra sock, and I thought it was the only decent thing I could do to repay the consideration they'd shown me.

He said that by being so gung-ho, I'd managed to make the others look bad… lazy, he said. What was I trying to prove? Did I think this would make extra points for me? Was I trying to impress Moshe, or just the whole kibbutz? Maybe I was looking for some kind of favoured treatment, or just a favour. Then he said that by wanting to go to work right away, I probably had opened the door to a better position. I'd be able to get more food, and maybe other things, too.

What was there to say? I'd done what I felt I should do, and I didn't want to hang around doing nothing. It was really that simple, but he was having none of it. So, I said that he was welcome to begin working right away too if he wanted, there was no one stopping him. All he had to do was to show up in the morning. I couldn't see anyone telling him they couldn't use his help. I told him to go and see Moshe, and see what he said.

"You'll be getting your first pay on Sunday, too. If you want to catch a bus into Tel Aviv to go to a show or something, you'll have the money to do so." I finished off the subject by telling him I thought it would be a good idea, to begin work in the morning… what did he have to lose?

Suddenly, there was a knock on the door, and when I opened it, there stood Bernie, his face flushed like it usually was when something was upsetting him. He stormed in.

"I want to talk to you, Wiener! Why on earth did you tell them you wanted to start working tomorrow? Now we all have to go to work at the same time! We had four days of free time that we could use however we liked, and you've gone and changed the whole deal, you little squirt. What's the matter with you, anyway?"

I asked him what he'd expected us to do over those four days. Did he want us to sit around doing nothing, eating their food and watching them work?

"Bernie, listen. Moshe told us the truth. This is the hardest kibbutz in Israel. The workers here are up from dawn to sundown. Then there's guard duty for them. These are just children doing a man's job, some of them. The least we can do is work four hours a day. Why can't we start right away? We've only been relaxing for several weeks. Besides, you're the one who was always complaining about me looking for a free ride. So, I'm showing you that's not altogether true. Funny, isn't it? I'm the one you've never been sure of, but I'm the only one who wants to start doing what we came here for! I just want to show them that we're not just a bunch of Canadian deadbeats. You shouldn't have any trouble with that, Bernie."

He tried a few more times to get at me, but I told him I really didn't have much more to say on the subject.

"Sorry, but it's a closed book, Bernie. You go ahead and do whatever you think your duty is, I'll do what I think mine is. You're not my boss any longer, remember? Not here, and not ever again. Moshe is my boss now, and what he says, goes. I don't have to listen to you... not that I ever did.

"I want to learn the ways of this country as soon as the opportunities present themselves. I'm just making that happen faster. The rest of you can do what you like. As for me, I've got to go to bed now, so I'll ask you to leave the cabin so I can get some sleep. In case you've forgotten, I have to work in the morning. So I'd like to go to bed now. When you leave, please don't take the doorknob with you. Don't slam the door, okay?"

He slammed it, all right. Bernie was stung by what I'd said, and stomped out, but not with the false righteousness he'd entered with. Irving said he thought I'd told him off pretty good. "He was really angry when he left, but how could he argue against what he's been preaching all along? Jesus, you really know how to get under that guy's skin, don't you?"

I yawned. Listening to Bernie had made me tired. I told Irving maybe he should write a letter home and let his folks know he was doing all right. Then I asked if he'd made his decision... would he come out to work in the morning?

"If I wake up early, I'll go to work."

I laid my head down on the pillow and turned on the radio. I liked going to sleep to music. Somehow, I thought Irving would be up before me, that he'd make a point of it, and would wake me up for work. He didn't like to freeload, or worse, to be considered a freeloader. Fiddling with the radio, I tried to pick up an American station, hoping to hear something recognizable. I didn't know it at the time, but it was a short wave radio. As I moved the needle through the stations, I heard the voice of Elvis singing 'You ain't nothin' but a Hound Dog', and left it there. I closed my eyes and slowly drifted off.

The next thing I knew, someone was shaking my shoulders. It was Irving. He was already dressed. The only facility we had in our cabin was a sink. For a toilet, there was an outhouse in the back. It was just like being at summer camp, I thought. Life here would be a breeze. After cleaning up, we headed off for the dining hall, where there were only six or seven people present. Bernie was not among them. The girl who worked in the kitchen came over to our table and asked us what we'd like for breakfast. We could have cereal (hot or cold), eggs, potatoes, toast and coffee. We could have it all, if we wanted. If we really wanted a nourishing breakfast, she said, we should have some halvah, which was available in two flavours... the white and the marble. I said I'd try a piece of each, along with everything else.

The meal arrived and we began to eat. Irving, who hadn't said a word yet, suddenly raised his arm and pointed toward the door. "Look," he said, "I don't believe it!"

There was Bernie, all dressed up in his work clothes. When he saw us, he came over to our table and the very first words that came out of his mouth, instead of good morning or how are you today, were,"Well, Larry. You certainly are a little son of a bitch, aren't you?"

I just laughed it off, not really caring what he thought. He may have been our leader on the way to Israel, but now we were here, and his position had dropped down to being an equal with the rest of us. He didn't like that idea, but there was nothing he could do about it. I hadn't thought he'd show up, but I guess his pride got the best of him. He couldn't stand the idea of anyone saying I was working, and he was shirking... though I doubt if anyone would have said it. I'd thought he'd take the four days off, but now he couldn't. In his opinion, I wanted to show everyone else up. He wouldn't stop, either, and as we tried to get through breakfast, he just kept on talking.

"So, Larry. We had a few nice days to rest from our boat trip, but you had to screw everything up, as usual. You can never leave well enough alone, can you?"

I put a forkful of egg down and looked up at him. "Listen," I said, "we're trying to eat here. Can't you see that? Why don't you just leave it alone, and let us get to work? It's only for four hours, you know, it's not forever. Why don't you go and get yourself something, and do the same? If you want to sit down with us and eat, fine. If you just came in to talk, you're at the wrong table."

Even Irving agreed. "Yeah, Bernie. If you're going to work in the fields, you're going to get hungry out there unless you have some breakfast."

Just as Bernie's big mouth opened to let some more flies out, Moshe walked in. He didn't seem to notice that we were being anything but civil to one another. Or, maybe he did. He was wearing that great grin of his, so that you could never quite tell what was going through his mind.

"Hello, boys. I'm very happy to see you're all so ready to go to work today. And so shortly after getting here, too! I'm very pleased with you."

He insisted on making one thing very clear, though, and went straight to the point.

"You must all be very aware of the severe heat here, because if you overdo it, exhaustion can... and will...set in very quickly. Your work consists of simply carrying aluminum piping out to the fields, and setting them up in furrows. There will be someone with you at all times, to turn on the water, and adjust the pressure.

"All you have to do is to wait approximately ten minutes until the furrows become filled with water. Then, you simply repeat the process. The water dries up quickly here, you see. So, good luck with your first day on the job. Again, I'm glad to see you turn out this morning."

I didn't know about anyone else, but every time Moshe left us, I felt like saluting, or bowing. He had a certain manner about him that let you know beyond any doubt who was in charge. There was no fooling around or arguing when he was nearby. His very presence wouldn't allow that. He may have smiled and laughed a lot, but he was all business. There was no doubt about that.

When we got to the fields, everything was as he said. He'd told us that as we progressed in our duties, we would be transferred into other positions. We could look upon this first job as a sort of test, a place for beginners to see how quickly... and where... we might fit into the general scheme of things at the kibbutz. This was fine by me... I was used to starting at the bottom. It's the best way to learn the ropes.

Our first day there, Moshe went out with us into the fields, showing us what was what, and introducing us to some of the other workers. Our main objective, he said, was to make sure that the proper equipment reached the right places in the fields.

"Just follow any instructions you are given. You'll have an hour to relax and think things over."

To our surprise, the job wasn't quite as hectic as we'd thought it would be, and the morning went by quickly enough... it was like we were only passing the time and not working at all. Nobody talked very much, which meant no arguing, which was nice for a change. As far as the other workers were concerned, it was as if we weren't even there... they didn't talk much either. I got the impression that they, too, felt much as we did. They were there to do their job, not to make friends. Looking at them, I thought of the old saying, "what must be done, must be done".

I must admit that the job was quite messy, but there was the consolation that a good, hot meal was coming up, and we all had washing facilities. You sure got covered with dirt, though. By the time we were finished, you'd have thought we'd been mud wrestling.

The strange thing about the washing facilities was that they were located almost in the centre of the working fields. I wasn't accustomed to having a shower in the middle of nowhere, and having females doing the same thing, with only a thin wall between us. Mostly, I was worried about the dirty clothes I was wearing. Apparently noticing my concern, one of the girls motioned to me, though.

"Just have your shower, put your clothes back on, and go to your cabin and change into something clean. You are finished here for the day. The new girl will pick up your dirty clothing and wash it, and return it before suppertime."

I grinned at the thought of Debbie having to wash my clothes, and went into the shower stall. Little did I know I was in the wrong showers! I soon realized my mistake, when a young girl walked in quite unexpectedly (and as naked as I was!). She just stood there, looking stunned. When she got over the surprise, she said, very calmly, in halting English, "Sir, do you realize that you are in the wrong showers? But, you look all right to me." She was laughing, and I was turning red. I grabbed my towel and wrapped it around me, and headed off to the cabin. I was so flustered by her appearance, I forgot to put my clothes back on!

I was thinking to myself that this little incident would be all over the compound by suppertime. I was embarrassed at being caught bare-assed, and wondered what I'd tell Irving, who had already gone back to our cabin.

Sure enough, when I opened the cabin door, there he was, seated at the table. Hearing me come in, he looked up and asked the obvious question, what the heck was I doing, running around with only a towel covering me. I told him what had happened, and tried to laugh it off. He accepted my explanation with a shrug, making me much happier than he knew. He said it was funny, and that was the end of it. I'd expected he'd go to town on me. Remember, we

were young, and this was exactly the sort of thing that one expected to be made fun of over. Irving simply changed the subject...
probably because there was no one else in the cabin to play up to.

After getting dressed, I asked him what he thought of our first
day on the job. He said it was basically what he'd expected.

"Maybe they're breaking us in slowly, giving us the easy stuff
first. I learned quite a lot about farming life here today, come to
think of it. I wouldn't want to spend my whole life doing it, but I
did enjoy the experience."

"Well, this is just the beginning," I told him. "We have three
hundred and sixty-four days to go yet. I'm not going to evaluate it
yet. We'll see how it goes."

"I'm sure, Larry, that the days will simply come and go, just like
any other days. We'll fit into the routine, and get used to it, whatever they give us to do. That's what I think. It doesn't look so hard.
They treat people well here, too. That's important."

"Well, you heard what Moshe told us... we'll be learning all
of the phases of kibbutz life, one after another. We're going to be
indoctrinated into it all. And he cautioned us that we'll be doing
a week here, a week there, doing different things, and then the
field hands will be doing our jobs and we'll be doing theirs. We'll
be getting an all around education, that's one thing for sure.
That's the way it will go, he said, unless there are specific tasks
that come up for us to do. He didn't say what they might be. If he
wants us to go plant land mines on the highway, he'll cordially ask
us to do it. If we're not up to the job, I don't know what will happen then."

It wasn't that I thought Moshe would ask us to do anything
dangerous but I've never been able to completely trust people who
wear a mask, especially one of joviality. You never know what's lurking behind the smile, and the Israeli government hadn't sent someone like Moshe out into the most dangerous part of the country
because he liked to laugh a lot. Young and naive as we were, even
we realized that Moshe was first and foremost a soldier. Whether
or not the workers of the kibbutz were expected to take part in that
aspect of Middle East life, remained to be seen.

"So, here we are, and the rest of the day is ours, Irving. I think

I'll grab a few hours of extra rest, since we were up so early this morning."

Really, I was bored, not tired. There didn't seem to be anything interesting to do when you weren't working. Then, an idea began to form in my mind. It would be very nice, wouldn't it, to write to my mother again, just to let her know what life on the kibbutz was like, how the first day of work went, and so on. I told her life there was very difficult, but otherwise enjoyable. I told her about the shower episode, too. I asked about my brother and how things were back home, and told them how hot the weather was out in the desert. I didn't tell them where we were, though... I didn't want anyone to worry.

As I closed off the letter, I glanced at the clock. Only twenty minutes had gone by. I realized that this was no good... I couldn't write home every time I got bored. If I did, I'd be sending out ten letters a day! I tuned the radio into a station beaming out some Rock 'n Roll, and laid back on the pillow.

I spent the first week working on the irrigation piping. Then one night in the dining room, Moshe beckoned me over to his table. He wanted to know how things were going. I told him that so far, I liked the work, and thought the others did, too. He smiled, and said, "Good! Now I have a question for you. Please answer it honestly. How would you feel about learning to utilize an Uzi rifle? This is the weapon used by those doing guard duty. Do you think you might like to try, or does your western background deny you the pleasures of life's more realistic moments?"

I didn't know what to say to that, but felt that he was making fun of the more peaceful nations like Canada where it was safe not to have a gun with you everywhere you went, where if you were attacked, it would be by an individual, not a whole nation or bunch of terrorists. I told him that I didn't know what to reply to a question like that. He said to think some more about it, and let him know.

He said that for the next few weeks, I would be working in the fields. I'd soon be starting in on picking potatoes. The reason, he said, he wanted me to climb so quickly up the ladder of kibbutz life was simply that I was showing interest in the farming community.

He laughed, and said that picking potatoes would not be like carrying irrigation piping.

"It's a little tough. Your back will let you know about that. But you are young and flexible, and you'll survive. Potatoes, and carrots, too, are a mainstay of our diet here, and we need young, strong people to help get them out of the ground and into our stomachs. So, what do you think? If things work out, you'll go on to a better position quickly here."

I still didn't know what to think. He was singling me out, and once the rest of the group got wind of it, they'd be upset. They'd say I was wheedling my way around Moshe for reasons of my own, and would never believe it was his idea, not mine. I told him I'd pick the potatoes and carrots, yes, I'd start in the next day, but as for learning how to operate a gun, or being a border guard... I just didn't know. I didn't like the thought of maybe having to shoot at someone... or being shot at, either! The closest I'd ever come to a gun had been in the movies, watching Roy Rogers or Gene Autry shoot at fictitious "bad guys". The idea of shooting at someone for real didn't much appeal to me, so I said as little as possible about it, and hoped Moshe would simply forget about it. It was a pretty wild idea.

And the group! They'd be jealous, furious to see me rise above them in any way. Especially, being able to do it without any real effort, while they got left behind. Moshe said there wouldn't be an opening for me for two or three months, and that first, I had to gain the confidence of the entire kibbutz by showing that I was reliable enough to act as a guard on their behalf.

"The most important aspect of guard duty, Larry, is that you be absolutely trusted by the rest of the workers. Once you have a gun in your hand, the kibbutzniks, as I like to call our little flock, will feel that you have been honoured by being chosen to protect them. There is a certain tradition to this, a ritual that goes back in our history a long, long way."

Moshe said I had plenty of time to think about all of this, and think carefully, please. You will still have your daily chores to perform. In the meantime, while you are thinking about these things, it would be prudent... and in your best interests... not to mention our little conversation to anyone. Just carry on with your work as

usual. You're doing a good job, you know. We have had a few people here who we've had to send back to their homes, because they
didn't appreciate the idea of having to do a little work for their
homeland. You are different, and you will learn that we value people like you. You don't mind getting dirty. I've watched you in the
fields, and you do your job well. Now, return to your friends and
finish your meal. We will talk again."

When I rejoined the group, of course they wanted to know
what was up. I told them Moshe had just wanted to know how we
liked it here, how we were getting along with the other workers.

"By the way," I said, "Moshe told me that tomorrow will be an
exceptionally hot day and that it might be a good idea if we worked
without our shirts on. Each of us will be working with another person, picking potatoes. One person will pick them from the ground
and the other will hold the basket, which will be placed in the fields
ahead of time, about twenty feet apart. We'll switch positions every
once in a while, when our backs get sore. This will go on all day, so
it'll be pretty boring work."

The next day proved Moshe's prediction about the weather
accurate. It was sweltering, and we did as he suggested, working
without our shirts on. It was dirty, sweaty work. At lunchtime,
when we went into the dining hall, one of the kibbutzniks, a young
girl, came over and began talking to us, giving us an impromptu
history of the farms, telling us where the food we were picking
would go... into the cities and towns. Some kibbutzim, she said,
grew large amounts of one particular product.

"As the rest of the world knows," she said, "Israel is famous for
its oranges. They know this because we ship them everywhere. This
is an example of only one item. Our potatoes are sent mainly to
England, because that is the most popular shipping port. The carrots go to big soup companies, and to markets for use in restaurants."

She had it all figured out, and it was intriguing listening to her.
We were not on one of the farms that grew mainly for export, she
said, "but we service the small divisions of the army. So, whatever
we do here on this kibbutz has an important purpose. Our food also
helps to feed the poor, those who come here from Europe, expecting Paradise." She laughed.

"They come here, but they are unable to work on the kibbutz. If you are over the age of fifty, you will not be accepted here, or anywhere else, unless it is for a specific reason. Kibbutz life is not unlike being in the American army. If you are young and healthy, you will be conscripted into service for the period of one year. Not every kibbutz, though, is for growing food. There are others, those that build things, things no one knows about. Maybe these are for military purposes, but no one really can say this as a fact."

I hadn't considered that, but now that she mentioned it, it made sense. Israel was a nation perpetually at war with its neighbours. For right or wrong, it always had been, and most likely always would be. This, you felt in the air. The tension of being in a war zone never left you, no matter how peaceful things might look on the surface. You knew there might be bombs exploding at any moment. Being young, I didn't mind this... it seemed like an adventure to me when I thought about it, though I tried not to think about it too often. Of course, I wasn't carrying a gun yet, and my thinking might change. Being somebody's target didn't sound like the kind of adventure I wanted to be a part of, somehow.

The girl continued. "I would like to say that life on a kibbutz is not as tough as you might think it is. The year you signed up for will pass very quickly. But you will find this out on your own. Now, I have a surprise for you. On Saturday morning, you will have two days free, to do as you please. There will be a bus that will pick you up and take you into Tel Aviv, Jerusalem or Haifa, wherever you like. The choice will be entirely up to you. Oh, and there's one more thing... you will be beginning lessons in Hebrew soon. This will be of great benefit to you when you go into the larger cities. It is quite easy, you see, to be cheated on your money, if you don't know the language. The merchants will take great delight in, how do you say... bamboozling you out of everything you have, so you have to be careful."

We all corrected her at once. "Bamboozling, you mean!" It was the first thing our little group of Canadian pioneers had done in unison for a long time. She smiled, and went on.

"The lessons will teach you how to speak small words that are easily understood by everyone, and you will learn the value of Israeli money, and how to use it. These lessons you can learn at night. Each lesson will be about an hour in length. We don't want to overburden you. The lessons are also free of charge, because we here in Israel think it is important that those who work with us for the common purpose learn to speak our language. It will also help you to understand us better, for it is said we are a difficult people to know, because of our history."

She then said goodbye to us, adding that she hoped she'd see us all at the lessons later. We nodded, and went our way back into the fields to work the rest of the day.

After we'd cleaned up and supper was over with, we talked together a bit about how the free Hebrew lessons would add to our general good. It could only work in our favour to learn the language, and to know how the denominations worked. "That's right," I said, "there's nothing worse than being fleeced by your own people." Irving shrugged, saying he thought it was great to have this opportunity to go to school. The rest of us agreed, but all four of us had a feeling that Debbie wouldn't show up, because of her position. She was alone with people who didn't speak much English, and would probably learn well enough on her own.

At our first class, we were greeted at the door by our teacher with, "Shalom chaverim. I'm glad you made it." She explained that our first lesson would be about how to communicate with other people, and proceeded to give us each a small handbook, a Hebrew/English dictionary.

"The most important word you must come to know is shalom, which can mean both hello and goodbye. The next most important word is boker tov, which means good day. Lie-la tov means good night. I'm not going to take up too much of your time trying to explain each and every word in the dictionary to you. Many you will have to look up for yourselves, but that's how you learn. These few I've already given you are the principal ones. You won't be able to get along without them. We Jews know there are many who do not like us, and those people seldom use these words, unless they are trying to deceive us. So, we tend to trust those who use them on a regular basis. It helps us to know they are at least friendly, if not sympathetic, toward us… on the surface anyway. That way everyone will get along on the surface of things. You will find much is done here on the surface that is important. In fact, it's how we survive."

I wasn't sure what she meant by that, but given the histories of Israel which I was later to read, I understand now. It's when you probe too deeply about certain questions or in certain areas that you get into trouble. People begin to question your motives. Are you for or against them? How should they respond? If they respond the wrong way, an ugly incident may occur, and it's always best to avoid one, because trouble can quickly spread. Riots have developed over a mis-spoken word here, over misunderstandings. I've come to believe that almost everything that happens in the Middle East is based on some misunderstanding or other. But, enough about that for now.

Our teacher went on, saying that some students always learn more quickly than others, depending on their aptitude and desire for knowledge. Personally, I knew I'd pick things up right away. I'd always had a flare for languages, enough to get by on at least. She told us we should take the dictionary with us, and study it whenever we had the chance. She emphasized that there was no hurry, as we had a full year to learn the language, but cautioned us again that if we went to any of the cities, we would need an elementary awareness of how to react when dealing with merchants and the like.

There would be another lesson the following week, she said, and after talking with us a bit more, and throwing a few new words our way, she said goodnight (in Hebrew, of course) and we headed back to our respective cabins. It was still quite early, but we all had to be up at the break of dawn.

Bernie asked me why I wanted to learn Hebrew. "You'll never learn anything, Larry. You're too dumb." He was just trying to draw me into an argument. He hadn't forgotten about his losing four days of doing nothing… the word "forgiveness" wasn't in his vocabulary. I was in a good mood, so I decided to take the bait and throw it back at him.

"Well, Bernie, I'll tell you. You may think I'm just a dumb schmuck, but I have a little surprise for you. You see the big, ugly lips on my face? They'll get me anything I like, and take me anywhere I want to go. I know how to use them, you see. I can flap them in ways you've never dreamed of, but in the direction of people who know how to listen, which is why I'm not going to waste the effort on you. You want to know why? Because, Bernie, I have a theory that the name you call someone is the name that applies only to yourself. So when you call me a dumb schmuck, I don't mind. I know the reason behind it, and it's plain for all to see."

Boy, did he get mad! He let loose with a barrage of curses... every dirty name that was in the book, and some that weren't. He'd walked right into it, so much so, I wasn't sure whether he was angrier with me or with himself. But it was his own fault. To me, it was just a humorous exchange, but he took everything seriously. He snarled, and said he'd get even with me if it was the last thing he did.

"You shouldn't make promises like that," I retorted. "It might turn out to be the last thing you do, you never know."

"I'll get even with you out in the field, Wiener. I'll find a way to make you do double duty!"

Looking back, I realize now we were both being childish, but he was much more so. He was older than I was, and should've known better. It was his pride, his ego that always got in the way. In the rules of the commune, though, there was no way anyone ever did double duty... the heat wouldn't permit it, for one thing. Whatever came out of Bernie's mouth, I decided, meant nothing anyway.

Even Irving said so. He told Bernie he was in the wrong this time, that if he was going to try to egg me on, he'd only wind up with the egg all over his face. I guess Irving had had enough of him, too, because he added, "In fact, you're no longer the boss. You can't impose anything on any of us. Those days are over and finished with. Larry is doing his job well, so why don't you back off and leave him alone. He's right, too. He isn't bothering you at all... you're bothering yourself. What do you expect him to do, jump every time you speak?"

Bernie was livid, and cursed us both. He must have known that if we wanted to make trouble for him, we could do so easily. For one thing, he was slacking off, and collecting money on the side for repairing small appliances. No one was supposed to know about this, but he couldn't keep his big mouth shut and had told Irving about how he'd found a way to make some easy cash. We didn't want to cause him any trouble, but we mentioned to him that we could, and Irving pointed out how, and that he'd better watch his step and keep his ugly thoughts to himself... at which point, he stomped off, muttering and kicking at the ground. We were glad to get rid of him.

We went to our cabin and started getting ready for bed. I thanked Irving for sticking up for me. He replied that he was just sick of listening to Bernie blowing off steam about nothing.

"This doesn't mean our own situation has changed, Larry. I still would like to be away from you. But I figure the sensible thing to do is to try and stick it out without going out of my way to look for trouble. Between you and I, it's simply live and let live. If either of us moves away from the other, it'll be with no love lost. I still don't much like you and I know you feel the same about me, and that's fine. But we have to live together."

I just grunted, and said, "Yeah, well... what do you say we forget this conversation, and call it a day?" I was starting to sound like a diplomatic Israeli already! Within ten minutes, the light was out and Irving was snoring. It wasn't long before I joined him.

Six in the morning arrived quickly. I was up at first light and felt I'd had a good night's sleep. By seven o'clock, I'd be back in the fields. After performing my morning rituals, I headed for the dining hall for breakfast. The group was already there. Just as I sat down to join them, Moshe appeared. He came over to our table and after saying good morning to us, said with a grin, "Larry, when you are through your breakfast, please don't leave the table. I have something very important to discuss with you."

I was sure I must have done something wrong. I glanced over at Bernie, wondering if he'd said something to Moshe about our argument last night... he'd been known to distort the truth by blowing things out of all proportion. But, Bernie looked puzzled, too. If he had told Moshe anything, he would have been gloating... that was his style. Guessing that Bernie had said nothing made me even more puzzled. When we'd finished our meal, Bernie confirmed it by asking what Moshe wanted with me. He had to know everything, but this time I had no answer for him.

"I have no idea," I said. In my mind, I knew I positively hadn't done anything wrong, but what could be so important? Well, I'd soon find out. The fact I really didn't know must have come across to Bernie, as he relented momentarily from tossing one of his customary snide remarks in my direction by saying, "Maybe it's some sort of news from home."

That got me worried. Maybe something had happened to Mother or someone else in the family. I hoped that wasn't it. Soon enough, though, it was time to go out into the fields, and people began leaving the dining hall. Soon, there was only the kitchen staff, myself and Moshe. He came over to my table and sat down, bringing me a fresh cup of coffee.

"Boker tov, Larry." I nodded to him. "Shalom."

Then, straight out of the blue, he said, smiling all the way, "So, Larry, the kibbutz staff have made a decision regarding you. They've chosen you for a specific job, that is, if you will have it. What do you think of that? Do you feel up to it?"

Too surprised to answer, I said nothing, but waited for him to continue.

"Well? How would you like to become a border guard?"

I didn't know what to say. This was something I had to think about, but by the tone of his voice, he wanted an answer right away. I asked him why they had picked me for this particular position, and he said it was because I was the youngest member of our group. He knew there were problems, he said, and thought this would be a way for me to get away from them. I think he had the impression they were picking on me, saying that the staff felt I was getting unfair treatment, that it had been observed that Bernie was pushing me around.

I tried to disagree with him, not wanting Bernie to get into trouble over me, because I knew that would make things worse between us. Moshe wasn't going to accept that, though. He told me that he thought Bernie had a chip on his shoulder, but figured he'd get over it. The more time the two of us spent apart, the better.

"Nothing will be said to Bernie," Moshe said. "This is between you and me. I am not stupid, and it is not difficult to see there is friction between you two. We want everyone here to get along peacefully. I told you that in the beginning. But if there is no way things will resolve themselves naturally, and it appears that is the case, we will do what we can by separating those who do not get along.

"What I have noted, I have noted. Your former leader still thinks of himself as a leader, but inside he knows he is not. This angers and frustrates him. Don't worry... I've seen it before! He takes this frustration out on you, because he cannot take it out on the others.

"There are two members of your group with the name of Irving. One is Bernie's peer, and resents being told what to do, so it doesn't work with him. The other, I think, takes orders only from his God, and that is commendable, if not very practical for our purposes here. The other member of your group, Debbie, is already separated from Bernie, is she not? So, he can exert no power over her. That leaves you, the youngest, and in his mind, most likely candidate to exercise his will upon. So, the tendency is to take everything out on you. We have eyes here, Larry. We can see how it is. A large part of the running of a kibbutz is to ensure that our members all work together, and sometimes they do not want to. We have plenty of experience. This is why I am asking if you would like to become a border guard. How is your coffee?"

"Hot," I said, not knowing what else to say. I took another sip, thinking for a moment.

"But why me? Why not Bernie himself? He'd love to have a chance like this. It's right up his alley."

Moshe sighed, "Yes, I'm afraid it is, but you see, you do not give someone like him a gun right away. He might use it without thinking, trying to prove himself to the workers that he is indeed the right person for the job. We've run across that before, too. It can be very dangerous. A man with a gun should be a man who knows how to use a gun, yes, and he should also know when to use it. But, he must know when not to use it, and that may be more important, in the long run. We aren't here to provoke incidents, but to help prevent them, and to fight back when they occur. We do not need a border guard who has a temper as hot as the sun above him."

That made sense, and Bernie's having a gun and a uniform would probably go to his head. He might make mistakes. As if reading my mind, Moshe laughed, and said, "There are mistakes and then there are fatal mistakes, my friend. On the borderline that separates the Jews from the other nations here, any error in judgment is usually a fatal one for one side or the other, and at times for both. It is said that we Jews despise our neighbours, but it is not true. We understand their need for land, too. We are all only trying to exist, but co-existence is not a simple thing, and must be well thought through, and planned as much as possible. Therefore, we need the right people in the right positions.

"No matter what our enemies say, we are not a nation of terrorists, any more than they are. But there are terrorist factions everywhere, and at times it is very difficult to tell who is who, what their intentions are. There are extremists and fanatics on both sides of the border, but the last thing any of us needs, our enemies included, is extremists of any sort guarding our borders. It just won't wash... it would be the end of everything, and things are bad enough as it is. When there is peace here, it is very, very fragile, as you must know. And I think our friend Mr. Bernie is not yet ready to walk on eggs, do you?"

I was beginning to see what our language teacher had meant when she talked about the surface life in Israel. I knew Moshe was right about Bernie, too. As they say today, his psychological profile just didn't fit into the kibbutz' plans.

"So, Lawrence, what do you say to my little proposition? You may rest assured, your friends will never pick on you again. But I want an honest answer from you. If you really think you're not up to it, please say so. I want you to think very carefully about this. You must understand that you will have to work nights only, you will need to sign a paper, giving us permission to notify your parents should something happen to you.

"Also, you must agree never to tell anyone outside of this kibbutz who you are, what your duties here are. This is very important. Being a border guard at a kibbutz is one of the most important jobs in all of Israel. The land depends on us, the people depend on us. If you should have to shoot someone, you simply shoot and that is that. You will never leave your tractor. You do not have to go and see who you shot. It won't be an Israeli, or an Israeli sympathizer, and that is all you will have to know.

"In the early mornings, we have people who work along the fence and if you have had a mishap during the night, it is their job to take care of it. Once you come in from your shift, anything may be discussed pertaining to your job."

He grinned again, waiting for an answer. I didn't know if I liked Moshe or not... he made it all sound so easy, so simple. But he was talking about killing people. About me killing people. I asked him if he didn't think the rest of my little group would find out what I was doing.

"It will make them very angry when they find out," I told him.

"We didn't pick you so that you could maintain a love affair, you know. So let your group think whatever they want to think. Why should it bother you? Everything that is done here is done for a very good purpose. If we need a few guns to help keep it going, so be it. If people have to die because they interfere, that is the way it has to be. As for you, you should feel proud to have been chosen in this way."

My new assignment, he explained, if I decided to accept it, was a step above the rest. Why he had chosen me, I still didn't understand. It really was beyond me, as there were a hundred other people who I thought more likely for the detail. Moshe explained that my age and my caring for what I did on the kibbutz were both factors. Then there was the group I was with. It was evident to him they were giving me a hard time. He figured the job would keep me away from them a great deal of the time, and why did it matter what they thought, anyway? Moshe was very persuasive, laughing all through the interview as if we'd been talking about gathering eggs or counting fish scales, instead of shooting people.

"Also, working here as a border guard will help increase your awareness of the importance of our kibbutzim, and you will become even more valuable to us. Those who live here now will come to respect you more, as they will depend on you for their continued safety and survival. When you are finished your shift, you will notice how the kibbutzniks will treat you with deference, with the honour due to your position. I think you will like it.

"When you walk into the dining hall, everyone will know you have lived through another night," he laughed. "You will see how they will treat you then. They will look at you, and remember the past, and think of the future. Your stature will be such that you will be foremost in their prayers. By the way, have you ever heard of an Uzi?"

Not knowing what he meant, I said, "The only Uzi I know of was a Carl Uzi. I saw him once on the *Ed Sullivan Show*."

Again the roar of a laugh from Moshe. "You Canadians! Are you so sure you're not Americans? The *Ed Sullivan Show*! Well, Larry, an Uzi is a multipurpose gun. It will operate under any conditions. Water, sand, dryness etc. do not affect its operation. It is not difficult to learn to operate, however. I think you'll like it. It will give you a new sense of freedom, and of safety. It is a gun our enemies do not like to see in our hands... they know then they are no longer dealing with a David carrying nothing but a slingshot. You will be a David with a powerful weapon, one that makes them hesitate and think twice about bothering us. It is a grand weapon, one that is full of passion!"

He talked about the gun for a while, and it seemed to me that this was a great love of his. He said that previously, those on the guard tractor used a Carl Gustoff rifle, but since the Uzi was invented, it had proved to be a much more effective deterrent. He kept insisting that I'd enjoy using it. I'd never so much as fired a bee-bee gun before, but to Moshe's way of thinking, a man with a gun was far above a man without a gun. As he talked, it made me think how different life in Israel really was from life back in Canada. It was like being on a different planet, with different rules.

"What I would like you to do today, Larry... since you now know what is ahead for you, is to take the day off. When you write a letter home, though, or to anywhere else, you must not mention your new job, or anything about what we have been discussing here. You must look on it as, in a way, a secret assignment. Is that clear?"

Moshe seemed to take my not giving him a direct "no" as a hearty "yes". Still, I said nothing, only asked more questions.

"What will I say to the group? They're sure to ask what we've been talking about. They'll be curious to know why I didn't show up for work, too."

He replied, "You just tell them that I gave you permission to take a day's rest. Tell your friend Bernie, if you like, that I said you were working too hard. Drop by the office later, and I will issue you a pamphlet on the Uzi and its operation. You may have a little difficulty in understanding it, but whatever you learn from it will be important and helpful. The rest, you can learn as you go along... on the job."

I didn't know what to think. Here I was, a young Canadian boy, not old enough to vote, and this Moshe character was almost begging me to take up arms against a foe I didn't know and really had nothing against. Was this the way they recruited people in Israel? Bring them in young from other countries, brainwash them and turn them into kibbutznik soldiers, fighting for the cause? When I signed up for this trip, no one ever mentioned anything like this. If Uncle had paid my way over here, or bribed the officials back in Canada, did he really hate me so much to send me off to a place where there was every possibility I might get myself killed?

I couldn't believe it, and concluded that probably, the officials at the Jewish Agency didn't know what happened at the other end, either. It wasn't hard to see that General Moshe (as I began calling him... behind his back) had a natural disdain for North Americans, and he was a little too friendly toward me, I thought. He also was a kind of tyrant in ways. I noticed how the other workers avoided him whenever possible, and went out of their ways so as not to cross his path. I wondered about that, and mentioned it once or twice to those working in the field, but they just looked away, and ignored the question.

But what if I said I didn't want any part of it? How would he treat me then? That was what I didn't know, and besides, the idea had its appeal. I'd have a story to tell when I got back home, for sure. No one else would be able to tell a story like it, I knew that much. Of course, I didn't know what was to come, but maybe even then, the germ was planted to one day write a book about it. I didn't ever dream that it would be fifty years before I actually sat down to write it, though!

So, I decided to accept Moshe's offer. I didn't fully trust him, but there was a certain indefinable something about him that made me feel good, made me feel important. Looking back, I suppose that had been his plan. Put it in the kid's head that he can be somebody a little higher than his peers, and he won't be able to resist. Give him a gun and he can become a hero, if only in his own mind. Like an old Mormon said once, "Bring 'em young!"

It wasn't long before Moshe sought me out again, and I told him I'd come to a decision.

"The right one, I hope," he chortled, pulled a big finger through his beard.

"To be honest with you, Moshe, I don't know. But I've decided to take you up on your offer. I always was the one for doing something different, and I'm not afraid to try out this border guard stuff, if that's what you want."

He slapped me on the back so hard, he almost knocked me over.

"Good fellow," he said. "I knew you were just the man for the position. Come with me into the office."

He led the way, and I followed... a young lamb to the slaughter, maybe. But, I went willingly, thinking of Bernie and Irving and how they'd be shocked all to Hell once they found out what was going on. I could almost hear them mocking me already: "What?! Give Larry a gun and he'll mow us all down! Or shoot himself in the leg!" I won't repeat their cursing, but in my mind, I could hear that, too... and plenty of it. Well, too bad for them. I was moving on. At least, I wouldn't be stuck in the fields pulling up vegetables day after day.

When we were inside the office, away from the hearing of others, Moshe filled me in some more about the job, my hours, and what some of the duties entailed. All through Moshe's introduction to a border guard's life, I kept thinking of Bernie, and how mad he would be. He'd be just fuming, mostly because it had been me that was chosen, and not him. He wanted to be the one, the main man among us, but it would be me instead. Little Larry Wiener, the brat, the guy who had joined up for a lark and a free vacation. I suddenly started to believe there might be some kind of justice in the world after all...

Moshe explained over and over that I had to understand what was happening, that anything could occur once I was officially on duty.

"It only takes one shot, one bullet, and you'll be done for. So, you have to be alert. Don't think so much of protecting the workers and the kibbutz, but think of protecting yourself. If you can do that, you'll work out well, and you won't get hurt. It's a serious undertaking, being a guard. It takes a special kind of person, but I believe you have it in you, and that's why you're getting the chance to prove yourself. If you do it as well as you've already done, and as I think you will, everything will work out well for you... and for us. But again I must emphasize, this is a deadly serious business we're engaged in here. In the middle of the desert, especially along this strip, anything can... and does... happen, so you have to know what's going on out there at all times. You have to learn what the desert looks like when someone is out there... even if they're virtually invisible, the desert can let you know. You have to look for the signs. A lull in activity, new sounds, or a different sort of silence than usual. But, these are things you'll take to naturally. Every good soldier does.

"The people here in the kibbutz, they understand the job you'll be doing. They won't bother you, but will help you at times. Those who pick up the bodies on the outside of the fence... and you may see them at times... they're not with us, and they're not with the enemy. They don't care whose side the dead bodies were on when they were alive... they're like vultures, birds of prey. They come to pick over the bones, so to speak. We don't care, either. Normally, the dead outside the fence aren't from the kibbutz, though they could be Israeli soldiers on patrol, caught, if they were unlucky.

"We're on the same side, but our jobs are different. They don't interfere with us and we don't interfere with them. I'm not saying we have no communication, but our missions don't normally overlap. What they do isn't our business, and vice-versa. I'm telling you this just to let you know. If you see someone out there, you have to learn to distinguish between what the Americans like to call *them* and *us*. It's not difficult, and you'll soon learn.

"As for the workers in the field, they depend on the border guard for everything, for their very existence. The people here, most of them, don't want to be here, but here they are. They don't like their jobs, they wish they were back in the cities. In the beginning, they thought it would be romantic, to work on a kibbutz, helping the country develop and get on its feet. It's not like that, though. It's a dangerous occupation, picking potatoes in the desert...

"Most of these people, you see, they're not healthy enough to join the regular army, but they want to do something to help things along. The kibbutzim are all there is for them, so here they are. This is their contribution, and we accept it as a good thing. We treat them well, and they plow our land and pick its produce."

Amazingly, Moshe was able to say all of this without laughing once, though he smiled a couple of times. I didn't see anything very funny about any of it. Maybe, I told myself, he's exaggerating. Maybe he's just trying to scare me, or find out what I'm made of. Well, he's got a surprise coming.

"Now that it's official, Larry, you'll be issued a passport immediately. You'll have the freedom to go anywhere in Israel you like, without anyone asking any questions of you. Your friends won't have that privilege, nor do any of the regular workers here. Being a border guard isn't all as bad as you may think. It has certain advantages, you will see.

"The only people who have the authority to question you are the MPs, and you'll see them everywhere you go. When you go to the cities, if there's trouble in the streets... and there often is... you may be stopped and asked to help; or they may simply want to know who you are and why you're there. But don't worry about it. Once they realize who you are and what your position is, you'll be treated with the utmost respect. We Israelis, you will see, have great respect for our soldiers. The worst that can happen, if there is real trouble, is to send you home for your own safety."

I commented that the passport must be worth its weight in gold. He replied that it was. "It may be worth much more than that. It may be worth your blood. You must treat it with respect, too, and use it in the proper manner."

He then presented me with a waiver or paper of consent to sign, and said he would see me the following morning for my first lesson in using an Uzi. I signed the paper, and he dismissed me from the office.

So. I was free for the rest of the day. It was only nine o'clock in the morning, and as I was walking away from General Moshe's temple (as I came to call his office headquarters)... I bumped into Rabbi Irving, carrying a large black bag. I was still in a bit of a daze, having had so much happen to me in so short a time, and when he first spoke to me, I barely heard him.

"I said, hello, Larry! Aren't you awake yet?"

I blinked out of the trance I was in, and replied, "Oh, hi Irving. How are you? Where are you off to? Is that your luggage you've got there? You leaving town, or what?"

He said he wanted to take a walk to the next kibbutz, because he had heard that it happened to be a religious commune, and asked if I'd like to come along with him.

"Just to see it, Larry. I don't expect you to join it!"

I considered. This might be a good chance for me to get off the grounds for a while, and why not? I told him sure, I'd tag along. The kibbutz we were headed for wasn't far away, Irving said, and was called "Kibuttzad". I asked him how he'd managed to find out about it... I thought we were out on the desert alone. He just smiled, and said that a rabbi had come to the kibbutz to stay overnight while travelling through, and he'd gotten wind of it and had looked him up.

"I was able to talk with him for awhile, and told him quite plainly that this kibbutz just wasn't for me. He asked why, and I told him that no one here seemed to have any religion at all. I told him it seemed to me that they're very confused about what they're doing here... they want to grow things, and kill people. So then this rabbi, whose name was Cohen, mentioned that this Kibuttzad is only a few miles from here, so I had to figure out a way to get off work so I could go.

"Since it's such a hot country here, I decided, and God will forgive me because He knows why I'm doing this... to use the excuse that I had diarrhea."

Then, he looked at me strangely and asked me how come I wasn't at work. I answered that I was just too lazy, and didn't want to work that day. He said they could throw me off the kibbutz for something like that. I laughed and asked if he thought his diarrhea didn't stink. He smiled, and we kept walking. As I said, the front of our kibbutz wasn't fenced off, and you could walk out into the desert anytime you liked, if you wanted to. Most people didn't want to, but we were a couple of what they called "crazy Canucks", and so we just kept on walking.

It took a while, and by the time we got there, we were pretty hot. Rabbi Schwartz' "few miles" seemed like very long ones, but eventually, we arrived. At least he'd pointed in the right direction. Irving took one look, and came right to life, hot and dusty or not. He saw people wearing religious garments, and pointed out how the boys had curls hanging down around their ears.

The girls wore long dresses, and had bandannas wound around their heads. Irving was in Heaven... he felt right at home. Almost skipping for joy, he turned to me and said, "Larry, I don't care what you tell them back at the kibbutz. You can say anything you like but don't tell them where I am... I'm not coming back. I'm staying right here! The Lord God led me here, I really and truly believe He did! I do! Don't try and stop me, Larry... this is it for me. This is my last stop in Israel, it's where I was meant to be in the first place."

Well, I wasn't going to argue with him, but I did think I should be heading back. It had been a much longer walk than I'd expected, and I was getting hungry. Besides, I didn't want to be missed... I hadn't told anyone I was going anywhere, either.

"You do what you think is best, Irving, and good luck in it. I think you're better off here, too. I won't say anything. Let them think what they like."

I wouldn't have said it to him, but I was thinking the others might think he'd flown off, been scooped up in a fiery chariot or spaceship or whatever it was that had taken Elijah into the clouds. When it came to religion, it was all a mystery to me (and to most everyone else, I realized... but at least I was able to admit it).

"So," yelled Irving as I started back, "goodbye, goodbye! I really think I'll be able to stay here and work for the Lord. I know they'll let me stay. It's my destiny, to be here!"

So goodbye already, Irving. I'd heard enough, and turned away from Kibuttzad. Kibuttzad the Sad, the Mad, the Glad, and headed back to my own kibbutz, the Bad. The walk took roughly two hours, and I was dragging my hot little feet a bit by the time it came into sight… it was about four in the afternoon by this time, and really hot.

When the workers returned from the fields for supper, there seemed to be something in the air, like they all knew something but no one would say what it was. I knew by the way they walked in, with their heads down, and by their silence. Something had happened out there this day, but they lived by the rules, and weren't going to talk about it. Probably, they had been instructed not to say anything to anyone.

That evening after supper, there was a movie being shown, and I took it in. It wasn't a James Dean film, and I can't remember now what it was, but I remember I liked it. I remember, too, when it was finished, Bernie approaching me like Big Brother in the flesh, demanding to know where I'd been, and why I hadn't been out in the fields. I was tempted to tell him I'd had diarrhea, but didn't, as he wanted to know why Rabbi Irving hadn't shown up, either. He looked at the sky, and asked very plaintively, "What has happened to our group? Two of them aren't even showing up for work, and the other is screwing her days away."

Whatever his last crack about Debbie meant, the skies didn't give him any answer, not that he thought they might. He made a big show about giving up on the Heavens, and turned back to me.

"So, Wiener, what the Hell's going on around here? Where were you all day? And where's Irving? He still hasn't shown up. He wasn't even at supper. I checked his cabin, too… everything's gone. His belongings aren't there, and neither is he! This has got something to do with you, I just know it, Larry! So where is he?"

I shrugged, and said I didn't have a clue, adding that he should know that, he'd said it often enough.

"Well, what about you? Why weren't you out with the rest of us today? Answer me that, wise guy!"

I simply told him that Moshe had given me another job, and that I couldn't talk about it. Let him guess. He'd find out soon enough. I told him that Moshe had decided I wasn't cut out for field work, that was all, and that he was going to get me off it before I took sick.

"So if you're not satisfied with that, I guess you can go and ask Moshe. Maybe he'll tell you what he has in mind. I don't have time for this, anyway, Bernie. Your line of questioning reminds me of something I read once about the Spanish Inquisition. Sorry, señor, but I'm going to the cabin and get some rest. My feet are tired, and you're making my mind tired, too. Just leave me be. I'm being trained for something else, that's all I'm going to tell you, okay? Good night."

Moshe

The first day of my new "job" began as usual. After breakfast, I marched out alone, heading for Moshe's office. All I can remember seeing was my little Canadian group standing by the edge of the field, staring after me, wondering what I was up to now. I knocked on Moshe's office door, and he answered, "Boker tov, Larry, come in, today will be an educational day for you." Even early in the morning, he laughed. It was like breathing to him.

"I can't teach you the operation of the gun here at the kibbutz," he told me. "I think your group would become very upset if I did that, so we will enter into a lorry, and go out into the desert where no-one will bother us. This way we will be alone. I'll bring along twenty-five clips of ammunition for you. It should be enough to get you started, unless you turn out to be, as the Americans say, trigger-happy. As for myself, of course I am very familiar with this weapon, and will not spend many shells. Come."

We walked out of his office and over to the LORI, an army vehicle, and drove off, leaving my group standing there scratching their heads. Soon, we were far enough away from the kibbutz, and Moshe stopped. We got out and he showed me the gun I would be using.

Not being used to handling weapons of any sort, my initial reaction was to pick it up very gingerly, as if I'd been reaching for a newborn baby. "Go ahead, take it," he laughed. "Don't be afraid to touch it. It never bites the one holding it."

The Uzi felt heavy in my hands, but lighter than it looked. Moshe showed me how to load the clips, holding the gun close to my waist, tightly. Then, he picked up the one he'd brought for himself, and stood beside me.

"Pick out an area in the sand, and visualize someone standing there, ready to shoot you. Use the area as your target... don't worry, there's no one here. You won't hit anything. You won't even damage the desert... it's been here thousands of years and is still doing well... better than some of those who claim it. Now go ahead, squeeze the trigger."

I did as he said. The noise was deafening. Much to my surprise, however, I found it exciting. I'd never even seen an Uzi before, let alone touched one. As Moshe showed me the weapon's abilities, I began to feel at home with the thing in my arms. Moshe was a master... really sharp. He could take out anything he aimed the gun at. It took me a while to even come close to the imagined targets I'd chosen. He said not to worry about it, I'd get accustomed to it, and my aim would improve quickly.

Listening to a man such as Moshe, it wasn't difficult to believe anything. He was so sure of himself, and I knew he'd trained many others before me. I didn't stop to wonder what had happened to them. As far as I was concerned, I only wanted to please him, and besides, I liked the feeling of holding a gun. It was true what the psychologists back home said... it gave you a sense of power, of being slightly higher than other people. I think Moshe counted on this, especially when he dealt with young people like myself. Make someone feel important enough, and just like a dog, he'll follow you anywhere, and do whatever you say.

Moshe explained that it had taken him many years to learn how to get full use of the Uzi, but that what I was learning that day was all I would have to learn.

"It has a number of subtle uses," he said, smiling his usual "I'm not telling you everything" smile. "But, for your purposes, all you need to know is how to load and reload, aim, and fire. If you turn your body slowly as you squeeze the trigger, you will be able to what we call sweep the area in front of you. Even if there are ten men coming toward you, once you master this technique, you will come out alive and they most likely won't. It is a good thing to know how to use your body as well as the Uzi. Turn from your waist, and keep your feet firmly planted on the ground if you are standing. If you are sitting, the same principle applies. Think of yourself as a part or an extension of the weapon. Make sure of your intended target, turn and fire. It is not so hard."

It's not so hard to shoot, I thought, but is it hard to kill? I said nothing, however, but listened to my teacher diligently, soaking up every bit of information he gave me.

As if reading my thoughts, Moshe slapped me on the shoulder, and said, "Soon you will be performing as anyone in the army would. You simply shoot to kill. If you hesitate, you yourself will be killed, or worse. Oh yes, there are worse things than being killed, believe me!

"The one thing that you must remember, aside from constantly being on your guard, is to keep your weapon clean at all times. Now, fire the remaining rounds. Practise until you get a real feel for the gun. Turn as you shoot, firing in a semi-circle."

The amazing thing to me was how I liked using the Uzi. I felt like I was in an old-time gangster movie, cleansing the neighbourhood of the bad guys. Or vice-versa. Or just cleansing the neighbourhood. It didn't matter. Maybe I was a killer at heart, maybe we all are. Maybe, reader, if I gave you a gun, you'd feel the same, who knows? At any rate, I felt as powerful as all get-out. While I was practising, I was supposed to envision a group of Arab terrorists coming across the desert. To me, they all had Bernie's face.

Every once in a while, I would have to stop and reload. At those times, out of the corner of my eye, I would see Moshe standing there, assessing me. Later, he told me I'd done exceptionally well. Of course, I wasn't shooting at anything, only imagined ghosts. It was all a fantasy to me, like giving a kid his first cap gun. I don't know if Moshe realized this. If he did, it probably wouldn't have mattered. All he wanted was a guard who would be reliable, one the kibbutz workers could depend on. I got the feeling he didn't care why the guard was doing it, as long as he could shoot straight.

We stayed out in the desert shooting for about three hours, Moshe showing me this technique and that, then Moshe looked up at the sky and announced it was time to be going back. He thanked my for showing such an interest in learning about the weapon and how to use it. As usual, I had asked a lot of questions, and this seemed to impress him. If you're not asking stupid questions, it usually impresses everyone… I'd learned that long ago. As far as the gun went, though, I was genuinely interested.

When we returned to the kibbutz, it was lunchtime, and Moshe asked if I'd like to join him. I assented, and took a step in the direction of the dining hall.

"No, no, Larry. We'll go to Beer-Sheva, to a restaurant. You get back in the vehicle, and I'll be out in a moment. I have to make a short telephone call."

When he returned, we drove off, heading back the way our group had come when first arriving in Israel. Soon we were in the town, and we pulled in at the same restaurant we'd stopped in on our way to the kibbutz. The proprietor recognized me.

"Allo, American! I know you from the taxicab, don't I?"

He asked where the rest of the group was, and how they were doing, and so forth. I responded in kind, making small talk about how well everyone was doing, which was what he seemed to want to know. Moshe nodded agreeably at everything I said. Clearly, he was pleased with the way I was handling myself.

The proprietor then asked Moshe why "this fine young man" wasn't with the rest of the group, back at the kibbutz, working in the fields. Moshe's response alarmed even me.

"It is because this young man is a killer, and killers have no place picking potatoes."

We were both carrying our Uzis, of course. It wasn't safe to leave them out of our sight, not when we were off the kibbutz. It was neither safe for us nor for the guns themselves. Things like that disappear very rapidly in the desert. The minute your eyes are off them, they vanish.

The restaurant proprietor smiled at Moshe's statement. Probably, I looked a little shocked.

"And he is so innocent looking," the man said. " My, my. Such a fine young man, a killer. Just think of it. It makes one proud to think he feels this way about his homeland."

"He's a tough boy," Moshe said, as jovial as ever, as if it were all a joke. "Our enemies will think twice when they see him with a gun."

Moshe ordered dinner, which didn't take long in appearing. We ate in relative silence, then as we were finishing with dessert, he looked over at the proprietor, who had been sitting at the counter watching us. When the man saw Moshe looking at him, he asked who would be paying for the meal.

Moshe stood up leisurely, and pulled at his gun.

"You yourself will pay for it, I believe."

The proprietor's face paled, and his eyes bugged out at the sight of Moshe fingering the gun. I didn't know what was happening, but with Moshe, I could believe almost anything. He was a man of surprises. In this case, though, he was only joking. He put the gun down, and started his crazy laughing again.

The proprietor's face broke into a grin, and the colour came back into it.

"Come with me," Moshe said to the man. We all went out into the street, and Moshe opened up the back of the vehicle and pulled down the rear seat, revealing a floor literally covered with cartons of cigarettes... at least seventy-five or so. Seeing this, the "restaurateur" immediately ran inside and returned with a couple of large boxes.

I helped pile the cartons into these boxes, and the man, looking up and down the street, cautiously carried them inside the restaurant. Then, he was outside again, standing between Moshe and myself, handing Moshe a wad of bills. My initial thought was that they must be into the infamous "black market".

Moshe then instructed me in my first Israeli economics lesson: "You have seen nothing here, except a meal. This sort of thing has been going on since time began, and for some, it is a way of survival. I do not want to see it come to an end, and you don't either, do you?"

Showing my usual youthful enthusiasm, I indiscreetly asked what I would have to do to get involved in this black market. He laughed, and then turned serious. "Well, what do you think you can do for me, Larry? Are you able to obtain American and Canadian cigarettes? They are a great luxury here, you know. What do you think? In America, they say a man will walk a mile for a Camel. Here in Israel, there is a variation on that: A man will walk his camel ten miles for any kind of North American tobacco."

Moshe stood there smiling, waiting for a response. I considered. American cigarettes were probably out of the question, but I sure knew how to get Canadian brands. I had some in my pocket, and showed him a pack of Export A. He seemed surprised to see it, and wanted to know where I'd gotten it.

"That's my little secret," I told him, "but I can get them for you, two cartons at a time. But what are they worth to you?"

Moshe said I could get up to five times their original price, and that sounded good to me. He had buyers who would want all he could get. He said that when I got them, to pout them in a bag and leave them at his office, and in exchange he would give me an envelope with my "pay" in it.

He grinned. "You must never mention this to anyone. It would be very foolish... and dangerous... if you were to do so, without question. If you meet me anywhere on the compound and you have a supply on hand, ready to take to my office, simply tell me what a lovely day it is, and I will make ready your cash. That is all we will say about it, nothing more unless we are alone, and unless I bring the subject up. You will not speak of it. Is that understood?"

I nodded. It was understood.

"Well, I think it is time we were getting back to the kibbutz, don't you?"

The restaurant proprietor was by this time back at his counter, waiting for his next customers. He had, after all, paid for the meal. At least, we didn't, unless he'd taken it out of the money he'd passed to Moshe. It didn't matter to me. Another free lunch, I remember thinking as we drove away. I was smiling, too... it had turned out to be a happy day for all of us.

When we arrived back at the kibbutz, I asked Moshe when I would start on actual guard duty.

"Today is Wednesday," he said. "There's no point beginning until Monday. You will have the time until then free."

I realized I had time to get away for a few days. I'd go to Tel Aviv, and enjoy myself. I asked Moshe about making arrangements for the trip, and he said it wouldn't be a problem, but I would have to find my own transportation there and back. I could start my little vacation the very next morning, he told me.

"Larry, you should go there and do nothing except have a good time. Meet the people, see the sights. You'll find it very different from Canada, I think. By the way, tonight, there is going to be a folk dance. People come from different kibbutz' and gather here. You should attend. The groups coming tonight are American and Canadian. Maybe you'll be fortunate enough to meet someone from your own area. You might be able to send a message home through someone, letting them know how you are getting along, that you like it here."

Moshe had already decided I was in love with the place. But to me, it was still on my "to be understood" list. Far from loving it, I found everything very puzzling, with all of the cloak-and-dagger stuff going on. But, Moshe wanted people to promote Israel's kibbutz life as much as possible, and to him, I must have seemed the perfect candidate. It wouldn't have hurt him, either, if a rabbi or a member of the Jewish Agency showed up and discovered that a Canadian kid was getting along so well. It would prove that what the agency was doing wasn't a waste of time and money.

I was hoping there would be some Americans at the dance. If there were, I could try to make some sort of connection to send a letter to my mother telling her I had been transferred from field work to Negev or border guard duty. I wanted her to know the truth, despite Moshe's warnings of secrecy. If I came back in a pine box, I wanted my mother to know why, and to be prepared for any eventuality. Not that I expected anything would happen, but one never knew.

Bernie, on the other hand, felt just the opposite... though he didn't yet know what my real role was. He didn't want anyone at home to know he was no longer the group's leader, and certainly didn't want anyone finding out he'd been reduced to taking the part of simply another farmhand. That was too far beneath him, and he wanted to keep his private fantasies alive, pretending he was still the big shot. He even had the audacity to say that he didn't think any of us should communicate with our families back home or anywhere outside of the kibbutz… "in the spirit of national unity". Yeah, right. I don't think anyone listened to him.

About seven-thirty that evening it started to get dark. We changed our clothes, cleaned up, and got ourselves ready to go on over to the main recreation hall, where the dance was to be held. When we arrived there, we noticed several people had gotten there before us, and they were all dressed up in various Israeli traditional costumes. They welcomed us warmly, and seemed very happy that we had come out to see them.

We liked it, too. It gave us the chance to stop thinking about our day-to-day chores and duties. We sat down to wait, to see what would happen next. A group of people suddenly piled into the room from a Sherut, or taxicab. The driver stayed to join in the fun until the party ended. By the sound of the voices of the tourists, they were mostly all American, and I was out of luck. I struck up a conversation with the driver, and asked if there were any Canadians in the crowd. He indicated that he thought there were, and volunteered to go back to the cab and check his logbook.

When he came back in, he found me and said that indeed, there were. There were a Mr. and Mrs. Solomon from a place called Toronto. I was surprised by this, and asked him if he would mention to them that the young blond boy… myself… would like to meet them, since I was also from there. I also told him that the "place called Toronto" was a large metropolitan city in the heart of Canada, and that there were a great many Jewish people there.

I didn't want my group seeing the Solomons talking with me, though, because they'd try and make something out of it, like, "There he goes again, trying to fleece someone"… or something like that. I did have ulterior motives, of course, but not at all what they might have thought. The driver disappeared into the crowd, and a few minutes later, returned with the Solomons trailing him, looking in my direction.

They were very friendly, and wanted to know all about kibbutz life, how I'd managed to wind up here, and what I thought of it all. I told them I worked in the fields, and nothing more. Moshe wouldn't have liked it, and besides, I didn't want anyone to know prematurely what I was doing. I mentioned, though, that it was very important I get a letter across the waters to my mother, and asked for their assistance in the matter. I told them the letter was already written, and I was carrying it with me. It was already sealed and addressed. I didn't want to send it by mail from the kibbutz, I explained, because "at times, the mail doesn't get through from here". I offered no reason for this, and the Solomons didn't ask.

They told me they would certainly take it for me. They had children, they said, and knew how important it would be to my mother. I gave them our family phone number, saying that all they had to do was call her, and she would come and pick it up. They agreed, and I thanked them for their trouble.

Meanwhile, the dance had begun, and I watched for a while. It really was quite entertaining. In between songs, one of the visiting women called out for no apparent reason, "You all have oil wells in this part of the country!"

Debbie was at the dance, as was almost everyone on the kibbutz, and she answered, "No, lady, you're wrong. There are no oil wells in this part of the country, only potatoes! To find oil wells, you have to go to Arabia!" She started to add something else, but the music started up again, and drowned her out.

Personally, I wasn't the dancing type when it came to anything other than Rock 'n Roll. Yet, when the kids from our group got up and started, Moshe nudged me toward them, and the next thing I knew, I was hand in hand with Bernie and Irving going around and around in circles, doing the Hora. Not wanting to lose face in front of Moshe, I put a smile on my face and went along with it. As it turned out, I enjoyed myself immensely. My letter-passing mission had been easily accomplished, and I settled back to enjoy the rest of the evening as much as possible, given whose hands I was being forced to hold!

A Bit of History

Israel is roughly the size of the state of New Jersey, and came into being for the second time in 1948. Thousands of years earlier, the land was built on faith in "the one God"; in its latter day, while faith still abounded, it might not be entirely unfair to say that faith was in military might and the power of money. One of the great minds behind the founding of modern Israel was that of a man called Theodore Herzl, who wrote a famous novel about the subject, calling it *The Old-New Land*. Herzl was considered a visionary, and died in 1904, never living to see his dream come true. If he'd been alive and writing in the late fifties, he might have reconsidered, and reversed the title… *The New-Old Land*, for that is what it seemed to be to me. The old traditions had been preserved, but what drove the people was a new way of thinking.

Israel's history had altered course, and maybe not for the best. But, times change, and you have to make the best of it. Especially after the horrors of World War II, it isn't hard to see why the worldwide Jewish population wanted a place of its own. The first kibbutz or collective settlement as it was called was built at a place called Degania, and dated back to the early 1900s. When I learned that, I began to appreciate the idea of working on a kibbutz, and that we hadn't embarked on anything new; we were simply carrying on the work started by others, long ago. We were cogs in a machine, spokes in a great wheel. There were plenty of ideas about what that machine might actually be doing, and where this new state of Israel was heading, no one really knew for sure, not even those who were behind the ideas.

By 1957, long working days and apprehensive nights had already become one of the legacies of life on the kibbutzim. You never knew if you were really safe or not, and guard duty was simply a part of your life there. Theodore Herzl would have been pleased to see the deserts turning into gardens, fulfilling old prophecies, almost as a by-product of the work being carried out. Whether he would have approved of the dangerous situation the entire nation was caught in, may be another matter. I think, though, he would have liked the little article I wrote about Nachal Oz.

The following has been reprinted from The Border, *a magazine that was published by the kibbutz...*

It could be that some readers have already heard about Nachal Oz, for its members featured in many television programmes in (the) U.S.A. and Canada, including Ed Murrow's *This Is Israel... Person To Person* show. However, just by way of introduction, Nachal Oz lies five kilometres from Gaza... until recently just 400 metres from the border, and 800 metres from the nearest Egyptian military position... one of the most dangerous positions in the tinderbox known as the Gaza Strip.

As can be imagined of a kibbutz just three years old, there is a great deal to be done here, but a bright future lies ahead. It has become the most well known kibbutz in Israel, if not the world, and I am glad of the opportunity to tell you as much as I can about it. There are 130 Sabras here, who, I might say, are very nice in their own way, and work very hard doing a great job for their kibbutz and Israel in the making of a great state. There are already 10 young natives of Nachal Oz, all under 18 months old. They have their own "children's house", and a nurse, too, so they live a grand and healthy life in the Israeli sunshine.

The work is not very hard, but there is a wide variety in the different jobs. One year-round job is the vegetable garden, and there is always work picking, planting and weeding potatoes, carrots, etc. Work commences at 6:30 a.m. and carries on until noon... there being a break for breakfast at 8 a.m. Work after a hot lunch in the communal dining hall ceases for the day at 4 p.m. After work there is much hilarity in the shower house.

For a three year old farming kibbutz, the facilities offered to someone making a life here are very good. There is a modern well-equipped laundry, a repair shop with the best tools, a carpentry shop and a metal shop. There are two combine harvesters, five tractors and many other Massey-Harris implements, which save many hours of manual labour. The grain store holds 300 tons of grain, and is one of the busiest places, for varied corn crops are the bulk of Nachal Oz's products. The farm has 15,000 chickens, which are mainly bred for eating purposes, so the Jewish custom of chicken on Shabbos is well and truly being carried on here. The methods used to look after the chickens have been praised by many a visiting agricultural expert... looking after them is the regular work of only two people. There is also a cowshed, with 60 cows and calves. One of the most important animals, however, is a little kid lamb, the pet of the children and adults alike.

The farm sells its products to Tnuvah, the central marketing body for all the kibbutzim, and the bulk of the profits is ploughed back into the farm, only a little being set aside for living purposes, housing, etc. The growing of cotton can be done successfully, the grade being of the highest, but labour costs make the growing of cotton on a large scale prohibitive. A newly planted orchard of over 3,000 trees is expected to yield its first crop next year, and a small vineyard has also been planted.

All electricity on the kibbutz is powered by its own generators, and is adequate for the needs. One of the most urgent needs of electrical consumption before the occupation of the Gaza Strip by Israel was the chain of high-powered lights that used to light up every inch of the fence surrounding the kibbutz, so that uninvited guests would be discouraged from using the fence for entry purposes.

Perhaps the most important of all the work carried out on any farm unit in Israel is that of irrigation, and this is certainly true of Nachal Oz. Nachal Oz receives its water through pipelines on the Yarkon-to-Negev water scheme. It should be noted that Nachal Oz is somewhere between the arid Negev and the fertile Coastal Plain of Israel - good irrigation is essential to prevent its land straying from the fertile plain to the Negev Desert wastes. The water is distributed on the farm by means of portable aluminum pipes, which have a simple connection device. Each pipe is 20 feet long, but a man can easily carry two at a time. Any area of the fields covered by the main pipelines can be watered at will by the setting-up of the water pipes with spraying devices attached between each pipe and the next.

This kibbutz is already self-supporting, and by the time it is the age of the already "well established" kibbutzim should be one of the biggest and best kibbutzim in the country. But most of all, it will stand as a symbol of true faith for those who put their work into it in times that once looked as if this farm would never be in the number one trouble spot in the world. The part that the members played in the recent Israeli Sinai Operations, in the three years that Nachal Oz was a border settlement, in the important work of guarding the borders of Israel against marauders sworn to hatred of Israel has deliberately not been mentioned in this article... a true reflection of the attitude of mind of the peaceful farmers (who want) to be able to build not only their farm, but their lives in peace.

Larry Wiener

Tel Aviv

The next morning, I awoke at my usual time, which was roughly six a.m., and headed over to the dining hall to get some breakfast. I felt a twinge of guilt about having free time while everyone else would be busy bending their backs, but I didn't let it get to me. In the middle of a couple of eggs and toast, Moshe sidled up behind me and said, "There will be a bus at the roadside at seven o'clock, if you are thinking of going to the city. You should, you know. It will give you a better feel of Israel, and more of a grasp of what we are trying to achieve here at the kibbutz. You will come to appreciate our work more, by seeing what it is like outside."

I had told no one that I was thinking of leaving for a few days. I thanked him, and went back to the cabin and packed a small knapsack to take with me. I made sure I had enough money, and headed out toward the highway. A few minutes later, sure enough, a bus came roaring along and stopped when the driver saw me. I climbed aboard, paid the fare, and asked how long it was going to take to get to Tel Aviv. He said we'd arrive in about an hour.

I found a seat next to the window and after a few minutes of enjoying the outside scenery, noticed a pretty young woman opposite me who was breastfeeding a child. It was a difficult decision, not staring at her, but I managed somehow. The hour went by pleasantly enough, and more quickly than I had anticipated. Moshe had given me a scribbled note, instructing me to go to such and such a hotel, which was supposed to be good, but not overly expensive. He'd drawn me a little map with instructions on how to get there from the bus station, and I made my way there.

After checking in and examining my room, which was not very large, but clean enough, I decided to go for a walk around town. The people on the street looked at me in an odd way, and I decided I just didn't look the part of a Sabra. I guessed they figured me to be a tourist.

I found a place down by the beach, where I heard music... Rock 'n Roll! Ecstatic, I walked, almost ran, toward it. It was like an open dance floor, out on the street. There was a jukebox by the cashier, and I was curious to see what was on the thing. To my glee, I quickly discovered that most of the songs on it were good old American Rock 'n Roll tunes, and started digging through my pockets to see if I had any coins that fit the slot.

While I stood there looking down at the song titles, out of the corner of my eye, I could see a number of young men lounging around. They all looked to be in their very early twenties. I wasn't sure whether or not I should approach them to try to strike up a conversation, but before I'd made up my mind one way or the other, one of them came over to me and began talking, in very good "English" English.

"Hey, Blondie, are you an American?"

"Sure am," I replied. "This is my first time here in Tel Aviv."

"So, what are you here for? Are you visiting on a vacation?"

"Sort of. I'm only going to be here for a few days... a present from the boss of the kibbutz I'm working at." This bit of news seemed to impress him... everyone in Israel at that time being very patriotic. I asked what he and the others were doing there, did they live here, did they work, was this a day off, what?

"My partner and I are doing quite well," he informed me, "in a very good business. In fact," he went on, "if you're interested in earning some fast money for fast work... there may be an opportunity here for you."

I thought I knew what they meant, and decided not to say anything about already being in cahoots with Moshe. I wasn't interested in what they were offering. But, I was curious to know what he was driving at... I might have been wrong in my assumptions... I was thinking cigarettes.

The youth opened his jacket, and showed me a small package, shaped not at all like a cigarette pack. This got me thinking, and the thing that came immediately to mind was drugs. And jail. I wasn't interested in either, so I just shook my head "no", and motioned to the girl behind the cash register, ordering a Coke (if you can't find anything else in the Middle East, you can always find a Coke!). Hoping the young man would get the message and leave me alone, I went back to looking at the titles on the jukebox.

Inserting a couple of coins, I pushed a few buttons and looked around for a seat. Over to one side, there was an empty table, with an attractive girl sitting next to it... I made my way toward her, and started to sit down. She stopped me, by getting up just at that instant and asking if I liked to dance. I wasn't sure if this was simply a question, or she wanted me to be her partner. I soon had my answer, though, when she, not waiting for a reply, grabbed my hand and dragged me out into the middle of the floor, and started jiving.

It had been a while since I'd been able to stretch my legs this way, but I got into the groove almost immediately, twisting my body to match her movements, and adding a few of my own. This obviously pleased the crowd, who were watching me intently. I was concentrating on the music... and the girl... but in the background, I heard clapping and the occasional "Go, man, go!"

When the number was over, I asked if I could join her at her table, and she nodded, "Yes, yes, please sit with me." She told me her name was Sarah, and that she was a Jewish Yemenite. I asked about her life in Israel. Did she like living here?

"It is good here, but I have never been anywhere else. But what are you doing here, please?" I told her about working at the kibbutz, and that I wasn't really an American, but from Canada. She didn't seem to know the difference, replying that she had never gone out with an American boy. I said this could be her opportunity, if she liked.

We left the little café and walked for a time on the beach, talking some more, and deciding where to go. As I didn't know what was available, I asked if she'd like to go and have coffee somewhere. She agreed, saying she knew of a place not far from there, on a side street.

Once there, she told me more of who she was. She explained that she did not come from a very well-to-do family, and therefore lived in one of the poorest sections of the city. It didn't bother her, she said, to tell me this... she wasn't ashamed of who she was. Later, I found out she was going to school, studying to be a nurse, but she didn't tell me this right away. When I asked how old she was, she said seventeen. I told her I was exactly the same age as she was.

Sarah had no telephone, but we agreed to write to me at the kibbutz, if I would give her the address. I did, and then we decided to return to the dance café to listen to some more music. It was more crowded than ever when we arrived, but there weren't many people dancing, so Sarah and I got up and started swinging each other around. Suddenly, a woman came up to me and asked, right out of the blue, if I would consider teaching people how to Rock 'n Roll American style, as she owned a dance club and noticed I was quite good at it.

She said she wanted someone to come a few nights a week, and that if I decided to, she would make it worth my while by paying me accordingly. I told her I was working at a kibbutz, and she said it didn't matter, that she would be willing to pay my transportation back and forth.

"You won't lose any time at the kibbutz," she said, seeming to know which one I meant. "The last bus out there is at midnight." I asked which days of the week she was thinking of, but in the back of my mind, I knew I would never be able to do it, because the guard duty I was about to start was at night. I didn't tell her this, only saying it would be impossible for me to help her after dark. I said I might be able to do something during the daytime, though, if that would be okay with her students... they could learn just as easily in the afternoons, couldn't they?

She wanted to know if we could arrange something for twice a week. I told her the very latest time I could leave Tel Aviv to get back to the kibbutz would be six o'clock in the evening. She smiled sweetly and nodded, asking for my name and mailing address. The only way I would work her for, I said, would be on a cash basis... I made sure to tell her that. No checks. No record of employment. I didn't want to get into any trouble with the authorities. This was fine with her, she said knowingly. She didn't need any trouble either.

Our conversation over for the time being, I excused myself and took Sarah's hand and started dancing again. When the dance club lady left, I asked if Sarah would mind giving me a tour of the city, as I didn't know anything about it. She said she'd like that, and off we went.

She showed me several points of interest... the parliament buildings called the Knesset. This was where there was a huge menorah set up; she showed me where the major synagogues were, and many other places. She was so nice to me, I could hardly believe it. I'd never dreamed of meeting someone like her, but had had visions of wandering around the city by myself, bored out of my skull.

"Are you going with anyone?" I asked. "Do you have a boyfriend, Sarah?"

She said no, she didn't. Her mother was very particular about who she went out with. Mother's main objective was to make sure her daughter became successful in her career. It was then she told me about wanting to become a nurse.

"Well," I asked, "do you think your mother would object to you writing me at the kibbutz, or how about your getting letters from there?"

"She will not object, I am sure of it. She would have no reason to, would she? We Israelis are well known for our hospitality towards strangers to our land, you know."

She then told me she knew about a nice quiet park where we might "get to know each other a little better". This got me to thinking, and I certainly didn't object to the ideas that were now beginning to form in my dirty little mind. The park turned out to by near a large hotel, and was very quaint looking to me, not what I considered to be modern at all.

We sat and talked for a time, and then I asked her what she would think if I felt I'd like to become more involved with her, "in a serious nature", as I put it, hoping she'd get my meaning. "I think you're very special," I told her. "You're also the first girl I've actually met in Israel, and that's special, too."

She replied that, of course, we would develop a friendship if we wrote back and forth. It went no further than that, though, as I suddenly realized it was time that I should be getting back to the hotel, and asked if she'd walk with me.

When we got there, I took a chance and kissed her lightly on the cheek, saying I hoped it wouldn't offend her, adding that I didn't think I'd be seeing her again in the near future. To my surprise... and delight... she kissed me back, hard, her arms around my shoulders.

"I will write you at your kibbutz, Larry, I promise."

We said goodbye, and she walked away. I went into the hotel, whistling, and had my meal. The man at the front desk suggested to me that since it was only about six thirty, I might like to see a film, as there was a theatre just down the street. I decided this might not be a bad idea, and went off to see what happened to be playing. I can't remember now what it was, but I remember enjoying it.

Afterwards, I returned to the hotel and went straight to sleep. The next morning, I felt refreshed, and happy that I had met a girl. I walked around for a while, heading for the beach area, and wound up standing in front of the same little dance café where we'd met, and went inside.

The same two guys were standing in the same corner they'd been in the day before. Maybe they were permanent fixtures. They spotted me right away.

"Hey, Blondie! How are you today? Do you remember us from yesterday? We were talking to you then."

I remembered, and said so.

"Well? Have you come back here to talk business with us now?"

It hadn't been my plan, but I thought that while I was there, it might give me the opportunity to find out firsthand how large black market operations worked. These guys seemed to know what was going on, or at least gave the impression that they knew. I asked where they were from, as they obviously weren't natives... their English was impeccable.

"Oh, we're from Britain."

"So in what way do you think I might be of service to you?" I asked.

"Well, we deal in practically everything... records, cigarettes, and... other items."

I figured my first assumption had been right... drugs, or maybe even guns. In which case, I wasn't interested. But, I wanted to know more, and decided to hear him out... curiosity didn't always kill the cat. I asked how much money I would stand to make, if I decided to do business with them.

"As you are American, of course, you will make good profits. We can get you anything you like, just tell us what it is. If there's anything... anything... that can't be had here, we'll find a way to get it. We have our contacts, and they're very reliable."

The other fellow spoke up then, asking if we could carry on our conversation over a cup of espresso. I figured if they wanted to spring for a coffee and give me some more information, I'd go along with them for the time being. So, off we went down the street to another café.

They wanted to know where I was staying in Israel, and I told them I was from a kibbutz and if they hung around this area, I would find them if I wanted to. I listened to their offers and stories... some of which I suspected were more boasting than anything... and said I'd have to think things over. They gave me the impression, though, that they realized I wasn't interested, so toward the end of our conversation, I told them straight out that I wasn't interested. Thanks, but no thanks.

One of them then put his hand into his pocket, pulled out his wallet, and showed me his I.D., informing me they were international police, on the lookout for dealers in contraband. I was stunned. Brother, was I glad I didn't accept any of their offers! There I'd been, thinking they were the bad guys, and there they were... thinking the same thing, waiting for me to make a slip and agree with them! It was entrapment, but if you were caught, I doubt there would be anything you could do about it, once they got you into a court of law.

They shook my hand, thanked me for my time, and said they hoped I enjoyed my stay in Israel, and that they thought I was a "good man"; but also said that I should watch out for people who approached me with offers like theirs... some of them might not take "no" for an answer. I believed them. After we parted, I began to shake a little, thanking whatever powers-that-be I had decided not to tell anyone about the little setup I had going with Moshe. Now, that would have been a fine fix to get myself... and him... into! He would've taken away my gun and sent me out into the desert with "JEW!" stamped all over me... right into the arms of the Arabs... or so I figured. It might even have been enough to make him stop laughing for once. So, I was lucky.

I was very happy indeed, when it was time to get on the bus and head back to the kibbutz, believe me! My tush had been saved, but just. With a little more persuasion, I might have tried to compromise with the two "dealers", talk them into "no drugs or guns, but how about cigarettes and music" or something, and felt extremely fortunate that I hadn't. So, I'd had enough of Tel Aviv for the moment... well, Sarah and the dance lady excepted; though suddenly I was no longer sure about the dance lady.

The bus rolled into the kibbutz at about eight in the morning... just in time for me to have breakfast. The group was sitting there looking morose and disjointed. I joined them. As I sat down, Irving asked why I wasn't working in the fields and how was it that I'd been given the day off, and they hadn't. He said in an angry tone, "So what's up, Wiener... have you been kissing tush again?"

I told him I'd been given a few days off in exchange for certain other jobs I had to do. I didn't elaborate.

"You're just trying to evade your duties," he replied.

"That's not it at all, Irving. I had something else to do, that's all. It's none of your business, anyway, what I do."

"I know what you're up to," he said. "You're up to no good. You've been in the city, haven't you? We saw you get off the bus. Since you've been here, you've done almost no work. You might think you're putting something over on Moshe, but it won't wash with us. We know you better. So what were you doing, trading with the Arabs? You're acting like a real traitor."

How he figured that, I don't know... it was just the way he thought. He couldn't say anything pleasant about anyone, especially yours truly. I'd heard enough.

I exploded. "Listen, pal, you'd better apologize right now for that comment. There's no call for this kind of bullshit. What I do is my business, not yours, and if you don't like it, too bad. But don't call me a traitor. You'd like to turn the whole kibbutz against me, wouldn't you? But you'd better get your facts straight first.

"Like you and everyone else here, I came to this place to do a job and that's what I'm doing. You're just mad because you don't know what it is… you haven't got the inside story. You're jealous, because Moshe has given me different duties, that's all. So leave it alone, okay?"

He wouldn't stop, though. "Different duties! What different duties? You're just trying to shirk your responsibilities, Larry. You're doing nothing and getting away with it, as usual."

I was trying to eat my breakfast, but he kept on nagging and making his stupid remarks. Finally, I overturned my bowl of cereal, pushing it toward him, making sure he got splashed. Then I stood up.

"Okay, let's finish this right now. It's time we got things settled once and for all. You," I said, pointing my finger at his astonished face, "are going to be mincemeat!"

"Name the place," he said.

"I've got the place, all right… we'll go out to the desert since I don't want to have to beat you up on Israeli property. Your blood shouldn't be spilled on holy land, that's what I'm thinking. So let's do it, right now. I've had enough of you and your insults!"

Bernie asked if we were really going to go through with it.

"If he's not afraid to," I told him, not taking my eyes off Irving. He wouldn't be able to get out of this without losing face with the others, so I knew he'd comply.

"Well, you'll need a referee," Bernie said, not wanting to miss any of the action.

"No referee," I said. "Only one of us will be walking back. This fight originated in Toronto, and it's time it happened. He doesn't like me, I can't stand him. That's how it is. We've been tolerating each other for too long a time, and it's time to call it quits and do something about it. Let's go."

Bernie cautioned Irving that I might not be as easy a win as he thought. "The kid's fast on his feet," he said, "and he probably knows some dirty tricks. So if you're going through this, be careful."

Irving finally said something: "Okay, Jewboy, you're on. I've had enough of you, too." To Bernie, he said, "I'm not worried. If I win, I win, if not… well, that's the way it has to be. But I'll beat him, you'll see,"

On our way out toward the desert, I felt like Gary Cooper in the movie *High Noon*. We went about a mile from the kibbutz, walking side by side, with about twelve feet between us. Neither trusted the other, which is why we kept our distance. I thought he might try to take a surprise swipe at me on the way, and I guess he figured the same about me.

We stopped when Irving suddenly announced, "Okay, this is far enough."

Neither of us had much experience with fighting, and we didn't know how to begin… sometimes it takes a hit or two to get your adrenaline up. There was a fairly large rock nearby. I suggested we both lean against it, and the first one to move it aside with our shoulders would instigate the first punch by the other. Irving said he didn't care how it started, he just wanted to get on with it, but he agreed.

We tried this, each pushing as hard as we could, but the rock refused to move. It was heavier than it looked. Then I came up with an even better idea of how to get things started.

"Well, Irving, this won't work, but I know something that will. You called me a traitor back at the dinner hall, so let me give you the compliment back. You're just a damn Communist, that's what you are… and what kind of a Jew is that? You don't love Moses, you love Karl Marx!"

That got it going. Irving cursed, and gave me a backhand smash in the side of the head. I returned it, by whacking him a good one right in the nose. It started gushing blood immediately.

He wiped his face with the back of his hand and stared at the result. "You little bastard," he shouted, and made a dive for me. "I'll kill you!"

The force of his leap knocked me over, and he started putting the boots to me, kicking me in the side. He had his work boots on. I was wearing ordinary shoes. A stray foot caught me in the side of the head, near my eye. I figured it'd be nice and black by the time we returned to the kibbutz. This got me mad, and I lit into him with all I had.

He got in a couple of good smashes, but I laid right into him, swinging my arms like a windmill. There was no turning back now. I caught him in the face five or six times, hitting as hard as I could. I was crazy with hatred. Whatever pain he'd inflicted on me with his fists and boots wasn't even close to the pain he'd caused by his mouth, his dirty little insinuations, his lording it over me whenever we met.

The fight went on for a while, until I realized the shouts were coming from Irving... shouts not of anger, but of submission. I kept swinging, but Irving had given up. His arms were in front of his face, but he wasn't responding with punches... he was trying to keep me from hitting him any more. Then, he dropped to the desert floor, like a stone falling from above. It was over.

He just laid there on the sand, curled up in a ball. I stood over him for a few minutes, gloating in the knowledge of what I'd done to him. It was sad, in a way, but at least it was over with, and I'd won the fight. I wasn't entirely void of compassion, though, and asked him if he was all right. He answered with a groan.

"Come on," I said, stretching out my hand. "It's over. Let me help you up. We'd better get back to the kibbutz. They'll think we killed each other."

Apart from the bruises he'd inflicted on me, I felt great. Irving knew there was nothing else to do or say. He slowly rose to his feet, and thanked me for the entertainment, saying, "The next time, you'll probably shoot me in the fields." How he knew I was going to become a border guard, I had no idea. Maybe it was just a wild guess. I just grunted.

It had been a fair fight, it was over, and in my books, that was the end of it... case closed. I hoped Irving would feel the same, though I doubted it. He'd think twice before taunting me again, that was sure. There would be no more arguments over nothing. We were still stuck together like Siamese twins, sharing the same cabin, and we'd just have to learn to live with each other.

We made it back to the kibbutz and realizing we hadn't been as long as we thought, went into the dining hall that was still open.

As we entered, dirty and bloody, everyone glared at us. Fighting among ourselves was not good for morale. One of the field workers said this out loud. We didn't know what to say, but hung our heads and tried to ignore the crowd.

Moshe was there, and came over to our table, wanting to know what had happened, asking in a voice that was for once not punctuated with spurts of his booming laughter. Obviously, he wasn't very happy about the situation. The idea of his workers fighting among themselves was beyond him… we should be concerned with the enemy, he said, which was all around us. We both looked up at him and smiled, saying it was nothing, just a "lover's spat".

Moshe shook his head. He gave Irving the day off, but as for me, he said we needed to have a private discussion. I asked him if I could clean myself up first. He just looked at me and said, "No." He motioned for me to follow him, and we went to a corner of the dining hall, away from the others.

He said, "Larry, you will be starting your guard duty this very night. You'll work from eight o'clock until six in the morning. You will present yourself at my office at seven-thirty to pick up your gun. The weapon must be returned every morning, before you go for breakfast. Now, you are free for the rest of the day. Go get yourself cleaned up, and you should get some rest later on in the afternoon, too. The first night is always the longest. Oh, and Larry…"

I'd been staring down at my shoes, half-expecting to be bawled out by him. I looked up. His old familiar grin was back. "Try not to get into any more scuffles, will you? I'd appreciate it." And, that was that.

Later, I learned that while we both had black, swollen eyes, Irving also had a busted ear drum. His face was a mess, and mine wasn't much better. It had been worth it, though. I didn't like fighting, but I'd taught him a lesson, one he'd never forget. He'd leave me alone after that. Never again would I let him intimidate or insult me.

I spent the rest of the day doing the big zero… nothing. I rested, and walked around for a while. It had been a hectic morning. During one of my walks, Bernie showed up, saying he wanted to have a word with me. He said he hadn't expected me to go through with the fight, figuring I'd chicken out at the last minute.

"Well," I said, "I don't like being called names, especially when they're the wrong names. I'm not a traitor, and he shouldn't have said it. Actually, the fight goes all the way back to Canada. It started up again when we were in Paris. Irving just can't keep his big mouth shut. He can't leave well enough alone, and I'd had enough, that's all."

Bernie agreed with everything I said, but had to get his two cents in anyway, saying I was brown-nosing Moshe, and that I brown-nosed everyone I thought I could get something from, or have my way with. I told him that was his opinion, but it wasn't true. But, I let it go because I didn't want any more fights that day. Sensing this, Bernie let it drop, too.

"I don't know what's going on with you, but I've had some good news," he said. "I'm going to get new duties... in the electrical field." He was pleased with this because he'd be working in an area he was familiar with, as he'd done this at home in Toronto for a time. I got the feeling Bernie had finally given up on pretending he was still the group's leader. Maybe it was a relief to him, too. His view of Moshe seemed to be that he was a natural for the job, and there was no need for anyone else. He was right, too.

It was almost suppertime now, and I had to go to the office where Moshe had left a uniform for me. I told Bernie I'd see him later, and we went our separate ways. I was excited about this idea of working as a border guard, but tried not to let it show... one reason because so far, no one even knew about it. I didn't want to have to try to explain to anyone why I was acting excited, when I couldn't tell them. It was no big secret, but I figured I'd let people find out naturally, without my telling them. That way, it wouldn't seem like I was bragging.

The uniform was in camouflage. I tried it on, and it was a perfect fit. When it came time to start my shift, I was a bit nervous. After getting dressed, I headed over to Moshe's cabin and knocked on the door. He let me in, with a big smile, saying he wanted to give me a few pointers or hints that would help to protect me when I was out in the field.

"When you sit up on the tractor, always remember... never touch the pipe, because it's very, very hot. The heat from that pipe is so severe that it will go right through your gloves and will burn the skin right off your hands.

"When you're holding the weapon, never point it down to ward the ground, or up into the air. Always... always!... keep the gun on your knee, with the barrel aimed outward, toward the field. You must keep these things in mind at all times.

"But, the bottom line, Larry, is that we want to see you come breakfast time. If you don't turn up, we'll know we'll have to send you back to Canada in a body bag, and nobody wants that to happen. So, look out for yourself. Your own safety is just as important as anyone else's... even more so, because a dead soldier can't ensure anyone else's safety."

I thanked him for the advice, and nervously asked, just sort of "by the way"... what had happened to the person I was replacing, my mind conjuring up all sorts of bad images.

"Nothing to speak of," Moshe replied. "He became frightened one night, and ran out into the desert to live with the snakes... he's been there a month or so now. He'll get used to it after a while, if the scorpions don't get him."

I could see he was having a hard time trying to keep a straight face, and finally he slapped me on the back and said, "No, Larry, I'm only joking... he went home, that's all. His time with us was over. For your information, there have not been very many of our guards who have been shot. Things are certainly bad here, but not as bad as you might think. It isn't open warfare yet, but don't fall asleep out there. If you keep on your toes, you'll be all right, and after a few nights, it'll all be routine to you."

I hoped so. I didn't completely trust Moshe, but he had a way about him that inspired confidence in people. He told me that the man I'd be working with went by the name of Samuel. He was a veteran who would help me with anything I asked.

"You can call him Sam if you like. He won't mind. He's been told all about you. He's a professional at his job. He puts his time in, and takes his duties very seriously. He'll depend on you to cover him as he makes the rounds on his tractor. You'll learn quickly enough. If you have a problem, ask him. He's a good man, one of the best we have.

"Your job, when he's doing his rounds, is to provide backup firepower for him in case he gets into a scrape. Samuel will stay on his tractor all night, and will go through the entire field, bit by bit. He's very thorough. But he can only do his job effectively, with all of his concentration, if he has full knowledge that you're behind him every step of the way. He has to have confidence in you.

"I told Sam that I had trained you personally, that he had nothing to fear. I told him..." and here, Moshe broke out into his disarming grin, and started laughing, "I said you're a professional killer, ready for anything, that you care about nothing except the safety of the kibbutz. I said your finger is always on the trigger, and it's usually itchy. Samuel was glad to hear that, I think... he gets nervous if he has any doubts at all about the person he's working with. I don't think you'll disappoint him.... or me. You won't, will you, Larry?"

I said I wouldn't, that he could count on me. Inwardly, though, I was wondering why he'd told Samuel I was a professional killer... I'd never killed anything in my life, and didn't want to start, either! I figured I could shoot back if someone shot at us, though. That was a matter of personal survival, and I'd always been pretty good at surviving.

Moshe continued. "I told Sam that you were also an easygoing person, that he wouldn't have to worry about being accidentally being shot at by you... something that happened to him once when a young recruit got the gun caught in his pantleg and instead of trying to free it the way anyone else would, panicked and clumsily tugged at it, and it went off. The bullets went into the ground, only a few yards away from Sam's tractor. That was a bad night for Sam, and his partner was lucky he didn't shoot back. The first few discharges of gunfire always make a man react too quickly, and sometimes you shoot at nothing until you've pinpointed the source of the fire. By that time, you may be dead, so your reactions are always to start shooting right away, out of self defense. It isn't a good practice, maybe, but that's how it is when your life is in danger.

"But, I know you'll work out all right."

Moshe walked me out into the fields. All I could see was darkness, except for one small, brief light in the distance... it looked like someone flicking a lighter. Moshe said it was Sam. We kept walking toward it, and suddenly, right in front of me, was the tractor I'd be using.

"Okay, Larry," he said, "it's time. Get up on the tractor, keep your weapon on your knee... always!... and, here... I've got some lunch for you. Save it for later on, when the cooler hours come. You'll want it then."

I thanked him, and climbed aboard the tractor. Moshe turned and walked away, wishing me "good luck" over his shoulder, disappearing into the darkness.

The next thing I knew, a voice came out of seemingly nowhere.

"Lawrence Wiener of Canada," it said. "I hear you like your new weapon. I am Samuel, your partner here in the fields. I am pleased to meet you. So, let us begin our rounds."

And with that, he climbed onto his tractor... I could just vaguely make it out in the darkness. I heard his engine start up as he turned the key. I fired mine up, too. So there I was, my first night of guard duty beginning for real. I was more excited than nervous. I saw Samuel's tractor stop, and made his arm out, motioning me to pull up alongside of him. I did, and we drove along together for a while.

He was curious to know about life in North America, wanting to know would he be able to find a decent job there, if he ever decided to leave Israel. I got the feeling he'd had enough of the hide and seek game everyone was playing. I told him it was unlikely he'd find the same sort of work.

"Fields don't have to guarded there," I said. "People are free to come and go as they like. Farms aren't run communally, but are privately owned and managed. No-one's at war there. North America is the land of peace."

"Ah, yes," Samuel declared, "Di Goldene Medina! The golden land... or fool's paradise, take your pick. No one fights there with guns, but instead with money. Is that true?"

I nodded my head in the darkness. "In America, anything is possible," I told him, "but not everything is probable. You might get work there on a farm... there are a lot of them, but I don't think the pay is very good... and it's seasonal work, too."

Samuel said it didn't matter to him. He'd had enough of what he called "our limited freedom", and wanted more. The more he talked, the more I sympathized with him. I thought, "What a gloomy prospect... a future of working in the fields here with nothing but a tractor and a gun. And what do you do, once that's over with?"

As we made our way through the fields, I started to get the feeling that Sam and I would become friends. I seldom saw him during the daylight hours, but at night, at least I'd have someone to talk with. It was good for him, too. Some of the things he told me... his private thoughts... I didn't think he'd be comfortable about sharing with his fellow Israelites. He seemed very bitter at times, and blamed his own people as much as anyone else for the trouble the country was in.

"We're getting into this thing deeper and deeper, Lawrence of Canada. It'll never be resolved. The more we dig in, the more the others would like to strangle us. There will be no end to it, except war. No one will win. The roots run too deep. Everyone wants the land, and for each foot of it that you win... even here in the desert... you lose another foot somewhere else. After a while, you become pessimistic, you don't care, you only want it to be over with... and you know it won't ever be over with. This is life in the Middle East, and it will never change. It is like a chess game that nobody can win, a real mishmash we're into."

Sam called me "Lawrence of Canada" right from the beginning. I didn't mind.

Working the fields on the tractor at night was a tremendous, if nerve-wracking experience. At times, I felt like a golem out there, waiting for other golems to appear so I could take a shot at them and frighten them off. Maybe, if we were all lucky, we'd return to the clay from which we were made. It's funny what sitting out beneath the stars with a gun can do to a person... I began to think of Moshe as my creator... a man gone slightly mad with patriotism and power. Whenever I inwardly questioned what I was doing there, I would remember a favourite saying of his, "gentiles are not used to Jewish problems"... and everything would seem to fit back into place. I was in the right place, after all.

That first month, I used the gun twice, firing into the darkness at some imagined or real sound... at any rate, no one ever fired back. Sam told me not to worry about it... maybe there had been someone there, it was always hard to tell. And maybe my firing had frightened them off. "If you think there is reason enough," Moshe had told me, "use your gun... and then your head. You'll be safer that way." Then he laughed, "Just don't mistake Sam for the enemy. He wouldn't like that."

One morning at breakfast, toward the end of the month, Moshe joined me at breakfast. I hadn't seen much of him, and I wondered how he thought I was doing. I didn't have to ask.

"Kid, you're doing a great job, but I think it's time you had a few days off. I've found a voluntary replacement for you, so you can begin right now, if you like." Thinking to myself, I hadn't spoken with Sarah for some time, the idea appealed to me. I liked guard duty, not only because of the special status it gave me, but for other reasons, too. It kept me away from our group as much as possible, I enjoyed working at night, and I had come to be good friends with Sam. If a few days off were in the cards, though, that was fine with me.

I decided I'd go into Tel Aviv - I had Sarah's address, and if I had to, I'd knock at her door, despite her mother's reservations about her seeing young men. Moshe told me there would be a bus leaving at 11:30, and he had my pay ready for me. It wasn't a fortune, he said, but it was more than I'd have made working in the fields... it would be enough to carry me through a few days in the city.

Moshe said he was very happy with my work. "You have accomplished quite a lot," he said. "Some people get spooked out there, and can't do it. Sam has said you are perfect for the job, and he's happy working with you. If you can keep him happy, I'll do my best to keep you happy." With Sam, although Moshe didn't know this, it was a two way street - he was showing me the ropes of guard duty, and I was teaching him English so he could eventually leave the kibbutz and Israel itself. In return, he taught me the basics of the Hebrew language. We both liked the arrangement. I felt I'd earned this little holiday, though, and was glad enough to be heading for the city.

After Moshe left, I looked around the room. There was Irving, sitting at another table. He hadn't spoken to me since the fight. Well, the Hell with him, I thought, and made my way to the table anyway. Bernie was seated beside him. He looked up at my approach. Irving just stared into his cereal. Of course, they knew by this time what my new duties were. If they were impressed, they weren't about to tell me… but Bernie was at least friendly on the surface.

He said he'd heard I was supposed to be guarding the place, and said he was surprised at the news. "You must have made quite a splash with Moshe, Larry. To tell the truth, I didn't think you'd last the month out there. It must be very lonely at night, and it could be dangerous, too. I wouldn't do it, no matter how much it paid. I'm not interested in getting shot at."

It was the first complimentary thing Bernie had ever said to me. When I told him I had a few days off and was going into Israel's largest city, he said he thought I deserved it. "Your nerves must be shot, Larry." He knew that when I went out there at night, he was one of the people I was protecting, so I guess he couldn't be critical.

Irving ignored us. Looking at him, a little wave of remorse went through me, and for a moment I was sorry about what I'd done to him, however much he'd asked for it. Bernie asked if I knew where "Rabbi Irving" was. Remembering our agreement, I said I didn't know, but that he had maybe he'd managed to get himself transferred to a religious commune somewhere, like he'd wanted. I was about to say something… I didn't know what… to Irving, but just as I opened my mouth, Moshe's voice came booming across the room, "Larry, your bus is here, you'd better get going!"

I said "Shalom" to everyone, and headed outside to the bus. As before the trip didn't seem to take long. You just got settled, and you arrived. It was about two o'clock. I got off the bus and headed straight for the dance hall, to see if I could find Sarah, but she was nowhere in sight. The two undercover cops were there, though. They nodded to me, and I nodded back. That was all I wanted to have to do with them, innocent or not.

Leaving the dance hall, I went down the street, looking for someone to ask directions of. A police officer was standing on a corner, and I approached him. I gave him Sarah's address, and asked how to get there. He told me, explaining that if I was walking, it wasn't so far. I thanked him, and went off in search. It wasn't long before I got there, but it certainly wasn't what I'd expected.

I'd figured Sarah would have lived in an apartment with her family, as most people did. This wasn't true in her case, not in this sector of the city. The place was like a disaster area... a pile of shingles lay by the front door, having fallen off the roof, an upstairs window was broken, and there was dirt everywhere outside the house. I couldn't believe such a good-looking girl as Sarah would have to live in such squalor! Maybe I had the wrong building.

An elderly woman answered to my knock, and said, in English, "Hello, who are you looking for?" I asked for Sarah, giving her last name as well, and the woman said, "This is the right house, but Sarah is not in at the moment. She is out shopping. But, may I ask your name, sir?"

I introduced myself, stating that I was from the kibbutz. She smiled, and said she'd guessed as much, adding that she was Sarah's mother. Apparently, Sarah had spoken to her of meeting me.

"You are a Canadian, aren't you? Well, come in and wait. Sarah should be along shortly. Is she expecting you?"

I said no, as I had no warning I'd be coming that day, and added I hoped Sarah would be glad to see me. Mother took me into the kitchen, made me a cup of espresso and we sat down to wait. She wanted to know all about life back in Canada. My home and native land had a very good name, she told me. I described Toronto to her as best I could, and she was very interested. Asking what we did for recreation, I thought it best to answer in a general way, and said, "Hockey is a favourite pastime in Canada." She'd never heard of it.

Sarah arrived just as I was explaining that although the sport of baseball had originally been invented by a Canadian, it was essentially an American game. She was surprised to see me, she said. Her mother told her... after being asked... it would be all right for us to go out to a café somewhere. I got the sense I was interrupting Sarah's daily duties, and that she was glad to get off the hook.

Sarah wanted to go to a Chinese restaurant called "The Rickshaw". This was a place, Sarah told me, that had acquired a reputation as a very good spot to eat. We didn't know exactly where it was, and set out to find it, with the help of a telephone book. Sarah knew where the street was... in a better section of town. We'd go there and have supper. She had to be back home by nine p.m., she explained, as she had studying to do for school the next day. She suggested we spent the rest of the afternoon in the downtown area, seeing the sights. I really hadn't done a lot of touristy things the first time I'd been there, and so this seemed like a good enough plan.

I put my hand out toward hers, and she took it. We did a walking tour of the city, bought ice cream, told jokes, laughed and enjoyed ourselves immensely. It was good to be with a girl again. Nights on the tractor, holding a gun on my knees, were lonely, with only Sam and the desert to talk to. The time went by quickly with Sarah, and before we knew it, five o'clock had rolled by and we headed for the restaurant. Sarah's walking tour had been gradually leading us toward it.

It had a good reputation, she said, but it was a tourist trap, and not many Israelis frequented the place. It was very busy, anyway... Tel Aviv attracted a lot of tourists in those days. After reading a (rather expensive) menu in the window, we went inside to find a seat. The maître d' met us just inside the door.

"Do you have a reservation?" he asked. I told him we hadn't thought to phone ahead, but that I was from Nachal Oz, a nearby kibbutz, thinking maybe this would help get us a table. The maître d' nodded, then bowed. "Very well," he said, "and what is it you do there?" I shrugged and said I was a border guard. This turned out to be better than having a reservation.

Everyone was familiar with the name Nachal Oz. The man knew of this particular kibbutz, he said, and we were most welcome at The Rickshaw. "Please to come this way," he said, and we followed. He led us to the best table in the house, as if we were celebrities, saying he was "very, very happy to see someone from Nachal Oz!" - it was like meeting a brother. I hadn't known what kind of reputation the kibbutz might have had in the city, but now I knew: we were heroes.

I tried to tip him, but he wouldn't accept any money. "No, no," he said, "please, you sit and enjoy yourself." He brought us flaming drinks, on the house. I was slightly embarrassed, but Sarah was very impressed. She'd never been treated so well in her life, she said, giggling. It was a new experience for me, too, and I revelled in it. The meal was fabulous, and as we ate, the waiter hovered around the table, filling our glasses from a carafe of their best house wine, asking every few minutes if everything pleased us. It certainly did. When we were finished, I left a tip anyway, sliding it under a plate. The food was delicious, the company was good, and we'd been given the royal treatment... what else could I ask for?

Well, I wouldn't mind seeing the theatre section of town, I said to Sarah... just to top off the evening. I wanted to see what sort of films were showing, whether or not they played American movies, and if they were in English, or had subtitles. We turned down toward the main street, Sarah leading the way. Although she couldn't afford to go to these places very often, she knew where everything was. I spotted a movie house right away, and noticed they were playing the American film *Giant*. I'd seen it in Toronto, and also on board the *Queen Mary*, and here it was in Tel Aviv. I felt as if it was following me around. I loved the film, and decided I'd see it again the next night.

Our evening had turned out better than I'd thought it would, but now Sarah had to go home, and so we headed back toward her place. I remember thinking along the way that our relationship hadn't turned out to be as "lovey-dovey" as I'd hoped, but we were becoming good friends instead, more like brother and sister. I really did like her, and I think she felt the same. I wanted things to develop into something else, of course, but had a strange feeling they would never do that, though there seemed no reason why not. When I left her outside her home, we kissed once, and that was it. She said good night, and went inside. I went my way, back toward the hotel. There was a funny feeling in my gut that I would never see her again, though I could think of no logical reason for me to feel that way.

The feeling stayed with me, though, as I walked along, away from her. All sorts of things were going through my head... would I be killed on the kibbutz? Would something drastic happen in her life, parting us forever? It was a crazy feeling, but I just couldn't shake it.

I returned to the hotel, and had a good night's sleep. My legs were tired from all the walking, and it had been a long day... I'd been up all the night before, sitting on the tractor, watching the fields for movement... not the world's most relaxing job.

Next morning, I was up early, and decided there was something I had to do... go and see the famous city of Jerusalem. It was a two hour bus trip, and the first thing I did after breakfast was to go to the station and purchase a ticket.

Jerusalem

Jerusalem is the city where Christ was crucified and then rose from the dead, and Mohammed supposedly rose to Heaven on a black steed. How much of either story is true, nobody knows. It's a city of mystery, where the past blends in with the present.

I asked a police officer where the holy wall was, something I'd heard about all my life and wanted to see for myself. He pointed the way, and when I got there, I saw that many people were davening, crying and praying, slipping notes in between the wall's cracks, just as I had heard they did. I wondered what good it all did, but then, people sometimes think they need a physical object in order to relate to their faith or beliefs. A lot of the people there looked like tourists, trying to act like the natives, as if they knew what they were doing. I had to smile at their naiveté. Like me, they probably knew very little about what was going on.

Not far from the wall stood the famed Temple of the Golden Dome. The more I watched the tourists gather around this part of the city, the more I wanted to erect a big sign reading, THIS WAY TO THE TEMPLE OF THE GOLDEN DOOM!" - just so I could sit back and watch the expressions on their faces. They were all so well dressed, these tourists, while some of the children and beggars I saw looked like they hadn't had a good meal in weeks. It was quite a contrast.

I wandered inside the Dome out of curiosity, and spent about an hour there. I liked the architecture, and marvelled, as did everyone else, at the incredible beauty of the place. I wished Rabbi Irving could have been with me, to interpret some of the more esoteric meanings of it all, and wondered how he was doing back on the farm. After purchasing a number of postcards to send back home, I left the Dome and went off in search of the policeman again to ask how to get to Bethlehem. He said it was just past the Mandelbaum Gate.

The area was Arab occupied at the time, however, and I wondered how I'd get inside to see it. Visiting Bethlehem was something I'd wanted to do ever since landing in Israel. Whether or not one believes in the story of Christ, it's still a rich part of the history of the land. I did manage to get inside the Gates, though, by simply walking through as if I was a tourist... which, that day, I really was. No one would be able to tell from looking at me that I was anything other than another North American come to see all of the sights.

Bethlehem was something else, and I don't know how to describe it other than "quaint"; the streets were very narrow, as they dated back as far as you'd care to go. I was very conscious of the fact that these were the same streets that Jesus had walked. Bethlehem has been so uniquely unchanged over the centuries, you half-expect to find his footprints in the dust.

I was very rushed that day, trying to get in as many sights as possible during my brief stay. I stopped and ate a falafel (and no, you don't "feel awful" afterwards... they're really pretty good!), then decided it was time to head back to the bus station. I had no trouble going back through the Gate. No one seemed to notice me at all, though I was sure there were plenty of hidden pairs of eyes watching everyone. That's the way it was there, and probably still is.

Jerusalem seemed to me to be a place for tourists, and for people from all religions to gather and make good their claims at having the "only truth" of it all. Me, I wasn't interested in things like that. Let them have their gods, I figured. I was more interested in finding some action, like a dance club maybe. After looking around for a time, I realized this wasn't the city for me, and I went my way.

Meanwhile, Back at the Kibbutz...

I headed for the bus, as it would soon be leaving for Tel Aviv. I caught a few minutes sleep on the way there, as I had a full night ahead of me. I wanted to see the James Dean film *Giant*. The bus pulled into the station about an hour before showtime, and I grabbed a bite to eat on the way, then settled in to enjoy the three hour movie.

As I left the theatre, I passed a small news-stand, and noticed the headline of the *Jerusalem Post*. I was shocked to learn that a tractor on a kibbutz had hit a land mine, and as I read on, I realized that this had happened at my kibbutz, and it was my tractor that had been blown to bits... not to mention the operator along with it! It only took a few seconds for the reality to set in... it could easily have been me! It was pure luck that Moshe had given me a couple of days off.

What made this episode so unique was the fact that it was the first plastic land mine ever to be exploded in Israel. Standing there reading the newspaper, I came to a rather sudden but not unexpected decision. I wouldn't go back to the kibbutz. I'd stay as far from it as I could get. The only way they'd ever get me back there would be if they arrested me and dragged me back. "Young pilgrim in the Homeland" or not, I was too young to die!

There was a slight hitch to this. I didn't have much money with me. I only had a few dollars. I'd have to find a job, quick... something unofficial, so they wouldn't be able to find me and take me back to Nachal Oz. I decided to return to The Rickshaw, and try to get some work teaching people how to Rock 'n Roll. In the meantime, I went back to my hotel to sleep on all these things. I don't remember sleeping much...

In the morning, about eleven o'clock, I went to The Rickshaw where I asked the doorman about the woman who was in charge of the entertainment... I'd forgotten her name.

"You're looking for Martha?" I was asked. I nodded, and asked if I could speak to her right away, adding that it was important. I was told she was not in, but would be returning shortly. The man offered me a cup of coffee while I waited. Finally, Martha arrived, just as he'd said she would. She recognized me right away.

"Hello, Blondie. What are you doing here?"

"So you remember me," I said. "Do you also remember asking me if I'd like to teach people how to dance American style? Well, if the offer is still open, I think I'll take you up on it, that is, if the price is right. What are you willing to pay?"

Having made my decision not to return to the kibbutz, I was desperate, but wasn't about to let her know that. She told me I would earn about thirty pounds a night. This didn't sound too bad to someone who had no income at all, but I managed to appear nonchalant about it, and didn't break out into a big, stupid grin.

"So, when should I start? I'd like to begin as soon as possible... you know, to get to know your customers, and feel my way around..."

Martha wanted me to start that very evening, which was fine by me. I then told her a little bit of the truth, that I needed some cash up front. I said something about not knowing I'd be staying in Tel Aviv and that all of my money was back at the kibbutz. I didn't tell her why I was leaving, but I think she knew. She'd seen the papers, too. She said that if I showed up that evening, she would give me a ten pound advance. That would get me some food and whatever else I needed. I promised I'd be there at six o'clock sharp. I asked how I'd be paid, and she smiled and said, "Every night, you'll get your money. I'll give you cash... it's the easiest way." I think she knew that was what I wanted.

Killing time in Tel Aviv without any money in my pocket

meant walking around and seeing the sights, and that was how I spent the rest of the afternoon. At six o'clock sharp, I returned to The Rickshaw. Martha was there, waiting for me. She frowned as she saw me, and I thought for a second she'd changed her mind. But, it was just that she didn't like the way I was dressed. I told her all my clothing had been stolen on the boat. She said I could wear one of the waiter's suits. There was a room in the back where I could change. I did as she asked, and came back to the table where she gave orders to one of the waiters to bring me some food.

"This is Larry," she told him. "He will be a new employee starting this evening," Martha said. The waiter was curious to know what I'd be doing. Martha explained I'd be a sort of dance instructor, that I would be teaching the customers how to Rock 'n Roll, "just like the Americans do."

That first night, time passed very quickly. As I finished my meal, people began coming in. At about eight p.m., the music began. Martha went up to talk to the disc jockey and a few minutes later, he announced that there was "a gentleman present who will be happy to teach you the basics of Rock 'n Roll dancing. He is seated over in the corner there, by the window. Please feel free to approach him if you'll like to learn. All you need do is ask. There is absolutely no charge for this service. We want our customers to have the best of everything."

I waved and nodded to the crowd as the man spoke. He added that if anyone felt like offering me a tip, that was entirely up to them, but there was no obligation. When the disc jockey was through talking, the music started up immediately. It was good old American Rock 'n Roll... Bill Haley, Chuck Berry, Brenda Lee, Connie Francis, Fats Domino, Buddy Holly, and of course, "the King"... Elvis Presley. The customers started coming to my table at once, and I got up onto the dance floor. At that moment in time, I was so glad to hear some music I was familiar with, I would have danced all night for free. Making money was the last thing on my mind.

It was great. To my amazement, I'd even made a fair amount in tips. Once I'd been out on the dance floor a few times and the customers had seen I knew what I was doing, they began lining up at my table. By the end of the night, my feet were sore, but I was happy. Martha came over to me and handing me the rest of my pay, said, "That was wonderful. I hope you decide to stay on with us."

I did. I went through the first few weeks without even caring or thinking about what might be happening back at the kibbutz. My financial situation was much better, too. I was working with two pockets filled with money. I had American tips in one, and Israeli shekels in the other. I had nothing to complain about.

As I only worked at night, I decided to use the daytime hours travelling and exploring. I would hop onto a bus in the morning and go to any city I wanted, as long as I could get back by six o'clock when my shift started. One day, I went to Ramat-Gan, and enjoyed it. I went to Natanya, and that was interesting. The Dead Sea was a favourite... there, you could lie in the water and float with no worry about sinking. The water was so filled with natural salt and other mineral deposits, you couldn't even swim in it. The water was very relaxing, and I was told it had been known to cure various ailments. I could believe it.

I visited museums, libraries, movie theatres... you name it. Time was passing by quickly, and I was really enjoying myself, but I had a feeling that sooner or later they'd catch up with me. After all, the Jewish Agency hadn't sent me there to teach people to Rock 'n Roll! But, I didn't care. Let them come and get me. I was having too much fun to worry about it. What could they do, anyway, except maybe send me back? I hadn't broken the law in any way... all I'd done was not returned from a bus trip; the only thing they could call me was "missing".

I didn't know it at the time, but when I was busy dancing up storm after storm, night after night, the kibbutz had sent someone out to search for me. They had my picture, and would use it to help locate me. For all they knew, I might be dead. One day, Martha drew me aside and said that someone had been to the restaurant looking for me. The person had shown her a photograph, and there was no doubt in her mind who it was.

"The man was looking for a young, blond Canadian who had left the farm and not returned. I asked him if the person they were looking for had committed any sort of crime, or was wanted for anything else, and he said no. But, he said, it was the kibbutz's responsibility to make certain any missing person returned, if they could find him. I told him I'd keep an eye out for you, Larry, and that if anyone fitting your description came to me seeking employment, I would let him know. He gave me a card with a telephone number."

When I went in the next night, however, Martha unexpectedly said it would be my last night's work.

"You'd better move on, Larry. That man was back, snooping around. He said he'd spoken with some of my customers, and they'd described you, though they thought you were an American youth, not Canadian. Who can tell the difference? But, you'd better think about what you're going to do next. If you stay here, they'll find you. They can be very thorough when they want to. Our people are very well trained.

"Unless you want to take your chances of being caught up with here," Martha said, "you might want to think about going to Haifa. It would be a good place to go… they might have a hard time finding you there. I want to tell you, though, it has been a real pleasure having you with us, and I wish you all the best of luck, whatever you do. You've shown us quite a lot. Everyone is always curious, you know, about life in North America. I think just talking with you, we've learned something. So, thank you."

She handed me an envelope and told me not to open it until later. She said, too, that I was welcome to keep the clothes. And then she said goodbye, and I walked out of The Rickshaw into the night, wondering what I would do next.

On to Haifa...But Not For Long

Haifa was a very fast moving city with all kinds of action, and the first thing I knew I had to do was to get a job somewhere. Just by the look of the place, I figured this wouldn't be easy, as I really didn't have any skills... I could do manual labour, but that was about it. Not being very fluent in, or able to read Hebrew, I needed to find an English newspaper. I could go through the "Help Wanted" section, and maybe look up some of the clubs. Maybe I'd get lucky and find someone who needed a dance instructor. The fact that I only knew the latest Rock 'n Roll crazes didn't deter me... it had worked once before.

I could also go to restaurants, as many of them had entertainment or night clubs, and ask around a bit. I had one good thing on my side... I wasn't shy or afraid to approach strangers. I could ask some of the customers where the best places were, and then try them out. Spotting a police officer, I figured I may as well start right away, and asked him if he could direct me to a good club in the area.

He wanted to know if I was an entertainer. I replied, "yes, in a way", and this made him curious. I told him the truth... I taught American Rock 'n Roll dancing. After thinking about this for a minute, he then told me about a dance studio his daughter attended occasionally. He gave me the address, and instructed me how to get there. Maybe I'd get lucky right away.

I found the place and went in and up the stairs. There was a reception desk, and a pretty young woman asked if I was interested in joining the dance club. I explained my reason for being there, that I was offering my services in the area of Rock 'n Roll, adding I'd recently worked in Tel Aviv, and could supply a reference, if needed. The young lady seemed pleased to hear this, but said she wasn't able to hire anyone herself, so I should speak with the owner of the club. The fact that I had experience might be helpful. If I returned in two hours, she said, he would be there. She'd tell him I dropped by. I thanked her and left the studio, headed for the docks, where I sat watching all the large ships coming and going.

The two hours passed quickly enough, and I headed back to the dance studio, where I met the owner. He said he was interested in the idea of having someone teach Rock 'n Roll to his clients, and asked when I could begin. "Whenever you like," I said.

"I'll have some advertisements done up," he said, "announcing that we now teach Rock 'n Roll dancing. This is something we've never done before, but students have been asking about it. I'm glad you showed up."

He shook my hand, and that was that. I started teaching the very next day. He took me entirely at my word, didn't want to see a demonstration and didn't care about a reference. "We'll let the students be the judge of your capabilities," he said.

The students said they liked me, and we got along well together. They gave me tips on top of my pay, as had happened at The Rickshaw. I enjoyed being there, and liked the atmosphere. Maybe I should have stayed longer in Haifa, but three weeks later, I was on my way again. Haifa was a "safe haven" for someone like me, kind of half-on-the-run, and I was hesitant about leaving, but I missed Tel Aviv - I used to call it the "blackboard jungle" of Israel. There was just something about the place that made me feel more at home there than anyplace else in the Middle East.

So, one day, I just up and left, catching a bus back to Tel Aviv. When I arrived, I stopped in a small café I'd frequented, and then headed over to The Rickshaw, to see Martha and the staff, to say "Hello". I sat down and started sipping a cup of coffee one of the waitresses had brought me. Suddenly, the door opened, and in walked two military police. As soon as they saw me, they stopped in their tracks, glancing at each other.

Finally, one of them nodded. I knew then that it was over. I was the one they were looking for. There was no place left to run.

One of them came over to my table and asked, "Is your name Larry Wiener? Are you from Nachal Oz?" I told him he had guessed right.. I was informed they'd been searching for me for the past two months, and I asked the reason. Had I committed a crime? He said, no.

"But your name is on the missing list, and everyone must be accounted for, especially foreigners. And in your case, especially those who have worked as border guards."

They knew I'd gone "AWOL", and said I'd caused them quite a lot of trouble by not returning or telling anyone where I was going. They didn't understand, they said, why I hadn't returned. I was about to reply that I hadn't come all the way from Canada just to be blown apart on a tractor by people I didn't even know, but decided to hold my tongue.

So, I had to go with them. There was no way out of it, they said. I asked if they were going to handcuff me, but they said they didn't have to. If I would please just get into their car and not make a fuss, everything would be all right. They had to return me to the kibbutz, they said, and they would like to be able to do that in a civilized manner. Whatever happened after that was not their concern. They were simply doing their job.

Back to the Kibbutz

They took me back to the kibbutz, where everyone, as you might imagine, was simply thrilled to see me... especially Moshe, who came out of his office as we pulled up. He took one look at me and beckoned. No smiles this time.

"I want to see you," he said.

I followed him into his office and as soon as the door was closed, he piled into me. He was really upset. I was a disgrace to the kibbutz. Everyone thought I was dead. What I'd done had been bad for morale. I was this, I was that. He tried every possible angle, short of calling me a spy, to get some kind of reaction out of me. I told him I didn't really care what he said or thought.

I told him quite bluntly I didn't like the place, and hadn't from the very beginning. All I wanted was to go home. I hadn't signed up with the Jewish Youth to shoot people. He'd coerced me into it. I hadn't wanted to go to Israel in the first place. For every insult and accusation Moshe threw at me, I had an answer. Who did he think he was, anyway? I couldn't stand the group I was with. When I'd gotten involved with them initially, it had all been a joke. So, the joke had backfired. So now what? Were they going to put me in front of a firing squad?

I will always believe that my mother and uncle pressured the Jewish Agency into accepting me, to get rid of me for the year. I was young and wild, and probably they thought some discipline would straighten me out. But, I told Moshe, they would never have

389

let me go if they thought I'd wind up with a gun in my hand. Besides, they knew I wouldn't really fit in, that I wasn't the sort of person you could push around or order about.

I had enjoyed parts of Europe, but after that, they could have put me on a boat and aimed it back toward America. I had no inclination to make much of a go of working in Israel, and I still felt the same way. I told Moshe he could do whatever he wanted with me, adding that I figured it was time I went back anyway.

"So what do you have for me? A letter of deportation? I've heard that's what happens to kibbutzers who don't follow the rules."

Moshe sighed, looking disgusted. "As a matter of fact, I do have a letter for you, Larry. I've been waiting for months to get this letter. We always have letters for non-conformists like you."

He told me then that he agreed with my group about me, adding that he personally had never liked me much, either. "You refuse to do what you are told, and I saw this, and so made concessions for you. I made you a guard because I thought it would straighten you out, that you would see the importance of your being here. And what happened? You ran away from your duties. I think from the start you were against us. Rules are meant to be obeyed. There can be no individualism here."

I almost asked him about the boxes of cigarettes he was selling, if he considered that in contradiction of his beloved rules, but thought better of it. He was really upset. He hadn't so much as grinned all the time we'd been talking. Best to leave well enough alone, I figured. Let him ramble on, and say as little as possible.

I had never been a religious person, and being Canadian, nationalism meant little to me. In Canada in those days, we didn't even have our own flag to fly... just a British one. Israel, to me, was just another patch of land somewhere. It meant nothing. Why should it? Just because I was born Jewish didn't meant I had to automatically race off to join someone's war, did it? Sorry, not me... you must have the wrong Wiener!

I knew this meant the end of my participation at the kibbutz, but the way I saw things, when I'd read about those bombs going off... I simply wanted to make sure I wasn't going to be in the next headline. I didn't come to Israel to be killed. I told Moshe how I felt, and why I hadn't returned. I also told him I'd done my part by protecting the kibbutz while I had been there, and that even he had agreed I'd done my work well enough. He just grunted when I said that, because it was something he couldn't argue about.

"I don't care if you throw me out," I said. "And as a matter of fact, I wish you'd done it a lot sooner."

I have to give Moshe credit. He didn't try to talk me into staying, but told me he had a letter stating I could leave the kibbutz in a week's time. This meant I'd be returned to tourist status, and would have to leave the country. This was all spelled out plainly in the letter. He handed it to me, and I folded it up and put it in my pocket.

"Thank you," I said. "Can I go now?

Moshe nodded his head. "Go," he said, "I'll speak with you another time."

I'd never seen him so subdued... he hadn't so much as cracked a smile. Obviously, he was taking this very seriously... maybe he was afraid I'd bring up the little item of the cigarettes, if he was too hard on me. He had his superiors, too. I got a certain amount of pleasure out of this, knowing that he was afraid of me.

I walked out of his office, and headed for my cabin. Irving was there, sitting on the bed. He looked up at my entrance and, not even bothering to say hello, began right away asking why I hadn't returned to the kibbutz from my trip to the city.

I repeated what I'd said to Moshe. He told me everyone knew I'd be deported. He tried his best to rub it in, not realizing that I didn't care.

"It's too bad, Larry. It really is. While you were working in the fields as a guard, your status was rising. Everyone thought you were something, that you were braver than you really were. You were gaining respect from the workers, and even from us."

Working guard duty had made me out to be a bit of a big shot, he said. I repeated that I didn't care.

"I read in the papers the other day, there was one of those big shots killed the other night, killed while sitting on his tractor. That was the same tractor I sat on, Irving. I'm not even twenty years old. Tell me what I should have done. What would you have done, or any of the others? We didn't come here to be killed. That's about all I have to say about it, really. I want to go home in one piece, and not in a pine box. That's not hard to understand, is it, Irving?"

I was a little testy with him, but I didn't feel like explaining any more. I had a week to go, and that would be it. I had nothing when I'd come to Israel, having lost everything on my way there, and would be leaving with nothing. That seemed somehow fair to me. Working on the kibbutz paid very little, and I had to put my life on the line. I'd done everything... and more... that I'd been asked to do, but I wasn't going to die there. I didn't feel ashamed. I'd done more than the others, so there was nothing anyone could say to me.

Those nights I sat out on the tractor in the field, not knowing... maybe not even realizing... it could be my last night on the planet... in the morning, no-one ever thanked me for it. No wonder poor Sam had wanted so desperately to go to America.

All of this I said to Irving, but it didn't make any difference to him. So, I told him I was in a better position than he or any of the others.

"I'm doing better than you guys," I said. "I'm getting out of here. They're giving me free passage back to Canada. I had a free trip here, and got to see Europe, so I can't complain. In fifty years, none of this will matter... whatever happens to the state of Israel is going to happen anyway. No one got to shoot me or blow me up, and I'm not going to be hung for a traitor, so I'm happy. I'll be even happier to leave, though. I mean, can you honestly tell me, Irving, that you or any of the others actually like it here, that this is what you expected?"

Irving stared down at the floor, and didn't answer.

"I didn't think so," I told him. "Well, I'm going to take a walk around the kibbutz. See you later."

I ran into Bernie out by the fields, where he was doing some electrical work. They'd offered him this job as they'd seen him puttering around in his cabin, fixing the wiring. He didn't want to talk about that, though. Like Irving, all he was interested in was what would be happening to me. What would I be doing until I left?

"Nothing, Bernie, absolutely nothing. What should I do, ask for my gun back? You'd like it if I was blown to smithereens, wouldn't you?"

I left before he could think up a smart answer to throw back at me. I'd had enough of trouble, and didn't need any more.

Close to supper time, I went into the dining hall and ate a nice meal. No one spoke to me, but I didn't care. An announcement came over the speaker system, saying there'd be a film shown that evening. I had never been to a movie at the kibbutz, so I thought I'd check it out. As it would be shown right there in the dining hall, I hung around and waited for it to start.

Though I can't remember what the film was, it wasn't so bad, but halfway through it, Moshe came into the hall, flipped the light switch on and turned off the projector. He had an important announcement to make, he said.

"The Arabs have struck on the Mediterranean, very close to Israel. Everyone hopes this situation will change, that they will stop before things get too out of hand. Otherwise, there will be war. I'm sorry to interrupt your movie, but I'm telling you this because we must be more careful than ever, especially those of you who," and here he gave me a very definite look of disgust, "have the privilege of helping guard this kibbutz against our enemies. That is all."

If this was an attempt to embarrass yours truly, it didn't work very well, because I no longer cared... if I ever did care. I wondered if the others did, either... as soon as he left the room, the lights went out again and the film came back on. I noticed no one was overly excited by this bit of "news" Moshe had brought us.

For me, it was as if I'd never left... I was stuck with Irving again, and while I had no job to go to, nothing much had changed. No one spoke to me, but then, no-one had spoken to me much before. Life went on as usual. The kibbutz was a dreary, somewhat lifeless place to be to start with. Aside from the occasional dancing, life there was pretty dull.

After the movie, I returned to my cabin. To my surprise, Moshe was there, waiting for me. I was surprised that he asked if I would consider doing guard duty again.

"I've been gone for two months, Moshe. Didn't you get anyone to replace me yet?"

He replied that he could have gotten someone very easily, but

Sam said he wanted me. I wondered out loud why Sam hadn't been involved in the bombing. Moshe told me. On that particular night, it just happened that Sam had the night off.

"So, Larry? How about it? Or did you mean it when you said you'd had enough? Someone has to guard us, you know."

I don't know why, but I told him I would do it. Probably, because Sam had requested it. I liked Sam... he was really the only one on the kibbutz who bothered to talk with me, and I liked him.

"In that case," Moshe said, "you begin at eight o'clock. Come to my office and pick up your equipment before then.

"By the way, Larry, I've already set out your midnight snack. How do you Americans say it...?... I had a hunch you'd say yes."

And, he laughed, just like that... like nothing had ever happened, as if I'd never left. I was amazed that he'd asked, and also that I'd agreed. I'd thought it was the last thing I would ever do again.

"You sure have a lot of nerve, Moshe."

"So do you, kid. I may not be crazy about you and some of your ideas, but you've got nerve. I'll give you that much."

Moshe must have been desperate to ask me to go back into the fields, especially after all that had happened. Either that, or he was a better judge of character than I gave him credit for, thinking I might even agree to do as he asked... which I did. I wanted to see how Sam was doing, how he felt about almost becoming a part of the garden. I wondered, too, what would it be like if the same thing happened again. I wouldn't be able to run this time. As I said to Moshe later, "Maybe that's the answer, maybe that's my punishment... to get hit after all, just because I listened one final time to you! Wouldn't that be ironic!"

He thought it was funny, me coming out with something like that, and it was good to see him laugh again... he wasn't as angry as he'd made out.

"But, remember, Moshe," I said, "you'll never get that lucky." His laugh stopped then, and he just said I'd better get going or I'd be late and the Arabs wouldn't know what to aim at.

Sam was waiting for me, and shook my hand. He smiled and said, "Back to the grind, kid. Our friends have missed you. So have I. It's good to see you." The night went by quietly with no mishaps.

I never did find out what Sam thought about almost being killed, because I didn't know how to ask. Maybe he was used to it.

A strange thing happened in the morning, at breakfast. The whole gang was there, and, one by one, they came over to me and thanked me for going back to guard duty. They didn't say why they did this, but I figured either Moshe or Irving had said something, because I really did feel they sort of took it all for granted. The guy guarding you gets blown to pieces one night, well, that's too bad... get another guard out there! I realized they really didn't feel this way, though, and it was good to know that if you did happen to be killed some moonlit night, at least someone would appreciate it.

A few moments later, to make the morning even weirder, someone came running into the dining hall yelling that Bernie had just been electrocuted. He'd been thrown off an electrical pole and was alive, but had been burned very badly. Everyone ran outside to the accident site, but there was nothing anyone could do. Bernie was conscious, barely, and one whole side of his body was black and charred. His clothing had been almost completely burnt off. The common consensus was that he might not make it.

By the time we got there, a doctor was with him, waiting for an ambulance to arrive. Later, in the burn unit of a hospital at Tel Aviv, they put him on an oiled bed to help the healing process. He lived, but his side would be a discoloured purple for the rest of his life.

Irving wanted to go in the ambulance with him, and Moshe said he could. Bernie was still in shock, and it was thought it would be best if, when he came around, there was a familiar face nearby. This was a totally unexpected turn of events for Bernie, far from anything he had thought might have happened to him in Israel. Electrical work was something he liked, and was pretty good at, but still, he didn't have his papers and I guess there were things he wasn't aware of, unless he had been careless...and it wasn't like him to be that. But, like they say, things happen. Even I felt sorry for him.

Later that day, after all the excitement and talk had died down and everyone had gone out to the fields, I went to my cabin and wrote a letter to Sarah to tell her "goodbye". I wanted her to know we'd never meet again, and how much I had enjoyed her company while we'd been together. I told her I'd never forget her and this book is proof that I haven't).

As I was signing the letter, there was a knock on the cabin door, and in stepped Moshe, back to his smiling self.

"I hear you put in a good night's work," he said. "The camp thanks you for that, but now I have a special request. I would like it very much if you would put in a week's work in the fields, in the daytime, just as a sort of special remembrance before you leave us."

We both knew I'd never do it again, not in Israel, anyway. I asked if there would be any restrictions put on me... could I come and go as I pleased, during this final week?

He laughed, and said, "You are free to do as you like, as long as you don't leave the compound. If you go from here again, I can't guarantee what will happen to you."

"So, what about being paid?" I asked.

"You've already been paid, Larry. I'm sorry."

And that was that.

I did one day on potatoes, one day on carrots, and so on, and then, the last day before I left the kibbutz, I was on irrigation duty.

At the end of my final day, Moshe called me into his office, and said he thought I'd done a very good job for someone who really didn't want to be there. Then, much to my surprise, he gave me sixty pounds cash, and wagged his finger at me.

"Now, don't you tell anyone about this, Larry, not a single soul. If you do, they'll have me out there on that tractor, with a flashing light around my neck, just so the enemy will see me!

"The bus will pick you up and take you directly to Haifa. From there, you'll catch the boat and proceed on your journey home. The only remaining thing you have to do now, is to sign this paper. Then, our business will be concluded."

He handed me a piece of paper, and explained: "This means the kibbutz will no longer be responsible for any of your actions after you leave here. You'll be on your own, and I'd advise you to keep out of harm's way. So, it's over. You're going home."

I left his office, and made my way around the kibbutz, letting everyone know that they were finally through with me and I'd be leaving the next day. I saw Sam and told him that even if he never made it to America, I would never forget him. He'd taught me how to stay alive out in the fields, and how, if I had to, to be able to kill. He said he was sorry to see me go, and shook my hand heartily.

The next morning, the bus pulled up to the compound, and I was waiting for it. I had no luggage at all. I'd arrived with nothing, and I'd leave the same way. Deep down inside, I was thinking that maybe this kibbutz wasn't so bad after all, but it was too late now to do anything about it. I was just making things harder on myself by thinking that way.

The only one at the bus to see me off was Moshe... maybe he wanted to make sure I was going. He shook my hand, though, and said the nicest words I'd ever heard him say to me: "Larry, you are one son of a bitch, you are. You did your job well, and I want you to know I'm proud of you. If we had more like you, our job would be that much easier here. And I want you to know, too, what you did was exactly what I would have done, if I weren't an Israeli. I just wanted you to know that. You did nothing wrong, and probably saved your life by staying away from us. I realize it might have been you blown up with that tractor. So don't feel too bad. But, we have to abide by the rules, and so you have to go. Goodbye, and have a safe journey."

"Thanks, Moshe," I said, "but I'll be forgotten after the next rain. I want to leave you with these words: Shalom Chaverim."

The door slammed shut, and the bus slowly crept out of Nachal Oz. If there was any part of the countryside I wanted to remember, this was the time to see it. There really wasn't much to see, however, and I dozed most of the way through it.

We arrived in Haifa around lunch time, and I went off to find a restaurant to grab a good meal. Thanks to Moshe, I had the money to be able to do this. The boat had let me off right at dockside, so after eating, I went off to see if I could find the boat I'd be taking. It didn't take long, and soon I was hunting down the purser.

I found him, gave him my ticket, and he showed me to my quarters. If I was leaving the boat, he said, I had to be back by five o'clock, as the ship was scheduled to depart at seven p.m. This gave me time to have my last look at Israel. I knew in my mind I would never set foot in the place again, so I walked around Haifa and had as good a time as a person can by himself, anyway, playing the tourist.

I had another good meal before heading back to the boat, and then, suddenly, it was five o'clock... time to get on board. Walking up the long gangway, I blew a kiss at the fabled land. I stood at the railing for a long time. It was a perfect ending, a view beyond comparison... the sun was just beginning to set, and Lawrence of Canada was going home. My time in Israel had come to an end. Goodbye, goodbye...

I stood there for a while, staring at the land and at the sea, and the widening gap between myself and the time I had spent there. I knew I'd never have anything like this happen to me again.

Many Jewish teens will come and go, I thought. Some will stay and help build up the country. Some will become patriots and maybe never return to their homes. As for me, though... the time I spent there would have to be enough to do me a lifetime. I was glad I'd come, but I was glad to be leaving, too. For all of the hype I'd heard about Israel a year earlier, back in Canada, I never dreamed my trip to the land of milk and honey... and land mines... would have turned out the way it did.

Build up your nation, yes, by all means, go and do it. But, don't forget... there will always be a Moshe, no matter what side of the fence you're on, even if you're straddling the middle. Don't fall off, because it won't matter where you land... the strife, the killing, the warfare, the hatred that has built up over the centuries won't be cured, and you'll become a part of it.

So, go ahead and dream your dreams, but watch out they don't turn into nightmares. Yes, good luck, and may God bless you... and if you find yourself going to the Promised Land, whatever the reason, whatever the season... I can't say what else you may find in the course of your travels, but one thing is for certain. There are no flowers on the desert. Maybe there never will be.